Praise, Praise, Praise for Dogs For

"Dog owners of the world, rejoice! Whether you are a dog owner, wannabe or a seasoned veteran, there is something useful, interesting, or entertaining in this handy reference. . . . Highly recommended."

— Edell Marie Schaefer, Library Journal

"*Dogs For Dummies* divulges all the secrets of the canine inner sanctum. Other books focus on breeds, health or training. Here is all of that and more."

— Vicki Croke, Boston Globe

"Written with intelligence, wit, and heart. If your dog had a credit card, he'd buy you this wonderful guide."

— Carol Lea Benjamin, author of *Mother Knows Best: The Natural Way To Train Your Dog* and the Rachel Alexander and Dash mystery series.

"*Dogs For Dummies* should be required reading for anyone considering purchasing or adopting a dog . . . comprehensive, yet concise and entertaining."

— Amazon.com

"*Dogs For Dummies* is anything but. It's an intelligent, thorough, and humorous reference that should be on any dog-lover's list of must-haves."

— Duncan C. Ferguson, VMD, PhD, Professor, University of Georgia College of Veterinary Medicine

"If you had to pass a test to be a dog owner, this is all the book you'd need to get your license. Your dog will be glad you read this. So will you."

— Gene Lock, Reigning Cats and Dogs Store, Sacramento

"This kind of owner's manual for dogs is indispensable, and I can think of no one more qualified to write it."

— Beth Adelman, former managing editor of the *American Kennel Gazette*, the official magazine of the American Kennel Club

"Owning a copy of this delightful book is one of the best things you can do for your dog."

— Maria Goodavage, author, *The California Dog Lover's Companion*

Dogs

2nd Edition

by Gina Spadafori
FOREWORD BY **Marty Becker, DVM**

A Wiley Brand

Dogs For Dummies®, 2nd Edition

Published by **John Wiley & Sons, Inc.** 111 River St. Hoboken, NJ 07030-5774 www.wiley.com

Copyright © 2019 by John Wiley & Sons, Inc., Hoboken, New Jersey

Published by John Wiley & Sons, Inc., Hoboken, New Jersey

Published simultaneously in Canada

For general information on our other products and services, please contact our Customer Care Department within the U.S. at 877-762-2974, outside the U.S. at 317-572-3993, or fax 317-572-4002.

For technical support, please visit https://hub.wiley.com/community/support/dummies.

Wiley also publishes its books in a variety of electronic formats and by print-on-demand. Some content that appears in standard print versions of this book may not be available in other formats. For more information about Wiley products, visit us at www.wiley.com.

Library of Congress Control Number: 2019941095

ISBN 978-1-119-60907-0 (pbk); ISBN 978-1-119-60909-4 (ebk); ISBN 978-1-119-60910-0 (ebk)

Manufactured in the United States of America

C10010425_052119

Contents at a Glance

Table of Contents

Foreword

These days, people's pets have become bona fide members of the family. Moving from the kennel to the couch, they share our beds, family rooms, and holidays and are recipients of our kindest impulses and utmost concern.

Yet pet owners know that a pet is also a big responsibility because they are dependent on us for almost all of their basic needs, including food, water, shelter, and love. A pet is a living being whose life your human family will shape, share, and nurture. A pet partnership is a lifetime commitment. Do it right, and your pet will become an important and valuable part of the family for years to come. Do it wrong, and you've broken a sacred covenant between mankind and man's best friend.

As a veterinarian who's done thousands of new puppy and kitten visits, and as someone who works with the leading veterinary experts at most of the major veterinary schools in the United States, I've had the good fortune to see firsthand what steps you can take to begin your pet ownership the right way. Luckily, they are all found in the wonderfully written, comprehensive book that you hold in your hands: *Dogs For Dummies*, written by Gina Spadafori.

Many veterinarians recommend this award-winning book to new pet owners because it so quickly and easily delivers the information that clients want — and pets need. It's a proven "in-the-trenches" look at the simple steps you can and must take to make your pet an "ideal" pet — one that is well-behaved, content, and perfectly integrated within the human family.

I enthusiastically recommend *Dogs For Dummies* to all of my clients and to millions of pet lovers through my work on television, radio, and in print because the book is both a comprehensive manual and a quick reference, is easily understandable yet authoritative, and is inspirational as well as instructional. Complete this educational book and you'll have an honorary "Dogtorate" degree *in The Bond*.

Buying this book is most certainly one of the greatest gifts you can give a beloved pet. By following the principles, plans, and proven positive approaches described in *Dogs For Dummies*, you'll be the owner every pet wants and deserves — informed, responsible, and loving.

Marty Becker, DVM

Introduction

Welcome to the second edition of *Dogs For Dummies*, the canine reference for those who want all the basics covered in one easy-to-use book.

Well, you've found it. Dog health. Dog training. Not to mention dog gear, dog grooming, dog breeding, and dog sports. Whether you're looking to adopt a dog, trying to improve your relationship with the one you have, or attempting to come up with fun things to do with your furry pal, this book contains something for you.

The first edition of *Dogs For Dummies* was the first of the *For Dummies* pet books, and the most common question I heard was: "Wait! Don't they just do computer books?" I don't hear that anymore, with *For Dummies* books available on just about any imaginable topic, and with lots more on the way!

Dogs For Dummies was more than the first *For Dummies* pet book: It was *my* first book. I'd written a pet-care newspaper column for many years, and I was featured in the pets area of American Online when I was asked to write the first edition of this book. I felt like my prayers had been answered when I was offered such a great opportunity.

The first edition of *Dogs For Dummies* was critically acclaimed, and named Best General Reference and Best Writing on Dogs by the Dog Writers Association of America. Even more important, I started hearing from lots of book buyers about how much my work had helped them.

Buoyed by the success of *Dogs For Dummies*, I co-authored *Cats For Dummies* and *Birds For Dummies*. I'm proud of them all, but this book will always be my first, and I'm so happy to have the opportunity to make it even better.

So make yourself comfortable and enjoy this comprehensive and easy-to-follow book *for* dog lovers *from* dog lovers. The dog you get — or the dog you have — will thank you, believe me.

We Love Dogs . . . to Death, Sometimes

In spite of the popularity of dogs, some numbers suggest we don't love dogs all that much. How can anyone explain a society where doggy birthday parties and doggy day care aren't all that rare, but millions of dogs are put to death every year in humane society shelters and municipal animal-control facilities?

Undoubtedly, some of these dogs are semiwild strays, some are psycho, some incurably ill, and some are ancient. But many are none of those things: They're healthy, young, beautiful dogs — mixes and purebred both — who will die because the people who took them in don't want them anymore, for reasons as frivolous as redecorating and as serious as biting.

And what about the puppies who won't make it? Where did they come from? Some end up in shelters as part of "oops" litters, others are leftovers from litters planned by people who overestimated the demand for Golden Retrievers or Poodles or Rottweilers and got tired of the extra mouths to feed.

Because no one wants to imagine the worst, everyone who has ever dropped a dog at a shelter imagines that he ends up in a perfect home.

For many, that home is in heaven. Such is the dark side of a dog-crazy society.

How Do Dog Disasters Happen

Too many decisions about dogs are made because of emotions, not facts. The truth is, most of us are suckers for a puppy face.

Few things are more adorable than a puppy, no matter the breeding. They are endowed with noses like licorice jelly beans, big eyes that sparkle with curiosity and affection, big paws and gangly legs that give them an adorably bouncy gait, and soft, fluffy fur that's better for snuggling than any teddy bear ever made.

Like human babies, puppies even smell special.

My own theory is that they are made this way as some kind of ingenious natural defense, to keep the humans they rely on from seeking revenge for every carpet soiled, every finger nipped, and every couch corner chewed during what can seem at times a very long babyhood and adolescence. You come upon your wondrous puppy in possession of your new and very expensive running shoes, the upper of the left one neatly severed from its sole by sharp puppy teeth. You feel the blood rush to your face. The puppy stops, a piece of fine leather dangling from an eye tooth.

Before you can snap his little neck, he's running toward you, stumbling over those big paws of his, every inch of his body happy to see you. And before you know it, you're smiling.

See what I mean? Do you think a wild dog would fall for cuteness? Think again. He'd nail him if they had been *his* running shoes. Or *his* tasty leg of rabbit. Cuteness counts for nothing in the wild.

The awwwwwww factor

It's a shame we aren't a little less impressionable where puppies are concerned. Every year hundreds of thousands of people bring puppies into their homes, many after little more than a moment or two of thought.

If you take away only one thing from this book, it should be that getting a dog on impulse offers low odds for a successful relationship. Still, it's easy to see how it happens.

Maybe you see a puppy at the mall, in a pet-store window that's emblazoned with the symbols of every credit card in your wallet. Or maybe you get waylaid by a couple of kids outside the grocery store, hawking a box of free puppies.

"And you say the amount of shedding isn't really that bad?" you ask the nice people at the pet store while cuddling a collie pup, thinking of your navy-blue couch and your closet full of basic black. The puppy sighs and snuggles against your chest. Soon you're adding a lint brush to the growing pile of supplies on the counter and, lest you start to worry about the cost, the sales clerk quickly points out that you can always breed your dog and get your money back with puppy sales. You look at that wonderful puppy face and imagine seven more just like her, and then seven times the purchase price in your pocket. A beautiful pet *and* a return on your investment? Sold.

Or maybe you're moved by pure altruism.

"Say, mister, that one really seems to like you!" says the kid in front of the market, as you stop just long enough to cuddle the pup with that amazingly adorable patch over his eye. The puppy is licking your fingers while your brain struggles to work this dilemma out. You know you ought to call your spouse. But hadn't you talked about getting a dog someday, now that you've bought a house? How much effort can a little puppy be? You always had dogs when you were a child; how can you deny *your* children that pleasure?

"Dad says if we don't get rid of 'em today he's going to drown 'em," says the kid, urgently.

"Not Patch!" you yell and, a little while later, you're driving home with a puppy in your lap and ten pounds of puppy food in the trunk of your car.

Puppy love is fleeting

When it comes to puppies, love at first sight is a disaster in the making. A year later, Patch and the collie touch noses at the shelter. On TV, Timmy never seemed to care about Lassie's fur on his jeans, but you can't stand it on your clothes anymore. As for Patch, who'd have thought he'd turn out to be so large? You have neither the kind of space nor the time for the exercise he needs. And you're tired of yelling at the kids over whose turn it is to clean up the yard. One dog isn't house-trained, the other never seemed to understand that chewing wasn't OK. Not surprising, because neither dog was ever trained as a puppy.

They're still nice dogs, though. Young, and apparently healthy. A country home, a little training, and they'd be perfect — for someone else. Problem is, they aren't so cute anymore. Maybe they both make it, maybe neither does. It's not your fault, is it?

A Preventive Approach

Nobody adopts a dog guessing that they'll be dropping him off at the shelter later. Just thinking about doing so is heartbreaking. You get a dog because you want a loving, well-mannered companion. A playmate for the children. A crime deterrent, perhaps.

The most important factors in determining whether you end up with your dream dog or an ill-mannered and possibly dangerous beast is how well you educate yourself before you buy and how well you educate your dog thereafter.

That's part of what this book is all about. Preparing you to make the right selection when you're ready to adopt a dog and giving you the information you need to make good on the bright promise of that first meeting.

Improving the Dog You Have

Of course, many people wouldn't dream of giving up on their dogs, although the infatuation stage is long past and the relationship is strained. They endure "bad" dogs the way they do bad marriages — and for many of the same reasons. Because the children would be heartbroken or because friends and relatives would be disappointed. Because it's the right thing to do, or because they don't want to admit they made a mistake. Because if they wish hard enough, maybe the situation will get better. Because maybe the problem is their fault, and they're sure that they still love him (or her).

Is this you? You may get points for being a good sport, but admit it: This isn't any fun. You want a *good* dog.

I can help you with that. Your marriage? You've got the wrong book. (Although there is a *For Dummies* book on making marriage work, and another on rekindling romance!)

Why You Need This Book

A saying in dog-training circles — "Every handler gets the dog he deserves" — refers to the fact that your chances at success are directly related to your abilities to choose, raise, and live with your dog properly. What you put in determines what you get out.

In the more than ten years that I've been advising people about dog problems, I've discovered that, more often than not, the lack of accurate information — *not* the lack of effort or concern — is the number one reason for doomed people-pet pairings.

What kind of dog do *you* deserve? I think you deserve a healthy, happy, and well-mannered canine companion, and I'm going to show you how to get one — or turn yours into one. And then I show you how to have a great time sharing your life with your wonder dog.

Becoming an Informed Consumer

Think about what you did before you bought your last car or television set. You probably comparison-shopped, trying to figure out which manufacturer made the product that was best for you in terms of its specifications, its reputation for reliability, and its cost to purchase and maintain.

If you're young, single, and in an entry-level job, I'm guessing you didn't buy a minivan. Likewise, if you spend a lot of time ferrying your daughter's soccer team to the pizza parlor on Saturday afternoons or buying plywood sheets for the latest home-improvement project, your choice wasn't a sporty economy car. As for the TV, you probably took a tape measure with you to make sure that it fit in your entertainment cabinet.

Now, consider the following: If things go right, you'll have a dog longer than you'll keep a new car and probably longer than a TV will work. So why should it come as a surprise that you need to shop carefully for a dog? Take your time, study the specifications. Determine the rate of defects, consider the cost of maintenance. Even do your homework on the person from whom you get a dog, because if you have a warranty, you want to deal with people who'll be there when you need them.

You need to be a savvy shopper — before you get a dog and every day after. Keep in mind that you'll be buying food and supplies for the life of your dog! (Don't worry, I'll give you tips.)

With that attitude and the information that follows in this book, you're well on your way to becoming a dog expert — and better still, a satisfied dog owner.

How This Book Is Organized

Dogs For Dummies is divided into five sections. If you're looking for a dog, you might want to start at the beginning. If you already have a dog, you can skip around, checking out the chapters that address your most urgent dog problems. If you want to impress your coworkers by explaining the difference between the two kinds of terriers, you probably want to read the whole book.

No matter the order you choose, here's what you'll find:

Part 1: Bringing a Puppy or Adult Dog into Your Life

Mixed breed or purebred? What size? What breed type? Puppy or adult? Male or female? Breeder, humane society, or pet store? Complicated as these decisions may be, they're also some of the most enjoyable ones you'll ever make. This section walks you through them, step by step.

Part 2: Getting the Relationship Off to the Best Start

Once you get your new puppy or dog home, there's everything you need to get the relationship off on the right paw, including house-training tips for little pups or big dogs. You'll find the information you need on dog supplies in this section, too, along with help on feeding your dog.

Part 3: Keeping Your Dog Healthy

Basic care for all stages and ages are outlined here, along with tips on choosing animal-care professionals. Learn how to groom your dog, spot health problems early, and choose the right veterinarian. Common health problems are covered in this section, as well as information on how to make your dog's senior years comfortable and happy.

Part 4: Living Happily with Your Dog

Basic training and problem-solving are covered in this part, along with what you need to know to get involved in dog sports. Traveling with your dog is the focus of another chapter. You'll also find an overview of breeding — along with reasons why your dog is almost certainly better off not becoming a parent.

Part 5: The Part of Tens

From protecting your landscaping to the best Web sites for dog-lovers, some of the best has been saved for last. Read these chapters with your dog in your lap — you'll both enjoy them more.

Icons Used in This Book

TECHNICAL STUFF

Maybe you want to know a little more *why* some house-training strategies work better than others. This icon is the place to look to find that sort of information. If you just want to catch the basic concepts, give this guy a pass.

TIP

This icon flags things that are especially useful for making living with your dog easier or making your dog happier and healthier.

REMEMBER

This icon reminds you of information so important that you should read it more than once, just to make sure it stays with you.

WARNING

This icon marks some of the most common mistakes dog owners make, along with tips for avoiding them.

How to Reach Me

I invite you to tell me about *your* dog and your tales of living with a canine companion. You can read the exploits of my animals — as well as up-to-date information on animal health and behavior — as part of my weekly column, *Pet Connection*, which is provided to newspapers by the Universal Press Syndicate and also appears every week in the Pet Care Forum (www.vin.com/petcare), part of the Veterinary Information Network (www.vin.com), a subscription service for veterinary professionals. I also write an exclusive essay on pets every week for Pets.com. You can e-mail me at writetogina@spadafori.com, but snail mail is just as nice to get, at the following address:

Gina Spadafori

PMB 211

5714 Folsom Blvd

Sacramento, CA 95819

Beyond the Book

In addition to what you're reading right now, this book comes with a free access-anywhere Cheat Sheet. To get this Cheat Sheet, go to www.dummies.com and search for "Dogs For Dummies, 2nd Edition Cheat Sheet" by using the Search box.

1

Bringing a Puppy or Adult Dog into Your Life

IN THIS PART . . .

This part explains where to look for your new puppy or dog, how to choose the right one for you, and how to get the relationship off to a good start. In here, you'll get the information you need to evaluate whether a male or female, puppy or grown dog, is a better fit with your family. If you want a purebred puppy, you get the facts you need to find a good breeder — and find out why you should avoid any other kind. Considering a grown dog? A mixed breed? Good for you! I give you plenty of information in this part to help you find a good source.

Chapter **1**

Considering the Canine Possibilities

You don't have to spend much time looking at dogs to realize that our canine companions may have started out as wolves, but we've meddled some since then with amazing results. No matter how many steps or how many hundreds of years passed, imagining the ancestor of a Maltese or Toy Poodle as a wolf is difficult at best. A Malamute, sure, a German Shepherd and maybe even a Collie — you can see the wolf in them. But a Maltese? Fluffy, sweet-natured, and small enough to fit in an oversized purse . . . it's hard to imagine such an animal chasing deer through a frozen forest or lifting a muzzle to howl at the moon.

But if you spend some time observing even the smallest, most adorable dogs, you will see the wolf. The same is true of every dog that has set foot on this earth since dogs began, generations of hounds and herding dogs, lap dogs and sled dogs. Despite the best efforts of our species to change their species, dogs are still, at heart, the animals they came from — pack animals with a language that's in many ways close to our own, making them a good fit in our own families.

That means Maltese or Malamute, Toy Poodle or Tibetan Mastiff, every dog is going to understand the meaning of a smile, both human and canine. Every dog is going to enjoy a good sniff of, and probably a roll on, the most disgusting, smelly thing available. And every dog, no matter the mix or breed, wants to be part of a family, a *pack*.

Considering Canine Packaging

Every dog may be a wolf at heart, but we've certainly done plenty to change the rest of the package, to soften some traits and strengthen others. No species on earth shows such diversity of size, shape, and purpose.

In my own home, I have dogs who'd crawl on their bellies for miles, skip meals, and forgo sleep on the off chance that someone, somewhere, will throw something into a body of water for them to retrieve, again and again and again until they fall over from exhaustion, still dripping the water that is as much their element as the air they breathe. One of my other dogs walks around puddles but has a tendency to herd children. My dogs are retrieving and herding dogs, in case you didn't guess. The behavior of one comes from the instinct to fetch prey, the other is motivated by an age-old desire to drive prey. Along the way, these hunting behaviors were separated — one to the retriever, one to the sheep dog — and bred to be stronger to give the animals a function in the human community.

TIP

Dog breeds and breed types differ in size, activity level, shedding level, and trainability. That means that becoming a canine expert is a good idea. Not for the opportunity to impress the family when you see a dog show on TV — "the Schipperke, a Belgian breed, first became popular as a watch dog for use on canal boats," you can say with authority — but for the ability to analyze how any particular breed or breed type will work as a member of your family.

REMEMBER

Choosing the right dog for you, your family, and your lives is the first step in acquiring the dog of your dreams.

Go back in time again to the wolf. Remember many of those desirable breed traits — chasing game, herding sheep, and protecting the pack — are wolf traits that have been strengthened or adjusted over time to make dogs a better fit in the human community. Other vestiges of other wolf traits live on in today's dogs, including the desire to know exactly where one stands in the pack, whether it's a canine or human family — and the accompanying desire to better one's status. (See how like us they are?)

Dogs, in general, are a little more easy-going than wolves, thanks to thousands of years of domestication. But you have to look no farther than dog-bite statistics to see that some problems still exist in the relationship between their kind and ours.

WARNING

The normal victims of these power struggles are children, the smallest, most vulnerable members of the "pack." When I read stories of a family dog — commonly an unneutered male from one of the currently popular tough breeds — that has attacked a child "without warning," I know that's not the whole story. While you may find some psycho dogs, in most cases the humans had more to do with the outcome than the dog did. They got a breed that was too much for them, compounded the problem by not socializing and training the animal, and then didn't recognize the warning signs of a dog looking to be leader. The result was a tragedy for both the child, who must live with the repercussions of an attack for the rest of his life, and for the dog, who usually loses his life in the aftermath. Need a better reason to proceed with caution in choosing a dog? I didn't think so.

Statistics show the dogs involved in attacks are most commonly unneutered males, especially young adults coming into their prime — just another reason why neutering is so important. For more reasons to neuter your pet, see Chapter 17.

WARNING

CALL OF THE WILD: WOLF-DOG HYBRIDS

We never seem to get the balance right when it comes to wolves. First we hated them, almost to extinction. Now we love them — and their close relatives, wolf-dog hybrids — with a devotion that is for many wolfdogs as lethal as the hatred it replaced.

The result of a breeding between a wolf and a dog — most commonly a Husky, Malamute or German Shepherd — the wolf-dog hybrid is a beautiful, intelligent animal and a potentially dangerous companion that few people can handle or adequately care for. They are often destructive and can rarely be house-trained. Determined and resourceful escape artists, they can be chillingly efficient predators.

On these points, virtually everyone agrees.

On the point of whether they should be allowed a place in human society at all, widespread and often heated disagreement exists.

The intelligence that fanciers adore, combined with size and strength, causes problems at maturity, when wolf-hybrids do what comes naturally: Try for a higher place in their social order, challenging the authority of their human "packmates." Human deaths and injuries are more common with these animals, as compared to domesticated dogs as a whole, and you hear many anecdotal accounts of vicious attacks — especially on children — by seemingly docile wolf-dog pets. It's not their fault: It's their nature!

Because of these problems, some communities have tried to ban the wolf-dog hybrids, many humane and animal control shelters will not put them up for adoption, and the few groups that do give permanent sanctuary to unwanted hybrids are always at capacity. As a result, many a wolf-dog hybrid has paid for the surge in popularity with its life.

All of which means the wolf-dog hybrid is a pet all but a few highly experienced and dedicated dog-lovers should avoid.

Always look at the history of your particular breed. A large, powerful dog developed to protect land or property, working on his own and making his own judgments, is not likely to accept your input graciously. He may be highly intelligent, and even biddable in the hands of experienced dog handlers, but in many situations, he's all too often a time bomb.

REMEMBER

For most people and most families, the best dog is one from a breed (or mix of breeds) that has been developed to be responsive to training and human guidance and isn't too hung up on being in charge. Dogs specially developed as companions, such as the toy breeds, fill that role, and so do some hunting and herding breeds, such as the Golden Retriever or the Collie.

Letting Go of Love at First Sight

In dogs as in humans, the one you're immediately and most powerfully attracted to may not be the best bet for a long-term companion. You may have grown up with Collies in a suburban home with a large yard and your mother home all day, and you may still consider the Collie your favorite breed. But a Collie may not be the best choice for you today if you live alone in an apartment and are fond of expensive clothes in dark colors. So start fresh, with a fair appraisal of your life and of the dogs who offer the best fit.

I grew up in a home where the undisputed best breed of all time was considered to be a Boxer. While I'm still fond of them — one of my "nephews" is my brother's Boxer, Taz — I haven't lived with one since I left home. The reason? Dog saliva gives me hives, and while Boxers aren't the drooliest breed around — the Newfoundland would probably win that prize — they are drooly enough to make me limit my exposure to them.

My mother, on the other hand, thinks nothing of carrying a towel to wipe off a dog, but the little "fur mice" that congregate in the corners of my house — my dogs shed so much I'm thinking of having sweaters made from the fur — would make her scream. I keep the hand-held vacuum close by but otherwise pay little attention to the fact that my medium-coated dogs drop black fur, hair by hair, every day, and the long-haired one produces enough gray, white, and tan fuzz during his twice-yearly big shed to fill a grocery bag a week.

Fur or drool. Sometimes choosing a dog that suits you comes down to something as simple as that.

Everyone wants the perfect family dog. But you must take into account many factors in choosing the dog who's a good match for your home.

Photo courtesy of Howell Book House/Mary Bloom

Starting from Scratch

Choosing a breed or breed type is one of the most enjoyable aspects of adopting a dog. You have a chance to window-shop on a grand scale, to discover dogs you've never heard of and imagine life with breeds you've never seen before.

Start with an open mind, and be honest about your own life, your own preferences, your own expectations. Keep these factors in mind: Size and space requirements; activity level, fur factor, and trainability and dominance.

Sizing up a breed type

The range of size in dogs is truly remarkable, so broad that even though they are the same species, it would be unthinkable for a dog from one end of the spectrum — say, a Saint Bernard — to mate with one from the other, like a Toy Poodle. (Although never underestimate the desire of any dog to try to make such a coupling possible!)

Some people who adore small dogs are scared of large ones. Some who adore large ones speak derisively of small ones, considering them less than "real dogs," and calling them "powder puffs," "dust mops," or "rats." Size doesn't seem to matter as much to the dogs themselves as to the people who own them; many small dogs have the pugnacious attitude that would be downright dangerous in a large dog, and many large dogs want nothing more than to curl up in their owners' laps.

REMEMBER

For the sake of practicality, size is the first factor you should look at when choosing a dog, if for no other reason than figuring out the cost difference between keeping a dog that eats one-quarter cup of food a day versus one that eats seven cups.

Dogs come in all sizes — even within the same breed, as shown by these American Eskimos.

Photo courtesy of Amanda Munz

My, that's a big dog!

For some people, only a large dog will do. Large dogs are the perfect choice for active people: joggers, hikers, and cross-country skiers. Even the friendliest large dog is a bigger crime deterrent than the surliest small dog (although crime-prevention experts say that even small dogs do a good job of alerting owners to the presence of strangers and letting the bad guys know that their approach has not gone unnoticed).

Should you consider protection training for your dog? See Chapter 14.

Large dogs can pull a wagon, walk for miles, chase a ball for hours. They are usually not so sensitive to the ear-pulls and tail-grabs of children, and a solid pat on the ribs will not send them flying across the room. Although a small dog may seem like a hot-water bottle if you let him share your bed, a large one may seem like a hot-water heater — as reassuring a presence and as loud (if they snore) as another human.

Still, there are trade-offs. The bigger a dog gets, the more food she eats and the more waste she produces. Big dogs can be more difficult to handle, more likely to knock over your toddler or your grandmother, more capable of destroying your home, more likely to inflict a serious injury should they decide to bite. A pushy small dog is amusing; a pushy large one is dangerous. Large dogs are harder to travel with and more expensive to kennel. If you don't own your own home, you may find securing housing that accepts a large dog nearly impossible.

Larger breeds generally need more exercise and are more likely to find other ways to shed nervous energy — like digging, barking, or chewing — if they don't get enough to keep them happy. Even the largest dogs are not impossible to keep in apartments, townhouses, and homes with small yards — if you doubt it, visit any doggy play group in Manhattan — but you have to work doubly hard to meet their exercise needs under those circumstances. Another thing to consider if you are an urban dog-owner is that a small dog can use a couple sheets of newspaper for relief on those blizzard days, while with a large dog the Sunday *New York Times* won't suffice.

Little things mean a lot

They may get their share of snickers, but little dogs don't care. They live a life big dogs can only dream about. Only a small dog can sneak into a department store hidden in an oversized purse. This kind of portability, the go-anywhere function-ality, combined with adorable faces and shoe-button eyes, makes the small dog a whole lot more fun to own than a lot of "real dog" people can imagine.

Some practical advantages exist, too. You can give a small dog a bath in the kitchen sink, without straining your back lifting the animal. A small dog can sit in your lap while you watch TV. They're no trouble to walk, even for small children. Food costs are low. Your walk is a rapid trot for them, so exercise is easy.

REMEMBER

On the negative side, toy breeds can be yappy, and they are definitely fragile, which makes them unsuitable for homes with boisterous children. They have to be protected, too, from large dogs, some of which may consider a powder-puff dog as an appetizer.

Keeping up with your dog

Activity level isn't tied to size, except at the extremes. Some of the largest dogs seem barely interested in getting out of bed in the morning, while some of the smallest are on the go practically 24 hours a day. In between are dogs of all sizes and various activity levels.

TIP

You can sometimes gauge a breed's activity level by looking at the work it was bred to perform but, still, all you're getting is an overall impression. Each individual varies by breeding, age, and health, although the general rule holds true: If a dog was bred to go all day long, a sporting breed, for example, it is going to be more consistently "up" than a large, heavy, guarding breed that only worked when intruders arrived. Dogs such as Dalmatians, bred to run for miles alongside carriages or horse-drawn fire-trucks, aren't likely to take a laid-back attitude toward life. Terriers, developed to keep vermin at bay, are always on the alert and ready to rumble.

Puppy-testing can also give you an idea about activity level and is especially useful when evaluating a pup whose parents are of different breeds. See Chapter 4 for more information.

Some breed types tend to be selectively active — on outside, off indoors. Many hunting dogs and their mixes are active in the fresh air and fields, but are fairly content to curl up in front of the fire in the house after their exercise requirements have been met. The world's fastest dog, the racing Greyhound, is so fond of lounging that one rescue group calls the animal "a 40 mph couch potato."

TIP

You can take the edge off the problems high activity can trigger — destructiveness and barking, for example — by giving active dogs enough aerobic exercise, daily, to keep them happy. When my retrievers don't get their exercise, they drive me crazy while I work. One good run, or a fast-paced game of fetch, settles them down just fine.

Activity level means more than exercise requirements, of course. Some breeds like not only to be moving constantly, but also to be keeping the world inform-ed of their activities. "Hyperactivity" and "yappiness" are also a matter of individual preference: One person's watchdog is another's yappy pest. For others, the playful liveliness of such breeds is ample trade-off for a little — or a lot — of extra barking. Again, be aware of what your tolerances are. Training can take the edge off the most undesirable of temperament traits, but nothing in this world can turn a peppy, barky Sheltie into a calm, quiet Bulldog.

WARNING

Some active breeds are so yappy that even their fanciers can't stand the noise and routinely have their dogs debarked. While the surgical removal of the vocal cords is sometimes the last chance for an otherwise good dog's survival (a discussion of barking problems is in Chapter 15), a breeder whose own dogs are debarked ought to give you pause. At the very least, debarked parents suggest that your puppy may grow into a dog who is unlikely to let a leaf fall without barking at it.

Greyhounds may have been bred to run, but when they retire from the track, most of them prefer to spend their days napping.

Beauty/photograph courtesy of www.greyhoundgang.com

Facing up to fur

Let me settle one thing up front: *There's no such thing as a dog with fur that doesn't shed.* (The slight hedge is for such breeds as the hairless variety of the Chinese Crested, a tiny little dog that can't shed what it doesn't have.) The corollary is that there's no such thing as a dog that's hypoallergenic. Some dogs do shed less and may be manageable for some asthmatics and allergy sufferers, but if you're not prepared for or capable of handling fur, you're better off with goldfish (not a cat and not a bird, because those can be even worse for many allergy sufferers).

The long and short of it

All dogs are covered with fur, except for the aforementioned Chinese Crested and a couple of other rare hairless breeds. But there the similarity ends, for the variety of coat lengths, colors, patterns, and textures is nearly endless.

Length? Think short fur like the Boxer to start with; then a little longer, like a Golden Retriever; then longer still, like a Collie; to the long-as-they-can-grow preferred locks of the show Komondor, a Rottweiler-sized dog covered with floor-length cords of twisted fur that looks like a cotton mop set in motion.

Color? Think sparkling white like some Samoyeds to glossy black like the Schipperke. Then think of everything in between, all kinds of colors with more words describing them than the marketing division of a fashion house could think up in a year. How about mouse-gray, fawn, wild boar, badger, and red stag? Wheaten and deadgrass, mahogany and chestnut? Medium brown? Too dull. Call the color *Isabella*; Doberman fanciers do.

Patterns? Spots, like the Dalmatian. Black with tan accents, like the Doberman, Rottweiler, Gordon Setter, or Manchester Terrier. Patches, like some Great Danes and Akitas. The tiger-stripes of the *brindles*, like Boxers or Pit Bull Terriers. The mottled mishmash of color known as *merle* in some Australian Shepherds, Collies, and Shelties. And don't forget the importance of accessories: white paws, white chests, white chest ruffs, and white head blazes.

And what about texture? Velvety short, long and silky, or wiry — and that's just in Dachshunds! Those coats exist elsewhere in the dog world, too, along with curly coats, wavy coats, rough coats, and smooth coats. Can you say lint brush? The short white hairs of a Dalmatian or the pale ones of a yellow Lab turn up on everything and are notoriously hard to get off. The Keeshond and the Collie, with luxurious coats so long and thick you can lose things in them, shed in the spring and the fall in clumps the size of hamsters — as do most of the breeds with a long, thick overcoat and a downy undercoat. The rest of the year, these fur factories shed "normally," as in a lot.

Some breeds shed so much long, silky fur that a small industry has sprung up to spin the hair into material for knitting, so dog-loving crafters can fashion their pets' fur into garments. A season's shedding is all they need to get enough yarn for a nice, toasty sweater.

More information on shedding is in the grooming section in Chapter 10.

REMEMBER

You can handle some of the fur preemptively by frequently combing and brushing your pet — what you pull out on a comb doesn't end up on your sofa — but you're still going to have plenty of hair with many breeds. If the hair is going to drive you crazy, think short-haired dog in darker color so the fur won't show as much.

Shedding isn't the only issue. Some dogs, such as poodles, have coats that need clipping every six weeks or so. You can learn to do the grooming yourself — your dog will probably survive the embarrassment — or you can take him to a groomer. If you choose the latter, that means money. Factor this in when deciding what type of dog to get.

Some pet-supply catalogs sell lint rollers in bulk at greatly reduced prices, as do pet-supply stores. You can also find a rubber squeegee-like tool that does a great job of pulling fur from carpets and upholstery, and vacuum cleaner attachments specially designed for dealing with pet hair.

When I bought my first long-haired dog more than twenty years ago, I left the breeder's home with pages of instructions — what to feed, what shots he'd had, how to get him registered, the names of trainers, the names of veterinarians, and the names of kennels. My head was spinning, and I paused on the porch, a puppy in my arms, and asked the breeder if I needed to know anything else.

She thought about it. "Yes," she said. "Never wear black."

Fashion dictates otherwise, so I became adept at using lint brushes. Years after Lance grew old and died, I was going through some financial records, looking for a receipt. In the file folder was a tiny tuft of dog hair. His. I almost cried.

I have a high tolerance for dog hair, but at least some of my dogs are now in sync with the trend: jet black. What they throw doesn't show, although the hair is still there.

Factoring in intelligence

People are always asking about how smart a particular dog is, as if that's good for anything more than bragging rights. Intelligence is fairly irrelevant when predicting how well a dog is going to work as a member of your family. What's more important is *trainability* or *biddability,* qualities that describe how much — or how little — a dog concerns herself with what you want her to do.

Part of the puzzle again goes back to looking at the job a breed was developed to perform. Some dogs — such as hounds — were developed to work alone or with other dogs but, in any case, independently of human control. The scent hounds — Beagles, Bloodhounds, and Basset Hounds — are more likely to follow their nose than your directions. Sight hounds — Afghan Hounds, Grey-hounds, and Salukis — aren't going to hear you at all once they get up to chasing speed. That doesn't mean that they won't wag their tail in rapt devotion after you get them back on a leash, but it does mean that in the heat of the chase, their instincts take over. Just as with a tendency to bark, training can take the edge off the tendency to ignore your wishes — but getting your dog to mind is going to be easier with some breeds than with others.

Consider three of the breeds most often touted as highly intelligent — the Border Collie, Golden Retriever, and the Doberman Pinscher. These dogs do extremely well in obedience competitions. Does that mean they're smart? Undoubtedly.

According to dog-intelligence expert Stanley Coren, these three breeds start to understand a command after they've had the command demonstrated less than five times. But something else is at work here, and if you think about how and why these dogs were developed, you can see what these breeds — a herding dog, a hunting dog, and a protection dog — have in common: They were all developed to work closely with a human handler. The successful performance of their work function — moving sheep around, retrieving downed game, and patrolling with a police officer or soldier — relied on teamwork between human and animal. They come prewired to look to a human for guidance, and if the human knows enough to provide that guidance, these breeds will gladly serve. That's their job, after all.

As with activity levels, intelligence and biddability are a little hard to predict in mixed-breed puppies. Puppy testing can help. See Chapter 4 for more information.

Decisions, More Decisions

You've probably got a breed or two in mind, or an idea of the characteristics you want in a dog — large, small, long-haired, or short-haired. Before you start looking for your pet, though, you should give a little bit of thought to some other details. What age of dog is right for you? What gender? And how much money is this going to cost, anyway?

WARNING

As with the people who want a Labrador Retriever because "we've always had Labs in our family," those who automatically choose a puppy, or always choose a male (or female), and aren't willing to be flexible on costs may be denying themselves the chance for a good dog.

Keep an open mind to the possibility that some details in the mental image of your dream dog should be left vague until you consider absolutely everything.

Puppy or grown dog?

The advantages of a puppy are obvious: Puppies are adorable, sweet, and cuddly. To look at them is to smile. A puppy is yours to work with, an almost-clean slate you can mold to fit perfectly into your life. (Or completely ruin if you're not careful!) Yours will be the only family she knows, as long as you keep up your part of the deal. That said, there are some real advantages to choosing a grown dog. They're often less expensive to acquire, and certainly less expensive to maintain, since their puppy shots and wormings are behind them. If you choose carefully, you can find one who's already house-trained, and maybe knows a little basic obedience, too.

So why don't more people consider a grown dog? The number one reason I hear is that most people believe that a recycled rover doesn't bond as well with their family as a puppy does. That's true if you intend to keep your dog in a barren backyard with little human contact. But if you welcome your dog fully into your life, she's yours just as much as the puppy you took from her mother at seven weeks. Some people say the bond is tighter because the dog has seen the world and knows how lucky she is.

I'm not sure about that, but I've seen plenty of both kinds of dogs. (And have some of each now.) The quality of love they show for their owners — and vice versa — is the same.

REMEMBER

A puppy is a good choice for you if you have the time, patience, and flexibility — not to mention the sense of humor — to deal with canine babyhood and adolescence. You won't find any shortcuts to the delightful business of puppy-raising. It's 3 a.m. walks and chewed loafers, endless hours of play and just as many hours of training. You don't really know what you're going to end up with until you end up with it — this is especially true of mixed-breed puppies, many of whom are bigger or smaller adults than anyone at the shelter could have guessed.

Puppyhood is a wonderful trip, full of surprises and delights, but one you shouldn't take if you aren't committed. If you don't put in the effort, you may end up with a dog who drives you crazy — or one you'll drive to the shelter when you can't stand him anymore.

Grown dogs have a bad reputation, one that's often undeserved. Aren't grown dogs that are up for adoption usually pets that *other* people couldn't stand? Is adopting one really such a good idea? It depends on the dog, of course. The real plus is this: While an adjustment period is inevitable with any canine relationship, it's a lot shorter with a grown dog.

Can you teach an old dog new tricks? She can be trained — all dogs, young and old, benefit from training — but you won't be able to influence her personality as much. If you've got a puppy with shy or aggressive tendencies, you can do things to help her before a problem arises (more on this in Chapter 9). If you have a shy or aggressive grown dog, change is a lot more difficult, and maybe not possible at all. Which is why you shouldn't be influenced by a sad story and big brown eyes when you're considering a grown dog.

REMEMBER

A grown dog is an excellent choice for situations where no one is home during the day. For retirees who love the companionship of a dog, but haven't the energy for a puppy. For someone who wants to feel good about giving a decent dog a second chance.

A puppy is an excellent addition to your family — and one that requires a lot of patience.

Greta/Photo courtesy of Stephanie and Michael Corby

There are so many mature dogs who deserve that second chance — mixed-breeds and purebreds both, retired racing dogs, service dogs, and show dogs. Dogs whose owners have died, divorced, or moved. Dogs who want nothing more than the chance to belong to someone.

In all the time I've been writing about dogs, I've watched lots of puppies grow up and disappear because the people who bought them did so because of emotion, not common sense. Consider your situation carefully, and if you honestly aren't up for a year of puppy antics, adopt a grown dog instead.

Male or female?

Does a male or female dog make a better pet? There's no way of settling that question for sure, so for most people the choice comes down to personal preference. You should consider *some* differences, however, because even spaying and neutering doesn't make males and females the same.

If you do not plan to spay or neuter your pet (more about that in Chapter 17) the differences are more distinct. Unspayed females are generally moodier than unneutered males. Although males tend to be more constant in temperament, they can be annoying in their constant pursuit of such male-dog activities as sex, leg-lifting, and territory protection. (Some would say constancy isn't a positive trait in these cases, and argue that some unneutered males aren't just constant, but rather constantly annoying.)

Unspayed females usually come into season for a couple weeks twice a year, during which time you need to deal with a varying amount of mess and the constant attention of canine suitors. Unneutered males may be less than attentive to your commands when the luscious smell of females in heat beckons. They can also be more likely to challenge your leadership — or anyone else's — at any time. Studies have shown, for example, that young, unneu-tered males are the most likely to be involved in attacks on children. Spaying or neutering generally evens things out a bit. It makes females more emotionally constant and males less likely to fight or roam. But differences remain.

TECHNICAL
STUFF

In some breeds, for example, males are considerably larger than females — as much as 20 or 30 pounds and two or three inches. *The Complete Dog Book,* available in most libraries and bookstores, contains the official AKC breed standards, the "blueprint" of each breed in all areas, including size. This should give you an idea of the size difference to expect, as in this citation regarding the Newfoundland: "Average height for adult dogs [males] is 28 inches, for adult bitches, 26 inches. Approximate weight of adult dogs ranges from 130 to 150 pounds, adult bitches from 100 to 120 pounds."

Other differences aren't so easily defined. In the more dominant breeds, such as the Rottweiler, a female may be sweeter and more anxious to please. In the more shy and standoffish breeds, such as the Shetland Sheepdog, a male may be more outgoing and friendly. In some breeds, such a Golden Retriever, you might not notice much difference at all, especially in altered pets.

TIP

It's a better idea to concentrate on the breed or breed type rather than the gender, since the toughest male of an easy-going breed is probably a bigger cupcake than the mildest female of a breed with dominant tendencies. Talking to reputable breeders gives you a clear picture how the sexes differ, not only in the breed as a whole, but also in particular breeding lines.

For some people, the choice comes down to matter of landscaping: Males kill shrubs by lifting their legs on them, females kill lawns by squatting. Although some males squat and some females lift (at least some of the time), the generalization is pretty much on the mark. For more on dogs and landscaping, see Chapter 22.

Cost considerations

How much should a puppy or dog cost? Prices vary so widely that you can pay anything from "free," to the (generally) less than $50 that shelters charge, to the deal-of-the-century price that breed-rescue groups charge for purebreds, to several hundred for an "ordinary" purebred, to several thousand dollars for a show-quality dog of a rare or red-hot breed.

In general, however, a purebred, pet-quality puppy from a reputable breeder costs between $400 and $1,000, depending on several factors:

>> Breeds that have small litters, such as many of the toy dogs, may cost more because there are fewer puppies to cover the costs of screening the dam for congenital defects, transporting her to the stud dog, paying the stud fee, caring for the mother during her pregnancy, and caring for the mother and puppies in the weeks that follow.

>> Breeds such as the Bulldog require high levels of veterinary care in the breeding process, including cesarean sections, and that, too, boosts the price of puppies.

>> Puppies with the potential to be successful in such canine endeavors as dog shows, field trials, or protection competition are more expensive, because these features are "add-ons" in the same way that a bigger engine or better options package drive up the price of a new car.

Bear in mind that a reputable breeder produces dogs hoping to improve her lines and, by extension, her breed, but she raises *all* her pups to be healthy companions first. More puppies end up with people who want a pet than with people who want a show dog, and a good breeder wants them all to be happy and well-cared for. If you want to lower your cost, consider this: Those things that distinguish the *pick* puppies — which can be something as unidentifiable to the majority of people as the correct placement of dots on a Dalmatian — are not really very significant to those who are looking for a companion animal. A knowledgeable breeder can explain those differences, most of which you can pick up by studying the breed standard.

REMEMBER

The true cost of a dog, of course, is in the upkeep, but at least you get to make payments on that. The most cost-conscious proper care — food, basic gear, preventive veterinary care, boarding or pet-sitting while you're on vacation — will cost you hundreds of dollars a year, and into the thousands for a 100-pound-plus dog who can consume 6 or 7 cups of high-quality kibble a day. Add in occasional veterinary emergencies and the strictly optional, but enjoyable, collecting of such tempting canine merchandise as a wardrobe of fancy collars, a softer, more decor-conscious bed, pictures with Santa, and breed wind chimes, and the cost of keeping a dog can consume a significant percentage of your budget.

As a result, you should keep the cost of acquiring a dog in perspective. A $500 purebred puppy from a reputable breeder costs $50 a year if you figure the cost over a ten-year lifespan. And $50 is about what it costs to keep my dogs in kibble for a month.

In the end, it's what you feel comfortable with, purebred or mixed, shelter dog or show dog. The price you pay has no bearing on the love a dog can offer.

Chapter **2**

Narrowing the Field

f I ask you to choose a subject you feel certain everyone has an opinion on, what would you pick? Politics? Religion? Sports?

I've never met a person who couldn't answer this question: What's your favorite (or least favorite) breed of dog?

Even people who'd never own a dog, wouldn't think of petting one, and cross the street when one approaches, are interested enough in dogs to know — or be misinformed about — the breed they'd least like to see off-leash. As for dog lovers, the topic of breed favorites can keep conversation going — civilly, one hopes — for hours. Even people who prefer all-Americans — the politically correct term for *mutt* — show a definite affinity for breed type: curly-headed little Poodle mixes, strapping Lab crosses, or scrappy terrier crosses.

TECHNICAL STUFF

What exactly is a breed? Do papers make the dog? Does popularity? Some crosses such as the cockapoo — one parent a Cocker, the other a Poodle — are so common that people start to think of them as a breed in their own right. And while the major purebred registries aren't in the business of recognizing such dogs, groups are springing up all the time to acknowledge their popularity.

Simply put, a *purebred dog* is one that when bred with another of its kind produces more of the same. Breed a Poodle to a Poodle and you get a litter of smart, curly-coated wonders. Breed a Cocker to a Cocker and you get long-eared, sweet natured pups with eyes you can get lost in.

Breed a cockapoo to a cockapoo, though, and you won't necessarily get more of the same. Some pups may look like the parents, some like Poodles, and some like Cockers.

The ability to produce predictable traits when bred is what defines a purebred. Which makes the Cocker Spaniel a breed, and so, too, the Poodle, but not cockapoos — or terra-poos, peke-a-poos, or labradoodles. Lots of mixes are out there, great pets one and all. But a breed? Sorry, no.

Playing Favorites

I became convinced of breed loyalty years ago when I realized that the dog show is the only sporting event where 90 percent of the spectators couldn't care less about the winner. People come for a variety of reasons, the following being only a few:

>> For the pure and simple pleasure of looking at the dogs

>> To talk about the dogs

>> To look at breed-related merchandise — key chains, books, and "I love my Doberman!" bumper stickers

>> To celebrate their last dog acquisition — "That Akita looks *just* like Kiro!" — or their next

>> To debate the relative merits of the three kinds of setters — English, Irish, and Gordon

>> To argue if taller, like the Irish Wolfhound, or heavier, like the Newfoundland, is the criterion for "biggest," and which one eats more

>> To marvel at the contrasts between long-legged and short-legged, between slender and stocky, between big and little

>> To celebrate the dog, in all its many incredible variations

But mark my words: No matter how many breeds they study, how many they talk about, how many they touch, the people leaving a dog show take with them the sure knowledge that *their* favorite breed — or favorite breed type — is best. Everyone believes that everyone else is slightly daft, or sorely misguided, not to share this point of view.

The difference of opinion makes for good-natured discussions, that's for sure. Although I lean toward hunting and herding dogs, some of my best friends are seriously into hound breeds, lovely long-legged darlings such as the Scottish Deerhound and the Greyhound. They roll their eyes when my retrievers run for a chance to swim, since their dogs don't even like walking through puddles. And my dogs' constant zest for life sometimes leaves them cold. "Retrievers!" they sniff. "Don't they *ever* settle down?" I give as good as I get, of course, and we all know we're only teasing. We may have different dogs, but we're all dog-lovers.

Reputable breeders strive to produce dogs that closely conform to a document called the *breed standard*, a blueprint that lays out the rules for things as major as size and as relatively minor as the distribution of dots on a Dalmatian. The breed clubs decide the rules, and organizations such as the American Kennel Club serve as the keeper of the standard. Dog show judges follow these standards to make their choices. American breed standards — along with official breed histories — are collected in *The Complete Dog Book* (Howell Book House), the American Kennel Club's bible. (Other registries will share their breed standards if you write to them.)

To find out more about what those judges are actually looking for and how a dog becomes a champion, see Chapter 16.

Mixed Breeds

Mixed breeds, mongrels, or mutts. Call them anything you want, but millions of them are out there, each and every one of them a true original.

Some people tell you that getting a mixed breed is a huge gamble. You don't know how big your puppy will get, or what she will look like when she's grown. You don't know if her father is a purebred dog with bad hips and a roving eye. You don't know if the circumstances of her birth and lack of early socialization by owners who wanted neither her nor her littermates and could not dump them fast enough will have long-term consequences that make her unsuitable as a family pet.

All of these statements are true. But let me clue you in: It's all a gamble, even with purebred dogs. You do the most you can to better the odds in your favor, close your eyes, say a prayer, and throw the dice.

And you can do things to improve your odds with mixed-breed dogs. Work with shelters and rescue groups that test the temperament and check out the health of the animals they put up for adoption. The best ones take the concept of *adoptability* a step further, putting dogs with problems through training and working with new owners after placement to smooth over the rough spots. You can find more on dealing with shelters and rescue groups in Chapter 3.

What you should *not* do is encourage irresponsibility by taking a mixed-breed puppy from the kids outside the supermarket, or the woman selling them for $5 at the flea market.

Why? Do you really think people who just want to "dump" puppies have taken care of the mother during pregnancy? Do you think they've given the puppies proper food and medical care, shots, and worming on schedule? Do you think someone who produces mixed-breed puppies intentionally — cockapoos, peke-a-poos, or super-sized pit bull mixes — is concerned with how many unwanted dogs die every year? What does that leave you with?

The roll of the genetic dice has produced some of the best dogs — oh so loveable mutts.

Emerson/Photo courtesy of Pam Mourouzis and Matt McClure

I'll tell you: People who shouldn't be breeding dogs. People who are contributing to the millions of dogs put to sleep as *surplus* or *unwanted* every year. People who haven't educated themselves enough to care, or have chosen to ignore the consequences of their actions.

Don't encourage this behavior. Do consider a mixed-breed dog, and look for one in a shelter or from a rescue group.

You can do more things with mixed-breed dogs than ever before. You can get them certified as a Canine Good Citizen (see Chapter 18 for more on this program).

You can train them and take them to the highest levels of national obedience competitions. You can train for the sport of agility. (More on these in Chapter 16.)

And you can love the heck out of them and be loved in return, which is, after all, the highest calling any dog can follow.

Who knows? You may even save on veterinary bills. While the evidence is far from conclusive, some experts assert that mixed breeds are healthier than purebreds. Don't count on it, though: Many mixed-breed dogs don't draw from a gene pool any larger than most purebreds: They're often cross-breds rather than true mixes, the offspring of two purebred dogs of different breeds. And as such, they've got a lot of the same inherited health problems purebreds do.

Evaluating Breeds

The rest of this chapter is a broad overview of the more than 150 breeds available in the United States and Canada today. And after I go over all the possibilities, I include a section on the purebreds most people will choose — the popular ones.

Dog breeds are divided by their original purpose into groups, including these AKC classifications:

- » Sporting
- » Hounds
- » Working
- » Terriers
- » Toys
- » Non-sporting
- » Herding

TECHNICAL STUFF

Why go with the American Kennel Club groupings? Because the venerable AKC is the Microsoft of the dog world, omnipresent and dominant, with an impact on all things dog. Only the Kennel Club, in Great Britain, can touch the AKC's clout. Other registries are out there, to be sure, including the Canadian Kennel Club, and, in the United States, the United Kennel Club and the American Rare Breed Association. But no canine organization, and there are thousands all over the world, is better known than the American Kennel Club, for better or for worse. I've used AKC rankings and groupings for examples in this chapter, but the popularity and availability of a breed in any particular country varies

Remember — no dog is perfect

REMEMBER

Every breed is perfect for someone, but *no* breed is suitable for everyone. Some breeds or breed types — because of reasonable size and activity levels, low-maintenance coats, high trainability, and low dominance — fit in a majority of dog-loving homes. Many of these breeds are not as well-known as others, and I've singled these and some others out for special consideration if you're looking to add a furry bundle to your home.

Still, no matter what any expert says, you're the one who has to live with your choice. So do your homework, be realistic, and proceed with caution.

I provide the background of the dogs in each of these groupings so that you can get a sense of what the breed was developed to do, which is an important step in determining how it will fit into your life. *Note:* When I mention breeds that are *good* or *bad*, the terms are not used to denigrate the breed itself, but rather to evaluate its suitability as a pet in an average family with neither the background nor the time to work with a less-suitable breed.

WARNING

WITH PUREBREDS, BREEDING COUNTS

If it were possible to have the sidebar title printed in red, with a red box and red arrows pointing to it, I would. That's because every day — yes, *every day* — I hear from a reader who has adopted a ton of heartache in getting the right breed from the wrong source. Health and temperament problems are *rampant* in purebred dogs, and your chances of getting a dog with a problem increase dramatically when you buy from a less than reputable source, such as a casual backyard breeder. This is especially true of popular breeds such as Labradors, Goldens, and Rotties.

Most purebred dogs in the United States are registered with the AKC, which also awards titles for show championships and other dog sports. Although the organization has assumed investigative and educational responsibilities over the years, the AKC is primarily in the business of processing paperwork. AKC is *not* a brand name, like Sony or Chevrolet. The organization, which is actually a federation of breed and kennel clubs, neither breeds dogs nor certifies breeders.

All the time you spend reading about breeds, considering breeds, and finally choosing a breed is completely and totally wasted if you rush out and buy from someone who isn't raising good examples of the breed. Your chances of getting a Labrador or Chow Chow or French Bulldog with the qualities associated with the breed rely on your ability to find a reputable breeder. Chapter 3 offers information on choosing a breeder.

Genetic defects are common in purebred dogs, thanks to unscrupulous, ignorant, or careless breeders. In addition to being a poor choice for a family pet, a sick dog can cost you lots of money. Among the most common inherited defects is *hip dysplasia*, a malformation of the hip joint. While hip dysplasia is widespread in medium- and large-sized dogs, other common congenital defects are more breed-specific, such as deafness in Dalmatians. You *must* become aware of which defects are common in whatever breed you choose so that you know to find a puppy whose parents are have been checked out by a registry such as the Orthopedic Foundation for Animals or the Canine Eye Registry Foundation.

The sporting group

Some of the best dogs for families are in this group, so you shouldn't be surprised that some of the most popular breeds, including the first and second most popular breeds, the Labrador and Golden Retrievers, call the sporting group home. One other sporting dog — the Cocker Spaniel — also routinely claims a spot in the AKC's top 10.

Sporting dogs such as the Labrador Retriever are a good match for active people.

Indy/Photo courtesy Alissa and Greg Schwipps

Like the hounds, these are hunting dogs. Unlike the hounds, sporting dogs cannot trace an ancestry to the earliest stages of human/dog companionship. Their development is more recent and is tied to the invention of the device that changed the world in so many other respects: the gun.

Sporting dogs — setters, pointers, retrievers, and spaniels — were developed not to chase and to kill game, but to help firearm-equipped hunters locate game birds, flush the birds from hiding places so that they could be shot, and bring back the dead and injured to the hunter's hand without further damage. While the traditional work of many breeds — such as the Bulldog, bred to fight a bull for the bloody amusement of the masses — is thankfully no longer available, many sporting dogs still practice their craft. Thousands are dual-purpose animals. Family pets who roll around with children by day and sleep on the beds by night, they are also working dogs who spend fall weekends joyously slogging through half-frozen fields with the hunter of the family.

Nor is their work confined to hunting. Within this group are two breeds — Golden and Labrador Retrievers — commonly trained to serve as helpers for people who are blind or use wheelchairs. In addition, the keen noses of many sporting dogs have been put to good use detecting drugs or explosives.

Most of these dogs are large, but not overly so, for a massive breed would possess neither the agility nor the stamina to survive a day in the field. Some smaller breeds are in this group, too — most notably the Cocker Spaniel, a happy little dog that doesn't do much hunting but has taken a couple of turns at the top of the popularity charts.

Coats are pretty reasonable in this group, as befits any class of dogs bred to spend time amongst the brambles — short, medium, and wiry coats are the rule. The exception is the Cocker Spaniel and, to some extent, the Golden Retriever, breeds that rarely hunt anymore and have more coat than would make sense for a field dog to bear.

WARNING

Popularity often breeds disaster, and that's certainly true of some breeds in this group. The Cocker Spaniel, in fact, could be the poster dog for the problems of popularity. What could be a near-perfect family dog should be sold with a warning label today because of health and temperament problems caused by bad breeders. Some Cockers are so unstable they cannot be trusted around children; others are made miserable by no fewer than a half-dozen common congenital problems. You have to be very careful when dealing with this breed, and find a reputable breeder. The same is true of others in this group, most notably the Labrador and Golden Retrievers. More on finding a reputable source for a dog is in Chapter 3.

TECHNICAL STUFF

In many sporting breeds, some dogs differ enough in body structure and temperament that they could almost be separate breeds. In most of these breeds the split is between *show* and *field*; that is, dogs bred with lots of coat and a more laid-back attitude for the show ring versus dogs bred for hunting instinct, a more practical amount of coat, and an intensity for work that is a must in field competitions. Unless you intend to hunt with your pet, a dog from a reputable show breeder is probably a better bet, because the energy and intensity of a field-trial dog can be a poor fit with all but the most active households.

SPORTING BREEDS IN BRIEF

History: The first dog registered with the American Kennel Club in 1886 was from the sporting group, the English Setter Adonis. The sporting group, which once included hounds, was one of two original groups — the other was non-sporting — and sporting dogs have been important in every imaginable canine endeavor ever since.

Most popular: Labrador Retriever, No. 1 in AKC rankings for 1999.

Least popular: Sussex Spaniel, No. 138 in AKC rankings for 1999.

Small- to medium-sized breeds (24 to 50 pounds): American Water Spaniel, Brittany, Cocker Spaniel, English Cocker Spaniel, English Springer Spaniel, Field Spaniel, Sussex Spaniel, Welsh Springer Spaniel.

Large breeds (50 to 80 pounds): Chesapeake Bay Retriever, Clumber Spaniel, Curly-Coated Retriever, English Setter, Flat-Coated Retriever, German Shorthaired Pointer, German Wirehaired Pointer, Golden Retriever, Gordon Setter, Irish Setter, Irish Water Spaniel, Labrador Retriever, Pointer, Spinone Italiano, Vizsla, Weimaraner, Wirehaired Pointing Griffon.

Activity level: Most sporting breeds have energy to burn, but the heavy, low-slung Clumber and Sussex Spaniels are relatively calm.

Some lesser-known breeds worth a good look:

- **American Water Spaniel.** A good-natured, easily trained, and adaptable dog, this smaller breed, developed by hunters in Wisconsin, is covered in short curls.

- **Nova Scotia Duck Tolling Retriever.** I'm breaking the rules here: The toller is registered by the Canadian Kennel Club, but not the American. Given the speed with which the AKC adds breeds these days, that may change in the years to come. This good-natured dog has a lot in common with Golden Retrievers, but in a smaller package, often with more energy.

- **Vizsla.** Think athleticism, brains, and an easy-care short coat in a manageable medium-sized dog and you'll be picturing this versatile and friendly Hungarian dog.

The hound group

The hound group consists of *scent hounds* (dogs who hunt by scent), *sight hounds* (dogs who hunt by sight), and one breed, the Dachshund that, based on its development to "go to ground" after vermin, arguably belongs with the terriers. Some of the oldest known of the world's breeds, such as the Saluki and Greyhound, are in this group, as well as breeds that have been in the United States since before the Revolutionary War. (George Washington kept Foxhounds at Mount Vernon; the records he kept on his dogs date to 1758.)

The size range is dramatic in this group, from miniature Dachshunds, about five inches tall at the shoulder with a weight of less than 10 pounds, to the tallest dog of all, the Irish Wolfhound, more than 30 inches tall and weighing more than 100 pounds.

For many of these breeds, you need look no further than their names to find the key to their origin: Otterhounds were developed in England to hunt otters; rabbits were the prey of Harriers. For other breeds this naming trend doesn't hold true; the Pharaoh in Pharaoh hound is a reference not to the dog's preferred game, but to his antiquity. The Petit Basset Griffon Vendeen was bred to hunt rabbits in France, but you wouldn't know that from the name, which means "small, low-slung, wire-coated dog of Vendee," (*Vendee* being a French province).

Two of the most recognizable breeds in the world are in this group — the Basset Hound and the Dachshund. So, too, is one of the world's most unusual breeds, the Basenji, which is incapable of barking and communicates pleasure by chortling or yodeling. Some wonderful potential pets are in this group, most notably the Beagle, a happy, sturdy dog considered to be an outstanding companion for children. Highly recommended, too, is the Basset Hound.

Do not expect hound breeds to watch your every step out of doors, however: They've got better things to do, following their nose and their eyes as their heritage demands. "Come" can be a difficult concept for many hounds. House-training can be tough with the scent hounds.

Coats are generally low-maintenance: Most, but not all, of these breeds are short- or wire-haired. The most notable exception is the Afghan Hound, whose long, silky coat tangles and mats quickly without constant attention.

TIP

Greyhounds don't rank that highly in AKC statistics — 129th in the most recent rankings — but that number is deceiving. Uncounted numbers of Greyhounds aren't registered with the AKC at all — they're racing dogs, coming straight off the track. With the growth of rescue organizations, these fleet-footed hounds are becoming an increasingly popular pet as word has gotten out on their generally sweet nature.

The working group

No doubt about it: Some pretty tough customers are in the working group, made up of no-nonsense dogs who earned their keep as protectors and load-pullers.

TECHNICAL STUFF

HOUND BREEDS IN BRIEF

History: The most ancient of all known breeds can be found in this group; the first hounds — a Basset Hound, Beagle, Bloodhound, Dachs-hund, Greyhound, and Harrier — were registered with the AKC in 1885. The hound breeds were originally classified with the sporting breeds, but got their own group in the late 1920s.

Most popular: Beagle, No. 5 in AKC rankings for 1999.

Least popular: Otterhound, No. 157 in AKC rankings for 1999.

Tiny breeds (less than 20 pounds): Dachshunds, standard and miniature.

Small- to medium-sized breeds (20 to 50 pounds): Basenji, Basset Hound, Beagle, Harrier, Norwegian Elkhound, Petit Basset Griffon Vendeen, Whippet.

Large breeds (50 to 80 pounds): Afghan Hound, American Foxhound, Black and Tan Coonhound, English Foxhound, Greyhound, Ibizan Hound, Pharaoh Hound, Rhodesian Ridgeback, Saluki.

Giant breeds (more than 80 pounds): Blood-hound, Borzoi, Irish Wolfhound, Otterhound, Scottish Deerhound.

Activity level: Most hounds have energy to burn, but most breeds are fairly calm in the house. Greyhounds, for example, are often called "40-mile-per-hour couch potatoes" for their decided preference for napping. Scent hounds tend to be more active than sight hounds.

Some lesser-known breeds worth a good look:

- Borzoi. A gentle, good-natured giant who's happy to nap the days away. If you're thinking of a manageable dog in a jumbo-sized package, this breed should be one you consider.

- Petit Basset Griffon Vendeen. Contrary to popular impression, this happy hound is *not* a wire-haired Basset Hound. The breed is considerably more agile and energetic than the Basset, a good choice for an active family. Plus, that fuzzy face melts your heart.

- Whippet. "The poor man's race horse," according to the breed standard, the Whippet is a lot tougher than his delicate looks suggest, yet gentle and quiet. He loves to snuggle, and his smooth coat is as close to low-maintenance as you could wish for.

Some dogs here relied on their size and untrusting attitude to keep the belongings of their employers safe. In recent years, the Rottweiler has been the fad protection breed of choice, their popularity fueled by fear of crime and the desire of some to own a formidable animal, whether they can control him or not.

Some of dogdom's gentle giants — the Great Dane and Newfoundland — are in this group, along with versatile smaller breeds developed for other work but who, today, excel in obedience and other dog sports. Modernity seems to have eluded the Nordic breeds, whose appearance and tendency to howl in the night are eerily reminiscent of the wolf.

TIP

If you like the look of the wolf but have wisely chosen to avoid the wolf-dog hybrid (see the sidebar on wolfdogs in Chapter 1), consider the Siberian Husky or Alaskan Malamute. They're still a lot of dog — and too much for many novices — but at least they're domesticated. In the right situation, both are good pets.

WARNING

With a few exceptions, the working group offers little for beginners. These breeds are powerful, intelligent, and prefer making their own decisions — unless you have the training skills and leadership ability to convince them otherwise. Despite their popularity, many of these breeds are best left in the hands of experienced dog handlers able to give these breeds the training and exercise they need to reach their full potential.

Also adding to the challenge, some of the more prolific shedders and high-maintenance coats can be found in this group. Other working dogs, however, are no problem in the coat-care department. One more caveat: This group includes more than a couple of world-class droolers, such as the Newfoundland.

Working dogs like having a job to do, even if it's not one they were traditionally bred for. The hardy Portuguese Water Dog was used in its home country — that would be Portugal — to assist fishermen by retrieving nets and other objects. What with the shortage of Portuguese fishermen and all, what's a working dog to do? The answer: Make do! In San Francisco, a handful of Portuguese Water Dogs have found a new outlet for their desire to work and love of swimming: They retrieve balls hit into the bay from the baseball stadium. The San Francisco Giants make a donation to an animal charity each time a member of the Baseball Aquatic Retrieval Korps (BARK, get it?) retrieves a ball from the bay. The BARK team has made a splash, to be sure.

REMEMBER

If you simply cannot live without some of the more dominant members of this group, you must be sure to socialize them early and often. Doing so will *not* hurt their protective instincts, but it *will* make them more discriminating in their uncharitable outlook on "strangers," a category that, for an unsocialized, untrained dog, may include your friends and relatives — or the neighbor's children. Early and constant obedience training is another must, not only to allow you to control these strong dogs, but also to keep them reminded of the chain of command. For more information, see "Early Puppy Training," Chapter 9.

WORKING BREEDS IN BRIEF

History: As long as humans have had property and goods, they've had dogs to protect them, so some of these breed are quite old. The first members of this group, the St. Bernard and Mastiff, were registered with the AKC in 1885. The working breeds were part of the non-sporting group until the early 1920s and then, for decades, remained the AKC's largest group. That distinction ended in 1983 when the herding breeds were separated from the balance of the working breeds and moved into their own group.

Most popular: Rottweiler, No. 8 in AKC rankings for 1999.

Least popular: Komondor, No. 133 in AKC rankings for 1999.

Small- to medium-sized breeds (20 to 50 pounds): Portuguese Water Dog, Standard Schnauzer.

Large breeds (50 to 80 pounds): Boxer, Dober-man Pinscher, Giant Schnauzer, Samoyed, Siberian Husky.

Giant breeds (more than 80 pounds): Akita, Alaskan Malamute, Bernese Mountain Dog, Bullmastiff, Great Dane, Great Pyrenees, Komondor, Kuvasz, Mastiff, Newfoundland, Rottweiler, St. Bernard, and Greater Swiss Mountain Dog.

Activity level: Many of these strong, powerful dogs are fairly laid-back, although exercise is still a must.

Some lesser-known breeds worth a good look:

- Bernese Mountain Dog. A good-natured family dog, the Berner's good looks — jet black with tan and white markings on legs, chest and face — has earned it a fair amount of work in advertising. This big dog is good natured and laid-back, and pretty trainable besides. Males can be really large, females less so. Although more difficult to find, the related Greater Swiss Mountain Dog has similar qualities with less hair.

- Portuguese Water Dog. Sometimes mistaken for a Poodle (to the horror of Portie fanciers) this curly- or wavy-coated rare breed was developed to help fishermen by retrieving objects, carrying messages, and doing other tasks that require swimming, which Porties still love. His fanciers tout his calmness and intelligence.

TERRIER BREEDS IN BRIEF

History: Terriers were developed from hounds to get into the places larger dogs could not when pursuing prey. The first members of this group, the Scottish Terrier, Bull Terrier, Fox Terrier, and Irish Terrier, were registered with the AKC in 1885. The terriers were part of the non-sporting group until they got their own group as part of the AKC's reorganization in the early 1920s.

Most popular: Miniature Schnauzer, No. 14 in AKC rankings for 1999.

Least popular: Sealyham Terrier, No. 140 in AKC rankings for 1999.

Small- to medium-sized breeds (15 to 50 pounds): Australian Terrier, Bedlington Terrier, Border Terrier, Bull Terrier, Cairn Terrier, Dandie Dinmont Terrier, Irish Terrier, Jack Russell Terrier, Kerry Blue Terrier, Lakeland Terrier, Standard Manchester Terrier, Miniature Bull Terrier, Miniature Schnauzer, Norfolk Terrier, Norwich Terrier, Scottish Terrier, Sealyham Terrier, Soft Coated Wheaten Terrier, Smooth Fox Terrier, Staffordshire Bull Terrier, Welsh Terrier, West Highland White Terrier, Wire Fox Terrier.

Large breeds (50 to 80 pounds): Airedale Terrier, American Staffordshire Terrier.

Activity level: The bull-and-terrier breeds can be quiet and calm. The classic terriers have energy to burn.

Some breeds worth a good look:

- Border Terrier. One of the softer terriers as far as temperament goes, this rough-coated charmer packs a lot of personality in less than 20 pounds. Some Borders do well in competitive obedience work and agility, which marks them as a cut above the pack in biddability.

- Soft Coated Wheaten Terrier. Another of the more mild-mannered terriers, this time in a medium package. Soft-coated refers to his trademark coat, which is silky and wavy, and *wheaten* notes the only allowable color, an eye-pleasing golden-brown that lightens as the dog matures. Unlike the Border Terrier, the Soft Coated Wheaten has the trademark terrier look: a long, fuzzy face with whiskers.

- Staffordshire Bull Terrier. The smallest of the bull-and-terrier breeds, this easy-care dog is a solid, go-anywhere companion. Deal with only a reputable show breeder, and be aware that you'll hear a lot of negative reactions when you're out with your pet. Socialize and train your dog; as the owner of the bull-and-terrier breed you have a responsibility to help improve the public's bad impression of any dog who resembles a pit bull.

The terrier group

Talk about moxie! These dogs, developed to go *mano a mano* with all manner of vermin, are not lacking in self-esteem. They know what they want, they're not shy about going for it, and they don't look charitably on those who get in their way.

Terrier fanciers call these qualities *fire*, but most terrier owners would call the traits unmanageable if these breeds weren't almost all small, and also possessed as good a sense of humor as you'll find in any dog, especially if the joke's on you.

The terriers should be looked at as two separate groups:

>> The first contains what most think of when they think *terrier:* Mostly small, mostly wire-coated breeds such as the Cairn Terrier and Miniature Schnauzer, dogs developed to dispatch rats, foxes, badgers, weasels, otters, and anything else people decided they could better do without.

>> The second group contains those breeds that resulted from crossings of bulldogs and terriers to produce animals such as the Bull Terrier that are as solidly built and heavily muscled as the bulldogs, but with the terrier's classic tenacity and boldness. These breeds, commonly — but incorrectly — lumped under the name *pit bull*, were developed to fight other dogs in cruel contests that have been illegal for decades.

Pet potential exists in both groups, but you do have to be especially cautious with the latter.

Classic terriers first. These dogs are tireless, plucky, and stylish, equally comfortable in city, suburban, or rural homes. Even small terriers are sturdy enough to be a child's pet, but their take-charge attitude can be a problem if they are not socialized and trained. If allowed to rule the roost, some of these little dynamos can become little despots, a dangerous role for any dog to assume, especially in homes with children.

Other common behavior problems come straight from the terrier's background: They dig and they bark. Key tools for a dog trying to out-burrow a badger or drive out a fox from the den, but not so appreciated in a suburban backyard. Some terriers may get a little glassy-eyed and drooly over the presence of rodents in the house — you may call hamsters, gerbils, rats, and mice "pets," but you'll never convince a terrier they belong. Terriers may also be less than civil to other dogs.

TECHNICAL STUFF

While you will find short-haired terriers and silky, long-haired terriers, most terriers have a wiry coat that needs *stripping* (plucking of the dead hairs) to keep them in show-ring condition. The owners of pet terriers usually skip this tedious task and use electric trimmers on their dogs instead or have a professional groomer do the job every couple of months. Aside from this factor, these breeds are pretty easy keepers in the coat department, and they don't shed much.

The bull-and-terrier breeds — the American Staffordshire Terrier, Bull Terrier, Miniature Bull Terrier, and Staffordshire Bull Terrier are the AKC versions — have come in for some bad press in recent years, and that's a shame, because these dogs were considered to be stable pets for generations. What prompted the change is they became popular with an element that broadened their traditional aggression toward other dogs, producing animals that would like as not bite people. Couple this trait with these dogs' awesome physical power and you've got an animal that justifiably should be feared.

If you buy from a reputable breeder, however, and socialize and train your puppy, you end up with a calm, sensible dog with an easy-care coat who provides good companionship for a human family — though he's still unlikely to be overly fond of other dogs, and people will be a little tentative because you own a "pit bull."

WARNING

Finding a reputable breeder is important for any dog you choose — Chapter 3 tells you just how important — but it's absolutely crucial with these bull-and-terrier breeds. Dogs from show lines are a better bet as pets. Good temperament is always on the mind of reputable breeders, who are anxious to prove their dogs deserve a chance in the face of legislative attempts in many cities and towns to ban these breeds. Buy from anyone other than a show breeder, and you may well end up with exactly the kind of dog these laws are aimed at. Make sure, too, that you socialize these dogs. More on that in Chapter 9.

Probably the most recognizable of all terriers is the Jack Russell, thanks to his starring roles in numerous commercials, on the TV shows *Frasier* and *Wishbone*, and in the movie *The Mask*. But just as you shouldn't expect a Collie to act like Lassie, you shouldn't expect a JRT to act like Eddie: It takes a lot of effort for any Jack Russell to sit still. A true terrier, this small dog is a barker and a digger, but his roguish charm makes up for it in the eyes of his devotees. Just make sure that you know what you're getting before you commit to a Jack Russell — or any dog.

The toy group

They're cute. They're feisty. They're often quite long-lived. And some places with "No Dogs Allowed" signs don't enforce the rules when it comes to these charming little dogs.

Toy dogs are the only ones who can routinely travel in the cabins of airliners because, generally, they're the only dogs whose carriers can fit under the seat.

They're special. Just ask them.

You can give them ironic names like Spike, Ripper, and Killer, and people will think you're clever. You can give them names like Daddy's Itsy-Bitsy Little Cutesy-Poo and people won't think you too addle-brained. You can dress them in sweaters. You can have their toenails painted bright red. You can laugh at their furious displays of territoriality when a large dog passes in front of your house, and you can pick them up to keep them out of trouble when that large dog decides he's not about to tolerate insults from a scrap of fur no bigger than his head.

TECHNICAL STUFF

TOYS BREEDS IN BRIEF

History: While toy dogs have been kept as pampered pets for centuries, the popularity of these breeds started to climb in the late nineteenth century. Although the AKC first registered a Yorkshire Terrier and a Pug in 1885, most early shows did not include classes for toy breeds. That changed in 1928 with the creation of the toy group.

Most popular: Chihuahua, No. 7 in AKC rankings for 1999, although Toy Poodles are counted together with the two larger varieties; as a single breed Poodles stand at No. 6.

Least popular: Lowchen, No. 134 in AKC ranking.

Size: All small, ranging from two pounds for some Chihuahuas to just under 20 for the stocky Pug. The group includes the Affenpinscher, Brussels Griffon, Cavalier King Charles Spaniel, Chihuahua, Chinese Crested, English Toy Spaniels, Italian Greyhound, Japanese Chin, Havanese, Lowchen, Maltese, Miniature Pinscher, Papillon, Pekinese, Pomeranian, Pug, Shih Tzu, Silky Terrier, Toy Manchester Terrier, Toy Poodle, and Yorkshire Terrier.

Activity level: Most toys are lively and energetic.

Some lesser-known breeds worth a good look:

- Chinese Crested. Looking for something a little out of the ordinary? The hairless version of this charming breed may fit the bill. With hair on their head, lower legs, and tail, these dogs resemble a prancing little pony. The crested also comes in a fully coated variety, called the *powderpuff*.

- English Toy Spaniel. Quiet, calm, and affectionate, this breed ought to be a little higher in the popularity parade. Pamper him all you want: He's unlikely to get an attitude.

- Papillon. This French breed was named for her large ears, which resemble the spread wings of a butterfly. Papillons do well in competitive obedience work, are happy to learn, and easy to teach.

Mostly what you can do with a toy breed is *enjoy*. Heaven knows they've enjoyed us. Most toy breeds haven't had to work for a living. While larger dogs were out pulling sleds, chasing deer, retrieving birds, herding sheep, or killing rats, these breeds spent their days being pampered and wondering when dinner would be served.

Smart dogs, no? Indeed, they've got brains inside those little heads, and they're anxious to use them. Toys are some of the brightest breeds around, and more than a few of them excel in obedience competitions. Better still, they love to be the center of attention and so are naturals when it comes to learning tricks.

Many of these breeds have luxurious coats that need either to be kept clipped short or groomed frequently to keep tangles and mats at bay. Some real shedders are in here, too, but because the dogs are small, so too, is the problem of dealing with the fur.

WARNING

These dogs are among the best for inexperienced dog owners, but some problems exist where children are concerned. Tiny dogs are fragile and not up to the rough handling that some children can dish out. You know your own children best: If they are gentle and thoughtful, a toy breed will do fine in your home. Otherwise, you may want to consider a larger breed or wait until your children are old enough to handle a little dog safely.

TIP

The hands-down best book on toy breeds — with lots of information on their special needs — is Darlene Arden's *The Irrepressible Toy Dog* (IDG Books Worldwide).

The non-sporting group

The only thing these dogs have in common is that they don't have enough in common with the breeds of any other group. This is the catchall group, and has been since the AKC had just two groups — Sporting and Non-Sporting.

You find dogs here like the Bichon Frise, who were bred to be pampered but are bigger than toys. A bird dog, the Finnish Spitz, is prized in his native land for his ability to bark his fool head off. (Go figure. At least he's cute, resembling a red fox.) You see the Poodle, a multipurpose breed that today is primarily a companion, but has worked as a retriever, truffle hunter, and circus performer. Then you have two bulldog breeds that have been without work for so long — bull-baiting long gone out of fashion — they didn't really count as working dogs any more. And although his official AKC history mentions nothing of it, dog experts say the Chow Chow was prized as much for his meat as for any other feature in his native China.

You can say one thing for sure about this group: Some top-notch companions are in it.

Primary among them in terms of numbers is the Poodle, a highly intelligent dog who has been the butt of more jokes than any other breed. Fortunately the Poodle enjoys laughter as well as any other dog, and if he knows he's the one being laughed at, he doesn't let on.

The number one reason Poodles are picked on is probably the way they are groomed for the show ring. While based on a theoretically useful clip that protected the chest and joints of a water dog, this style has been taken to the limit by fanciers. The hairstyle may be a plot to keep this popular breed out of even more hands, for underneath all this foppishness is a dog that even the most avid Poodle bashers would admire if they'd allow themselves to, especially if they considered the medium-sized Standard Poodle — a dog the size of a "real dog."

Coats run the gamut in this group, from the profuse shedding of the Chow Chow and Keeshond to the easy-care glamour of the dog who wears a tuxedo to even the most casual of occasions, the Boston Terrier.

WARNING

This group seems to have more than its share of congenital problems, some caused by irresponsible breeding, others a result of breeding for a body shape that, while distinctive, isn't really conducive to the normal patterns of canine life. Many Dalmatians are deaf; Bulldogs are prone to heatstroke and breathing difficulties; and a half-dozen congenital problems frequently show up in Poodles. The sometimes difficult Chow Chow has a reputation as the breed veterinarians like to work with least. As with all groups, the larger breeds here are candidates for hip dysplasia.

The herding group

Not many people keep sheep and cattle these days, but that doesn't bother the herding breeds much. These versatile and intelligent dogs have made their mark in the modern-day world as police dogs, drug-detection dogs, search-and-rescue dogs, and even movie stars.

Most of them, however, will serve as pets, and some wonderful breeds can fill that role in this group.

The work of the sheep dog is older than the Bible and almost as widespread. While many countries have native sheep dogs — including the United States, where the Australian Shepherd was developed — most of the commonly known herding dogs come from the United Kingdom and France. Some of these breeds are now counted among the glamour-pusses of dogdom, but for generations they were just plain and humble working dogs whose ability to do what humans could not — control large herds of animals — was essential in the development of civilization.

TECHNICAL STUFF

NON-SPORTING BREEDS IN BRIEF

History: The AKC's class for dogs that don't fit anywhere else, this group has been around since the AKC began. The first member of this group to be registered was a Bulldog, in 1886.

Most popular: Poodle, No. 6 in AKC rankings for 1999, although the ranking includes Toy Poodles, as well as the Miniature and Standard varieties seen in this group.

Least popular: Finnish Spitz, No. 142 in AKC rankings for 1999.

Tiny breeds (less than 15 pounds): Tibetan Spaniel, Schipperke.

Small- to medium-sized breeds (15 to 50 pounds): American Eskimo Dog, Bichon Frise, Boston Terrier, Bulldog, Shar-Pei, Finnish Spitz, French Bulldog, Keeshond, Lhasa Apso, Miniature Poodle, Shiba Inu, Tibetan Terrier.

Large breeds (50 to 80 pounds): Chow Chow, Dalmatian, Standard Poodle.

Activity level: All across the board. Poodles at the high end, Bulldogs at the low end.

Some breeds worth a good look:

- Boston Terrier. They got it half-right. This smart-looking dog was developed in Boston, but he isn't a terrier. Sometimes called a Boston Bull Terrier, which makes a little more sense, because he does have bulldog in his background. A playful, lively breed, if you don't mind a little wheezing.

- French Bulldog. Another wheezer who may steal your heart. He's playful and sweet, an outgoing character who has no idea a lot of people think him homely, with his squat body, pushed-in face, and bat ears.

- Keeshond. Yes, they have a lot of fur. Are you going to hold that against a breed that actually pulls his lips back and smiles? This medium-sized breed is amiable, reasonably trainable, and gets along well with most everyone, including other pets.

The herding breeds are among the most intelligent and biddable of all dogs, developed to work in partnership with a human handler as the sporting breeds were. The nature of their work, however, demands a dog a little more aggressive than the setters, retrievers, and spaniels who serve hunters. Herding dogs work through intimidation and harassment to control animals sometimes larger than they are. This job is not for wimps and, indeed, the herding instinct is a toned-down version of techniques used by wolves working a herd of prey animals, looking for a weakling to kill. Sometimes a hard–driving herding dog gets so seriously annoyed at an animal who isn't moving where he wants that he takes a hunk out of him — although this technique is frowned on!

HERDING BREEDS IN BRIEF

History: Herding was the first new AKC group in more than 50 years when these breeds were pulled out of the oversized working group in 1983. The Collie was the first breed in this group to be registered with the AKC, in 1885.

Most popular: German Shepherd, No. 3 in AKC rankings for 1999.

Least popular: Canaan Dog, No. 141 in AKC ranking.

Small- to medium-sized breeds (15 to 50 pounds): Australian Cattle Dog, Bearded Collie, Border Collie, Canaan Dog, Cardigan Welsh Corgi, Pembroke Welsh Corgi, Puli, Shetland Sheepdog.

Large breeds (50 to 80 pounds): Australian Shepherd, Belgian Malinois, Belgian Sheepdog, Belgian Tervuren, Bouvier des Flandres, Briard, German Shepherd Dog, Old English Sheepdog, rough Collie, smooth Collie.

Activity level: These agile breeds have energy to burn.

Some breeds worth a good look:

- Bearded Collie. The bright, sweet-natured breed with the fuzzy face is occasionally mistaken for an Old English Sheepdog. A Beardie fancier will probably put the record straight by pointing out that this herding dog is one of the U.K.'s oldest breeds, older than the Old English, which isn't very old at all. The only thing bad about this breed is that their silky coats — especially profuse on their legs — means hours of dematting should you be foolish enough to take your dog into the fields. They're also a tad barky.

- Smooth Collie. Call it the Collie-with-a-haircut if you like, these short-haired dogs should be more popular. They still shed, but nothing like their long-haired relatives. Although you shouldn't expect your Collie to pull children out of wells Lassie-style, the generous Collie temperament is preserved in the smooth Collie. However, some say smooths are a little more *reserved*, which is breederspeak for a little timid.

- Welsh Corgis. Cardigans have tails, Pembrokes don't, but all Corgis have attitude, and you gotta love them for it. These dogs are smart and highly trainable, but they're as likely to train you as the other way around if you're not careful. The short-legged dynamos are sturdy enough for children. Get two, because few things will make you smile faster than seeing a pack of Corgis run.

This combination makes for a great working dog, but should raise a flag of caution if you're looking for a pet. The herding breeds that still work today — as herding or protection dogs — may be a little much for novices to handle. What's arguably the dog world's whiz kid and best sheep dog ever made, the Border Collie, doesn't take well to the confines of a suburban backyard and a life without challenges. The same goes for the German Shepherd and the three Belgian shepherds, the Tervuren, Malinois, and Sheepdog, breeds with so much potential that denying them a chance to fulfill it ought to be a crime.

Other dogs in this group, although plenty smart, have not nearly as much drive. Some of them have been cultivated primarily as pets for generations. Long before Lassie came home, Queen Victoria took a liking to the Collie, and the smaller herding dogs are well-loved companions in many homes.

Almost every one of the large breeds in this group is prone to hip dysplasia, and the German Shepherd is susceptible to a half-dozen additional congenital defects.

Coats vary in this group, including many profuse shedders, such as the rough Collie (which many don't realize comes in a short-haired variety, called *smooth* by fanciers) and the Shetland Sheepdog (which is, please note, a notorious barker). You do find some easy-care coats here, as well as the second of the AKC's two Hungarian corded breeds, the Puli. (The other, the Komondor, is found in the working group.)

Many of these breeds still demonstrate a strong desire to keep things in a nice, tight herd. They do so with toys, other pets, children, and even party guests. An acquaintance of mine's Australian Shepherd once demonstrated this trait at a backyard party. The dog spent the early part of the event nudging guests, slowly and oh-so subtly working around the group until they moved unwittingly toward the center of the yard, realized what the dog had done, and had a good laugh. Then they spread out again — much to the shepherd's frustration, no doubt!

A world of other breeds

Just slightly more than 150 breeds in the seven different groups are allowed to compete for American Kennel Club championships; at least twice that many breeds are in the world. That leaves a whole lot of purebred dogs unaccounted for, although the AKC seems to be quickly bringing many of them into the fold. Border Collies and Jack Russell Terriers are two breeds to have gained full AKC status in recent years — often over the howls of protest of some fanciers, who believe AKC recognition will ruin their breeds.

Information on non-AKC breeds is a little harder to find, but you must make an effort if considering one of these breeds. Your library may have the AKC's book of breed standards, *The Complete Dog Book,* but it is considerably less likely to have standards from the Canadian Kennel Club, the United Kennel Club, or the American Rare Breed Association, much less those from breed clubs themselves or the kennel clubs in other countries. A reputable breeder will have those standards, so ask. Ask, too, about congenital defects, dominance and trainability, activity levels, shedding, and grooming requirements.

TIP

The Internet is a great place to research any breed, but it may be the *best* way to find out information on a rare one. Because book publishers are in the business of selling books — big surprise there, huh? — you'll likely never see *Otterhounds For Dummies.* There just aren't enough Otterhounds to make it profitable to produce a book on them. But the Internet always amazes, with Web sites developed by breed fanciers to educate and celebrate the less common breeds. (For more on dog-friendly Web-surfing, see Chapter 23.)

Popular Breeds: The Rundown

We like to consider ourselves rugged individualists, and yet we find ourselves wearing clothes that look like everyone else's, driving what everyone else drives, watching the same TV shows, and noshing on the same trendy foods. It shouldn't come as a surprise to anyone, then, that we tend to choose what's popular when it comes to dogs, too. The American Kennel Club registers some 150 breeds of dogs, but nearly three-quarters of all the dogs registered come from the breeds in the top 20. Even more telling: Better than one in ten dogs registered is a Labrador Retriever, and one in five dogs registered is either a Labrador or a Golden Retriever. So much for rugged individualism!

Now, these retrievers are wonderful pets, to be sure. But is there really a good reason for a Golden (AKC's No. 2 breed in 1999) to be 136 times more popular than the Flat-Coated Retriever (AKC's No. 100 breed in 1999), since the Flat-Coat isn't really all that different a breed? Why are Cocker Spaniels everywhere and Field Spaniels seen only at shows, and rarely at that? Why don't more people like smooth Collies, dogs with all the virtue of their Lassie-look relatives and none of the coat?

Okay, enough of my little rant. Three out of four of you are going to end up with one of the top 20 breeds, so let me give you a snapshot of what you're in for, a basic overview of the good and not-so-good on each breed.

WARNING

Remember — more than remember, *burn it into your brain* — nothing I've said here counts for squat if you buy a pup from anyone but a reputable breeder — look for more on that topic in Chapter 3.

TIP

Dogs For Dummies is a basic reference, and as such I don't have room for a complete run-down on every breed, nor even for a detailed analysis of the most popular breeds. Fortunately, it's easy to find some great books on nothing but evaluating dog breeds. Among my favorites: *Your Purebred Puppy: A Buyer's Guide*, by Michele Lowell (Henry Holt); *Paws To Consider: Choosing the Right Dog for You and Your Family*, by Brian Killcommons and Sarah Wilson (Warner Books); and *The Perfect Match: A Dog Buyer's Guide*, by Chris Walkowicz (IDG Books Worldwide).

Now that I've gotten all these little niceties and caveats out of the way, let's jump forward with my helpful, educated, and perhaps scandalous overview of the 20 most popular breeds. Hate mail can be directed to me at the address at the end of the introduction. And remember: If you sic your Rottweiler on me, that just proves my point.

The breeds appear in order of their 1999 popularity with the American Kennel Club. It's a given that these popular breeds have congenital health problems: Ask the breeder what they are, and insist on health certifications on both parents. Or walk away. Quickly. Again, remember that my comments are about dogs from reputable breeders. Which is the only kind of breeder you should be considering (have I stressed that enough?). Oh, and I've marked as *Dummies Approved* the breeds that are versatile, good-natured, and easy enough to care for in terms of shedding (low to moderate), health, and ease of training (especially housetraining) to fit into nearly any household.

TIP

Labrador Retriever. Good-natured, great with children, highly trainable. Energetic youngsters mature into thoughtful and devoted adults — after a couple of years and with consistent, persistent training and lots of exercise. Easy-care short coat. Dogs bred for field work are lankier, leaner, and higher energy — fine for an active owner, but too much for others. Other lines may be more laid-back, but they still need exercise — Labradors have a tendency to put on weight like nobody's business. Shedding is minimal. Barks to alert, but may help the burglar out with the silverware. Size: Big, 60 to 90 pounds.

TIP

Golden Retriever. The biggest problem with the Golden Retriever — next to shedding, which they do lots of — is that people buy one expecting their pup to turn automatically into a paragon of easy-going canine perfection. This transformation from adorable puppy to perfect pet doesn't happen without effort on the owner's part. The good news is that the effort will be a pleasure, for a good Golden loves to learn and lives to please. Congenital problems include those of the hips, heart, and eyes, so insist on health certifications on both parents. Barks to welcome the burglar, and will then help him out with the silverware. Size: Big, 60 to 90 pounds.

German Shepherd Dog. An intelligent, versatile, and protective dog, there may be nothing like a well-bred German Shepherd. Unfortunately, plenty of dogs out there are indeed nothing like a well-bred German Shepherd, even though their paperwork and appearance says that's indeed the breed they are. This breed has been nearly destroyed by popularity, and if you want one, you must — *absolutely must* — shop carefully or risk getting a sick, shy, or downright dangerously aggressive dog. Year-round shedder, shedder, shedder. Barks to alert, and willing and capable of putting some bite into the threat. Size: Big, 60 to 90 pounds.

Dachshund. The Dachshund is a lot of dog in a small (and funny-shaped) package. As it is, this clever and sometimes willful breed comes in three coat types — smooth (or short-haired), long-haired, and wire-coated — and two sizes, standard and miniature. The wire-coated look like long-backed terriers; the long-haired look like short-legged setters. Those long backs can give them problems, and do, so you must be careful to keep their weight down and discourage jumping. Good with children, although children aren't always so good with them — a dropped dog can hurt his back pretty easily. They can be yappy and hard to house-train. Not much of a shedder. Size: Tiny (for the minis) and small (for the standards), less than 10 pounds to more than 25.

Beagle. Oh, what a happy dog! Sturdy and compact, the little hound wants nothing more than to follow his nose. Can't blame them, really, but the trait can get them into trouble — Beagles can be roamers, escape artists, and house-training challenges. Independent of spirit and a tad hard to train, as well. Their friendliness and size makes them a good children's pet, especially for the youngster who needs a leashed companion for wandering. Easy-care coat, not much shedding. Barking? Beagles don't bark, really: *They give voice,* a howling and persistent arooo-arooo-arooo that is music to the hunter's ear but may get on the nerves of others. Size: Small, 20 to 30 pounds (but these food lovers bulk up easily, so watch 'em!).

TIP

Poodle. The Poodle is loathed by some men who seem insecure in their masculinity and fussed over constantly by some women who really need to get out more. People ought to be ashamed of what they do to those Poodles unfortunate enough to be show dogs — it's grooming gone mad, I tell you! Mad! The Poodle — all three sizes count as a single breed — was the nation's top dog for years, and with good reason. Poodles are brilliant, easy to train, fun to be around, and possess an exceptionally low-shed coat (which must, please note, be professionally groomed at six-week intervals). Minis and Standards are great with kids; Toys are too delicate for all but the gentlest and most respectful of children. Barky, especially the small ones, but not all that protective. (Although I know of Standards who have been protection-trained!) Size: Tiny (for Toys), small (for Miniatures), big (for Standards), less than 10 pounds to around 70.

Chihuahua. *Yo quiero "enough already"?* A clever advertising campaign (or TV show or movie) is not a reason to get a dog. Honest. You'll find plenty of other reasons to get a Chihuahua, though, if a bright, clean, and loyal (some say possessive) toy dog is what you fancy. Some can be barky, and more than a little bit protective, although at less than 10 pounds no Chihuahua will be able to mount a formidable defense. Comes in the popular and easily recognizable short-haired version and a fluffier, long-haired variety as well. Too delicate for all but the gentlest and most respectful of children. Size: Tiny, less than 10 pounds. One of the weirdest stories you'll hear about this breed: Some people claim they cure asthma. Sorry, 'taint true.

Rottweiler. The Rottie caught fire in the 90s, climbing all the way to the AKC's second most popular breed before bad press and worse dogs started the breed on the inevitable move downward. Breeders of the clueless, careless, and opportunistic variety have nearly laid waste to a noble breed, and my advice to most people who ask me about a Rottweiler these days is to consider something else. Even the good ones are often too much dog — too big, too strong, too willful, and too smart. Sweet-natured Rotties? You bet they're out there. But also out there are lots of poorly socialized dogs with hair-trigger tempers that are a danger to society. If you must have a Rottweiler, you need to find a good breeder, and you need to socialize and train your puppy from the day you bring him home. Easy-care short coat. Drooly. Size: Big to Giant, 75 to more than 100 pounds.

Yorkshire Terrier. Bright, affectionate, willful, and very, very yappy. Protective and plucky, sometimes foolishly so. Charming but manipulative — Yorkies are adorable, know it, and are not above using their adorability to get what they want out of their owners. If you let them, they will become horrid little brats. Spoil them, sure, but don't let them get away with *everything*. Set some limits and stick to them. You'll have a better relationship with your little wonder as a result. Not a lot of shedding, but you'll want to have your Yorkie professionally clipped every couple of months. Too delicate for all but the gentlest and most respectful of children. Like many toy breeds, Yorkies can be a challenge to house-train. Size: Tiny, less than 10 pounds.

Boxer. I grew up with Boxers, learned to walk holding onto the collar of one, and still light up when I see one. Smart, loyal, protective, playful — and more than a little bit willful. Great with children, although a bit bouncy and strong for toddlers. Now for the really bad news: Boxers are prone to cancer and heart problems, and tend to die young. Still, a few years with a good Boxer is likely better than a few more years with many other breeds. The Boxer seems to be the up-and-coming breed of choice for those who want a "macho-looking" breed, so beware: The quick-buck breeders are out in force. Easy-care coat, not much shedding. Some boxers drool; others snore. Some drool *and* snore.

TIP

Shih Tzu. Smart, quick to learn, friendly to just about anyone, the Shih Tzu is the epitome of what toy breeds are all about: Companionship. If you spoil them, they won't take quite as much advantage of you as some of the more dominant toy breeds — but keep the spoiling to a minimum, anyway. As with many toy breeds, housetraining can be challenging. They don't shed much, but are best kept clipped short by a professional groomer every couple of months. A little larger and more robust than the tiniest of toys, the Shih Tzu is okay with all but the most rambunctious children. Size: Tiny to Small, under 20 pounds.

Pomeranian. A lot like the Yorkie in temperament, the Pomeranian is another dog we should be glad doesn't come in a large size. The Pom can be a foxy-faced brat if spoiled without limits, and a marvelously spunky companion if raised sensibly. House-training can be a problem, especially with males, who like to mark territory inside. Barky, bold, and not too sensible when it comes to larger dogs. That lush coat does shed, but remember that the most active small shedder is still small enough so that the mess isn't really much of a problem. Pomeranians are pretty tough characters, which makes them okay for all but the most rambunctious children. Size: Tiny, under 10 pounds.

Cocker Spaniel. Another top dog almost ruined by bad breeding. Aside from having too much coat — these dogs are best kept clipped — the Cocker should be everything you'd want in a canine companion. Perfect size, neither too big nor too small, plus a happy, outgoing, and loving temperament, brains, and a desire to please. That's what Cockers *should* be, but a lot of them aren't. Instead, the world is full of neurotic and sickly Cockers, and some that are so snappy they're dangerous. It's hard to imagine a better dog for children than a well-bred, well-socialized Cocker Spaniel; hard to imagine a worse one than some of the ones offered up by careless breeders. Not an overbarker. Size: Small, under 30 pounds (but Cockers are another of those breeds with a tendency to pork up, so watch the diet!).

Miniature Schnauzer. This breed has a face that perfectly captures the little devil inside each dog, complete with shoe-button eyes that make it impossible to do anything but forgive any transgression. The Schnauzer is a terrier, and like all terriers he's a busy, smart, and fun little dog with a high opinion of himself and a desire for playful, active companionship. A robust little dog who can handle the rough-and-tumble of life with children easily. A trip to a professional groomer every couple of months is a must. The worst trait: barking. Miniature Schnauzers are very yappy. Size: Small, less than 25 pounds.

Shetland Sheepdog. Beautiful, devoted, brilliant, and playful — what's not to like about a Sheltie? Unfortunately, a lot. I've had Shelties all my adult life and spent a few years rescuing and placing homeless ones. Dozens of foster Shelties have passed through my doors, with an appalling amount of downright annoying and neurotic behavior. Some of these dogs can be very shy, snappy, and very, very yappy. Oh, but when you find a good one, your heart will just melt. Shelties love to learn, and make training seem easy, they pick things up so quickly. Even the best ones can be hesitant around strangers — breeders call it *reserved*, and consider it proper temperament. I call it *shy* and would like to see a move away from it by those who care about this breed. Shedding is seasonal — twice a year Shelties *blow coat*, which means losing it in handfuls. Otherwise, shedding isn't so bad. Children are fine for this breed; in fact, training a Sheltie is a great project for any child. Size: Small, less than 30 pounds.

Pug. The largest of the toy breeds, the Pug has been growing in popularity, and with good reason: This is a great little dog. Sturdy, funny, easy-going, and loving; great with children; and at home in any family situation. The short coat is easy-care. Not much of a barker, and friendly to all. Is there a downside to the breed?

TIP

Snoring, maybe, but I think it's adorable. The Pug is the only breed I know of with a Latin motto: *Multum in parvo* (meaning "a lot of dog in a small space"). Oh, absolutely. Small, under 20 pounds (but with a tendency to eat his way larger, so beware!).

Miniature Pinscher. The lively little Min-Pin looks like a tiny Doberman, but the breeds aren't related by anything but appearance and the desire to protect. The little dog is has been around forever, while the Doberman is a modern development. Min-Pins don't seem to realize they're small, and will joyously defend you to the best of their ability. Fine, but all that energetic protectiveness has a downside: These dogs are horribly, horribly yappy and can be rather snappy. They're naturally strong-willed, and can be impossible to housetrain. Too delicate for life with all but the most gentle and respectful children. Easy-care coat. Size: Toy, less than 10 pounds.

Siberian Husky. The Sibe is a fish out of water in a suburban backyard, and will express his discontent with howling, digging, and chewing. Getting out and roaming is a favorite pastime, too. Don't blame the dog — this breed was developed to be on the move for hours, at an effortless trot that chews up miles while pulling a sled. If you aren't going to make an effort to see that those exercise needs are met, you'll likely be unhappy with this dog. The Sibe is good-natured and easy-going, not much of a barker and not very protective. Independent and smart, but not that interested in obedience. Twice a year comes the big shed, when handfuls of coat the size of kittens will come off your dog. Fine with children. If you're active — running or, even better, cross-country skiing — you couldn't ask for a better workout partner. Otherwise . . . maybe not the best choice. Size: Large, 50 to 70 pounds.

TIP

Boston Terrier. Bostons are another breed that deserves its popularity — they're a good, solid dog in a reasonable size, loyal, bright, loving, and playful. The good ones have an air of outgoing self-confidence fitting of any dog who wears a tuxedo every day of his life. Good with children, not too noisy, and comfortable in most any living situation. They snore and snort, but it's cute, really. Coat care is effortless. In all, just a neat little dog. Size: Small, less than 30 pounds.

Maltese. Smart, loving, and bubbly, the Maltese is another of those little gems you find among the toys. In the show ring, these dogs look like little angels in their flowing, floor-length white coats, but they do best with regular, professional clipping — those coats are impractical for everyday life. The Maltese is so smart that they seem to train their owners — I know of more than one who has her people completely at her beck and call. Fortunately, they're good-natured despots, so spoil away. Too delicate for all but the gentlest and most respectful of children. Like many toy breeds, the Maltese can be yappy. This little dog has a mind that's too keen to waste: They love to learn, and live to show off. Size: Tiny, less than 15 pounds.

Chapter **3**

Finding Out about Breeders, Shelters, and Other Sources

You've done your homework. You've evaluated your likes and dislikes, and you've taken a good, hard look at which breeds or breed types mesh with your lifestyle. (And if you haven't, you may want to take a look at Chapters 1 and 2 for guidance.) You're ready to move from picking the kind of dog you like to picking the individual dog you want to share your life with.

Where do you find that dog?

You can find puppies and dogs through many sources — examples include breeders, shelters, and pet stores. Although locating the perfect pet is at times trying and difficult, someone, somewhere, has a wonderful pet for you. There is no "right" source, and it's possible to get a good pet from a source that seems less-than-ideal. But *possible* and *probable* are two different things, and as an informed consumer you want to work to narrow your risk so that you increase the chances of coming up with a healthy and temperamentally-sound puppy or dog.

Welcome to Today

Finding a family pet used to be so easy. Did your parents go through much when they chose a family dog? Probably not. Your mother noticed a classified ad in the paper, or your father's coworker talked up the litter of puppies he was selling or giving away. Until fairly recently, few dogs were spayed and almost none were neutered, so puppies were everywhere.

When your folks decided it was time to get a dog, they probably rounded you and your siblings up and went to take a look at a litter they'd heard about. The puppy that came home that day was your closest pal until you went off to college, a perfect dog and stalwart companion for years. Things worked out great.

You may be wondering whether you really have to go to all the pet-purchasing efforts I advocate later in this chapter, (carefully selecting a breeder, for example). You know the breed you want, you should be able to open the classifieds, call a number or two, and have a pet by the weekend. Or if you're not quite sure about a breed, but probably have it narrowed down to two or three breeds, why not go to a pet store where you can see different breeds at the same time?

Before you do either, think about how much the world has changed — how different the home you can offer a dog is compared with the one your parents offered. Dogs are different, too, especially purebreds, as I discuss in the section "Different dogs" later in this chapter.

A different world

For many people, caring for a dog is more difficult today than it would have been in the past. Twenty or thirty years ago, dual-income couples were not as common, whereas today, both parents (or the only parent in the home, in the case of so many families) often work outside the home to make ends meet. More people, too, are delaying marriage and family — or are choosing to skip them entirely. All these changes mean that more homes than ever before are empty for hours, except for a pet. The stay-at-home mom of the *Leave It to Beaver* era was ready with milk and cookies when the children came home from school — and she was also home for the family dog. Even as today's parents struggle to provide quality time for their children, today's pet owners have to do the same for their "fur children."

Work patterns aren't the only things that have changed. Land is more valuable (read: expensive), making homes on immense suburban lots less common than apartments, townhouses, condominiums, duplexes, and single-family homes with drastically reduced lot sizes to increase affordability. The yard of the suburban house my grandparents bought new in 1954 was so deep I couldn't throw a tennis ball to the back fence when playing fetch with their spaniel. The house I live in now has a yard so small that when we play fetch, the dogs play the back fence as outfielders do, waiting for the ball to bounce before catching it — which means we go to the lake or the dog park for my big dogs to get the exercise they need. The outings are rewarding for all, but they do take time.

Different dogs

The growing number of two-career couples, hard-working singles, and smaller yards aren't the only things that have changed since your first dog was a pup. Dogs have, too.

In 1955, when my parents got their first Boxer ("our oldest child," my father called him, because the dog came along two years before I did), the AKC registered 359,900 individual dogs. In 1981, when my parents bought their last dog (now retired, they prefer freedom and travel to pets), the number had jumped to 1,033,248.

In the years before World War II, purebred dogs belonged primarily to people with names like Rockefeller and Belmont. In the years after, when U.S. government-mortgage programs and well-paying jobs expanded the home-owning middle class, young families wanted a dog in their new backyard, and they wanted the same kind of dog as the rich had: a purebred.

The number of AKC-registered purebred dogs grew in the time span from the '50s to the '70s, mirroring the growth and the prosperity of the middle class. The purebred dog boom finally leveled off not too long after the baby boom did. Since then about a million purebred dogs a year have been registered with the American Kennel Club — in 1994 the figure was 1,345,941. Any way you count 'em, that's a lot of dogs.

The boom caused purebred dogs to become a commodity. Instead of a hobby the wealthy indulged in, the breeding of dogs became big business. Commercial breeders and casual ones started producing puppies, often without regard for health and temperament. The quality of purebred dogs fell as a result, to the point where "puppy lemon laws" started showing up in the '90s.

You don't need laws to protect you if you inform yourself before buying a puppy. Your odds of getting a healthy, happy purebred puppy improve when you seek out a reputable and knowledgeable breeder. And I'm going to tell you how to find them.

The work of the reputable breeder hasn't changed much over the years: They're in it to preserve and improve the breed they love. When they breed, their goal is to end up with animals who more closely conform to the ideal for their chosen breed or who demonstrate working ability that can be proven in competitive events — for winning is a part of the appeal, too. The pet puppies who come out of these litters are a by-product of these competitive endeavors, in a way, but the animals benefit from the knowledge and expertise of their breeder. And so do you, when you buy a puppy from a good breeder.

The odds of getting a healthy, temperamentally sound pet depend on your ability to find the right source for a puppy or dog.

Photo courtesy of Heidi McClure

If you choose a purebred puppy from another source, you're more likely to end up with a dog who's sick, or whose temperament is undesirable — either too shy or too aggressive. A dog like that will cost you money — in veterinary bills or even lawsuits — but he will also break your heart.

REMEMBER

The bottom line is this: Meeting the challenge of keeping a dog has never been more difficult, and you can make the wrong choice in more ways than ever before — which is why *where* you get your dog is every bit as important as *what kind* of dog you get.

Purebred Puppies: Going to the Source

The time to start looking at puppies and dogs has finally arrived. Suddenly, everyone has a dog for you to look at — "my neighbor's moving and can't take her dog" — or a litter of puppies, any one of whom would be perfect for you, you've been told, even though they're not the breed or breed type you've chosen.

Listen politely, smile, and thank them for thinking about you. Who knows? The dog your coworker's neighbor is leaving behind may be exactly the dog you have in mind.

But don't count on it. It's time to go . . . dog shopping!

Breeders: The good, the ignorant, the unscrupulous

The words *champion lines* and *AKC-registered* sell a lot of puppies. So does the word *extra* (as in extra-large Rotties or extra-small Teacup Poodles). And so do the words *rare* (as in rare white Boxers), and *see both parents, home-raised, must go now!,* and *will deliver.*

You should not consider most of these terms incentives. Some of these "extras" — like *AKC-registered* — should be what you might call "standard equipment" for a purebred dog. Other terms aren't so good at all: They, in fact, advertise breeding practices that may not be in your best interest as a puppy buyer.

A lot of reputable breeders don't have to advertise at all: Their reputations, secured by years of producing healthy, temperamentally sound puppies for show, work, and home, is such that business comes to them. They breed few litters, and they often have waiting lists for the puppies they produce.

REMEMBER

A *reputable breeder* is the kind you want to find.

So what are the differences between a good breeder and the others? Look at the words you may find in a classified ad or flyer on the bulletin board at work and see why they may mark the seller as someone with little real experience with purebred dogs or the breed they're producing:

>> **Champion lines.** The only thing it takes to get *champion* on a pedigree is to buy a poor-quality dog whose great-grandfather earned that title. Less than two or three champions on a pedigree — and on only one side of the pedigree, either the mother's side or the father's — indicates a seller who isn't taking her dogs into the show ring to see how judges think they compare to the breed standard. She's breeding dogs who haven't been judged to be good examples of their breed. So ignore *champion lines;* look for *champion-sired* or *champion parents.* These words are the sign of a reputable breeder, as opposed to a casual one.

>> **AKC-registered.** Big deal. Almost any breeder will sell you a purebred who's eligible for registration with the American Kennel Club or another registry, although a good breeder may hold back that registration until certain conditions — such as spaying or neutering — are met.

>> **Extra.** You see this a lot with the protection breeds, with people trying to produce super-sized Rottweilers and other dogs with a scary reputation. The aim is to produce the biggest, baddest dog around, but the result is likely a dog who's not going to move as well as he should, or a dog with bad hips or other problems. Size limits in the breed standard exist for reasons; deal with people who do not know about them or do not care, and you've got to wonder what else is wrong with the dog.

>> **Rare.** *Puh-lease.* I recently saw this in a classified ad for Shar-Peis. These dogs may have been the rarest in the world when they were first introduced in the U.S. in the early '70s, but the breed's in the AKC's top 25 now. This seller has been either asleep for two decades or is hoping to make a little extra money off someone who has been.

>> **See both parents.** What could possibly be wrong with this statement? Maybe nothing. You should *always* be able to see the mother, but many times reputable breeders *don't* have the father on hand. That's because they research and scour the country for the male they consider to be the *best* mate for their female, a dog they hope will enhance her strong points and reduce her weak ones. That dog may be across town, across the state, or across the country; wherever he is, they send their female — or they arrange for artificial insemination.

WARNING

If both parents are on hand, you may be dealing with a seller for whom the only qualities important in a stud dog are proximity and price: The stud dog was there. He was free. So he was bred.

>> **Must go now!** and **Will deliver.** These are people who want to get rid of their puppies *now.* Where will they be when you have questions or when problems pop up? Not available, or trying to move the next litter just as fast. And how are you going to see the conditions under which your puppy was raised or meet your puppy's mother or siblings if the seller arrives on your doorstep as if she's delivering a pizza? A reputable breeder wants you to come over. She's proud of her dogs. She wants you to take your time, come over a couple of times, ask all the questions you need to — not just now, but six months or six years from now.

You're probably getting the idea. The thing I like to tell prospective puppy buyers is that you're probably on the right track if the breeder asks *you* more questions than you can think of to ask her. She knows her breed, and she knows what sort of homes work best for it. She knows which puppies are better in a quiet family, and which ones in a rambunctious one. She wants to make sure you know what you're getting into because she feels personally responsible for the dogs she has brought into the world.

Thinking of breeding your dog? In Chapter 17, I show you why breeding dogs is both less profitable and more effort than you realize, how it puts your own pet at risk, and how it contributes to the problems of surplus pets — even if you're thinking of breeding purebreds.

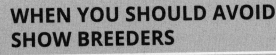

WHEN YOU SHOULD AVOID SHOW BREEDERS

WARNING

You ought to beware of some breeders of show dogs as well, no matter how long they've been turning out champions. For puppies to be proper companions, they must be around people from the day they are born. They must be handled by children and by adults of both sexes. They need to hear the ordinary sounds of life among the two-legged. This is true of all breeds, but it's especially true of those dogs who tend to be shy or aggressive — extra socialization is especially important in their upbringing.

Ask your questions about screening for genetic defects, about whether the breeder shows or otherwise competes with her dogs, about papers, contracts, and guarantees. But don't forget to ask where and how the puppies were raised.

If the breeder says "in my kitchen" and stresses how much they've been handled, you're on the right track.

If she says "in my kennels outdoors," and doesn't talk about how the pups were socialized, well, you can do better.

If you still want to breed dogs, that same chapter includes a basic primer on canine matchmaking, puppy raising, and placement — the "good breeder" way.

Finding a good breeder

A reputable breeder can be very hard to find and may not have a puppy available when you want one, like now. Those facts alone send many puppy buyers to other, less-than-ideal sources.

If everything goes well, you'll have your dog for more than a decade. Doesn't taking a little time to find the right breeder seem reasonable? To make a few phone calls, take a few field trips? To ask questions of a person who has lived for years with the breed you want, so you can get more answers than a book provides? To see for yourself how some dogs shed hamsters, and others drool rivers? To get a sense of what it's like to live with a canine dynamo, a dog who's always on the go, go, go?

The serious breeder, on the other hand, can tell you more than you possibly imagined about the breed. Their commitment to the puppy you buy doesn't end when the sale is final. You get a healthy, well-socialized puppy, as well as technical support that would be the envy of any software company. A serious breeder is just too good a deal to pass up, believe me.

Maybe you still think one AKC Labrador Retriever puppy is about the same as another. Maybe you think I'm putting too much emphasis on tracking down the elusive "reputable breeder." The fact is, I can't emphasize it enough. In almost two decades of writing a syndicated newspaper column on pets, I've talked to thousands of people about their pet problems. And I know that what breed or breed type you choose and where you get the puppy or dog has a great deal to do with how happy you'll be with the dog later — and even if the dog will be with you later.

I'm just trying to save a little heartbreak all around.

Perusing the periodicals

Attending a dog show is probably the most enjoyable way to start tracking down a breeder, but other ways exist.

The canine magazines — *Dog Fancy, Dog World, the AKC Gazette* and *Dogs In Canada* — have breeder advertisements, as do a couple of notable annuals: *Dogs USA* (put out by the *Dog Fancy* folks) and the *Dogs In Canada* annual.

These magazines do not screen breeders, however, so proceed with caution. If you can't find anyone locally for the dog you want, call the nearest breeder. If he's a reputable breeder, he likely belongs to a national or regional breed club and can give you a referral to a breeder nearer to you — if there is one. If he asks for your Visa card number and says your puppy will be on the next flight, thank him politely and move on to the next ad.

Finding a breed club

Joining a breed club is another way to come in contact with reputable breeders — or find out more about your chosen breed while you wait for your puppy. National clubs for AKC-recognized breeds are members of the American Kennel Club, which is a club made up of smaller breed and activity clubs, run by delegates from its member clubs. (The Canadian Kennel Club offers memberships to individuals; the AKC does not.)

How much assistance you get from a national club varies widely by breed. The corresponding secretaries of clubs overseeing the standards of popular breeds may send out little more than an information sheet. The clubs for less popular breeds may send you a list of club members actively breeding. Joining the club gets you a subscription to the newsletter, which is a wonderful resource for finding a breeder. Many breeds have local or regional clubs as well; the national club should be able to point you in their direction. If nothing else, belonging to a breed club gives you a built-in circle of acquaintances who think your breed is every bit as perfect as you do!

SHOULD YOU BUY A PUPPY SIGHT UNSEEN?

While you'll likely find a reputable breeder in your area, or within a few hours drive, that's not always going to be the case — especially if you've your heart set on a puppy of a less popular breed. In such cases you'll have to decide if you want to buy a puppy you've never met and have him shipped, probably by air.

Buying a puppy unseen may seem a risky business, but it's perhaps not so much as you may think. Before you consider this option, you'll have checked out the breeder thoroughly and talked to references. The breeder considers it a big jump, too, so she'll have had plenty of conversations with you. Pictures of the parents will have changed hands, along with the array of documentation and contracts good breeders provide.

Experienced breeders are used to dealing with airlines and will work to minimize the risk of air travel. (Shipping tips are also in Chapter 18.)

So if everything seems in order, go for it. It's likely better to deal with a reputable breeder a time zone or two away than a clueless one in your home town.

Even better: Go get your pup, and bring him home, on an airplane if need be. Even large-breed puppies are tiny enough when young that you can make arrangements to bring them into the cabin with you. What better way to use your frequent flyer miles than to get your puppy off to a good start?

The American Kennel Club maintains a list of contacts for its breed clubs, as do other registries; write to them or visit their Web site at www.akc.org for a particular listing.

Surfin' for a dog

A more recent way to connect with reputable breeders is though the use of the Internet, especially an e-mail list. An e-mail list is like an ongoing group discussion, except that it's carried out over the Internet and shared among those who have joined the list electronically. Many e-mail lists have sprung up to focus on a single breed, such as Dobermans, or breed group, such as spaniels. You can find a lot of them on the E-groups Web site, at www.egroups.com. Chapter 23 has more great dog-related on-line sites.

WARNING

Bad breeders have discovered the Internet and will be happy to sell you one of their puppies. Auction sites have also popped up, where the puppy or dog in question goes to the highest bidder, no questions asked. Good breeders use their Web sites to educate; bad ones to move the merchandise. Proceed carefully!

Some warning flags

A very few breeders are downright evil and fail to provide for even the basics of their animals' needs. A few more are mentally ill, living in filthy homes packed to the rafters with freely mating dogs. These people are fairly easy to spot and avoid — unless their pups are cleaned up and sold elsewhere.

Maybe I believe too much in the essential goodness of human nature — or the goodness of those who love dogs — but I think the majority of "bad" breeders — *backyard breeders*, they're commonly called — are not uncaring; instead, they're uninformed. They don't know that many of the dogs they produce can end up in shelters or spend their lives in pain from a congenital illness. They just want a litter "so the kids can see," or because "puppies are fun," or because they heard breeding dogs is an easy way to make a little money. They aren't bad people, but they're still not good breeders.

Following are a few things that should give you pause when dealing with a breeder:

» **Lack of knowledge about the breed.** Someone who doesn't know about the history of the breed or how suitable it is for different homes probably isn't someone who's too concerned about producing puppies that are fine examples of the breed.

» **Ignorance or denial of genetic defects.** Every breed has some problems, and some of the most common ones — such as hip dysplasia — can cause great pain and cost big bucks. A person who isn't aware of congenital defects almost certainly isn't screening breeding stock to avoid the defects.

» **No involvement in dog sports.** Every dog doesn't have to be a champion before he's bred, but you improve the odds of getting a high-quality purebred if you buy from someone involved in showing or otherwise competing with their dog. The point of a dog show, in fact, is to evaluate breeding stock.

» **Not letting you observe the litter, meet the mother or other dogs, or see where the puppies were raised.** Healthy, well-mannered adults and a clean, well-run set-up are a breeder's best testimonial. If a person doesn't want you to see anything except the puppy she's trying to sell, you ought to be wondering why.

» **No documentation.** If the purebred puppy's represented as "AKC-registered" then registration papers should be available. (This goes for other registries, too.) So, too, should papers backing up health claims. A sales contract spelling out the rights and responsibilities of both parties is highly desirable. Such a document provides you with recourse should the puppy not turn out as promised — if he has congenital health problems or isn't suitable for showing, if that was part of your intent in buying him.

>> **Doesn't seem to understand the importance of socialization.** Puppies need to be nurtured, loved, and handled to make good pets. Someone who can't explain what they've done in this area, or who tries to sell a puppy less than seven weeks old, probably doesn't understand enough about puppy-raising to be breeding dogs.

Again, it's all about increasing the odds of success. Can you find a good puppy from a backyard breeder advertising in your local newspaper? Yes, it's possible, but there's also a better chance that you'll end up with a dog who has health and behavior problems than if you go through a breeder with a well-established reputation. Which is why I think it's important, when shopping for a purebred puppy, to do everything you can to make sure you're getting the best puppy you can in terms of health and temperament. *Find a reputable breeder, and avoid the others.*

The Poop on Papers

A purebred dog's "papers" consist, at the very least, of two elements: a pedigree and slip that allows you to register the dog as yours with an entity such as the American Kennel Club or Canadian Kennel Club. A reputable breeder likely sends you home with far more. Here's a rundown of what you may get:

>> **Pedigree.** A diagram of your dog's ancestors for three or more generations, listing the registered names of these dogs, as well as the titles they earned. Although you can order a certified pedigree from the AKC or other breed registry, in practice most pedigrees are written out by the breeder.

You can learn a lot from a pedigree, and reputable breeders study pedigrees for hours when planning out their breeding programs. What you should see: a lot of titles. You want to see them in recent generations, on both the mother's and the father's sides. You want to see *Ch.*, for *champion*, a "looks" award, and you want to see working titles, for obedience or for such breed-specific endeavors as herding and hunting. A reputable breeder is able to explain any abbreviations on a pedigree; her dogs are likely to have plenty for her to explain, and she's happy you asked.

>> **Registration application or certificate.** A pedigree is a tremendously useful source of information for a buyer, but it doesn't mean a thing at the AKC, which is looking for a different piece of paper to register a puppy or dog. The registration slip is one of two kinds: Either an application to name and record a puppy for the first time, or a certificate that is used to transfer the ownership of an already named and registered dog. (AKC rules say once a dog has been given a registered name, there's no changing it. What you actually *call* him, of course, they don't care about.)

If you're buying a puppy, you'll probably get a registration form, commonly called a *blue slip*. A grown dog should come with an official registration certificate, white with a purple border. The transfer of ownership form is on the back. Other registries have rules of their own and can assist you with their paperwork.

>> **Health records.** This sheet shows when your puppy was vaccinated and wormed. (Many breeders take care of this themselves, so don't be surprised if a veterinarian is not mentioned on the records.) Certificates clearing the puppy of a particular defect, such as deafness in the case of Dalmatians, should be included.

   Your puppy's parents' health clearances may show on the registration application; if not, ask to see the documents. You're looking for letters such as *OFA* (Orthopedic Foundation for Animals) or *PennHIP* (another kind of health certification developed at the University of Pennsylvania's School of Veterinary Medicine) in breeds prone to hip dysplasia; *CERF* (Canine Eye Registration Foundation) in breeds with congenital eye problems; or *BAER* (Brainstem Auditory Evoked Response) in breeds where deafness is common.

>> **Sales contract.** This document defines your responsibilities — such as to spay or neuter your pet, or to inform the breeder if you can no longer keep the dog. The breeder spells out her role in the transaction, too: health and temperament guarantees and the remedies the breeder will offer if problems arise, such as replacing the puppy. The contract for a companion-quality dog sold on a spay-neuter contract is pretty basic, and grants you full ownership of the animal. If you intend to buy the dog to show and, ultimately, hope to breed her, the contract is considerably more complicated.

TECHNICAL STUFF

   A breeder's reputation is on the line when an animal capable of reproducing leaves her place, and she wants to ensure her kennel name doesn't end up on the pedigree of a puppy-mill dog. She may refuse to give you full title to the dog — a situation known as a *co-ownership* — and she may additionally stipulate that she has a major role in deciding when and to whom the dog is bred. If you've never shown before, co-ownership may be the only way to acquire a dog of a quality capable of earning a championship. If you can work within the confines of co-ownership and feel a rapport with the breeder, you can learn the ropes under the tutelage of someone who knows the breed and the sport. (Often when the dog's show career is over and the animal is spayed or neutered, the breeder will "sign off" on the dog and leave you as sole owner.)

>> **Care instructions.** Finally, the breeder often sends you home with directions on what to feed and how often, when to visit the veterinarian, and so on. Some breeders even provide booklets on puppy raising and basic obedience.

Perhaps you think this is a lot of paperwork, but paperwork, it seems, is one of the hallmarks of modern life. You never have to look at any of it ever again if you don't intend to exhibit or breed your dog. You don't even have to register your dog with a registry — many people never bother.

But that thick file you take home with your puppy is important because its very existence speaks volumes about the quality of the breeder you've just done business with. She's done her job, and you have the paperwork to prove it.

The rest is up to you.

TECHNICAL STUFF

BREED REGISTRIES

Most people have heard of the American Kennel Club, but the AKC isn't the only outfit in the business of registering purebred dogs. In the United States, the United Kennel Club labors in the shadow of the larger organization. Many countries have national kennel clubs of their own, such as the Canadian Kennel Club.

All of these organizations do pretty much the same things: They maintain the breeding records by registering the offspring of already registered purebreds and the change of ownership of adult dogs. They also oversee canine competitions, from dog shows like the Westminster Kennel Club's to obedience and agility competitions. Finally, they award titles like *Champion* to animals who have met the requirements for each title.

These organizations also fight for the rights of dog-owners, educate people on proper care of dogs, and investigate cruelty and registration fraud.

Breed registries — especially the AKC — have come under fire for not doing enough to stop puppy mills and discourage the breeding of dogs with inherited health and temperament problems. They've stepped up their efforts considerably in recent years — with an interesting side-effect.

Puppy-millers not happy with the crackdown are supporting registries that have virtually no standards. A puppy or dog registered with one of these outfits should be carefully investigated.

The AKC, UKC, and CKC, along with the national registries of other countries, are well-established organizations with the best interest of dogs and dog-lovers at heart. While they're not perfect, their inititals are still worth looking for when it comes time to get a pup.

Expanding the Possibilities

Please don't think because I go to such great lengths explaining how to buy a purebred puppy, I think purebred puppies are the only way to go when looking for a dog. Nothing could be further from the truth.

But from my experience, when most people start thinking about a dog, they think about a purebred puppy. There are so many ways to mess up this purchase I wanted to cover these folks thoroughly. Now it's your turn. If you're willing to open your heart a little wider, a whole new world of wonderful dogs suddenly opens for you. Want to talk about the appeal of a rare breed? How about taking that extra step and going for "unique," that 100 percent original, one-of-a-kind, never-seen-anything-like-it canine companion: the *mixed breed*.

But you have even more to consider. Depending on your lifestyle, what respected dog trainer and author Carol Lea Benjamin calls a "second-hand dog" may be a much better choice for you than a puppy. And these come in both purebred and mixed-breed varieties. Chosen carefully, your second-hand dog can become just as cherished a family member as any purebred you started with as a puppy.

TIP

Dog trainer Carol Lea Benjamin has written two wonderful — and inexpensive — paperback books that are must-haves for anyone thinking of adopting from a shelter or rescue groups: *The Chosen Puppy: How To Select and Raise a Great Puppy from an Animal Shelter* and *Second-Hand Dog: How To Turn Yours into a First-Rate Pet* (both from IDG Books). The pair are endorsed by shelters and breed-rescue volunteers across the country, some of whom sell them or give them out with their dogs. I buy *Second-Hand Dog* five copies at a time and hand it out when placing the strays that always seem to find their way to my door. (How do they do that?)

Shelters: A good choice and a good deed

Shelter is the word that often links *mixed-breed puppies*, *older dogs*, and *depressing*, but if you haven't been to a shelter lately, you'll find traditions are changing fast.

TIP

Creative outreach programs working in partnership with the media and with businesses such as pet-supply superstores take pets where the people are to increase the volume of adoptions. And shelters themselves are changing — after years of listening to people talk about avoiding the gloomy surroundings, progressive organizations are giving their buildings a face-lift to make them light, bright, and inviting. One such shelter belongs to the SPCA of Oakland, California which, in 1994, opened their PeopleSoft Adoption Center, a place so decidedly upbeat that schoolchildren go there on field trips to enjoy the interactive educational displays. Across the Bay, the refurbished Maddie's Pet Adoption Center at the San Francisco SPCA has opened to rave reviews. The best shelters these days have well-trained, caring staffs, and a healthy core of volunteers to keep dogs socialized and counsel potential adopters as to the animal that will provide the best match with their circumstances.

In short, today's shelter pets are more adoptable than ever before, thanks to programs that temperament test and perform basic health services — and some extraordinary ones — before animals are made available to the public.

To be sure, not all shelters are the same. Some shelters are run by municipal animal-control facilities, and some are run by nonprofit humane organizations. Some of the latter have widely different policies that affect the kind of dogs they have available for adoption, which means that doing a little checking first pays.

BUYING FROM PET STORES

Buying your puppy from a reputable breeder is always your best bet for obtaining a healthy, happy dog. But what happens if you absolutely fall in love with that face in the pet store window, and just can't get beyond those huge brown eyes? Here's some suggestions on how to be sure your fantasy doesn't turn to heartache and lots of vet bills down the road.

- **Establish some background on the puppy.** Keep in mind that many pet stores won't have the kind of detailed information and pedigrees that are available from a breeder. The pet store should be able to provide you, however, with a medical history including shot and wormings that have been done; infomation on whether or not the puppy can be registered and if so, with which registry; age of the puppy; and a list of medical problems, if any. It probably won't be able to provide much in the way of a personality profile, so it will be up to you to try to determine if the puppy's demeanor suits your family.

- **Give the puppy a good inspection.** Look at the puppy to be sure that his eyes are bright, there are no signs of fleas or other insects on the puppy, his skin is pink and healthy, and he shows no raw or hot spots on his back or legs. His gums should be pink and his teeth free from any buildup. He should appear energetic and inquisitive without being sluggish or overly aggressive. If the pup strikes you as being quite calm or lackluster, I suggest passing on this puppy, even if you have your heart set on him.

- **Ask what kind of guarantee comes with the puppy.** In other words, what happens if you get your dog home and a week later he inexplicably dies or ends up in the vet's office with a list of complications? You should be able to get some remedy from the pet store if this occurs. Most reputable pet stores offer some type of guarantee as to the health of the puppies they sell. If the answers are hedgy, I'd suggest going elsewhere.

Remember, your dog will be with you for years to come. Proceed with caution!

Still, good puppies and dogs are in any shelter, no matter how rundown the facilities and uncaring the staff. After all, a dog cannot help where he's dumped, sometimes for the most capricious of reasons. But just as you can improve your odds of buying a healthy, happy puppy by choosing a reputable breeder, you can better the chance of a successful adoption by choosing a progressive shelter.

WARNING

Making a decision about a shelter dog is often difficult. You want to take them all, and the realization that some of these dogs aren't going to find a new home softens even the hardest heart. But you aren't doing anyone any favors if you let your heart make your decisions here. If you pass over a dog who suits you better because of one you felt sorrier for, the dog you should have taken — the one that would have worked — may not make it. And you may end up miserable with your choice to the point where you take him back and don't try again. So instead of one happy ending, you've got at least three sad ones — yours and the two dogs'.

TIP

Take a friend to keep you from making a foolish decision. And take your time. Go back a few times if you have to. Play it cool. After your new dog settles in you can make up for it by spoiling her like crazy.

Be aware of some potential problems with going to a shelter. Shelter puppies are at risk for contracting highly contagious diseases such as *parvovirus*, and the considerably less serious *kennel cough* (More on these in Chapters 12 and 18.)

In addition, you probably won't be offered the choice of not spaying or neutering your dog, since most shelters either do it for you or require it done as a condition of adoption. Some also screen you almost as thoroughly as an adoption agency might, to make sure you're "qualified" to have a dog — and turn you down if they decide not! Like them or not, these are understandable policies for organizations in the front lines of fighting pet overpopulation. These should not dissuade you from considering a shelter when choosing a puppy or dog. Shelters are a good source for puppies and dogs — and a reasonably priced one when compared to the cost of a purebred puppy.

TECHNICAL STUFF

Shelters are not just for mixed breeds. While most young puppies in a shelter are mixes, the supply of grown dogs in any given shelter includes plenty of purebreds — up to 25 percent in some areas. And not just common breeds such as Labrador Retrievers, German Shepherds, and Poodles. Shelter workers have dealt with breeds so rare they had to look in books to identify them. Said one shelter director, whose family ended up with a fairly rare but nonetheless unwanted Schipperke, "Every breed shows up in a shelter eventually." It's sad, but true.

Animal-control shelters

Municipal animal-control facilities are perhaps the easiest to figure out. Finding homes for pets was not the reason they were founded and is not their primary purpose to this day — although many of them do a good job of it, nonetheless.

Animal-control departments were formed to protect people from animal menaces — primarily rabies. They pick up dead animals and enforce animal regulations, such as those regarding licensing — a rabies-control measure — and how many animals (and what kinds) people can keep. They respond to calls on vicious animals, as well as calls involving animals disturbing a neighborhood because of noise or odor. They also serve as a "convenience," disposing of unwanted animals through adoption, euthanasia, or, in some locales, through sales to biomedical research.

Animal-control shelters have never been well-funded operations, and this situation has not improved in recent years. With so much required of them and so few resources, readying animals for adoption and counseling prospective adopters cannot be number-one on the animal-control director's list of priorities. And yet, because of caring people in many of these departments and in the communities they serve, some decent volunteer programs are in place to fill the gap.

Because of these programs, municipal animal-control shelters can be good places to adopt. But many of the nonprofit humane society shelters are better shelters, because their mandate has always put helping animals at the top of the list.

WARNING

"HE FOLLOWED ME HOME"

It must be fate. Here you are, thinking about getting a dog and one follows your daughter home from school (with the aid of half a bologna sandwich). Or a dog is in the parking lot at the supermarket. Or your neighbor found one on his front porch.

Before you start picking out names, consider two possibilities: 1) He may not be the right dog for you (check out Chapters 1 and 2); and 2) He may already belong to someone.

You may not think the second possibility could possibly be the case with a dog who isn't wearing a collar and looks as if he is malnourished and, possibly, maltreated. But a lot of people — promise me you won't be one of them — never bother to put collars on their dogs, much less an ID tag or license. And it only takes a few days on the loose to make even a previously well-cared-for dog look dirty, tired, and sick.

If you find a stray and want to do what's best, try everything you can to find the owner first. Put up fliers in the neighborhood — most dogs stay within a couple miles of home when they get out — take out a classified ad in the newspaper and post "found" notices at local shelters and animal-related businesses such as groomers and veterinary hospitals.

Give locating the owner your best shot for a week or two and then if you decide to keep the dog, feel free. If by then you've decided he's not the pet for you, guidelines for finding a dog a new home are in Chapter 17.

Private nonprofit shelters

Nonprofit shelter groups run the gamut from squalid outfits that serve as little more than a fund-raising gimmick for the people in charge of them to organizations with well-funded endowments and programs that not only help homeless animals but also work to improve conditions for all animals — and animal-lovers — in their communities.

Most shelters fall somewhere in the middle: Their buildings could use some work, their budgets are always tight, and they do the best with what they have to provide for the animals in their community. New buildings don't necessarily a good shelter make, but you certainly want to work with a shelter that clearly cares enough for its charges to make sure they are kept in areas that are clean and don't facilitate the spread of disease.

Shelter work is difficult and stressful, and employees and volunteers can suffer burnout quickly. A well-run shelter is as compassionate to its staff as it is to the animals, because one has a lot to bear on the treatment of the other. Look for a shelter where employees are helpful and knowledgeable and clearly interested in helping the shelter's animals find new homes and responsible owners.

The best shelters have a good handle on a dog's history, health, and temperament before putting her up for adoption and have done what they can to enhance her chances of success in a new home, through socialization and screening for the right home. They provide not only preadoption counseling but follow-up help, with behavioral advice or reduced-cost training classes.

These are the shelters you should seek out when looking for a dog or puppy. If you want to go one step better, look for ways to help the shelters that don't measure up. Usually it's a question of money and volunteers, and you can do a lot to contribute in these categories. Contact your local shelter to find out how.

"Humane Society" and "Society for the Prevention of Cruelty to Animals" ("SPCA") are generic terms freely used in the United States and Canada by animal organizations that have no connection to one another or to national organizations such as the Washington, D.C–based Humane Society of the United States (HSUS) or the American Society for the Prevention of Cruelty to Animals (ASPCA) in New York City. And yet, local shelters are often stymied in their fund-raising efforts by people who have "given to the national organization" and consider their charitable efforts complete — even though money given to the HSUS and ASPCA is used to fund their own programs, not the local shelters'.

TIP

Which is why it's important not to forget your local animal shelter when giving. For an overview of how the national groups spend their money, check out the annual report from the newspaper *Animal People,* which is itself a nonprofit organization. To get the "Where the Money Goes" issue, contact Animal People, P.O. Box 960, Clinton, WA 98236-0960; 360-579-2505; www.animalpepl.org.

A bit of a war in the animal-welfare community occurs over those organizations that call themselves *no kill* shelters. There are more pets than there are suitable homes, which sets up a grim game of musical homes resulting in the death of millions of animals every year. Some no kill shelters get that way by refusing to accept animals that are not adoptable or by refusing all animals when they are full. The turn-aways often end up at another shelter, one whose staff often very much resents having to be the bad guy.

To be fair, an increasing number of no kill shelters have a fairly broad definition of *adoptable* that includes those animals that can be made adoptable through medical care or training. As someone who's looking to adopt an animal, you shouldn't get distracted by policy debates. Look for a shelter offering healthy, well-socialized animals and adoption counseling to help you pick out the right one for you. These shelters, with well-trained staffs and a solid volunteer corps, are your best bets for a successful adoption, no matter their policy on euthanasia.

Breed-rescue groups: A first-rate source for purebreds

One very positive change in the handling of homeless animals in the last couple of decades has been the growth of the volunteer, grass-roots breed-rescue movement. If you're looking for a purebred, and are willing to accept a grown dog instead of a puppy, then choosing a breed-rescue group is a good deal and a good deed.

Breed-rescue groups work with a single breed, such as the Basset Hound, or a couple of related breeds, such as one group I know of specializing in Collies and Shetland Sheepdogs. (In some areas, all-volunteer groups also foster and place mixed breeds.)

These groups range from one-person operations placing a few dogs a year to a few massive nonprofits with their own sheltering facilities, boards of directors, and well-organized volunteer networks dedicated to stepping in when one of their particular breed needs a hand. Some breed-rescue groups work by referral only, keeping lists of dogs in private homes and shelters that need homes and referring potential adopters. Others take in dogs from shelters and private individuals and foster the dogs, a policy that allows them to get a good feel for an individual animal's personality.

While such diversity of policies makes it impossible to describe a "typical" breed-rescue effort, probably the closest description of one would be a group consisting of two to four volunteers who work together to foster and place dogs of their chosen breeds and are both affiliated with a local breed club and loosely tied to a national network of rescuers for that particular breed. They typically offer dogs who have been vet-checked, vaccinated, and spayed or neutered, and the adoption fees they charge cover these veterinary expenses. Transportation and foster care costs often come out of the volunteers' pockets.

The nature of breed rescue creates both advantages and disadvantages for a potential adopter.

The advantages include getting a vet-checked, altered purebred at a very reasonable price — commonly, just the cost of the veterinary care. You also get more personal service with a breed-rescue group than with a shelter. A breed-rescue group puts you on their waiting list if they haven't got a dog who suits you, and also works with other rescuers in the region to find what you want. Breed-rescue volunteers have often lived with the dogs they're trying to place, and so they are more keenly aware of how each dog handles a home situation — such as how she gets along with cats.

Getting a dog through a breed rescue group has drawbacks. Breed-rescue groups rely on volunteers, and volunteers can easily get in over their heads and burn out quickly. These groups start up and stop and regroup and drop out at a surprising rate, which makes tracking down a current breed-rescue contact in your area a little difficult, as well as dealing with the same person you worked with if you have problems a year or two down the line, or need to give the dog up.

But don't let these problems dissuade you if you're looking for an adult purebred. Shelters, veterinarians, and reputable breeders often can provide you with a referral to a breed-rescue group and, if not, you can start at the national level and work your way down. Many AKC and CKC breed clubs have national rescue coordinators who maintain a current list of local and regional efforts. To find the national coordinator, write to the breed registries or visit the AKC's home page on the Web.

TIP

You may be lucky to live in an area with a well-organized umbrella group of breed-rescue volunteers. One such area is greater Seattle, where Seattle Purebred Dog Rescue (SPDR) has served for years as a model organization for other communities. For more information on SPDR, call 206-654-1117, or point your browser to www.spdrdogs.org.

Other Possibilities

You should consider a couple of other sources for healthy, adult dogs before you make your final decision.

Career change dogs

Groups that train service dogs to work with people who are sight- or hearing-impaired or who use wheelchairs demand a great deal from their dogs and, so, have a high rate of *washouts,* or animals who didn't quite make the cut.

Service-dog organizations often maintain their own breeding programs, producing animals of exemplary health, intelligence, and temperaments. These dogs, mostly Labrador Retrievers, Golden Retrievers, or German Shepherds, have such wonderful potential for pets that there is often a waiting list for those animals who, for one reason or another, didn't make it through the rigorous selection and training process. Placement procedures vary from group to group. Contact the service-dog training organizations in your area for details.

People who actively compete in dog sports, whether in showing their dogs or working with them in obedience, agility, or other events, sometimes are looking to place dogs who didn't quite make the cut as competitors or are retired from the ring — but still young — and not needed in a breeding program. These dogs can be real gems to find, animals who have had a lifetime of care and training, and who'd love nothing more than to be the only dog in someone's life.

Another excellent source of pets: Groups that rescue and place former racing Greyhounds. These groups — both industry-sponsored and independent — have sprung up in response to increased public awareness of the fate of Greyhounds who don't cut the mustard on the track. These gentle and elegant creatures used to be killed by the thousands every year, but more and more retired racers are finding happiness as treasured pets.

TIP

A few dozen organizations in the United States rescue, foster, and place former racing Greyhounds; one with affiliations nationwide is Greyhound Pets of America, (800) FON-1-GPA (366-1472). Cynthia Branigan's *Adopting the Racing Greyhound* (IDG Books) is a superb little paperback that helps potential adopters decide if a Greyhound is for them and helps smooth the transition afterward. *Note: Retired Racing Greyhounds For Dummies,* by Lee Livingood, contains expert tips for living with a retired Greyhound.

Private parties

Finally, you can't rule out dogs offered by private parties who aren't breeders (those private parties who *are* backyard breeders I've covered elsewhere in this chapter). Oodles of dogs end up advertised as "free to a good home" in newspapers and on office bulletin boards, or for sale at what may seem to be a good price. These people aren't trying to move the merchandise, but have just a dog or two who needs a new home.

Some of the people who put up these ads are trying to find homes for a stray, or help out a friend or neighbor in a pinch who has to place a dog, or are giving a dog they can no longer care for another shot at a good life. Some good dogs have turned up this way, but remember to let your head, not your heart, be your guide. Ask your questions, and if you don't get the answers you want, don't consider adopting the dog, no matter how sad the story.

I hate to generalize — but I'm going to, anyway. I advise people to avoid dealing with people who are just looking to get rid of a dog. That's because some people out there are constantly getting and dumping animals, and as long as there's an easy, guilt-free out for them, they will never see the error of their ways. (It's the same reason I discourage people from getting a kitten from a kid who brings a box of them and stands outside the door of a supermarket — if it's easy to get rid of of the kittens, why bother spaying and neutering the parents?)

Better you should patronize a shelter, or a breed-rescue group, than the person who's just trying to dump another dog — another in an unending string of animals who become unwanted because the owners decided they would rather have a puppy or another breed of dog.

REMEMBER

Working with a shelter or rescue group won't cost you any more money, even if you're passing on a "free to a good home" pet. The person who's giving a puppy or dog away may not have taken care of vaccinations, heartworm tests, and spaying or neutering — you'll have to pay to have those things taken care of. A puppy or dog from a shelter or rescue group can be had for a small amount — and the preventive care is often already done.

Offering puppies or dogs "free to a good home" is a sure way to attract people who are looking for dogs to sell to research, or as sparring partners for fighting dogs. What's the best way to find a home for an animal you can no longer keep? See the sidebar "Older dogs need homes, too" in Chapter 17 for help.

Chapter **4**

Choosing and Bringing Home a Puppy

"Acquiring a dog may be the only opportunity a human ever has to choose a relative," writes author Mordecai Siegal, and that may explain part of the excitement that goes with bringing home a new dog of any description, young or old.

Add to this thrill the natural charm of all puppies — those round bellies, those shining eyes, that wonderful puppy breath — and you've got all the ingredients for a day that ranks up there with the most anticipated events of our lives. The moment you lock eyes with the puppy who will be yours is sweetly perfect, one to remember forever.

REMEMBER

I want you to enjoy your perfect puppy moment, really I do. But, because I want you to have a lot more great moments with your dog than the first few, I want you to be sure you're considering your decisions carefully. Don't check your common sense at the breeder's or shelter's door. Take your time and bring a friend to help you if you think you may be too impulsive. Choosing your puppy is just the first step in a lifetime together.

The second step, surviving that long first night, makes you wonder if you've made the right decision — even if you have, for sure. It's tough on your puppy, too, but you both get over it.

From the minute you bring your puppy home, keep your eyes open. Puppies are an unending source of wonder and delight, and they grow up so fast! Do your best not to miss one precious minute for, once it's gone, it's gone forever.

Before you pick out a puppy, be sure you get the breed or breed type that's a match with your personality and lifestyle, and be doubly sure you're going to a reputable source. Check out Chapters 1 and 2 for help in considering such things as size, fur, breed type, and trainability, and Chapter 3 for the sources that give you the best shot at acquiring a puppy or dog with good health and a sound temperament.

If you're adopting a "teenage" dog, or an adult dog of any age, tips on choosing a dog and getting that relationship started properly are in Chapter 5.

Puppy Preparations

Is your house ready for the running, jumping, chewing machine that is a healthy, happy puppy? Are you? Before you bring home your special pup, you need to look your home over, and make some changes.

Puppy-proofing

One of the first rules of making a home safe for a puppy — and keeping a home safe *from* a puppy — is to start him out with a small, safe area. That means keeping the doors closed to the kids' bedrooms for a while, lest pieces of a cherished action figure end up in your puppy's stomach, to the horror of your children. That means using *baby gates*, expandable barriers you can put in any doorway or at the top of a stairway to further limit your puppy's options.

In the parts of the house you have left, get down on your hands and knees and take a look at things from a puppy's point of view. Conceal those tasty electrical cords under furniture and carpets, and put away any low decorations or bric-a-brac for now. Think toddler-proofing and you're on the right track, except with puppies you're thinking of things they can chew, not places they can stick their fingers.

Puppy gear

WARNING

Since you shouldn't let your puppy venture into places where other dogs have been until he's through with all his vaccinations — see Chapters 9 and 11 for more on socialization and vaccinations — you should make your first run to the pet-supply store without him. If you've already chosen your puppy and are just waiting for him to be old enough to come home, you can get everything on the list. If you're going to the shelter and don't know for sure who you'll come home with, make your supply run after your dog comes home with you.

TIP

Don't worry that you haven't named your pup yet. Let his first ID tag just say *REWARD* instead of a name. The important thing is to get one on him, right away.

Here's your shopping list:

>> Brush and comb

>> Chew toys

>> Dishwasher-safe, nonchewable bowls: one for water, one for food

>> Pet stain cleaner

>> Flat or rolled collar, buckle or snap-together — *not* a slip (choke) collar — with an ID tag

>> High-quality puppy food, as recommended by the breeder, shelter, or veterinarian

>> Lightweight leash, six-feet long

>> Nail trimmer and Kwik Stop powder

>> Pooper scooper and plastic bags

>> Properly sized shipping crate, for house-training

>> Puppy shampoo

The low-down on all these items, such as the proper kind of brush or comb, and the proper type and size of shipping crate, is in Chapters 6 and 10.

Puppy Picking

The day a puppy comes to a new home is one of great promise. You can't wait to get through all the paperwork. You don't want to read the information you've been given. You just want your puppy. Now.

You'll soon have all the time in the world to make a fuss. But you should keep your enthusiasm in check just a little while longer.

Before you get down to bringing home the puppy who'll share your life, take a second to confirm that your bases are covered. Go back and read Chapter 3 and be sure you're dealing with a reputable source — a good shelter or a reputable breeder. You don't want to fall in love with a puppy who has health and temperament problems, after all. Before making your final choice, review these good-puppy criteria:

>> **Be sure you're getting your puppy at the right age — between his seven-week and eight-week birthdays.** Some breeders, especially those with toy breeds, insist on holding their puppies longer — because they're small and delicate, primarily, and that's fine, but only if the breeder has continued to socialize the puppy with people. While you want a puppy who can get along with other dogs, you don't want one who's too dog-oriented to bond well with you, and that's what you get when puppies are left with their littermates too long and not socialized. Age is not as big a concern with a shelter puppy: He has probably been handled by staff and volunteers since the time he came in.

>> **Look for a puppy who has been raised as a pet — in the kitchen, ideally.** You want a puppy who has heard the normal sounds of living with people from the day he was born — talking, laughter, and even fights, the TV, music, and the sound of the dishwasher. Health screenings and good breeding are *very* important, but so, too, is socialization. Don't buy a puppy from someone who has raised them in a kennel, barn, or basement. If you don't know how he has been raised, check out his temperament with the tests located elsewhere in this chapter.

>> **Check for signs of good health.** While your puppy will be seeing a veterinarian within 24 hours — you should make a health check a condition of sale or adoption — you should be able to spot any obvious signs of disease on your own. Your puppy should be plump and glossy, with eyes, nose, and ears free of any discharge. He should seem upbeat and happy, not listless.

If you have questions, ask the seller, and make sure you're satisfied with the answers. Above all, don't let your enthusiasm override your common sense. It's hard to say no to a puppy, but you must if the puppy's not the right one for you.

TECHNICAL
STUFF

Sometimes a pup is alone in this world, a single pup born to a mother who died in childbirth. Should you avoid such a puppy? That depends on the breeder. A knowledgeable breeder does his best to make up for the shortcomings, taking over the role of the mother and, later, giving the puppy exposure to other dogs. Single puppies are often sent to be "adopted" by dogs with puppies close to the same age or at least given the opportunity to socialize with other puppies after weaning.

If this socialization has been done, you should have no qualms about adopting such a puppy, but you should continue to look for as many opportunities as you can to expose your puppy to other dogs as he grows up.

IS A CHRISTMAS PUPPY A GOOD IDEA?

The image of a beribboned puppy and delighted children on Christmas morning is both endearing and enduring.

Never mind that humane societies, trainers, veterinarians, and reputable breeders say that Christmas morning is just about the worst time to introduce a puppy to the family. To parents with camera at hand, the scene seems worth the trouble of an energetic ball of fluff rolling around on one of the year's most hectic days.

But is it really?

Getting a Christmas puppy is okay — if you get one before Christmas or after. Introducing a puppy on Christmas Day is very stressful for all concerned: The puppy needs your attention — but so does everything else.

Even if you get your pup before or after the actual holiday, you have some challenges. The first may be finding the right puppy. Many shelters and reputable breeders will not place puppies right before Christmas, because they believe the time is just too high-risk. That leaves you with less-than-ideal sources for your pet.

And that's not all: Consider the problem of socializing and training a puppy in the dead of winter, if white winters visit your corner of the universe in December. By the time the snow starts to melt, you could have a half-grown canine terror on your hands.

Giving up that Norman Rockwell moment when your children discover that St. Nick has answered their pleas for a puppy is difficult. But if you want a better chance of still having that pet as a well-loved member of the family at future Christmases, consider this option:

Wrap a collar and leash and a dog book for the children and put that under the tree — promise your children that their puppy had to wait to be born, but will be with them as soon as she can.

As far as holidays go, I like Easter a lot better for starting a puppy out. Your camera works just as well then, your children will be just as happy, and your puppy has a better chance at getting the attention she needs.

Working with a breeder

If you've found a reputable breeder, you may not have much to do when it comes down to choosing your puppy. You've let the breeder know if you prefer a male or a female, and whether you want that puppy to be more than your pet — you're considering showing, for example, or some other canine competition (more on these in Chapter 16). Maybe the litter has different color puppies, and you have a strong preference for one or the other, or you may have your heart set on one gender over the other. All these factors can narrow your choices dramatically (even when considering a very large litter).

Puppies learn as many lessons from each other as from their mother, including how to get along with other dogs.

Photo courtesy of Gina Spadafori

The breeder has been narrowing the choices, too. He's talked with you enough to get a feel for the kind of home you offer, whether you'd be too demanding for a shy puppy or too easy on a bossy one. In the end, you may have a choice between two or three puppies — or maybe just one fills the bill.

This is a give-and-take process, of course, and you may decide to broaden your selection criteria a little when faced with a squirmy litter of fat, healthy puppies. Suddenly a black Lab may seem perfect when before only a yellow one would do. The breeder, too, should be open to discussion. Just remember that he has a better idea of the personalities of his puppies — he knows his dogs, after all, and has been living with *these* pups for weeks. If he suggests the bold puppy who's crawling all over your son may not be the best bet for your family, believe him — he has probably learned from a past bad call and ended up with an unhappy family and a dog that was returned.

TIP

While it's a pretty good bet that there'll be plenty of puppies for you to choose from in a litter of Great Danes, that may not be the case if you're dealing with a toy breed, where small litters are the norm. You may want to hedge your bets a little by dealing with more than one reputable breeder. Chances are the breeder you choose already has that in mind: Good breeders are active in their local club and are likely to know who else has a litter that may suit you if theirs does not. Just ask.

Puppy testing

What if you aren't dealing with a breeder, you're not selective as to gender, and couldn't care less about your puppy's color or markings? What if you're offered the pick of any pup you want, not just from one litter, but from a whole shelter full of them. How can you decide?

By testing the personalities of your prospective pet, that's how.

TIP

Remember that even though you can, potentially, find a good puppy anywhere, making the most of any help offered is a good idea. Good breeders and good shelters test their puppies, and many shelters offer adoption counseling. If you're dealing with one that doesn't, you have to wonder about what else isn't top rate. And you may want to go back to Chapter 3 and take a shot at finding a better source.

Puppy-testing methods vary widely but, in general, the purpose of testing is the same. The goal is to determine the following:

>> **A puppy's level of dominance.** How bossy or shy is he? While a lot of people are inclined to pick the boldest pup of a litter — because he seems to pick *them* — he's probably not the best choice for most homes. He *may* be just the ticket for someone with a great deal of dog-training experience who intends to compete with her dog, but for an average home, a less-dominant dog's a better choice. Avoiding the shyest, least dominant puppy, which some people pick "because he needs us!" is best, too.

>> **A puppy's level of interest in people.** Some puppies are more dog-oriented or really don't care much about anything at all. A puppy who's not curious and interested in people — perhaps because of little or no socialization — isn't a very good prospect as a pet. You want a pup who wants to be with you, because that's the pup who'll be loving — and trainable!

>> **A puppy's trainability.** The goal here is a puppy with the ability to concentrate — as much as any baby can — and absorb information. A puppy who is so busy bouncing off the walls that he can't give you even a moment's attention is going to be one you want to avoid.

TIP

Take each of the puppies you're thinking about to a safe, secure area away from littermates. Observe how the puppy reacts to the change — tentative exploration is okay, but beware the puppy who's so terrified she won't move. Look, too, for how busy a puppy is: Playfulness is fine, but full-out go-go-go is maybe a little too much.

Your observations should ideally be compared and discussed with the observations of others who have looked at these puppies, such as the volunteers and staff at the shelters or the breeder.

TIP

Try to see the litter you're considering more than once. If all the puppies seem lethargic, ask the breeder if you've caught them just after eating. Puppies have two speeds, after all: Completely on and completely off!

REMEMBER

Keep in mind that the puppy who's probably going to be the best for you — after you find the right breed or breed type, the right source, and decide between male and female — is going to be "medium" in personality. She may not be the smartest in the litter, but she may be more interested in your point of view than the one who is the smartest. She's got moxie, but not so much that she'll drive you crazy. She's willing to try new things — she's no shrinking violet — but she'll like the new things better if you're with her

Although a particular breeder may *always* test his puppies at a particular age — six weeks, say — you may not have this luxury. Anything in the five-to-twelve week range is okay, but remember if you're testing puppies in their eighth week, they may all be a little skittish because they're in a *fear period*, where they're a little leery of new things for a few days. Testing before or after this stage is a better idea.

You can size up a puppy's personality in several ways, but here are a few exercises anyone can do well:

>> **Interest in people.** Put the puppy down facing you. Walk a few steps away, bend over, and call to him. (Bending over makes you less intimidating.) If the puppy seems a little tentative, crouch and open your arms. You're not ordering the pup — he doesn't know what you want, after all. You're trying to see how attracted he is to a nice person. So be nice. Call gently, click your tongue, rattle your keys. The medium puppy you want will probably trot over happily, perhaps after a slight hesitation. The bossy puppy may come over and nip at you, and the shy one may not move except to shiver in terror. The one who doesn't care a bit about people may go investigate a bug in the corner of the room.

A puppy should be interested in you, and come to you when you beckon.

>> **Accepting authority**. Gently roll the puppy onto his back and hold him there with your hand. The medium pup you're looking for will fuss a little, settle down, and maybe even lick your hand. Bossy pups usually keep struggling, and the shyest ones generally freeze in terror.

>> **Praise and petting response**. Praise and petting are integral parts of training and communicating with your dogs, and so finding a puppy who wants affection enough to earn it is important. Talk to the puppy lovingly and stroke him, but let him decide whether he stays with you or not — don't hold him. The medium puppy will probably lick your hands and be glad to stay with you. Rolling over is okay, and don't be surprised if he urinates a little — called *submissive urination,* this gesture is kind of a canine compliment, a recognition that you're top dog. (More on submissive urination in Chapter 8.) A puppy who bites hard is probably dominant and unsocialized, and the one who wants nothing to do with you probably isn't people-oriented enough. Stay away, too, from the one who's terrified of being touched.

WARNING

Listen to your head, not your heart. Doing so is really, really hard when you're in a shelter and thinking the puppy you don't pick isn't going to get picked at all. Don't play the guilt game. Pick a puppy with a temperament that's likely to produce a good pet. You're still saving a life in the case of a shelter puppy, still providing a good home in the case of any puppy. Keep that in mind and pick the best puppy you can

You may be tempted to take two puppies home, with the grand idea that adopting littermates will keep them from being too lonely while you're at work and will give them something to do besides pester you.

Give this idea a lot of thought. I mean, a *lot* of thought.

Raising two puppies together means twice the work, twice the craziness, and twice the mess. Most people barely have time to properly socialize and train *one* puppy, much less two. Plus, two puppies raised together may remain more bonded with each other than they are to you.

If you want two dogs, consider waiting until your puppy is grown to add another puppy. Adding a grown dog at the same time you add a puppy may be okay, but still, puppies are such work that you're better off getting your little one squared away before you add to your pack.

TIP

One of the best things you can do to get this special relationship started out properly is to take time off work when your first get your puppy. Call it *pupernity leave* if you like, but take the time if at all possible. A week — two is even better — gives you time to get house-training off to a great start and to enjoy your puppy while easing the transition for her between life with her littermates and life with you. For more on early puppy training, see Chapter 9.

Puppy Comes Home

The day your puppy comes home is a big step for both of you. She's leaving her littermates and throwing her lot in with yours. You're taking on the huge responsibility of raising a dog.

You want the transition to be as smooth as possible, and yet you want to make sure that from that very first day you're laying the groundwork for a wonderful life together.

Repeat after me: *I will never let my puppy do anything I wouldn't want her to do as a grown dog.*

Good! You're ready to be a full-fledged puppy parent now, heaven help you.

When you go to pick up your puppy, bring towels, both old bathroom ones and the paper kind. Chances are your puppy will get carsick. (This doesn't mean she's going to be carsick her whole life.) Don't go alone, either. If you're a single person, have a friend drive so you can hold your puppy. Have a spouse or kids? Take 'em. This moment is one you'll want to remember.

But don't let your children fight over the puppy. She's not a football. *One* person can hold her, on a towel, for the ride. You can draw lots and make it up to the other kids later. Remember that you want to lay the groundwork for your puppy from the beginning. You want to do so with your children, too, by insisting on gentle, respectful handling.

If the puppy throws up, or makes any other kind of mess, don't make a fuss of any kind. Change to a clean towel, and clean it all up when you get home.

TIP

WATCH THE BIRDIE, PUPPY!

Don't forget to bring your camera and record the special day your puppy comes home. And keep it at hand, because over the next couple of months you're going to kick yourself for missing some great shots if you don't — and hate yourself later for not having pictures of your wonderful dog as a baby.

Here are a couple of tips for taking great puppy pictures:

Head outdoors. Natural light — early morning is best — avoids the dreaded red-eye shot, where the flash makes your beautiful puppy come out as a monster. Taking pictures outside gives your new pet a more natural, healthy look.

Get down and get close. If you want a good puppy picture, you're going to have to go where your puppy is — on the ground. Shoot at just below your puppy's eye level and zoom in as closely as you can for good detail. If getting down isn't something your back will tolerate, bring the puppy up: Have someone hold him — this has the added benefit of keeping him still — or put him on an elevated surface, such as an outdoor table.

Watch your backgrounds. I have a wonderful picture of my first dog, Lance. He's freshly groomed. He's standing perfectly. His ears are up, his mouth smiling, his eyes bright. And he has a telephone pole growing out of his back. Be sure you have an uncluttered background, so your dog can shine!

Be creative. If you want your puppy to kiss your children, do as the pros do: Put a little dab of butter on your children, and let the puppy kiss it off. Another professional's trick: Just before taking the picture, rattle keys, squish a squeaky toy, or throw something in the air. Your puppy will come to attention, splendidly.

Get your children involved. This is a special day, so if you have kids, let them make some memories, too. Get them each one of those throwaway cameras and take pictures of their new puppy. You'll be delighted at some of the shots you get back — and they'll be doubly so!

The *first* thing you should do when you get home is to take your puppy outside and praise her for relieving herself, if she does. More on house-training in Chapter 8.

The name game

Naming a dog has to be one of the most delightful parts of getting one. It seems not a year goes by without a new book of dog names being published, including ones that specialize, such as a book on Irish names. I have no fewer than six books of names on my bookshelves, most meant for the parents of human babies, not canine ones.

Do you need to keep anything in mind when naming a dog? Yes. Avoid names that sound like common obedience commands. A friend of mine who had worked in Alaska adopted a beautiful Husky mix and wanted to name her Sitka, after a place he'd loved visiting. After I pointed out she'd have a hard time telling the difference between "Sitka" and the command "Sit," he named her Juneau instead.

Keep names short, one or two syllables, and easy to pronounce. I tend to use "people" names for my own pets, but you don't have to limit yourself. Name books are a good start, but don't forget atlases or special dictionaries such as those for foreign words or a book of baseball, railroad, gardening, or music terms, if your interests lie in any of those directions

Make your puppy love his name as much as you do by making sure that it has a positive association. *Never* scream your puppy's name at him or use it in punishment. The late dog trainer Job Michael Evans used to recommend making up a song with your dog's name in it and singing the song to him. Commercial jingles are wonderful for this, he said, because they're catchy and you can put the pet's name in where the product is mentioned.

And yes, I do this. "You Are My Sunshine" becomes "You Are My Andy" ("you make me happy/because you're gray") and Benjamin gets regaled with the Monty Python, "Spam" song, with *Ben* substituted for *Spam* — "Ben, Ben, Ben, Ben, Ben, Ben, Ben, Ben, Wonderful Ben . . ." Heather has her own song, too: "Heather! I love Heather," sung to the tune of "Heaven! I'm in Heaven."

Yes, it's silly. But try it anyway. You'll both smile. The songwriters may be horrified, but what they don't know won't hurt them.

The name your dog hears — his everyday name — is what fanciers term a *call name* as in, it's what you call your dog. If you have a purebred dog, he'll have a *registered name*, too. You get 28 letters and spaces with the American Kennel Club to come up with a registered name for your pet. If you choose a name someone else has already chosen, the AKC issues it along with a number to distinguish your dog's name from the others, so unless you want your Collie to be the AKC's 897,042nd Lassie, use all those spaces to come up with something sure to be unique.

Puppy's first night

Your puppy will probably be so overwhelmed by the new sights, sounds, smells, and all the attention that she won't much miss her littermates and her old home. Don't worry, that will come soon enough — and last most of the first few nights.

Keep things nice and easy to start out with. Everyone will want to hold the puppy and play with her, and that's fine, but remember she's still a baby and gets worn out quickly. She needs to sleep, but she may not eat on that first day. She has a lot to get used to; don't worry about it very much. Let her explore.

WARNING

Puppies aren't stuffed toys, and you must help your children to realize that. Small children — especially those under five — can't really help being a little rough with puppies (and dogs) and must be carefully supervised to ensure that neither hurts the other.

Where should your puppy sleep? I think dogs should always sleep in the bedroom, not on your bed in most cases, but in their own. Allowing the dog to sleep in the bedroom is especially important for households where a dog is left alone for hours at a time when the family is at work and at school. Letting your dog sleep in your bedroom — or in your child's bedroom — counts for time together, even though you're all asleep. It can go a long way toward building and maintaining a strong bond, assuring your pet that she's an important member of the pack.

If you want your dog to sleep in the service porch, though, that's your business. But please don't start on the first couple of nights after you bring your puppy home. She needs you now.

Those first couple of nights are very tough on a puppy. The reassuring warmth of her littermates is gone and everything has changed. She's going to have a lot to say about this, so be prepared. She will fuss less if she's in your presence, if she can be reassured by your smell and the sound of your breathing.

Set up her crate next to your bed, and prepare it with a soft blanket to sleep on and a chew toy or two. Tell her "crate" firmly, put her inside and close the door. And then open a book, because you won't be sleeping for awhile. (For more on the use of crates in puppy-raising, see Chapters 8 and 9.)

TIP

Endure the cries and whines as best you can, but don't punish your puppy, and don't take her out when she's carrying on — you'll teach her that all she need do is fuss and she gets what she wants. She'll probably settle down and then wake once or twice in the middle of the night. Take her out to relieve herself — and praise her for doing so — and then put her back in her crate.

In a day or two, the worst of the heartbreaking crying is over.

Chapter **5**

Adopting and Settling In an Adult Dog

We tend to be so nostalgic that it's sometimes hard to believe that the "good old days" weren't always so great. That's certainly true when it comes to dogs. Societal attitudes have changed, in many cases for the better.

Not very long ago, the experts were adamantly against adopting a grown dog. If you adopted a puppy, you could train him the way you wanted to, the thinking went, and the puppy would bond to your family more closely than a fully grown dog.

No doubt a puppy offers more of a clean slate than the sometimes sadder-but-wiser older dog, but a grown dog offers many advantages, especially for someone who hasn't the time or the experience to raise a puppy properly. And as for bonding, let me assure you that you won't find any difference. If anything, I sometimes believe a dog adopted as an adult seems *more* devoted, because he knows what being without people who love him is like. As with puppies, however, you want to learn a little bit about adult dogs and take your time in selecting one.

Grown dogs, like puppies, come from many sources — shelters, private parties, breeders of all kinds, and breed-rescue groups. Some dogs walk into your life as strays. To learn more about sources for finding a dog, see Chapter 3.

The Adult Dog Defined

The break between puppyhood and adulthood is at sexual maturity, which is a far cry, as is true with humans, from emotional or physical maturity. For most dogs, sexual maturity happens somewhere around six months of age, a time when the once roly-poly pup already appears a gangly adolescent. Although different puppies mature at different rates — small ones grow up more quickly than large ones — a dog isn't really an adult until sometime between 18 months and two years. Around this time your dog's difficult "teen" stage finally ends and your dog settles down — if you've raised him right, that is — into the companion you were dreaming of.

A dog's time at the peak of his abilities varies, too, according to his breeding. Giant breeds such as the Irish Wolfhound start aging as early as four or five, while a small breed like the Chihuahua won't start slowing down until after 10 or even 12 years. Dogs in the medium-to-large size range have six or seven years of prime adult life — but you can greatly extend those years by providing your pet with proper veterinary care, nutrition, and exercise (discussed in various chapters of this book).

While adult dogs of all ages become available for adoption, convincing people to take a dog over two is often difficult. Over five is even harder, and over ten — forget it! And that's unfortunate, because the dog over two is often an easier animal to work into your family, and dogs over five — or even ten — can be wonderful, calm pets with a great deal of high-quality life still ahead of them.

REMEMBER

In case you didn't catch my subtle endorsement, let me spell it out: *Don't rule out a dog because of her age.*

TIP

When I was volunteering for Sheltie rescue in my area, we often had prospective adopters who initially insisted they didn't want a dog more than a year old. It's almost as if they thought they were dealing with a used car, with newer models being more valuable than older ones. This thinking is simply not the case in dogs — or humans, of course. After some convincing, we placed many older dogs into homes that initially wouldn't consider them. Two of these dogs — a 7-year-old named Spencer and a 9-year-old named Major — lived in my neighborhood, and I can report that they both blossomed into perfect companions in their respective families and lived happily for years. Strike a blow against ageism! You may end up with a better dog as a result.

You don't have to start with a puppy. Adopting an adult dog can make a lot of sense.

Photo courtesy of HSUS

The canine adolescent

Most adult dogs available for adoption are young ones, for a couple of reasons. One is that shelters with limited space put out the dogs with the greatest chance of being adopted. People want young dogs, so that's what shelters tend to offer. Older dogs too often go straight to the euthanasia room, unless they've charmed the staffers into giving them a chance with their beauty or good manners. (This unhappy situation is *not* the shelter's fault, please note. The shelter's staff didn't bring these dogs into the world, and they're not the people making them homeless. They're just coping as best they can. If adopters were more interested in older dogs, shelters would be, too.)

Adolescent dogs are also in abundance because dogs just beyond puppyhood are the most likely to be dumped, for some of the following reasons:

>> **Bad fit.** Because all puppies are adorable, people easily forget to think about what they're going to have when their sweet little fuzzball grows up. About the time a pup reaches physical maturity is when her owners first realize they've taken on more than they can handle and recognize that they ended up with a dog who's too big, too active, or too dominant for them.

>> **Poor upbringing.** Puppies grow up too fast, and too many people put off until tomorrow the socializing and training they should do today. These birds come home to roost during adolescence, when people end up with an out-of-control dog who's a nuisance — and possibly a danger. Lots of these overgrown puppies just need a little work, some basic obedience, and problem-solving, but that's more than many people want to bother with.

>> **Novelty wears off.** The cuteness that keeps people from strangling puppies doesn't protect the formerly fuzzy when they get a little older. Gangly and out-of-proportion, with thin coats you can practically see through, these ugly ducklings show little sign of the swans they'll one day become. And that's not the only problem: The kids that begged for a pup and promised to care for him are now more interested in video games, the parents get tired of nagging, and the dog is suddenly shelter-bound.

REMEMBER

Does this mean you should avoid an adolescent dog? Not at all. But you should know that they're bound to be a little more high-spirited and distractible than a mature adult of two or more. An adolescent dog still has some growing up to do, and you're going to need to put some extra effort in to help turn a doggie teen into the pet you want.

Young adults

Dogs who have matured into adulthood and are in their prime years are among your better choices when looking for a pet to adopt. If you choose carefully, you can find a nearly flawless dog here, calm and sensible, sometimes with basic obedience training. Of course, you can also find a dog who's settled into some very bad habits, which is why you should take your time and not let love at first sight or a sad story affect your decision.

Senior dogs

Why take a chance on an older dog? Because it's the right thing to do. And because he may be perfect for you. And because counting a dog out because he may have a couple less years to spend with you is not fair.

My favorite example of why an adult dog should not be counted out comes from some friends of mine who adopted a Collie of about eight years old. The Collie died a few years later and, when she did, the friend told me she was the most wonderful dog she'd ever owned. Consider this: The five years that family had with the dog were wonderful, perfect, even. Fifteen with another may not have been so special. So consider quality, not just quantity. And figure you get extra points toward an afterlife for giving a special dog a chance.

TIP

One group of people older dogs are perfect for is older people! Many seniors would like a dog as a companion, but are afraid of what would happen to their pet should he outlive them. An older, sweet-natured, small dog is a perfect match for such a person, easing his worries and providing him with love and companionship. An added bonus: An older dog is bound to be more docile, less destructive, and require less exercise than a young one.

At 11 years old, Zoe is still young at heart.

Photo courtesy of Scott Barnes

New Dog Comes Home

While adopting a grown dog often isn't nearly the work that introducing a puppy is, you should still follow some guidelines to ease the transition. Your new dog will be a little disoriented under any circumstances. But if spaying or neutering was done just before adoption, the post-surgical fog may add to the stress and confusion.

REMEMBER

Remember the saying: "You never get a second chance to make a first impression"? The idea works with dogs, too. No matter how happy you are to bring him home, no matter how much you want to make up for the shabby way he was treated before you got him, start him off right from the beginning. Decide what the house rules are and stick to them, for the first couple of months, at least. Let him know that even though you're the nicest person on earth and the best human he could ever hope to find, your house does have rules, and he must follow them.

TIP

FIVE QUESTIONS TO HELP YOU EVALUATE AN ADULT DOG

No matter the age of the dog you're interested in adopting, you must do what you can to find out everything possible about her. While expecting to work on some things as your new dog gets used to you is reasonable, you want to avoid those animals who have too many problems, especially if one of them is aggression. Here are some questions that will help you:

- **What do you know of this dog's history?** You may be dealing with a shelter, a rescue volunteer, the dog's original owner or breeder, or a nice person who found a stray. If you discover the dog is well-bred and his parents have been certified free of con-genital defects, more's the better! If you find out nothing about him, though, because he was a stray, don't count him out. If he's healthy and friendly and otherwise fits your size, coat, and activity criteria, he's a contender.

- **Why is this dog available for adoption?** Dogs become available for lots of reasons, some as frivolous as a change in decor. "Losing our home," "divorce," and "death" are some of the ones that suggest a dog is free of blame; "bit our daughter" obviously is not (even if you don't have children). Listen, too, for what isn't said: "He needs more exercise than we can give him" may mean "He needs more exercise than anyone could possibly ever give him, and he eats furniture when he doesn't get it."

- **What behavior problems does this dog have?** Many things are fixable and worth considering if you honestly believe you'll take the time to work with the dog. "Pulls on the leash" is fixable. "A little aggressive" is not, at least not by the average pet owner's standard, and not to the extent that you should take a chance on a dog like this. Remember, too, that some problems are the owner's fault, not the dog's. "Won't stay in the yard," for example, may be easily cured by a decent fence and neutering.

- **How is he with children? Other dogs? Cats?** Even if you don't have children, you're going to run into some from time to time. The same is true with other dogs. You can successfully avoid cats if you don't have them, but make certain your prospective pet at least tolerates them well if you have a cat in your home. If you're getting an animal from a shelter, the organization should have asked the former owner to fill out a card on such things as problems with children or other animals. If you're adopting from a foster home, ask if the family has other animals and children. If there's no way to determine the dog's attitude toward children and other animals but he seems friendly, he may be okay. If you have doubts, however, hold out for an animal that you're sure fits well with your family.

- **What if it doesn't work out?** Obviously you're on your own if the person is moving out of state, but you need to know what your options are up front. You need to know what time frame you're dealing with for returning a dog who's not working out and whether your adoption fees — if any — will be refunded or if you'll be allowed to choose another dog at no charge.

Be what dog trainer Carol Lea Benjamin calls a *benevolent alpha* — a nice boss, but still a boss. Your dog will understand, respect, and love you for being his leader — it's the way dogs are. If you're not in charge, your dog will be. No democracies here. I always figure until my dogs pay our mortgage, the person who makes the tough call is me.

It just works better that way. Honest.

Introductions

Before choosing your dog, remember to ask if she gets along with what you've got. Make sure by arranging introductions with the people in your family before accepting the pet. The dog who seems perfect with a woman may be afraid of men and downright hostile toward children. The time to find out is before your new dog comes home. If you're childless and single, you may consider bringing a friend of the opposite gender along for introductions, just to be sure. Kids, too, if you can manage it. You never know: You may end up with both a spouse and children during your dog's lifetime.

WARNING

If your new dog shows aggression toward family members after you get him home, take him back. Yes, in some cases you can train a dominant dog to be more tolerant and build self-confidence in the case of fear biters or growlers. What's more likely to happen, though, is that you end up with a dog who is fine most of the time, a dog with whom you'll fall in love. And that dog, the one you love, is going to bite your child someday, when whatever triggers his aggression — taking away a toy, playing too close to the food dish, whatever — finally happens in your house. Don't take a chance. Leave training the aggressive dog to the people who train dogs for a living.

The following sections offer some tips for handling other introductions.

The original dog

If you already have at least one dog in your household, arrange to have the new dog meet him on-leash in neutral territory, such as at a nearby park, and walk them home together. Try not to telegraph your nervousness to the dog at the end of whichever leash you're holding: Be matter-of-fact but alert, and be sure that both leashes are loose. If either dog reacts aggressively, consider another dog — or no second dog at all, if your existing dog is too dog-aggressive to accept another one. Experienced dog handlers and trainers can keep dogs who don't like each other under control, but the average dog lover isn't up to the task.

Introducing a new dog into the family requires a period of adjustment for everyone.

Friday, Edgar, and Moose/Photo courtesy of Joyce Munz

That said, some jockeying for position is bound to occur in a two-dog household once the new dog comes home. Let them work it out themselves as long as jockeying doesn't escalate to growling — or fighting. If either happens, call in a trainer to help.

TIP

One exercise that helps two dogs learn that it is your wish that they get along — and that you won't tolerate anything else — is side-by-side, half-hour "Down-Stays." The late trainer Job Michael Evans believed this exercise to be a good way to build biddability in a dog from the inside out. Side-by-side "Down-Stays" say to the dogs, "Look, I don't care *how* you feel about each other, this is my house, and you'll behave yourselves in it."

For tips to teach the "Down" and "Stay" commands, see Chapter 14. What to do in the event of a dog fight — and how to protect both yourself and your dog — is in Chapter 15.

Cats

Put the dog on a leash when your cat and dog are first introduced, and be prepared for your cat to freak, especially if the presence of a dog in your home is a new experience. Correct the dog for trying to chase — as long as he's good-natured, don't be overly concerned — and ask him to "Sit," instead, and praise for proper behavior. If you have any doubts, let the dog drag his leash around in the house so you can quickly step on it and correct him if he starts to chase the cat.

Cats can take a long time to get used to having a dog in the house — a couple of months, in some cases. Be sure that your cat has a place to eat where he can feel secure — such as a tabletop or in a room the dog can't get into — and likewise take steps to make sure that his litter box is out of bounds. (If you know you're getting a dog, make these changes many weeks beforehand so your cat doesn't have to deal with too many new things at once.)

Again, the long "Down-Stay" can do wonders. Put your new dog on one while you pet and massage your cat so that your cat knows he's still loved and your dog understands that no matter what *he* thinks, the cat is to be left alone, because you say so.

TIP

Although it doesn't seem fair to our human sensibilities, your cat may prefer to spend the adjustment period sequestered in a small room with food and water, toys, a litter box, and a scratching post. A quiet, orderly life helps many cats ease through the transition: When you open the door after a couple of weeks, let your cat choose how much or how little interaction he wants to have with the new dog. Put a baby-gate across the door to the room, so your cat can always escape.

TIP

Cats don't always react well to changes in their lives, and sometimes behavior problems such as litter box-avoidance result. *Cats For Dummies,* which I wrote along with Dr. Paul D. Pion, a top veterinarian, has the information you need to solve feline behavior problems. The book was named the Best Work on Feline Behavior by the Cat Writers Association.

Small household pets

This one's an easy one. *Never* trust a dog around loose pets of the smaller variety — rats and hamsters, guinea pigs and rabbits, ferrets, birds, and reptiles. After all, some dogs believe smaller pets to be prey, and they can be very efficient at hurting them — or killing them. A fatal accident can happen in the blink of an eye. Don't take the chance.

Some breeds or breed mixes are worse than others when it comes to small pets. Terriers, for example, were developed to hunt and kill vermin. You may consider your rat a pet, but a terrier will consider it a rat, and rats are to be killed, no two ways about it.

Even the most docile dog can turn into a predator when his instincts are properly triggered. A pet rabbit sitting on the lawn may not warrant so much as a sniff from an easygoing dog. A pet rabbit *running* across the lawn may trigger a dog's chase instinct.

LOST DOG!

While any dog can become lost at any time, sticking around home isn't something that's easy for a newly adopted dog to do. After all, he's still not sure where "home" is, so he may take off for who-knows-where — at high speed.

The best time to protect your dog — old or new, young or not — is before he gets out. Here's a checklist of things to do, just in case:

- **Check your fences and gates.** Are there loose or missing boards or enticing gaps at the baseline that could be opened up with a little digging? Are latches secure, with locks in place? Fix them all. If you have children going in and out all the time, invest in a device that pulls the gate closed automatically.

  A special summertime hazard in the United States is the Fourth of July. The noise of fireworks can put pets in a panic, so the best you can do is go for a bowl of cool water and complete confinement in a crate, in the house, or in the garage, until the festivities are over. The same goes for New Year's Eve or any other event when noisemaking is the norm.

- **Check your dog.** Don't waste time before getting him a license and an ID tag. If your pet ends up in the shelter, a license buys him extra time. And if someone finds him when the shelter's closed, an ID tag with your phone number speeds up the reunion. Instead of your pet's name and your address on the ID tag, use the word "REWARD" and as many phone numbers as you can fit. Also recommended: A 24-hour tracking service such as 800-HELP4PETS.

  Microchip implants, which carry ID numbers, are a great idea. Make sure that your pet's permanent ID is registered so if someone discovers it, a fast reunion is possible. The AKC's Companion Animal Recovery service can help in the United States and Canada — they don't just deal with purebred dogs and not just with the kind of microchip involved in the program. Call 800-252-7894 or ask your veterinarian for more information.

- **Plan for the worst.** Keep current, clear pictures of your pets on hand — you need them to throw together a flyer in an emergency. If you lose your pet, put flyers everywhere you can and place a lost ad in the newspaper right away — don't waste precious time hoping your pet will wander home. Describe your dog as the general public would see him: To most people, a Belgian Tervuren looks like a Collie-Shepherd cross, and a Flat-Coated Retriever looks like a long-haired black Lab. So say that, too.

My brother's family has had two generations of mellow Labradors who allow the family's bunny, Ginger, to roam unmolested in the yard. I think they're just lucky.

I love dogs, but I never, ever forget that they are indeed predators. You shouldn't either.

Indoor livestock

Pot-bellied pigs and miniature horses are probably big enough to look out for themselves, but still, I'd never leave a dog unsupervised with one. As with introducing a new dog to another dog or to a cat, start the introductions out on a leash, and make sure that your dog understands that your pet is a pet, not a pork chop — aggressive behavior won't be tolerated.

WARNING

Chasing livestock is serious business. In rural areas, farmers often lose livestock to wandering pet dogs. You are responsible for any animal your dog hurts, and your dog may pay an even bigger price. In rural areas it's common — and legal — for a farmer to shoot any dog seen messing with livestock.

TIP

If you end up with a dog who wants to chase horses, cows, sheep, goats or whatever exotic creatures lurk in the nearby pasture, engage the services of a trainer who will work on countering your dog's predatory impulses — usually with the aid of an electronic collar. And don't let your dog roam.

Establish a routine

While every dog is an individual, most adult dogs start feeling comfortable in their new homes in about a month. You can do a few things to help him understand that yours is his new home and he is a loved member of his new family, but he also has to understand his place in the family.

Model your leadership in front of him. Doing so is easy and works great as long as you're consistent. Here are a few exercises to try:

- » **Leash-bonding.** For an hour each night, attach your dog's leash to your belt — or to a cord around your waist — and go about your business with the other end snapped to the dog's collar. Don't call him along with you and keep your hands off the leash. Just move about your house as you normally would — putting dishes in the dishwasher, paying bills, putting in a load of wash. Don't pay the dog much mind — just let your body weight remind him that he'd better go with you. The payoff is that he learns to pay attention to where you are and to think you and what you're doing are significant.

  Leash-bonding can also be used to help house-train an adult dog. See Chapter 8 for details.

- » **Sit for what you want.** Your dog should get in the habit of sitting for the good things. Ask him to "Sit" — and praise him when he does — before putting down his food dish, before petting him, and before letting him walk out the door on a walk. He'll start to think all good things come from you, but only when he behaves as you ask.

- » **People first.** In the dog world the higher ranking animal goes first. You want that higher ranking animal to be you. So your dog should eat after you do, and he should walk out a door after you do. For the latter, have him "Sit" and "Stay," and then step outside and invite him along. *Never* let him run past you — out of a car, into your yard, or into the park — as if he owns the joint. He doesn't. It's that simple.

- » **People food, dog food.** Don't share your meals with your dog, and don't add your table scraps to his. Feed a high-quality diet and leave it at that. If you share, you have no one to blame but yourself for his begging. Plus, your food is boss food. Yours and yours alone. (For more on choosing food for your dog, see Chapter 7.)

- » **People bed, dog bed.** Get your dog a comfortable bed or crate and make him sleep in it. Let him sleep in your room so he can be near you. Your bed is the most prime piece of real estate in his world, and it should be yours alone. He should have access with your permission only.

"Oh, c'mon!" you're saying, "who died and made you a drill sergeant? I want to spoil my dog!" Sure. Later. When your dog has impeccable house manners and you have nothing to complain about. Do my dogs sleep on the bed? You bet! But they don't come up without permission and they know it's a privilege, not a right. Do I share my carrots sticks with them while I write? Of course! But they sit for them, every one. And when I tell them I'm done sharing and to go to their beds, they do. Set the ground rules early and stick to them fairly and consistently. You can always loosen up, but tightening up is awfully hard after your dog's out of control.

2

Getting the Relationship Off to the Best Start

This part explains everything you need to know about getting your relationship with your new dog off to the best possible beginning. You'll find the rundown on dog gear — what you need, what you don't, and what's just plain fun to have. Everything you need to know about canine nutrition is in here to help you choose the right food for your puppy or dog. A whole chapter on housetraining, too, along with more tips on training and socializing your puppy.

» Sniffing out the coolest products

» Picking leashes and collars

» Finding fun dog stuff for you

Chapter **6**

All the Right Stuff

dog can get by without much in the way of material belongings and a great many of them do. A collar. A leash. A container for water, and one for food. A warm, dry place to sleep. Something to play with or chew on.

Add love, training, and attention to the list and, in truth, a dog doesn't need much more. But oh, how we love to spend money on our dogs! Pet supplies is a multi-billion-dollar industry, with so much money spent on dog-related furniture, food, and toys that I often joke the only difference between having a kid and having a dog is you don't need a college fund for the latter. That, and no matter how many things you buy your dog, she never gets spoiled.

REMEMBER

Your dog couldn't care less if the collar you buy her is jeweled. A crystal bowl or a stainless steel one, it really doesn't matter to her, as long as you put food in it. Color-coordinate her leash to match her collar and to complement the interior of your sport-utility vehicle; it won't impress her. Most of the dog-accessories decisions you face you make to please *yourself*. And that's fine, as long as your dog's needs are met with gear that is well made, practical, and appropriate for her size and temperament.

At the most basic level, your dog needs food and shelter. That's about the most any dog could ever have hoped for during the thousands of years humans and dogs have worked and lived together as companions and workmates. Everything you add to those basics is designed to make your dog's life — and your own — safer, more convenient, and more enjoyable.

And I know that you want safety, convenience, and fun — so get ready to go shopping.

For information on canine nutrition and what food to buy your dog, see Chapter 7. How to keep your dog well-groomed — including the tools you need to buy to accomplish the deed — is covered in depth in Chapter 10, along with what you'll need to buy to control fleas and ticks.

REMEMBER

Your dog needs more than you can buy her at a pet-supply store. She needs a healthy relationship with a veterinarian, and she needs socialization and training.

Houses, Beds, and Barriers

You have a responsibility to provide a safe, dry place for your dog, one that's cool in the summer and warm in the winter. One that keeps him from roaming the neighborhood, and protects him from cars, thieves, and assorted sickos. Those are the basic requirements, but you'll have a much better relationship with your dog — and he'll be much happier — if you take him out of the doghouse and into your house.

REMEMBER

I'm going to be blunt here: What's the point of keeping a completely outdoor dog as a pet? Protection? Fat lot of good that big dog will do you outside when burglars are inside your house. Companionship? You work all day, you come home, feed the outdoor dog, and maybe play with him a little. Then you go in and watch TV and he sits outside alone.

While some dogs handle the outdoors better than others, they still can cause a lot of problems. They bark, day and night, out of boredom and loneliness. They dig. They chew the siding off your house. They can teach themselves to be overzealously protective to the point of dangerousness.

A lot of people with outdoor dogs didn't start out intending for them to live outside. The dog was never fully house-trained, perhaps, or was never taught to not jump on guests. Perhaps he doesn't know how to behave himself around children. Perhaps he's destructive and you figure that it's better if he eats the picnic table than the coffee table. Perhaps he flat-out smells horribly rank.

Look, these things are *fixable*. Behavior problems can be solved by training, and smell problems — well, did you ever hear of a bath? Grooming tips are in Chapter 10; behavior problems are explained in Chapters 14 and 15. You owe it to your dog, your family, and your neighbors to do what you can to avoid leaving your dog outside all the time.

THE DANGERS OF CHAINS

In many parts of the country fenced yards are uncommon, so many people keep their dogs on chains. Tethering a dog for a short while is okay in a pinch — never with a choke collar, though — but a tethered existence is not a good one. And a chained dog should never be left unattended.

Dogs who spend their lives on chains are more likely to become dangerous, biting anyone who comes onto their turf. The profile of the average dog in a vicious bite incident, in fact, is a young, unneutered male on a chain.

And chaining is dangerous for the dog, too: I know of a handful of cases where a dog tried to jump a fence, didn't have enough chain to clear and ended up hanging himself from his collar on the other side of the fence. Dogs have also wrapped their chains around trees and died because they were unable to get to water on hot days.

If you don't have a fenced yard, walking your dog or buying a kennel run for him is better than putting him outside on a chain.

REMEMBER

If you must leave your dog outside, you must do your best to bring a little joy into your lonely dog's life with time and outings to strengthen the bond between you. Don't just throw some food out in the yard and forget him.

Good fences make good dogs

Still, unless you're an apartment-dweller, your dog spends a certain amount of time in your back yard, ranging from a few minutes a day to do his business to the hours while you're at work. You want to make his time outdoors as pleasant and safe as possible.

The ideal setup is a fenced yard away from the street. Solid six-foot fencing is best to protect your pet from the view of people who might tease or steal him and to give him fewer reasons to bark. If you're a gardener, consider breaking off part of the yard for your dog and keeping the rest of it off-limits unless you're with him.

TIP

My favorite example of dog-safe yard design comes from a friend and her architect husband, who designed their yard with a U-shaped area around the outside for their Airedale, and an interior courtyard that was kept safe from his big paws. (For more on dogs and gardens, see Chapter 22.)

Kennel runs are fine, too, for keeping dogs out of trouble when you're not with them. Keep the kennel run well-protected from heat, cold, and wind, keep fresh water and toys always available, and be sure that the time in the run is kept to a minimum. Remember that a 10-x-6-foot run is a safe place to spend a few hours, but it's no place to spend a life.

Electronic boundary systems that use shock collars to teach dogs the property lines can be useful in some situations, but they have some serious limitations. First, some dogs choose to be shocked if the temptation is great enough on the other side, and once out, avoid taking another hit to get home.

WARNING

An electronic boundary system does not protect your pet from animals or people who enter your property — so your dog can be easily attacked, poisoned, or stolen. And it does *not* protect people from your pet. I know of one case where a child was viciously bitten after coming onto the territory of a dog behind an electric boundary system. A solid fence would have spared the child the injury, and saved the dog's life, since he was put down after the attack.

REMEMBER

Good fences make good neighbors. Sturdy, solid-wood fences also make good dogs.

TIP

Two products that make the ins and outs a little easier to handle are dog doors and baby gates:

>> Most *dog doors* consist of a flap of metal or plastic that a pet can push with his nose or paws to open. They are great for anyone who doesn't want to get up every time the dog scratches at the door, and even better for people who leave a dog alone all day and want to provide access to the outdoors while they're gone. They can be set up between house and yard, or between a garage and yard. Some people build chutes with dog doors at both ends to cut down on drafts.

For the sake of security, have your door installed where your pet's comings and goings aren't so noticeable, and close and lock it when it's not needed, such as when you're on vacation.(Do remember, though, that a dog door — especially a large one — always carries a certain degree of risk. A young burglar — or a thin one — can easily gain access to your house through the flap.

When my dog door was put in, I had it installed through an exterior wall rather than a door, so I needed the help of a contractor. The man pointed out that the door was large enough for a criminal to wiggle through. "Yes, I see your point," I said. "But don't you think the person who looks at a dog door that large will wonder how big the dog waiting on the other side is?"

>> *Baby gates* — available in pet-supply catalogs or anywhere children's things are sold — can be used to limit a pet's access to certain parts of the house.

I use the two products in combination to provide a safe and secure place for my pets when I'm away from home: Baby gates to keep them in the kitchen, and a dog door to allow them to go to the part of the yard that they're allowed in when I'm not with them.

Doghouses: Protection from the elements

If your dog spends much time outside — while you're at work, perhaps — he needs shelter from heat and cold. One of the easiest ways to provide this is a doghouse. Your choices here: wood or high-impact plastic.

TIP

No matter the material you choose, a doghouse should fit your pet snugly — he should be able to stand up and turn around, but not much more. Providing your dog with a house that's too large makes staying warm inside of it difficult for him. It should have an entrance that's off-center so the dog can curl up in one end for warmth. A removable roof is helpful for easy cleaning, and the doorway should have a flap over it to keep drafts out.

Building a doghouse is an easy weekend project for anyone with basic carpentry skills; plans can be found at libraries or building-supply stores. You can also buy wooden doghouses, including some that are extremely fancy and designed to match your home's architecture — Cape Cod, Georgian, ranch, and so on. What a great project for the kids to help with!

Several manufacturers offer doghouses of molded, high-impact plastic that are in some ways superior to traditional wooden ones. They clean easily, do not retain smells and offer no place for fleas to breed — as long as the bedding is kept fresh. (More on bedding in the next section.)

TIP

Where you place the doghouse has a lot to do with how comfortable your dog is when in it. In winter, it should be in a spot that's protected from the wind. And in summer, it should be in the shade.

Every dog needs a bed (even if it's yours)

Indoor dogs need a place to sleep, too. Unless your dog has impeccable manners and respects your authority, he shouldn't be on your bed — it gives him the wrong idea concerning who's the Top Dog in your family. (More on this in Chapter 15.) Don't feel sorry for him, though: More beautiful and comfortable beds are available today than ever before, to fit every dog, every budget, and every decor.

TIP

One possibility for a bed is a *crate*, probably the most versatile piece of dog gear ever made. Once used primarily for transporting dogs on airlines, the crate in all its varieties — open mesh, solid metal, or high-impact plastic — is now widely used and recognized as one of the best tools for making living with your pet easier. The crate is the easiest and fastest way to house-train a puppy or dog — for more on that, see Chapter 8 — and it's also a decent whelping box, should you ever breed your pet. With some modifications to cut down on the drafts, it even makes a decent doghouse.

TIP

If your dog misbehaves, it's a good place to put him for a "time out." If for any reason you don't want him underfoot — a guest with allergies, a contractor marching in and out — the crate is a godsend.

The crate is also perfect for its original purpose: transporting your pet. A loose dog in the car can be an annoyance, even a danger. Everyone is safer when crates are used. And talk about safety! In an automobile accident a loose dog is as vulnerable as an unbelted human. Crates are tough, so much so that a crated dog once survived an airline crash with near-total human casualties. When traveling with your pet, you'll find showing up with a crate will endear you to hotel owners, some of whom can be sweet-talked into lifting "no dog" rules if they know your dog will be crated in the room — as opposed to chewing up the bedspread.

Dogs who are used to crates love them. It's a room of their own, cozy and secure, so much so that many dogs seek out their crates voluntarily. In my house, where an always-open, retriever-sized crate serves as an unconventional end table in the den, a dog is always snoozing inside, by choice. To increase comfort, you can buy pads to fit the floor of crates, make your own without too much difficulty, tuck a washable blanket inside — or you can just leave them empty, especially in warmer weather.

Need another reason to buy a crate? In times of disaster — floods, earthquakes, hurricanes — a crate can save your pet's life by keeping him secure and providing you with alternatives should you have to evacuate your home. The cages of veterinary hospitals and animal shelters adjacent to a disaster area fill up quickly, but there's always room for the pet that brings his own shelter. More on disaster planning is in Chapter 21.

Consider what you'll be using a crate for before you buy one. If you ever intend to ship your dog by air, be aware that not all crates are intended for this purpose. Some are designed for light use — house-training puppies in the home, for example — while others are designed for car travel, a medium-grade use. If you intend to use a crate for house-training, a bed, travel, occasional confinement and, possibly, a whelping box, you're better off buying a top-quality crate of high-impact molded plastic, approved for air travel.

Buy a crate to fit the size your puppy will be. A grown dog should be able to stand, turn around and lay down comfortably. When house-training a puppy, make the crate smaller by using a panel. An alternative: Borrow a puppy-sized crate from a friend or the puppy's breeder.

A crate is a big-ticket item, so shop aggressively. One important source: garage sales and classified ads. When I was fostering dogs as a breed-rescue volunteer, I owned close to a dozen top-quality crates, many of them constantly on loan to adopting families. I picked up most of them second-hand at less than two-thirds of the best retail price I could find.

The use of a crate in solving house-training problems is in Chapter 8; other training uses for the crate are in Chapters 4 and 9, for puppies, and Chapters 14 and 15, for adult dogs.

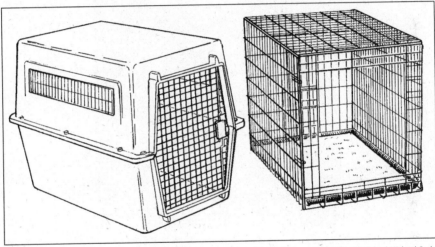

Crates are both a comfortable place for a dog to sleep and an invaluable training tool.

Greta/Photo courtesy of Stephanie and Michael Corby

While a crate can be used for almost anything, it's not the only choice when it comes to a bed. Beds keep floors and carpets cleaner, provide a cushion that makes all dogs more comfortable (especially older or arthritic ones), and allow you to live without guilt for keeping your dog off *your* bed.

Every dog needs a bed, even if it's just an old blanket. Two of the most popular varieties: Oval *cuddlers* designed for dogs to curl up in and lined with plush or polyester sheepskin; and stuffed cushions that resemble '60s bean-bag chairs, albeit in more muted colors than those popular then. The most important thing to remember when picking out a bed is that it must be *washable*, or at the very least have a removable, washable cover. You'll almost certainly have a problem with fur, smells, and fleas if you don't wash pet bedding on a regular basis — weekly is ideal.

Washability is why I don't recommend carpet remnants. You just can't keep them fresh and clean-smelling, and they're like a welcome mat for fleas.

TIP

Some of the handsomest and sturdiest beds are available by mail order, in a wider range of colors and sizes than you may be able to find locally. Doctors Foster and Smith, a mail-order pet-supply firm in Wisconsin, has some of the nicest. Another great source: L.L. Bean!

Every dog should have a comfortable bed of her own. This one provides necessary cushioning for an old dog's joints.

Photo courtesy of Gina Spadafori

You can also find great beds at dog shows — two of the nearly dozen dog beds in my home were handmade and sold only at dog shows. Those two — one a platform bed made of PVC pipe and the material found on outdoor furniture, the other a pellet-filled cushion in a handsome houndstooth cover — have outlived two dogs, hundreds of washings, and more than a half-dozen beds of lesser quality.

Bowls and Waterers

In dog dishes, too, you have a lot of options, from using an old pot to buying a hand-thrown ceramic bowl with your dog's name painted on it. Dishes designed to store up to a couple of days' worth of food or water are available, as are paper bowls good for one meal only (the latter most commonly used at boarding kennels and veterinary hospitals).

I prefer sturdy dishes of molded, high-impact plastic or stainless steel that resist chewing or scratching and can be sterilized in the dishwasher. These dishes — stainless steel especially — retain their good looks, handle any abuse a dog can dish out, and last forever. (I have one that's 22 years old!) Dishes that damage easily are hard to keep clean and invite the buildup of food and bacteria in the dents and scratches. Some dogs also have a sensitivity to flimsy plastic bowls.

TIP

For dogs with long, silky ears — like Cocker Spaniels — look for bowls with a narrow opening and high, sloped sides to keep that fur out of the muck. If your dog is a ravenous eater, a bowl with a nonskid base will help keep the dish from ending up in the next county.

Some people are a little squeamish about putting dog dishes in the dish-washer, but, honestly, if your dishwasher's doing its job right, the water will be hot enough to render everything in it clean enough for *you* to eat out of.

One of my favorite dogs and dishwasher stories involves my sister-in-law's parents, who swear the "Labrador Prewash" extended the life of their dishwasher. Although not allowed to beg while people were eating, their chocolate Lab helped with after-meal cleanup by licking the plates clean before they were loaded in the dishwasher. During California's drought years, they argued it was a real water-saver, too. These days, my sister-in-law carries on the tradition: Duncan, the family's yellow Labrador, does the Labrador Prewash in the family's home.

While your dog's food dishes should be picked up, washed, and put away after meals, water dishes need to be kept full and available at all times. Here, too, stainless steel is your best choice. Dishes with reservoirs are fine, but I find they're hard to keep clean. And, unless your dog needs a lot of water, these products get mucky before the water needs to be refilled.

TIP

For outside water, the *Lixit*, available in any pet-supply store or catalog, has long been a popular device. Attached to a faucet, it releases fresh water when the dog licks or nuzzles the trigger — and stops the flow when the dog is through. They need to be installed in a shaded area, however, for the metal can become frying-pan hot if exposed to full summer sun.

WARNING

All water sources need to be sheltered from both heat and freezing cold, or they won't be available to your dog at all times — a potentially deadly situation in extreme weather. A couple of blocks of ice — you can make them by putting water-filled margarine tubs in your freezer — will keep a shaded water supply cool for hours. As for keeping water warm, there are heated bowls available to keep water from freezing, as well as special devices designed to fit into buckets to do the same thing.

If you and your dog are constantly on the go, look into a more portable water source. Several different kinds of traveling bowls are designed to reduce splashing, and some collapsible products can be put away in a space as small as a fanny pack. You can also use a squeeze-type bottle like bicyclists use — your dog will quickly learn to catch the flow. A tip, though: You may want to mark it with indelible ink so everyone knows it's dog water.

A friend of mine had her dogs in mind when she remodeled her kitchen. The three bottom drawers of the center island pull out to reveal recessed dog dishes — stainless steel pop-outs, for easy cleaning — and secure storage for 40 pounds of kibble. On the other side of the kitchen another stainless steel bowl in a recessed bay provides the dogs with fresh water and keeps most of the drip off the floor.

It's one of the best ideas I've ever seen, and it keeps things neater in her lovely kitchen.

Collars and Leashes

A confession: Collars and leashes are the things I most like to buy for my dogs, even though it has only been relatively recently that I got a dog who shows off a nice collar well. My retriever has medium-length glossy black fur. Every collar and every color looks nice on dogs like these, and so they have a couple each, plus some bandanas for special occasions. Leashes simply *must* coordinate, of course, so we have plenty of those, too. My current favorite collar on the older retriever — his, too, I think — bright red with silhouettes of black Labradors. Stunning, simply stunning.

Fashion aside, collars, harnesses, halters, and leashes perform a very vital function: They help you to train your dog and allow you to keep him out of trouble in public. Collars also protect your dog when you can't, by carrying identification that will get him home should he ever slip away from you.

When ordering a collar — buckled or quick-snap — for regular wear, measure a couple of inches down the neck from your dog's head, and then add two inches. For tiny dogs, add an inch. When trying on collars, you should be able to fit two fingers snugly between collar and neck; one finger on a small dog. The goal is to have a collar snug enough so your dog can't back up and out of the collar, but loose enough for comfort.

A slip collar — commonly called a *choke* collar — should fit a little more loosely because it fits over a dog's head instead of being wrapped around the neck. Add an inch-and-a-half for small dogs and up to three inches for large ones — you should just be able to slip it over your pet's head and no more. (Some slip collars use a snap connection to allow them to be wrapped around and more closely fitted, riding behind the dog's ears. If you're working with a trainer who uses this type of collar, ask to make sure it's fitted properly.)

Match the width of the nylon or leather — or the heaviness of the links — to the size of your dog: Narrower measures and lighter lengths are for smaller dogs. Too light a link on a slip collar can dig in to a large pet's neck, plus the chain may not be strong enough to hold him should he lunge.

The everyday collar

A collar is an essential purchase for your dog, but if he's wearing the wrong collar at the wrong time, your dog could end up hurt or even dead. Which is why learning a little before you go shopping is important.

Your pet's everyday collar, the one you put her tags on, should be a buckled collar, either flat or rolled, made of nylon web or leather. Either a flat collar or a rolled collar will work fine on dogs with short or medium fur, but rolled collars are preferable on dogs with thick, long fur at the neck, such as Collies.

I like nylon web collars because of the incredible variety of colors and patterns, and because some dogs are more apt to chew off the leather collar of another family dog. Other dogs may find a nylon collar irritating, and do better with leather. As long as the collar is well-made, both nylon and leather will last for years. In recent years, quick-snap closures have become popular, especially on flat nylon web collars. And it's easy to see why: Press in at the edges and the collar's off easily for baths and changing tags. Press the tips together and *snap*, it's on again. For most dogs, these collars present no problems. Because they are so simply adjusted, they're ideal for growing puppies. Some trainers think buckled collars are more secure for large, strong, and impulsive dogs, but a high-quality quick-snap collar should be just as sturdy.

While some people may think that elegant canine collars are a recent development, it's simply not true. Those who can afford it have always put ritzy collars around the necks of their prized canine companions — gold and silver, pearls, and gems have been part of the society dog's wardrobe for centuries.

Today's dogs don't have it so ruff, either. Some of the loveliest collars around can be found in specialty catalogs and pet boutiques, for prices that would keep some dogs in kibble for months.

Want one? Oh, why not? Just make sure that you make a matching donation to your local shelter so the guilt doesn't get you down.

Training collars

A properly-fitted buckle or quick-snap collar — with tags and a license — is all a puppy needs for the first few months of his life and maybe all that he ever needs. But most dogs need a collar for training, or for you to be able to control yours better on a leash.

The most commonly used — and misused — training collar is the *slip*. This collar is a length of chain — and sometimes nylon — with rings at both ends. To use, you drop the length of chain or nylon through one of the rings and then slip the resulting loop over your dog's head. The leash is attached to the moving ring, not the stationery one.

The choices in collars have never been greater, including some so beautiful they're practically works of art.

Beauty/Photograph courtesy of
www.greyhoundgang.com

WARNING

The most important thing you need to know about a slip collar is that it *never, ever* should be your dog's everyday collar and *must always* be removed when you're through training or walking your dog.

That's because the moving ring of the collar can get caught on just about anything — even the eye-tooth of another dog in play. Once caught, a dog's natural reaction is to pull away, a move that tightens the collar, which panics the dog into pulling away more. Even if you're there, you may not have the strength to rescue a terrified dog in this situation — and if you *do* have the strength, you may be badly bitten while trying.

A great many dogs have died because of the misuse of this common piece of training equipment, and the near-misses are even more common.

This risk to your dog's well-being is one of the easiest in the world to avoid.

You can call it a choke collar if you want, but know this: If you're choking your dog, you're using it wrong. That's not training, that's cruelty, however unintentional. More than half the time this happens because pet-owners put the collar on upside-down. See Chapter 14 for more on using this collar.

The moving part of the training collar should *go over* the dog's head, not under it. When positioned properly, the collar tightens when you pull on the leash, and releases when you slack off. If the moving part of the collar is *under* the dog's head, when you tighten, the collar tightens, but it doesn't release when the pressure's off.

How to get it right? With the dog sitting on your left — in "Heel" position — hold the collar in a P shape, with the loop away from you and the back of the P on top. Slip it over your dog's head, and it will be in perfect position.

The slip collar's by far the most common for training and control, but there are a few others you should know about:

>> **Partial slip collars** can be a hybrid between a flat collar and a slip collar, part flat nylon, part chain, or all chain. They are designed to limit the choking action of a slip collar — they tighten, but only so much. Some trainers use them all the time, others recommend them for people who have an exceptionally difficult time with the release of the slip collar's snap and release motion.

>> **Pinch** or **prong collars** are more popular than ever before, because they are an efficient way of dealing with large dogs with especially well-muscled necks, like the Rottweiler. Like a partial slip, they can only be tightened so far, but, unlike the partial, they have blunt metal prongs evenly spaced along the inside of the length of the collar. When tightening, these prongs press into the flesh of the dog's neck.

These collars are very controversial, in part because of their cruel appearance — which is probably why some people like them: They look macho. They should not be a first choice training collar, but in the hands of a knowledgeable trainer, they can help with a powerful dog.

>> **Head halters** are another device with a public-relations problem; this time completely unwarranted. The problem: They look like muzzles. In fact, they

operate on the same principle that has worked for years with horses: Where the head goes, the body follows. The leash is attached to a ring under the jaw, and when pulled, pressure is placed around the muzzle and around the neck — both important in canine body language.

Properly fitted and used, a head halter can make even a large, powerful dog controllable enough to be walked by a child — but then, so can a proper course of training!

» **Electric collars** give a shock either automatically, such as when a dog barks, or manually, at the trainer's discretion. They are widely used in training dogs for hunting and field work and for correcting some serious behavior problems, such as perdition. Although widely available in pet-supply stores and catalogs, they should *not* be used by pet owners except under the guidance of experienced trainers. Without a thorough knowledge of training theory and a perfect sense of timing, this training tool is more cruel than effective.

» **Harnesses** for walking a dog are best left on little dogs, since they offer nothing in the way of control and give up a great deal in the way of leverage. Some small breeds — such as Poodles — have a tendency toward *collapsing tracheas*, where the rings of cartilage in the neck collapse temporarily when the dog's excited. These dogs are ideal candidates for harnesses to relieve the pressure on their necks from pulling. (Again, you can train your dog not to pull, but people with tiny breeds don't really have to, so they rarely do.)

Your veterinarian may suggest a harness if your dog is of a breed known for neck or back problems, or if your dog has had a neck trauma or surgery.

A couple of harnesses are on the market that do offer some control, tightening around the dog's chest as he pulls. These are an option even for larger dogs.

Some harnesses are made for dog sports — tracking, or pulling sleds or wagons. For more information on these sports, and others, see Chapter 16.

Leashes

The choices aren't as varied in leashes (also called *leads*) as in collars. There are a lot more colors and designs than there used to be, but the same basic choices remain: leather, nylon, or chain.

You can use anything you want when your dog is trained, but until you reach that point, the standard, six-foot, leather leash is your best choice. Nylon is a very close second — it's what I use on my trained dogs, because I like the colors — but it's not so easy to grip as leather and can give you burns if your dog takes off suddenly and whips the leash through your hands. Chain is a horrible thing to train with: It'll cut your hands to pieces, and your dog will confuse the noise of the leash with the noise of the collar.

The prong (also called the pinch) is an increasingly popular option for large, strong dogs. Although it looks formidable, it doesn't choke a dog the way a slip collar can.

Chula/Photograph courtesy of Ben Silverman

Other lengths are available, from a one-foot *traffic lead* that's useful for moving a large dog quickly from one place to another, to long leads for training or to give a dog a little more room to roam without unleashing him. For walking or training, the six-foot is still best: It lets you give your dog some freedom while leaving you with plenty of control. It's also the length spelled out in most leash laws.

Leashes are sold in ¼-inch, ⅜-inch, ½-inch, ⅝-inch, ¾-inch and 1-inch widths, with the two middle sizes the most commonly used in obedience training because they're easier to grip than the other sizes. The weakest parts of a leash are where the snap's attached and the handle is formed. Look for sturdy stitching or, in leather leads, one-piece construction.

TIP

One of the most popular pieces of equipment introduced in recent years is the reel-type Flexi lead that offers a dog up to 32 feet of freedom and yet can be shortened with the touch of a button on the plastic handle. While it's not meant to help you teach dogs to walk without pulling, it is commonly used to help teach them to come when called. It's great for travel, too, or for dogs who can't be trusted off-leash but still need to stretch their legs.

These leads, widely available in different sizes and lengths, are wonderful for letting a dog sniff around in areas where it's not safe or where you're not allowed to let him off-leash.

LASSIE COME HOME!

Your young daughter leaves the front door open or the wind blows down the fence: A lost dog can happen to the most conscientious of families.

For this reason, your dog's collar should always have tags. An ID tag with your phone number. A license. Getting a new tag should be the first thing you do when you move. Checking the tags frequently is important to ensure that the information is still readable. Even better is to subscribe to a 24-hours-a-day, seven-days-a-week tracking service, like 1-800-HELP4PETS, which will not only reunite you with your dog if she becomes lost, but will also arrange for boarding or medical care if you cannot be immediately found.

There are other ways to ID your dog, of course. Tattooing, with your driver's license number or another traceable number, like a registry number from the American or Canadian Kennel Clubs, has been popular for years, and microchipping has come on strong in the last decade.

The microchip is permanent identification no bigger than a grain of rice, which your veterinarian imbeds under the skin over your pet's shoulder blades using a large needle. (But don't worry: One yip is about all you'll hear, and then it's done!) Microchips have been of dubious value for returning lost pets because one company's chips couldn't be read by another company's scanner, and shelters couldn't and wouldn't cope with competing systems.

That's changed recently, with moves by manufacturers toward one industry standard and with the entry of the American Kennel Club as a registry of microchipped animals in the United States and Canada — any animals, not just AKC registered purebred dogs. It'll cost anything from $20 to $50 to have your pet chipped by your veterinarian, but it's a good investment in your dog's safety.

If you're going to have your canine companion microchipped — and I highly recommend it — find out what, if any, chip scanners are in use at the shelters in your area, and make sure your pet is implanted with a chip that can be read using that brand of scanner. You also should register your pet with AKC Companion Animal Recovery — 800-252-7894 — which offers 24-hour match-up service, 365 days a year. Although the service was set-up in conjunction with one manufacturer, you can register the number of whatever chip — or tattoo — you use. If someone calls to report your pet has been found, the service will release your number so you can be reunited quickly.

Flexis aren't designed to give you control over your dog, especially if he's large and strong. It's easy to lose your grip if the dog hits the end of the line running. For these reasons, I discourage the use of a Flexi in areas where it would be dangerous if your dog got loose.

Toys

Every dog needs toys. They keep your pet occupied and amused when you cannot, and they provide you with another avenue for interacting and bonding. Toys give your pet something to chew on besides your toes (or shoes, furniture, or books), and they are absolutely essential to puppy-raising, making puppies feel better when their teeth are cutting through. Not only that, but they are great fun to choose and buy. A couple of cautions in the toy area exist, but not many. Enjoy!

Chewies

The kind of chewie you buy has everything to do with the size of your dog and how aggressive a chewer he is. Some of the toughest chew toys on the market are made by Nylabone, in a variety of sizes, shapes, and colors.

The king of chew toys is the Kong, a hard rubber toy that looks a little like the Michelin Tire man. Not only are Kongs almost impossible to destroy, they bounce in a sprightly manner, in unpredictable directions.

Chewies designed to remove plaque and stimulate gums are a popular recent development. They have nubs along their length, or indentations designed to be filled with canine toothpaste.

Rope chews — some of them adorned with hooves at the ends or rubber balls in the middle — are popular, but some trainers think they're too much like things you *don't* want your pet to chew on, like carpet fringes.

Monitor your pet's chew toys. When they are worn or chewed to the point where they can be swallowed, replace them.

Squeakies

Puppies and dogs alike love toys of either plush or vinyl that make noise when squeezed. These can be a very expensive proposition if you own a dog who isn't happy until the squeaker is "dead." My older dog once, with surgical precision, removed the squeakers from four green vinyl frogs in under 20 minutes — at $8 each — and the youngest one, who adores stuffed toys, will treat one like a cherished love for days and then shred it looking for that squeaker. One beloved hedgehog, which roared rather than squeaked, lasted two whole weeks, a record.

TIP

One of the nicest and sturdiest plush toys is the Vermont Chewman, solidly made of thick, fake lambskin and available in catalogs and pet-supply stores.

Fetchies

Fetch is an outstanding way to exercise your dog while reminding him of your role as pack leader. Many people use flying discs for this and, while it's great fun, you should be aware that some dogs have been injured while leaping after flying disks, to the point of needing surgery on their knees and backs.

WARNING

Tennis balls are another common toy with built-in risks. *Never* let your dog chew on a tennis ball or play with one unattended. Some dogs have died after a tennis ball, compressed by powerful jaws, popped into the throat and cut off the air supply.

Does that mean you should avoid playing with flying discs or tennis balls? No, but use some common sense. With flying discs, avoid the acrobatics that wow spectators at half-time shows but have your dog leaping, twisting, and landing hard. Work on low throws in front of your dog, to encourage him to run, but not to jump. (I like to use the floppy discs made of fabric, not plastic.) Tennis balls are fine for fetch, but put them away when the game's over.

You can, of course, buy solid rubber balls. And for water retrieving — a great exercise for the dog who enjoys swimming — Kong makes a floating variety with a rope handle that's easy to throw a long way on land or in water. Since I got my first retriever a few years back, I seem to go through about a half-dozen of these a year — they're always getting caught in currents and swept downstream.

WARNING

If you buy a toy that invites tug-of-war games, it's fine to let your pet pull against another dog. But *never* play tug-of-war with your dog, and make sure that your children don't, either.

What seems like an innocent game could be a setup for tragedy. That's because tug-of-war can teach your dog to be dominant. Here's how it works: You play with your dog, pulling against him in a battle of dominance, however playful in appearance. You get bored, the phone rings, and you drop your end. You think: Game's over. Your dog thinks: I win — exactly the opposite of the message your dog should get, and one that may lead to other dominance challenges.

Chapter **7**

Feeding Your Puppy or Dog

U p until this century, the feeding of dogs wasn't that carefully thought-out an affair. They ate what we gave them. They ate what we left behind. They ate what other animals left behind. They killed things to eat, and they ate the remains of what other animals killed.

Dogs are not the pickiest of creatures, as anyone who has ever watched their pooch gobble rotting fish on a beach knows. Unlike cats, who are *obligate carnivores* — they need meat — dogs are omnivorous. They can survive on all kinds of foods, if they need to.

The hit-or-miss approach to dog feeding worked well enough for generations, especially when most dogs lived in rural areas, with access to rodents in the barn, rabbits in the fields, or leftovers in the farmer's kitchen or from the butchering of livestock. But then things changed, and more dogs assumed the role of companions in an urban environment where living off the land isn't such an easy thing to accomplish. At the same time, the burgeoning interest in animal husbandry has the men and women who are developing and refining breeds wanting their prize animals treated appropriately, with the best food that can be provided.

Dining Dos and Don'ts

"There is no doubt that a great deal of a dog's goodness goes in at the mouth," says Vero Shaw's The *Illustrated Book of the Dog*, first published in 1879 and reissued, as a novelty, more than a century later with the title *The Classic Encyclopedia of the Dog*. "We do not, certainly, advocate the feeding of dogs wholly upon meat . . . we do recommend meat to be given, in addition to the meal or biscuits which form the staple portion of the daily meal."

The book describes the ingredients and preparation of a dog's diet, the careful and considered mixing of grains such as rice and barley with vegetables such as cabbage, broccoli, and turnip-tops, and, finally, with the different kinds of meat available. "Horses suitable for slaughtering can usually be bought for from one pound to thirty shillings," notes the author.

Decades later, after untold hours of research by thousands of universities and pet-food manufacturers, Shaw's advice holds true: Most dogs today are on a diet that's a combination of grains and meat products. The difference: Today's pet-owner doesn't have to find and mix ingredients. And even better — doesn't have to kill the occasional horse to provide the meat!

The industry that's grown to supply your dog's needs is very, very big. How big? Try billions of dollars spent for dog food just in the United States, from tiny pop-lid tins of the most delectable gourmet meat chunks to the biggest bags of the least-expensive generic food.

Providing food for pets is such a big business that some of the most significant corporations around are involved in it. Not just the obvious ones such as Purina, but also Proctor & Gamble (which owns Iams), Mars (which owns Pedigree), and Colgate (which owns Hill's Pet Foods, the maker of Science Diet and other foods), to name but a few.

If you doubt the vastness of the pet-food industry, do a little research on your own. You won't have to go any farther away than your local supermarket or pet-supply warehouse. Pet food takes up as much space in your supermarket as any product line there, with the possible exception of cereals and candy — made, in many cases, by the same companies! And at the pet-supply warehouse, so much pet food is sold that it must be moved around by forklift.

And don't forget veterinarians, who often sell both premium brands as well as therapeutic diets meant to help your dog deal with various health problems from obesity to kidney and heart disease to plaque buildup on his teeth.

So many manufacturers. So many places to buy. So many *choices*! Where do you begin to find the food that provides your dog with what he needs: the essential elements of nutrition found for generations in the bodies of prey animals? Can you really find such nutrition in a can, box, or bag?

Read on! You'll find out what's known, and, more important, what isn't known about canine nutrition; what your dog needs and what's being marketed di-rectly at *your* desires, not your pet's; how to keep your dog eating correctly after you choose the right foods — so that your pet doesn't get too fat or too thin.

REMEMBER

Is all this information important? You bet, especially if you want a dog in good health, with a shiny coat, bright eyes, and energy to burn. Good nutrition is one of the basics of preventive health care for any animal — people, dogs, cats, you name it! Choosing good food is as important as anything else you do in the hope of providing your pet with a happy, long life.

The "perfect" dog diet

Part of the challenge of manufacturing a dog food is that what people will tolerate handling is usually a long way from what dogs would choose on their own. While few dogs would turn up their noses at fresh meat, they'd also drool over a carcass that's a whole lot further along than the human palate would appreciate.

My dog Andy, for example, once happily dug into the decomposing carcass of a beached and very disgustingly dead seal. I dragged him away from it after he'd taken a bite or two only, but in so doing, got close enough to the poor, dead creature that I started gagging from the sight and the smell. Revolting to me; yummy to a dog.

Until the day when dogs can buy their own food, they're going to have to make do with the meals people can stand to prepare — no rotting meat, and lots of convenience. That's probably why, instead of the rotting seal he'd choose, you're going to give your dog a dry food, where the label lists the first five ingredients as corn gluten meal, ground yellow corn, chicken, brewers rice, and wheat flour. Or you're going to feed him a canned food that lists wheat gluten and brewers rice just a notch or two below turkey.

Rice? Wheat? Corn? What gives? Are dogs carnivores or herbivores?

Well, actually they're omnivores, like humans. They like and can exist on meat or plant material — although they prefer meat. Dogs love treats of carrots, celery, or apple, but meat is a lot closer to their heart.

REMEMBER

Balancing convenience and nutrition, while appealing to both human *and* canine tastes, is a lot harder than it looks. All in all, commercial pet food has to be considered one of the great marvels of living in our modern age — and it keeps getting better, as our knowledge of nutrition increases.

Fulfilling basic nutritional needs

A lot of different nutritional elements (about 60) go into keeping your pet healthy, all working together to keep his body working as it should be. These nutrients each play a role, and although some seem to have a bigger part than others, each is necessary to keep your dog's body functioning. I touch on each of the main canine nutrition needs in the following sections.

TECHNICAL STUFF

When you're reading labels, you may notice that the percentages don't add up to 100. That's because the labels record the percentages of the food that are nutritionally available to the animal. Whatever isn't usable is what comes out the other end, as waste. That's why food with higher-quality ingredients usually produces less to clean up in the yard.

Protein

Perhaps to distract people from the fact that commercial pet foods contain a lot of grains, manufacturers like to play up the protein content in dog food. They crow that meat is the first ingredient on the label — even if they have to break the grains into smaller categories to make their relative percentages follow meat in the order of ingredients. And it's not just in advertising — some of the very product names tout the protein in the bag.

Protein is important, make no mistake. While dogs don't need as much protein as cats do, dog food still contains healthy levels of protein — from 14 to 21 percent of their diet, for older dogs, to 25 to 42 percent for growing dogs or dogs who still put in a full day's work, such as herding dogs or sled dogs.

Protein provides the *amino acids,* which your dog reassembles into the protein parts of his body — his own flesh, for example. All animals require these life-giving nutrients. Some amino acids, called *nonessential,* are synthesized in the dog's body; others, called *essential,* must be obtained from food. Variety and quality are the important things to remember when considering protein sources. A combination of meat, poultry, fish, dairy products, and other sources of protein ensures that your dog is getting all the essential amino acids he needs in his diet.

TECHNICAL STUFF

Protein comes from both animal and plant material, and varies in *digestibility,* or the amount of protein that's available to your dog as his body makes use of the food he eats. Meat, poultry, dairy products, and eggs are highly digestible and, therefore, are high-quality sources of protein; some other parts of animals, such as feathers, beaks, and bones, are not as highly digestible. Grains are somewhere in the middle in terms of digestibility.

Carbohydrates

Carbohydrates — sugars and starches — are a source of energy. Of all the ingredients in prepared dog foods, carbohydrates are probably not what a dog would choose to eat in the wild — although as opportunistic eaters, they take what they can find.

Dogs are indeed able to use the carbohydrates found in commercial foods, and that's a good thing, because by weight these carbs are the largest component of most commercial dog foods

TECHNICAL STUFF

Carbohydrates are listed on pet-food labels as part of what is identified as *fiber*. In the list of ingredients, they take many forms, including corn, soybeans, sorghum, beet pulp, barley, and rice. The percentage of fiber in dry food usually runs from 5 to 10 percent, with so-called "diet" foods on the high end of the scale.

Fats

In our society, we worry endlessly about the amount of fat in our diets, which experts say is too high. Dogs are often consuming more fat than they should be, also. But don't go crazy cutting it out — fats are an important part of a dog's diet (and your diet, too).

TECHNICAL STUFF

DO DOGS REALLY NEED MEAT?

Can a dog be a vegetarian? Although many may be surprised, the answer is yes. Unlike cats, who are true carnivores, dogs can thrive on a carefully balanced vegetarian diet. Even their needs for protein can be met without meat.

A dog would probably not choose to live without meat, however. The choice is made for them by owners, usually those who, for ethical reasons, are against the killing of other animals for food. (For some dogs, though, vegetarian diets are a way to fight food allergies.) Vegetarian diets are popular enough that some companies include no-meat dog foods as part of their product line.

I used to get a lot more questions than I do now about vegetarian diets for pets. Now the trend for those who like to feed their pets a noncommercial diet are so-called "biologically appropriate" foods — flesh, bones, and vegetables. (For more on this topic, see the sidebar "BARF: Food for a dog?" elsewhere in this chapter.)

Fat is essential for the absorption and movement around the body of certain vitamins — the *fat soluble* vitamins. Fat also provides food with much of its appeal to the canine nose and palate, and with essential fatty acids which play an important role in coat quality.

TECHNICAL STUFF

Fat percentages in dry dog food run from 5 percent to more than 30 percent. Diet foods have less fat, and foods for working, growing, or pregnant dogs have more fat.

Vitamins and Minerals

Vitamins are divided into two categories — *water-soluble* and *fat-soluble*. Both are important to your dog's health, and the lack of any vitamin in your pet's diet can have dire effects. Water-soluble vitamins include the B vitamins, niacin, panthothenic acid, folic acid, biotin, choline, and vitamin C. Fat-soluble vitamins are vitamins A, D, E, and K.

Mineral nutrients your dog needs include potassium, magnesium, zinc, calcium, iron, phosphorus, sodium, chloride, and others. Like vitamins, they make up a small part of your pet's diet, but they're essential for good health.

REMEMBER

The important thing to know about vitamins and minerals is that your dog needs the correct amount — but not more. "If a little is good, a lot must be better" simply doesn't apply in the case of vitamins — and nearly all other nutrients. An oversupply of vitamins and minerals can prove dangerous, which is why you should not give your pet supplements unless you've discussed it with your veterinarian first. Although excess amounts of water-soluble vitamins are passed in the urine, fat-soluble vitamins can — and do — build up to toxic levels.

Water

Do you think about nutrition as just being what your dog eats? Don't forget that what your pet drinks is just as important to her well-being. Water — clean, fresh, and ever-present — is essential to nearly every process of your dog's body, which is, after all, composed of 70 percent water.

The tiniest cells of living beings cannot survive without water. Nutrients are carried and wastes removed by water. A dog can go without eating for weeks if need be (please don't test this fact, though), but without water, death comes in days.

For information on choosing the bowls to feed and water your dog out of, see Chapter 6. You'll also find tips on keeping water at a drinkable temperature — neither too hot nor too cold.

CONCERNS OVER FAT PRESERVATIVES

In the last few years, a lot of controversy has been generated over the use of preservatives — primarily BHT, BHA, and ethoxyquin — to keep the necessary fats in pet foods from going rancid. These synthetic preservatives have been blamed for just about every pet health problem, not to mention the increase in violence on our streets and the perceived decline in traditional values. Those who hate these additives *really* hate them.

Many manufacturers have adopted the "if you can't beat 'em, join 'em" approach, which is why some products are now labled *ethoxyquin free* or *naturally preserved*, usually with vitamins C and E. And some canned products boast of being completely free of preservatives of any kind.

But here's something to bear in mind: *No good scientific evidence exists to support the decision to avoid synthetic preservatives.* If the issue worries you, choose a food that doesn't have these preservatives. But be aware that you have likely fallen prey to marketing strategies and fear rather than scientific fact in making your decision. In fact, more data exists supporting the *beneficial* effects of these products in foods (reduced cancer rates, fewer birth defects, and so on) than the negative effects.

When it comes to choosing a food for your dog, chances are you will be far pickier than your pup.

Star/Photo courtesy of Joan Mahone

Choosing Food for Fido

Pet food is more complexly regulated than human food is, and most passes the testing of the *Association of American Feed Control Officials* (AAFCO). This may sound impressive, but critics charge that some problems exist with the system.

TECHNICAL STUFF

Manufacturers have two ways to go when substantiating their claims about a food's nutritional value. One is based on a chemical analysis of the food, and some say that motor oil plus a few vitamins and minerals could pass these tests — not very impressive! The second approach is more sound and is based on feeding the food to dogs. To pass these feeding tests, the pet-food manufacturers provide their products to dogs in order to ensure that the products maintain good health.

Some experts say that these tests aren't enough, arguing instead that all foods should be required to keep two generations of dogs in good health. In other words, a food would be fed to adults, who then produce puppies, who are raised on the food, grow into adults, and produce their own puppies. If no health problems occur at any stage of the process, the food passes. This testing would provide pretty conclusive evidence that the food has nothing significant wrong with it.

The problem with these tests is that they would take almost two years, which would be quite expensive in terms of direct costs and more so in terms of the time it would take to bring a product or a reformulation of a product to market. Fortunately, the competition in the pet-food industry has heated up to the point where the major companies have decided that they cannot afford a huge mistake, and many pursue studies that are, in essence, similar to the two-generation test.

The brand-name manufacturers can afford long-term feed trials — and, more importantly, they can't afford not to do them, with their reputations on the line. Some manufacturers report the testing they have done right on the bag, but if you're in doubt as to the kind of testing a manufacturer does, ask. The most-valuable information on the bag of food is the company's phone number. Use it to ask what the company has done to ensure that their food meets all your dog's needs. You can hope your pet-food company will have gone above and beyond the requirements of AAFCO testing.

Are all brands equal?

You could perform hours of research on all the ingredients in dog food. Whole books are available on the subject; you could go to the library at your closest school or college of veterinary medicine and lose yourself in the stacks for days.

FOR THE SPORTS MUTT IN YOUR FAMILY

TECHNICAL STUFF

Dog-sports enthusiasts are often much more aware of trends in nutrition than some veterinarians. That's because they demand more of their dogs than do most of the clients a veterinarian will see. They want glossy coats on their show dogs, and energy to burn from their field, agility, or obedience dogs. They are always looking for an edge, and that makes them good people to talk to when it comes to choosing a food. Bear in mind, however, that dog-sport competitors can be a little *too* trendy when it comes to food, adding many concoctions to a high-quality kibble. And that's usually not necessary. Some supplements may even be dangerous, depending on what's being added. So here's my advice: If you don't know what you're doing, don't do it. Buy a top-quality food and leave it at that. And if you have questions, ask your veterinarian.

TIP

You don't need to go to such lengths, however, to make sure your dog's eating right. You can do just fine if you follow some simple guidelines:

>> **Choose brands that are appropriate for your dog's age, breed, and condition.** Look for the words "Complete and Balanced Nutrition" on the label, as well as the AAFCO animal-feeding tested statement "for all life stages." Talk to your veterinarian about what food is appropriate for your dog, especially when it comes to levels of protein and fat. Current research suggests that large breed puppies grow too quickly on foods with high levels of protein and fat. Some breeds, notably Dalmatians and Dalmatian mixes, have lower protein requirements than other dogs. Also, consider your dog's lifestyle: Animals who lead a sedentary life will gain weight on a food with high levels of protein and fat that is designed for active, working dogs.

>> **Choose brands from major manufacturers.** Older pet-food brands were hurt by the growth of the premium pet-food market, but long-established manufacturers have done a lot to improve their product in recent years. Another change: Some premium brands that were once available only in pet-supply stores are now on grocery shelves. Whether you buy your dog's food from the supermarket, a pet-supply store, or your veterinarian, as long as you're dealing with a major manufacturer's food that carries the "AAFCO animal tested" statement, you should be fine.

Large, established pet-food companies have a huge investment in maintaining the quality of their products, and they test them constantly in feeding trials. Don't choose generic or store brands unless you know for certain what manufacturer made the food, and if they did so in the same way as the manufacturer's regular brand. Store brands are usually just major brands that have been relabeled and are less expensive — and if they are, who am I to suggest not saving a few pennies? Skip trendy brands from unknown manufacturers, though — the accountability is just not there.

BARF: FOOD FOR A DOG?

A great many dog lovers have embraced the raw-food diet known as *BARF* with a near-religious fervor, while a great many veterinarians shake their heads in disbelief and even horror at what they see as a dangerous fad. (BARF stands for *Bones and Raw Food*, or *Biologically Appropriate Raw Food*.)

Australian veterinarian Dr. Ian Billinghurst is the creator of the BARF diet, but raw-food diets have been around for years, primarily promoted by American holistic veterinarian, Dr. Richard Pitcairn. Earlier raw diets included carbohydrates from grains, while later incarnations are made up almost exclusively of raw, meaty bones and vegetables. The idea is that the diet is most like what a dog would eat in the wild: raw flesh and bones, along with vegetable matter from the bellies of their prey.

A BARF diet requires a leap of faith for many pet lovers: The first time you hand a whole chicken wing or turkey neck to your dog, you're certain that you're killing him. After all, how many times have we heard that poultry bones can kill? (Which is very true, by the way, of cooked ones. They shatter easily and take on the properties of an ice pick once inside a pet.)

Worries or not, an ever-growing number of dogs are getting raw provisions every day. Advocates argue that a diet of cooked meats and grains, which is what goes into commercial foods, is both unnatural and to blame for many health problems. And they also question the quality of the meat, which often ends up as pet food because it's deemed not fit for human consumption.

On the other side of the issue, many veterinarians aren't satisfied with the data to support the claims of the BARFers, and point to feeding trials conducted by commercial pet-food manufacturers that show generations of healthy pets. They also worry that most pet lovers aren't capable of preparing a proper pet diet on their own. (The convenience of a commercial diet, after all, is a pretty strong selling point, considering how busy our lives are.) Finally, veterinarians worry about food contamination such as salmonella.

Raw-food advocates have good answers for every one of these concerns. One thing is certain: The debate will rage for years.

Anyone who is considering a raw-food diet absolutely *must* do some homework first. Required reading: *Give Your Dog a Bone*, by Dr. Ian Billinghurst (self-published, $27.95), and Dr. *Pitcairn's Complete Guide to Natural Health for Dogs & Cats* (Rodale, $16.95). *Give Your Dog a Bone* is available from DogWise at www.dogwise.com, or by calling 1-800-776-2665.

Should you pop the extra dough for more expensive premium foods? That's up to you. Some owners like them because they often contain higher quality, more digestible ingredients that are more easily absorbed. These foods often require less volume — both going in and coming out. But other than that, the fact is these diets offer no proven health advantage.

Ask your veterinarian or other animal-care professional — groomer, trainer, or reputable breeder — for a recommendation, and stick to it after you're satisfied it's working well for your dog and that he likes it. Dogs don't need variety, and they don't get bored with the same ration day after day. When a healthy dog is a picky eater, it's usually because the owners taught him to be that way, by adding tempting tidbits at the least sign of reluctance to eat.

Focusing on food: What types are there?

The food-processing industry, so busy providing convenient foods for the human population, also is active in manufacturing affordable, convenient food for pets. The commercially available choices for your dog's main diet are:

>> **Dry food.** Also called *kibble*, this variety comes in a box or a bag, and is the least expensive. Dry food also helps reduce tartar buildup on your pet's teeth. Dogs generally aren't as crazy about dry food, however, as they are about freshly-opened canned food.

>> **Canned foods.** Ranging from meat-and-meal diets to preparations meant to be mixed with kibble, this stuff is loved by dogs. It's expensive to feed because you're paying for a lot of water. It also becomes unattractive quickly if left to stand by a dog who is a less voracious eater. Canned food can be great for nursing ill or older dogs, however, especially those whose teeth make dry food hard to handle.

>> **Semi-moist foods.** This is a more recent development, often designed to look like people food — hamburger patties or sausage. Sort of a midway point between dry and canned in terms of ease of use and cost, semi-moist foods are often criticized for appealing more to humans — with clever shapes and artificial colors — than to dogs.

Most dogs will do just fine on a steady diet of kibble, with nothing at all added.

TIP

If you're house-training a puppy or dog, feeding them kibble can help. The water content of canned foods can make a dog need to urinate more frequently. This consideration is especially important if your dog is left home alone for several hours at a time, like while you're at work.

If you prefer canned food, you can always make the change after the puppy's a little older and able to hold it longer, or until your adult dog completely understands what the house rules are.

Don't think it's too dull if your pet's food is just plain brown: Fancy shapes and chunks of meat or cheese — or bits made to *look* like meat or cheese — are put there for *your* benefit. As long as it smells good, your dog doesn't care what it looks like. There's no evidence these people-pleasing touches will hurt your pet — unless they're too high in sugar, fat, or salt — but they're nothing you need to seek out, and you certainly shouldn't pay extra for them.

Some people just can't believe a dog can be happy with plain kibble, even of a top-quality variety. If it makes you happy, add some canned food to the kibble and maybe a little water, and briefly microwave the mixture. You'll likely get the enthusiastic response you're looking for. (Don't forget to cover the leftover canned food and refrigerate.)

Before you start feeding this way, however, consider that if you ever want to travel with your dog, or need to leave him with your veterinarian, at a boarding kennel, or with a house-sitter or friend, he'll do better if he's used to eating kibble.

Should you buy veterinarian-prescribed vittles?

Under certain conditions, your dog's veterinarian may recommend one of several specially formulated diets, if your dog has a health problem that one of these foods can help. These foods come in both dry and canned varieties, so you can choose the kind that you and your dog prefer.

For some medical conditions, your dog's time on these foods is temporary; for others, your veterinarian may suggest that your pet stay on the diet for the rest of his life. Any situation that requires your pet to be on a special diet for any length of time also requires you to work with your veterinarian to ensure the management of the disease in other ways. Make sure that your questions about the course of the disease are answered by the veterinarian, so that that you know what you're getting into.

Although your veterinarian has all the best intentions in recommending special diets, you should be aware that, other than those designed for patients with obesity, bladder stones, and, perhaps, kidney disease, no scientific data is available to support the medicinal value of these foods. Until such data is available, press your veterinarian for information as to why you're being asked to spend the extra money for these diets. This will, in turn, push your veterinarian to pressure the manufacturers to generate and provide the necessary data — or to stop trying to convince veterinarians and pet owners to buy their product.

How much food, and when?

The label provides a guideline on the amount of food recommended for your dog. It's just a start, though. Dogs who are highly active, pregnant, or are nursing puppies have higher energy requirements than the average couch-potato canine. In the wintertime, indoor dogs often need less food because they're less active, while outdoor dogs need more because staying warm burns calories.

TIP

A good guideline is to feed two-thirds of the daily ration in the morning, and the remaining one-third in the evening. Since dogs have a tendency to sleep after meals, this technique is especially useful for animals who have to stay alone all day — a sleepy dog is less likely to chew or bark. (If you're working a night shift you want to turn this around and feed the larger portion at night, before you head for work.)

WARNING

Another reason to divide your dog's daily ration is that doing so helps your dog avoid *gastric torsion*, otherwise known as *bloat*. This potentially lethal medical emergency can hit many larger breeds and can be triggered when a dog wolfs down a huge meal. (More information about veterinary emergencies is in Chapter 12.)

You need to feed puppies more frequently than older dogs — three or four times a day, depending on their age. For a feeding schedule for puppies, see Chapter 9.

Some people can get away with letting the dog decide when and how much he eats. Keeping a constant supply of kibble available (known as *free-feeding*) works in some cases, usually in single-dog households where there's no competition for food.

If you find your pet can maintain his own weight and you aren't having related behavioral problems like house-soiling, then free-feeding is fine. But realize that you will not be able to pick up on some subtle changes in your pet's eating habits that may be an early indicator of health problems. You also won't be able to use giving your dog food — after he sits — as an effortless way to reinforce your role as pack leader. (For more on this, and for other strategies for dealing with problem dogs, see Chapter 15.)

Also, it's hard to keep kibble fresh when free-feeding, and the constant availability of food may attract other animals, such as the raccoon who used to pop through a friend of mine's cat door at night for an evening snack. When a rat started visiting, she put up the food for good.

Treating Your Dog

Giving your pet a little something special from time to time isn't going to do him any harm and can be very useful in training situations, or when you're trying to keep him occupied while he's home alone. Here are a couple things to keep in mind, however:

>> **All things in moderation.** Treats, whether store-bought or from your dinner plate, don't make a good diet for your pet. Make sure the majority of his food doesn't come from extra goodies.

>> **Avoid some foods entirely.** Food that's heavily spiced or fatty can upset your dog's digestion, leading to diarrhea, vomiting, or even a life-threatening ailment such as pancreatitis.

>> **Think before you treat.** If you give your dog treats from your plate, you can't complain that he's a pest at mealtime. And if your dog's supposed to be losing weight, you shouldn't give him any treat at all.

TIP

Treats are an important part of dog training — more on that in Chapter 14 — but remember that it doesn't take very much to get the job done when it comes to rewarding your dog. Give her a tiny corner of a biscuit, or a little piece of hot dog, instead of a whole biscuit or an inch-long chunk of sausage.

We humans often express our love through food. Special family times have food at the center of the activity: Think about the mother of all pig-outs, Thanksgiving. Food plays an important role on Passover and Easter (forget the yams; give me those yellow marshmallow chicks!). Even Halloween is an excuse to treat yourself a little. Meals prepared, and meals shared, loom large in our memories. But here's a warning: Don't love your dog too much. Excess amounts of treats only hurt your canine companion.

The way to a man's heart is said to be through his stomach, but is it the way to a dog's heart, too? It certainly seems that way. Treats fill whole aisles of pet super-stores and whole pages of catalogs. They come in all shapes and sizes and dogs certainly love to get them as much as people love to give them. Every dog deserves a few, so put them on your shopping list.

WARNING

Treats don't have to meet the same stringent nutritional requirements dog foods do; in fact, they don't have to meet any requirements at all. So if you're giving your pet too many — some sources say anything more than 10 percent of a dog's diet — you may be throwing complete and balanced nutrition out the door.

Another problem: Treats add calories, and calories add weight. Obesity is the No. 1 food-caused health risk veterinarians see in the United States.

SLIMMING DOWN A PUDGY DOG

Just like humans, too much food and too little physical activity has led to an increase in pudgy pups. And that increase means a lot of dogs are dealing with health problems related to the extra fat they carry, such as extra strain on the joints. Some breeds — Labradors and Beagles are commonly mentioned — show a marked tendency to get chubby easily.

Is your dog fat? A normal-weight dog has ribs that don't show, but can be easily felt beneath a thin layer of protective fat. From the side and from above, you should be able to see a *waistline* — an area just behind the ribcage where your dog's body should tuck in.

If your dog's fat — or if you're not sure if he's fat — ask for your veterinarian's opinion on the subject. Your veterinarian can guide you in helping your pet to lose weight. In extreme cases, that might involve a total change of diet. In many dogs, though, the problem can be taken care of easily by deleting a few extra snacks — or substituting lighter treats, such as carrots or ricecakes — in combination with an increase in exercise.

Whatever you do, don't ignore obesity. Proper nutrition and fitness will help your pet to live a happier, healthier, and longer life.

So treat your dog, but remember: A little goes a long way.

A handful of toys are designed to use treats to keep your pet busy while you're away. The Buster Cube is one. When filled with kibble, the toy will keep your pet occupied with trying to roll the cube to release food, one piece at a time. Clever! While not specifically designed to hold treats, the Kong toy is often recommended by trainers who suggest filling its inside with all manner of goodies, from biscuits to peanut butter.

Biscuits and cookies

As with dog food, the marketplace for biscuits and cookies has changed dramatically in recent years. You used to be able to sum up your choices pretty much this way: Milk Bones, small, medium, or large. My grandmother kept a box of the small, multi-colored Milk Bones in her cupboard for decades, for her dog and, later, for mine when we dropped in to visit. (She always thought they liked the liver-colored ones best, the green ones least, but I don't think that dogs are anywhere near that picky. And I've always suspected that all Milk Bones taste the same, although I never personally tested my theory.)

Milk Bones are still around, of course, and doing well. You still find them in my cupboard, a gift from a friend's dog on the occasion of my oldest dog's birthday. But you find a lot more in my cupboard, too. Like peanut-butter flavored gourmet cookies, a dog-warming gift from a reader when my youngest dog appeared in print for the first time. I also have organic treats with a list of ingredients so healthy I could probably stand to gnaw on them a little.

At least one manufacturer offers a line of treats to complement dogs' regular diets, with formulas designed for puppies, active and older, or overweight dogs.

Experiment all you want. Your pet will help you, that's for sure!

If you don't have enough to do in your busy life, you can always make cookies for your dog. A handful of books offering treat recipes exist, and you can find more with a little digging. Dog-treat recipes turn up in newsgroups and e-mail lists on the Internet, and chances are that your groomer, trainer, or veterinarian's receptionist has squirreled one away. The classifieds of dog-magazines offer them, too, for a small price.

Preparing dog treats is a fun project to do with children and a great way to come up with holiday gifts for the pets of your friends.

WARNING

One treat you should not share with your pet is chocolate. Although your pet would have to eat a lot of chocolate to get into the toxic range — more than 10 ounces of milk chocolate, but considerably less of baking chocolate — even a nibble can make a small dog mighty sick. If your pet gets into chocolate, call your veterinarian right away.

Animal-based chews

While rawhide — made from the skins of cattle — has been a popular dog treat for a long time, in recent years there doesn't seem to be any part of any animal intended for human consumption that hasn't ended up being marketed as a dog treat.

I think the trend started with beef hooves, discovered, as the story goes, by some savvy dog lover who noticed that dogs enthusiastically devour the pieces trimmed off hooves when horses get new shoes. (If I were a horse, this would have made me a little nervous around dogs, but many people are into both horses and dogs, and they say everyone gets along just fine!)

Horse-hoof parings weren't easy to find, but beef hooves were plentiful. The product was a smash, and manufacturers started looking for opportunities to duplicate the success. Next up: pig ears, another hit.

No matter how unappetizing some of these products look to *us*, they're certainly a favorite with our dogs. As a result, there seem to be plenty of takers, not only for pig ears but also dried beef neck muscles, lamb ears, beef ears, and sterilized bones.

Fresh bones are available, too, from your local butcher or grocery store.

All of these treats are fine for your dog, but you have to take into consideration your dog's size and chewing style. The bigger and stronger your dog is, the bigger and sturdier you want these treats to be.

THEM BONES, THEM BONES, THEM FRESH BONES

Cooked poultry bones are a ticket to the veterinary emergency room, and should be avoided at all costs. There are some other fresh bones out there, though, that are real special treats for your dog.

Beef bones, big and sturdy, are your best choice. Oxtails are good for small-or medium-sized dogs, but don't hold up too well to big, aggressive chewers. Beef knuckle or leg bones are good for all dogs. Leave them whole for big dogs, or have them cut to a more manageable size for smaller ones.

While grocery stores often have these bones — if you don't see them, ask! — I've had the best luck with small butcher shops. One in my area saves a huge piece for me with a leg bone in the middle and knuckles on both ends, and cuts it into smaller pieces — two half-knuckles and a leg bone — for my dogs.

Some people like to cook them first, but I don't bother. I let them chew on them for a day or so and then out they go.

A couple more cautions about bones: If you've got a multi-dog household, you may want to forget fresh bones entirely because they can cause fights. Likewise, unless you're 100 percent sure of your dog's gentleness, I wouldn't give bones to your dog if children are around — a snap could result. For your dog's safety, trim the fat off the bones first or the fat could end up triggering diarrhea or worse.

On a less serious note, remember that bones are messy! This treat is best left outside or in the kitchen, and if you don't believe me, I've got a stained carpet to prove it.

WARNING Rawhide, hooves, and bones can cause problems with aggressive chewers. Some large dogs are capable of chewing off and swallowing big chunks of rawhide, and pulverizing bones and hooves. This can cause internal problems, like when bone bits reform as a blockage that may even have to be surgically removed.

So know your dog's chewing style. Pressed rawhide and large knots are best for hearty chewers. Watch to see that big chunks aren't being swallowed, and discard these treats when they become worn enough to be swallowed in one big gulp.

Chapter **8**

House-Training Puppies and Dogs

Dog training has changed a great deal in the last couple of decades, and in no area is this more true than in house-training.

For generations house-training was done almost by the process of elimination, if you'll pardon the pun. The puppy-owner screamed when she found a mess, dragged the puppy over, shoved his nose in it, and swatted him. "Well! I can't go there!" thought the puppy, who was also thinking that this newspaper-wielding crazy woman was really not the nicest of people. Eventually, the puppy figured out the place where he *wouldn't* get punished for going — by accident, as much as anything else.

Maybe he got over the idea that his owner was dangerous, maybe not, but one thing for certain: House-training was a nasty business for all.

Today's training methods are kinder, faster, and less messy. And for that, you can thank both a shift to training by positive reinforcement and the widespread use of the crate.

Things are so different now that even the vocabulary has started to change. The battle-of-wills sound of the term *housebreaking* is now frequently replaced by trainers with the more positive term, *house-training*. And so it is in this book. You don't want to *break* your puppy or dog, ever. *Training* — consistent and positive — is the key.

A Positive Approach

In recent years, the use of a crate to house-train puppies and dogs has become standard among knowledgeable trainers and breeders. Crate-training allows you to shape your puppy's potty behavior by limiting his options to three. During training he's either

>> On empty and loose under your supervision

>> Relieving himself, where you choose

>> Confined to his crate

Confined to his crate? Isn't that cruel? For you, maybe, and for me. But you have to look at things from a dog's point of view. Dogs appreciate the idea of a *den*, a small area they can call their own, in which they can feel perfectly safe. Their wild cousins raise their young in dens, and domesticated dogs still instinctively prefer areas that remind them of a den. Like the cave behind the sofa. And like a crate.

Information on crates — what they are, and which kind and size your should choose — is in Chapter 6.

How much do dogs hate crates? I wish you could ask dogs that question. In my house two crates are set up permanently in the TV room — the larger one functions as an end table next to my chair. The doors to the crates are always open, and there are always dogs inside — by choice. Any experienced dog person will tell you the same story. *Dogs like crates.*

Another instinct is at work in using a crate for house-training. Because a den would quickly become unusable if its inhabitants messed in it, a dog is predisposed to keep his sleeping area clean. His mother teaches him this lesson when he's little by eating — disgusting, but true — the messes her puppies produce. Later, her puppies learn to eliminate outside of their den, as she does. Which is why your puppy will avoid messing in his crate, if he can help it — and you can help make his success possible.

THANKS, MOM!

Some puppies come to their new families with a head start on house-training, thanks to the diligence of their mother and their breeder. Dog mothers like to keep their living area clean, and will do their best to pass on this desire to their babies.

Good breeders help the mother dog by keeping the puppy area scrupulously clean, so no puppy ever gets used to the feel of wallowing in mess. When puppies are older, good breeders set up a puppy pen in such a way that there's an area that's designated for pottying — through an open door, or over a low division to an area filled with sawdust or shavings.

By the time a pup leaves his littermates, he'll have grasped the concept of house-training — even if his little body isn't yet ready to be perfect in the practice of it.

Your puppy naturally wants to relieve herself away from her sleeping and eating areas — and you can choose the place.

Photograph courtesy of Richard D. Schmidt

These complementary instincts — the desire to use a den and the wish to keep it clean — form the basis of house-training by using a crate. A crate encourages your puppy to hold it until you can take him to the place where you wish him to relieve himself. And once there, you can attach a command word to his relieving himself — and then praise him for obeying. Positive reinforcement. Fewer messes. What could be better?

EASY CLEAN-UPS

When accidents occur, you must clean them up promptly and thoroughly, and not just because doing so is better for your carpets. Dogs are attracted to sites of past accidents and will keep soiling the area if they can. Even if you clean up all visible signs of the mess, enough smell may remain to keep the area attractive to your dog. Here are a few tips on mess clean-up:

- **Don't use ammonia-based cleaners.** They smell like urine to a puppy — ammonia being one of the by-products of decomposing urine. So instead of making the area smell clean, ammonia products make a mess site seem even *more* attractive.

- **Use products designed for pet mess clean-up.** These liquid products contain enzymes that break down the waste and neutralize odor. Crystallized products work well, too, by absorbing the liquid in a few minutes so that you can vacuum the mess up.

  You can also make a fairly effective cleaner for a fresh urine accident with water, white vinegar, and a gentle soap such as Ivory. Dog-lover Anne Cotton of Massachusetts has a recipe I've used with good results: One quart hot water from the faucet, one teaspoon Ivory, one teaspoon white vinegar (it neutralizes the odor). Shake a bit. Blot the area with paper towels, and then wet with the cleaner to cover — but not enough to soak the area. Let it sit 15 minutes, and then blot again. Finally, follow with a disinfectant spray.

- **Clean up the area as soon as possible.** Do this before the mess has a chance to soak through to carpet padding, where getting the smell out is very hard. Once the urine soaks through, you have to pull up the carpet to ensure that the area's truly clean.

- **Search for and destroy old stains.** Even if you can't smell anything, old stains may still have a lingering odor that can attract your puppy. Pet-supply outlets offer black lights that show old messes you may not be able to see. Veterinarians and trainers sometimes have these available for rent. Enzyme cleaners will do the best on old stains, but you may need to treat the area a couple of times.

When your puppy's completely house-trained, you'll most likely want to have the carpets cleaned; but, if you are diligent during the training period, you'll probably end up with no permanent stains. Keep clean-up supplies on hand, though, because accidents and illnesses occur throughout your dog's life.

Why would you want a dog to go on command? The owners of city dogs are probably ahead of me here: If you can communicate to your puppy that it's time to get down to business, you spend a whole lot less time outside waiting for your pet to get busy. Your pet knows what's expected — and does it! A dog who eliminates on command is also a lot easier to travel with, and walk with, too, because *you* can pick the time and the place for him to relieve himself, pick up his mess, and get on with your lives. "Hurry up" is the command I use, but you can use anything you aren't embarrassed to say in public. "Do your ootsie-bootsie puppy poo!" isn't something I'd pick, but if you can stand it, that's your business.

I *guarantee* you house-training is faster, neater, and easier with a crate. If you use one for nothing else buy or borrow one for the first few weeks of puppy-raising. Chances are you'll recover the cost of the crate in things your puppy *doesn't* ruin — but would have ruined without a crate.

Puppies naturally want to eliminate away from sleeping and eating areas, but some are raised in ways that make that impossible. Puppies who can't avoid their messes get so used to the sensation of standing in filth that they can be exceptionally difficult to house-train. You may need to hire a trainer or behaviorist to help you with the task.

Whatever kind of food you end up feeding — a discussion of food is in Chapter 7 — feed a high-quality kibble during house-training and nothing else. Canned foods are high in water, and other foods aren't as efficiently digested, and so don't produce small, neat stools that are easier for a puppy to hold as he learns what's expected of him. (Neat stools are easier to clean up, too.) Changing foods or adding table scraps may give your pet diarrhea, and that is guaranteed to be both a training set-back *and* a mess. Also: Make sure your pup is free of intestinal parasites. Worms can make it very difficult for a pup to learn how to control his bowels.

A Puppy Potty Strategy

Crate-training limits a puppy's options and sets the stage for training that uses positive reinforcement. Puppies need to relieve themselves after they wake up, eat or drink, or after a period of play. Set up a schedule to accommodate his needs — puppies can't go very long without eating, drinking, sleeping, or relieving themselves — as you work to mold behavior.

TIP

You may well end up *free-feeding* your pet when he's a grown dog; that is, leaving food out at all times. I don't recommend it, however, because free-feeding prevents you from spotting some potential health problems and denies you the ability to use food as a tool for enforcing your status as boss. You do, however, need to have water constantly available to your housetrained pet.

When you're house-training a puppy, however, you need to regulate both food *and* water. That's because if your puppy is eating and drinking constantly, he's going to need to relieve himself constantly, and that makes house-training very difficult. For the first couple of months, a puppy needs to eat three times a day — before you go to work, at lunch, and as soon as you come home in the evening. By the time the puppy's four-months old, he should be nearly house-trained and you can switch to two meals a day and an always-available supply of water.

If at all possible, come home, beg a neighbor, or pay a pet-sitter to come in at lunch during the first couple of months. Your puppy's *social* development will survive without a midday break — assuming you adopt an ideal schedule on the weekends, and make up for the lost opportunities for socialization. He will *not* make it through the day without relieving himself, however, and that will set your training back.

REMEMBER

If you have to leave your puppy alone all day, be fair: You'll have to set his crate up with the door open and access to water and food and to a small area covered with newspapers. When you come home, you'll find a mess. Clean it up without comment, because it's not your puppy's fault.

TIP

How long can a puppy stay in a crate? A good rule of thumb is the same number of hours as his age in months. So a two-month-old puppy can be confined for two hours, a three-month-old puppy for three hours, and so on. No matter how old your puppy gets, I wouldn't recommend confining him in a crate for more than six hours at a stretch, however.

Here's an idea of what your puppy's ideal schedule should look like:

>> **First thing in the morning:** Take your puppy out of the crate and coax him to follow you outside to the spot you have chosen for him to relieve himself. If he starts to relieve himself on the trip outside, give him a firm "no" and take him to the *potty zone* in your yard. Give the command you've chosen — "Hurry up," "Do it," or whatever — and praise him for going. Take him inside and give him food and water, and then go outside again immediately — a full tummy puts pressure on a puppy's bladder — give the command and praise him when he goes.

If you're going to work, put him back in the crate. If you're not going to work, let him play for a couple of hours, but don't give him full run of the house. Close doors or use baby gates to keep him where you can see him, such as in a kitchen/family room area. After an hour or two take him outside again, and repeat the command and praise. He'll be ready for a little nap, so put him in his crate until lunchtime.

>> **The midday break:** Take your puppy out of the crate and head outside for another round of command, relieve, and praise for a job well done. Then back inside for food and water. Then back outside.

- If you're home on your lunch hour, play with him a little before you put him back in his crate.

- If you're going to be home with him, leave him out to play where you are, under your watchful eye. Take him out in mid-afternoon, and then crate him for his afternoon nap.

>> **Dinnertime:** Same as at midday. Take him out, feed him, take him out, and let him play. Leave him out for play and socializing, in an area where you can watch him. Offer him a little water a couple hours before bedtime, but no more food.

>> **Bedtime:** One last trip outside. You may be tired and cranky at this point, but don't let your puppy know it. Be *consistent*: Give your command, and after your puppy does what you want, praise like the dickens. Then bring your little genius inside and put him in his crate for the night. If he doesn't relieve himself within a few minutes, put him in his crate anyway. You'll be up again, soon enough.

>> **Middle of the night:** If it makes you feel better, dealing with a puppy is not as difficult as dealing with a human baby. But for the first week or so, you may also have to add a wee hours outing. Sometimes you have to do that when your puppy's a little older, too, because he is so busy exploring that he doesn't get around to relieving himself. If he sleeps through the night — roughly defined as after the 11 o'clock news until the alarm clock goes off for work at 6:30 the next morning, then fine. But if he wakes up and fusses at 3 a.m., put your shoes on — you're taking him out.

Housetraining can be tiring work for a young pup.

Sydney/Photo courtesy Debbie Bacon

HOUSE-TRAINING WITHOUT A CRATE

Of course house-training without a crate is possible — it's just harder, more time-consuming, and messier. You still should use a positive approach, though.

Keep your puppy where you can keep an eye on him — and keep him in a small, safe area when you cannot. Baby gates are ideal both for keeping a puppy near you and creating an area for him to stay in while you are gone. Unlike a solid door, which isolates and upsets him, a baby gate allows him to see and hear and smell his family.

Use the same schedule (described earlier in this chapter) for going out — first thing in the morning, after play and eating, at lunch, dinner, and last thing at night — give your command and praise, praise, praise for going in the right place.

Because you are keeping a closer eye on your puppy, you can tell when he's making "gotta go" motions — sniffing and circling — and can whisk him outside. Other times you won't be fast enough. If you catch him, say "no" sternly, and then take him outside to finish the job. Clean up the area thoroughly and without comment.

House-Training the Adult Dog

The first step in turning an adult dog into a reliable house pet is for you to embrace a key concept:

There's no such thing as a partially house-trained dog. He either is, or he isn't.

Why is realizing this concept important? Because if you have a dog who is sometimes reliable you have a dog who really isn't getting the picture, probably because no one took the time to teach it to him properly in the first place. To do that, you're going to have to go back to square one.

Before you do, though, make sure you're not dealing with two problems that usually aren't a factor when you're house-training a puppy:

>> **Illness.** If you have a dog who was perfectly house-trained and is no longer, you *must* be sure that what you have really is a behavior problem and not a physical problem. Check with your veterinarian. If you've just adopted an adult dog who seems to be urinating several times a day, you should have her checked out, too, before assuming she's not house-trained. She may have a bladder infection or other medical difficulty.

>> **Leg-lifting.** If your male dog is marking in the house — but defecating and also doing some urinating outside, your best chance at fixing this problem is to neuter him and put him on a regimen that will help to convince him that he doesn't run the show in your house. See the "Establish a Routine" section in Chapter 5, and start training basic obedience to establish your role as boss. Another must: Aggressively and thoroughly clean any area your dog soils; if you don't, the smell will bring him back.

Leg-lifting in the house can be a very difficult to cure, since it's tied to dominant behavior. If you're getting nowhere with a leg-lifter — and especially if you're having other problems with potentially aggressive behaviors — call in a trainer or behaviorist.

If you've ruled out medical problems and you haven't got a leg-lifter, house-training an adult dog uses the same principals as house-training a puppy, except you have to be even more diligent because you need to do some *untraining*, too.

You need to teach your dog what's right, though, before you can correct him for what's wrong. To do this, spend two weeks ensuring that he has nothing but successes by never giving him the opportunity to make a mistake. Here's how:

>> **Leash him to you in the house so you can monitor his every move during his training period.** If he starts to mess, correct him with a sharp "no," take him outside, give your go command and praise him for doing right.

>> **Crate him whenever he's not on leash with you.** A grown dog can wait a lot longer than a puppy in a crate, and it's not unfair to leave him in one for four or five hours at a stretch — assuming, of course, that he's getting his regular exercise. If you go to work, you can leave him in the crate with a couple of chew toys to keep him busy and a radio playing to keep him company.

>> **Take him outside first thing in the morning, as soon as you get home from work, and just before you go to bed (when you put him in his crate for the night).** *Always* remember to give your go command, and praise when he does as you wish.

REMEMBER

The most difficult part of house-training an adult dog is your attitude toward limiting his options in such a way as to make success possible. And that means a crate and a leash. People seem able to accept a crate more with puppies — perhaps because they enjoy the respite they gain when their little terror is confined. You may not like the idea of crating your adult dog as much, but bear in mind that you won't need to do it forever. But you need to do it for now.

WHAT ABOUT PAPER-TRAINING?

Letting your puppy relieve himself on news-papers — or in one of the new canine litter boxes — is really only practical if your dog is very small, since the volume of waste makes paper-training an unsavory option for large dogs.

Sometimes people make the task of house-training much harder by insisting on using papers as if they were the first step. If you don't need papers, don't start using them. Take your puppy or dog outside from the first day.

If you choose to use newspapers or a litter box (you have a small dog in a city apart-ment, for example) training your pet to relieve himself on a certain spot inside is done the same way as training him to go outside — take him to the newspapers, give your go command and praise him when he does the deed. You must remember, however, that once a pet is trained to use newspapers, he has to be *retrained* to go outdoors. Retraining is not that big a deal — just follow the directions I give earlier in this chapter — but you can't expect him to figure it out on his own.

THE "MISTAKE" THAT ISN'T

Your pet seems to be flaunting his bad behavior. He comes up to you and piddles right in front of you! Don't lose your temper: Your dog is acting out of fear and trying to placate you with a classic canine show of submission.

Trainers and behaviorists call this behavior *submissive urination*, and it's something another dog would recognize as a show of respect to a more dominant member of the pack. In many cases, this display is offered to the man of the house — usually the biggest member of the family and the one with the deepest voice.

If you punish your pet for this behavior, you're making yourself seem even more powerful — and making matters worse.

A puppy or dog who has this problem is very sensitive and lacks confidence. Recognize that submissive urination is not a house-training problem: It's a relationship problem. This puppy needs gentle obedience training and lots of encouragement to under-stand that while you're indeed the boss, you're a kind and benevolent one.

Don't punish your pet for submissive urination. As you work to develop a loving and trusting relationship with your puppy, his confidence will grow, his fear will decrease, and his submissive urination will stop.

If you've been consistent, your dog likely has a good idea of what's expected of him at the end of the two weeks, and so you can start to give him a little freedom. Don't let him have the run of the house yet: Keep his area small and let him earn the house, room by room, as he proves his understanding of the house rules.

Accidents happen. If you catch him, correct him with a sharp "no," take him outside and give him the chance to set things right. Give your go command, and praise if he does. Clean up the mess promptly and thoroughly, so he won't feel so inclined to refresh his smell there. If you aren't catching him, you're not keeping close enough tabs on him: Go back to the crate and leash and start over.

REMEMBER

Consistency and patience are necessary for house-training an adult dog. If you have both, you're likely to succeed. Without them, you may have a very difficult time getting the results you hope for.

Special Tips for Owners of Toy Dogs

Toy dogs have more than a few special things about them, most good, some not so good. The upside: They're adorable. They're portable. They're usually long-lived. On the downside, they seem to be exceptionally hard to house-train.

The problem is mostly human. People tend to dote on toy dogs, and overlook or be inconsistent in dealing with problems that the owners of your average large dog wouldn't dream of. (After all, a pile from a Toy Poodle just doesn't seem as awful as one from an Irish Wolfhound.)

You have to start by looking at things from a small dog's point of view — and that can be very hard for people who think their dogs are little people. Here are some tips:

>> Limit your dog's range in the house. Close doors and use baby-gates to keep your dog where you can see him. It's easy for a little dog to slip away unnoticed and mess.

>> Make sure your dog can feel safe in the outdoor spot you've chosen for him. The act of elimination is one when a dog's guard is down, and when you weigh 10 pounds or less, it's important to feel you're not going to be attacked. And keep the grass short so the dog doesn't feel as if he's hacking through a jungle.

>> Keep your little dog warm. Cold weather can make house-training more difficult. Little dogs lose heat rapidly and would rather use a nice corner of a warm house than venture outside. Sweaters are not silly for the little dog and can help with house-training.

>> Use a schedule consistently to monitor feeding and trips outside. It's not fair to decide you'd rather not take your dog out one day and punish him for using the carpet the next.

>> Praise for good behavior, but don't punish for mistakes. If you keep an eye on your dog, you'll be able to spot a mess in the making. Don't yell: A big person is pretty scary to a little dog. Instead, whisk your pet outside and praise him for finishing up outside.

TIP

Housetraining isn't the only area where toy dogs are different. The best book out there for anyone who has or is considering a toy dog is Darlene Arden's *The Irrepressible* Toy Dog (IDG Books Worldwide).

» Teaching your puppy the basics

» Dealing with your puppy's shortcomings

Chapter **9**

Early Puppy Training

You can see in your puppy today what our ancestors saw when this astonishing trans-species relationship was just forming. In the eyes of that wolf cub thousands of years ago was the same thing anyone who has ever taken home a puppy since can't help but notice: the beginning of a beautiful friendship.

Many of these beautiful beginnings go wrong, however, and people in a lot of different areas — behaviorists, shelter directors, sociologists, and veterinary epidemiologists — spend a great deal of time trying to find out why, in hopes of stemming the flow of half-grown dogs into the nation's shelters. Wrong choices, bad timing, and poor planning all play a part, but in many instances "too little" is the sorry epitaph that marks the end of a once-promising relationship. Too little time, too little training.

You don't want this to happen to you. Your concern is for your puppy and making sure she turns out the way you want her to. You don't want to be living with a canine terror a year from now, and you certainly don't want to be finding her another home because you can't handle her anymore.

You can make up a lot of ground with a puppy who wasn't raised under the best of circumstances before you got her, or you can totally undo the careful breeding and handling of your pup by a knowledgeable and reputable breeder. The decision is completely up to you. Ignore your puppy or raise her wrongly, and you'll both be sorry.

REMEMBER

Love your puppy, play with your puppy, enjoy your puppy. But you should always — *always* — be thinking of how you're molding this little baby into the confident, obedient dog of your dreams. It takes socialization, and it takes training. And most of all, it takes *time*. Time passes all too quickly in the life a puppy. A couple of critical weeks, once past, are gone forever. So take the time. Make the effort. Your work in the first few months of your puppy's life will reward you many times over during the life of your dog.

Shaping Good Behavior

Forget everything you ever heard about starting training at six months. Your puppy starts learning the moment he's born, and by the time you get him — seven to ten weeks of age — he's as absorbent as a bath towel, taking in the sights and sounds of his world and trying to figure out his place in it. The position he decides he has may be quite different from the one you want him to have, which is why you need to be involved in the process as he learns to live with his new, human family.

It's not that complicated, really. Your puppy wants to be part of your family, and he craves loving leadership. Just keep a few things in mind as you enjoy your youngster:

>> Socialize your puppy and bond with him.

>> Never let your puppy do anything you wouldn't want a grown dog to do.

>> Teach your puppy using positive methods — make training fun!

>> Realize your puppy will make mistakes, and don't get angry when he does.

>> Remember always that *preventing* bad habits is easier than fixing them later.

Every minute you spend with your puppy is not only delightful but also an investment in the future. What will happen if you let your puppy grow up without you? A visit to any shelter provides the answer. You can find step-by-step instructions for training adult dogs and puppies in Chapter 14 and a guide to puppy house-training in Chapter 8.

Bonding

One of the reasons dogs have adapted so well to being human companions is that the social needs of both species are similar. Dogs and wolves live and work together in social unit called a *pack*, which is really what we would call a *family*. Because their very survival depends on working together, they have evolved a system of communication emphasizing social order and cooperation. From families to soft-ball teams to corporations, so have we. Both dogs and humans count on others to raise us and help us throughout our lives.

REMEMBER

When you take a puppy into your home, you are asking her to accept your family in exchange for a canine one. And she will, quite happily and with amazingly few problems, if you hold down your end of the deal — provide her with companionship and a proper place in the social order.

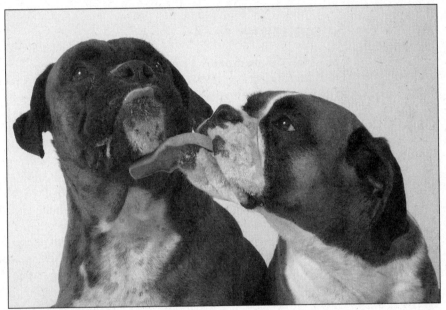

A wellsocialized puppy deals gracefully with his other family members.

Photograph courtesy of the HSUS/Joseph R. Spies

She cannot find her place in your family unless you make your puppy part of your life. Simply put, a puppy cannot bond with people she barely knows.

Bonding isn't hard to accomplish. Spend time with your puppy. Talk to her. Sing to her. Put your hands on her. Use baby gates instead of closed doors if you don't want her in certain parts of the house, so she can hear you and see you and feel part of the crowd. You are the only family she has from the time you take her home. Make her part of that family, and she'll be a better pet.

TIP

One of the easiest ways to promote a fast, tight bond with your puppy is to have her sleep in a crate at the side of your bed. It's almost like cheating: You sleep, she sleeps, but as she sleeps, she bonds. She smells your wonderful smell and hears every sound you make, all night long — and she won't mind your snoring!

When I say *in the bedroom,* I don't mean *on the bed.* Sleeping in your bed gives a dog a rather elevated idea of her station in life, and that can lead to problems. You want your puppy to know from the first that you are the boss in your house. You're a nice boss, however, which is why you've provided a snuggly crate or soft bed for her to sleep on. But you're still the boss. Period.

When your puppy's all grown up and perfectly behaved, you can invite her on your bed. That's where mine sleep. But they understand it's a privilege, not a right. They are not allowed up unless invited, they are not up there every night, and they are never allowed up unless I'm already there.

Socializing

You simply cannot expose a puppy to too many new things — people, places, and other animals. And yet this is one area where puppy owners undo the good work of many reputable breeders. When a puppy is not continually exposed to new things, her social development stops — and in many cases regresses. The goal is to have a confident, outgoing dog, not a shy or aggressive one. The way to accomplish this is through socializing.

We ask a lot from our dogs, a lot more than their wild cousins need for survival. Wild dogs and wolves live in harmony with others of their pack and are important members of their ecosystem. They know their own family, and they don't have to get along with members of other packs. No one ever asks them to live in peace with other predators and the only relationship they have with prey animals is when one of them becomes dinner. Wild dogs and wolves know the seasons and the smells of their environment and are able to run when anything unfamiliar turns up.

Contrast that picture to what domesticated dogs are expected to endure with good grace. Born of a dog mother and raised among dog siblings, we ask our dogs to form a family relationship with members of another species. We ask them to live peaceably in this strange family, and we expect them to be docile with humans who are outside their pack. We ask, too, that they remain able to get along well with others of their own kind, both in the family and at such events as dog shows. We ask, further, that they abide the presence of a competing predator — the cat — and ignore the presence of what any wolf knows is good eating, although we call them pets: rabbits, birds, and other smaller animals. We even ask that our dogs travel with us.

Dogs are genetically predisposed to have more potential to become part of human society than wolves or coyotes, and some breeds within the family of domesticated dogs find doing so easier still. For example, compare the companion ability of a good Golden Retriever, which was bred to work closely with humans, with the suspicious nature of breeds such as the Rottweiler or German Shepherd, which were developed to protect people, livestock, or property.

So part of it's genetics, but the other part is you. Get your puppy out! The more people and animals he comes in contact with as a pup, the better he'll be able to socialize as an adult.

WARNING

The world is full of scary things, especially to a little puppy. At times, even the boldest of puppies is paralyzed with uncertainty when faced with something he's never seen before. Your response to his fear is *very* important. Do not soothe him.

Petting him and saying, "It's okay, baby" or something similar gives your puppy the idea that being scared is okay, that you're rewarding him for the behavior. Be matter-of-fact and encouraging. Let him know that you think there's nothing to be afraid of. Let him work it out and when he takes that step forward, praise him for his courage. And then move on.

Your veterinarian knows what's best for your puppy, and she likely told you not to take him *anywhere* until the complete course of vaccinations has ended. I'm telling you to socialize him. Are you facing a conflict here?

Yes and no. Your puppy *is* at risk for contracting diseases from other dogs before his full immunity is in place. This is why you shouldn't go anywhere where dogs you don't know hang out — parks, dog events, or pet stores — until your veterinarian gives the go-ahead. You *should* take him to places that are probably safe — to see friends and play with their healthy, vaccinated dogs, for example, or to places humans frequent, such as the outdoor seating area of a sidewalk cafe. Why take any chances at all? Because doing so is *important*. Behavioral problems present as great or greater a risk to your puppy than do contagious diseases.

So use common sense. Plan safe outings, and carry your puppy to keep him from picking up diseases on his feet if you're not sure. And when that last puppy shot is in — at 14 to 16 weeks — then really pull out all the stops when it comes to socialization.

TIP

Be creative when it comes to letting your puppy experience new things. One of my favorite experiences for a puppy is to take him through a drive-through car wash — lots of noise and motion, but absolutely no danger!

Consistency

Puppies are adorable, even when they're naughty. Maybe *especially* when they're naughty. You catch your little fluffball with your slipper in his mouth, or halfway through the destruction of yet *another* roll of toilet paper and, instead of being upset, you smile. And laugh. And head for the camera.

Although this reaction is normal, it's definitely *not* the way to raise a puppy who knows to leave slippers and toilet paper rolls alone. If you want your puppy to learn, you need to be *consistent* about what's acceptable behavior and what's not.

But you know that, which is why sometimes you keep your face as stern as you can for as long as you can, until . . . well, who wouldn't laugh, the way that toilet paper's wrapped around his cute puppy body?

REMEMBER

Look. I *know* it's hard. He's cute, and you want to let him have his way. But you're going to be sorry a few months from now if you don't remember this one little rule: *Never let a puppy get away with what you don't want a grown dog to do.*

Developing a consistent approach to naughtiness requires a little thinking and effort on your part.

TIP

PUPPY CLASSES

Many times when I recommend early socialization and training for puppies, people act surprised. A typical reaction is, "I thought the experts say you aren't supposed to start training until a dog's six months old!"

What the experts meant was *formal* training, as in a class. And even *that's* not true any more. Almost every trainer offers classes for puppies as young as 12 weeks of age.

I highly recommend them.

Understand this: These are not boot camp classes for problem pooches. The goal here is socialization and lots of fun. Big puppies play with little ones, and everybody gets to pet everyone else's pup. And along the way, puppies pick up a few nice tricks — sometimes all the basic commands, taught in an encouraging, reward-centered way.

Puppy classes are good for your puppy and good for you, too. A puppy class gives you the opportunity to talk to a trainer every week about difficulties you may be having at home and get tips on how to keep puppy problems from becoming dog disasters. For your pup, the class is a megadose of socializing, an ongoing lesson that learning is a pleasure, and the foundation for a lifetime of canine good manners.

The bottom line on puppy classes: Make sure that you're dealing with a trainer who asks for proof of vaccinations (for the protection of *all* the puppies in the class), who trains in a secure place, and who does not use harsh corrections or slip-chain training collars on the puppies. Watching a class or two will give you a better idea of the trainer's skills and philosophies than any phone call or brochure. A good trainer welcomes observers.

First, envision the kind of pet you'd like to live with. Some people are considerably looser with their dogs (and kids) than others. If you think that allowing dogs on the furniture is okay, then let your puppy up on the furniture. But if you think it's only okay for *puppies* to be on the furniture because you want to snuggle yours, then you're not being fair.

Second, follow through with the ground rules, every time. No letting things slide because you're tired. No letting him get away with things because he's cute. When he jumps on the couch for the first time — and he will try it, at least once — tell him "Off" and set him on the floor. Praise him for being a good puppy on the floor. When he jumps on you or the kids, tell him "Off" and "Sit" and then take his collar and show him what you mean. Praise him for sitting and for keeping all four paws on the ground.

TIP

Consistency also means that every human member of the family is clear on puppy rules and helps the puppy learn and live by them. If you've decided you don't want your dog to beg for food, you're going to have a hard time enforcing the rule if your son is slipping the puppy french fries while watching TV. Set the rules, and make sure everyone follows them.

Loosening the rules is easier than tightening them. A puppy who grows up thinking every obnoxious thing he wants to do is fine is going to grow into a dog you're not going to enjoy living with or be able to take places. Once your puppy is a well-mannered dog, you can invite him up on the couch or teach him to put his paws on your shoulder and give you a big slurpy kiss. The distinction between him doing what he wants and him doing what he wants *with your permission* is a big one.

Praise — and correction

Millions of words have been written in the last couple of decades on the theories of dog training. I'm going to sum it up a little more simply: Dog training is a carrot-and-stick endeavor which in recent years has become a whole lot more carrot and a lot less stick. This evolution has come about because of two things: First, no humane person wants to punish a dog, and second, any intelligent person realizes that rewarding good behavior is more likely to produce a strong, trusting bond than is constant punishment.

Physical correction — but not physical abuse — has a place in dog training. I go into that more in Chapters 14 and 15. Dog training has become more positive than negative recently, and puppy training has become more positive still.

WARNING

Never strike a puppy: not with your hand, not with a rolled-up newspaper. *Never* scream at your puppy. If you do either to show your puppy "who's boss," you'll end up with a puppy who's both leery of you and convinced you're something of a jerk. You want your puppy to love you and respect you, to know his place in the family, and to feel secure and happy in it. Doing so takes encouragement and lots of loving praise.

TIP

Don't be stingy. When your puppy does something right, let him know it. The first time the little light bulb goes off in his head connecting the word *sit* to the lowering of his rump — if you watch, you can see the workings of his mind in his eyes — be ready to tell him he's the smartest, most perfect, most beautiful, and best-loved puppy in the whole history of the world the instant that little puppy-butt hits the ground. Croon to him like Bing Crosby. Pat him and stroke him.

At other times, your puppy won't be perfect, and you need to correct his bratty behavior. Remember: Let the punishment fit the crime. A verbal correction, properly timed and correctly delivered, is the gentlest. Done properly, this type of correction may be all you need in most puppy-raising situations. Here are few more ways to send a clear message of disapproval:

>> **The ol' switcheroo.** Especially useful for the young puppy, this technique stops a behavior you don't want and provides the puppy with one that's acceptable. For example, if your young puppy's chewing on your nice leather shoes, make a noise to startle and distract him — slap the counter or clap your hands — and then give him something you do want him to chew on, a toy. When he takes it, praise him!

>> **Ask for another behavior.** With older puppies, you can stop a bad behavior by asking for a better one. Tell the puppy who's jumping up "no" and then "Sit" — and praise him for doing so. Tell him once, and if he does not — to be fair, be sure that he understands what you want — gently push him into a sit, and then praise.

>> **The big squirt.** Get an inexpensive plastic squirt bottle and fill it with water and something distasteful — lemon juice or vinegar, a tablespoon or so to a 12-ounce bottle. Tell your puppy "no" and then squirt. Try to hold the bottle close to your side so the stream seems to be coming from nowhere.

>> **The time out.** This technique has two levels, and you need to pay attention to your puppy to choose the appropriate correction. Puppies thrive on your attention, even if it's negative. The time out removes this reward and gives him a few minutes to think things over: "Oh, I can't stay with them if I do that!" he'll realize. This technique is especially good for a puppy who doesn't want to keep his mouth to himself, a bad habit for any dog to get into where people are concerned. When the puppy starts nipping, tell him "no," and them clam up, pick him up, and put him in his crate for five minutes. Ignore the cries and whimpers. After a few minutes, let him out without much fanfare and let him hang out with you gently for a while.

WARNING

NO, NO, NO, NO, NO, NO, NOOOOOOOO

Almost without fail people use one word too much and incorrectly when raising a puppy. The word? "No." Some puppies hear it so often they think it's part of their name: "JoeNO!" "MeganNO!" Used constantly and especially if used in a whiny, pleading manner, "no" loses its value as a training tool.

"No" should be delivered firmly and sharply, as guttural as a low, barky growl — comparable, in other words, to how a puppy's mother expresses her displeasure. Don't whine your correction: "No, no, no, *no*. Mommy's fluffums is bad, bad, *bad!*" Instead, *throw* the word at the pup.

Some trainers suggest using another sound especially for correction, something that lends itself more naturally to sounding like a growl, like "arrrggghhh." I use both "no" and a guttural "argh" sounds as a correction words, but I don't use "no" as a warning word. I use "I wouldn't" when a dog is contemplating something like a second assault on something he has been told to leave alone. Again, the delivery is the key: I drop my voice and growl, "I WOULDn't."

They try by their innocent expressions to assure me they were not even thinking about it. But I know better.

If your puppy has been running around for a long time and just seems bratty, he may be tired. If that's the case, put him down for a nap in his crate, along with a chew toy. Again, ignore his fussing. Chances are he'll be asleep in a few minutes.

WARNING

If you're finding you need to do a lot of stern corrections, you've probably been sending your puppy mixed signals. You've probably led him to believe he has a chance to be boss — or at least go up a notch or two in pack order — and he's trying the higher position on for size. Discuss the situation with a trainer, and soon. You may have some big problems developing if you don't learn how to correct your puppy in an effective way.

Teaching What Every Puppy Should Know

People sometimes tell me they don't believe in dog-training because training will break their puppy's spirit. "I want him to be *free!*" says the person whose dog is running amok. While this attitude was a lot more prevalent during the '60s and '70s, when free-roaming canine nuisances played fetch in the common areas of college campuses, it remains even today, despite the enthusiastic enforcement of leash laws in some areas.

And it's not just running amok that's the problem. The late trainer Job Michael Evans used to say that when your dog jumps in a guest's lap, and that guest says, "Oh, it's okay. I *love* dogs" she's probably just being polite while wondering why you don't teach your dog some manners.

REMEMBER

No dog in the world has more freedom than one with good manners. And no dog is easier to live with. These dogs can go in to stores and on vacation. They're welcome at the veterinarian's and the groomer's. Well-mannered dogs are helping to *reverse* the trend of antidog laws, including opening the minds in some communities to the possibilities of dog parks where good dogs can be rewarded by running . . . free!

About a million and six good reasons exist to train your puppy, and only one exists not to: foolishness. Do both you and your dog a favor and train. Remember my motto: *It's easier to raise a puppy right than to fix problems later.*

Getting used to a collar and leash

Your puppy can start wearing a buckled collar from the time you bring him home. I like lightweight nylon collars, inexpensive to replace when a puppy grows, and they come in oodles of fun colors. Quick-snap collars are fine, too, and easy to adjust to larger sizes. Check the collar frequently to ensure a good fit. (And don't forget to attach a small ID tag!) For more on collars and IDs, see Chapter 6.

By the time your pup's ten weeks old, you can introduce a leash, for a few minutes at a time. Instead of using the leash to get the puppy to go your way, go *his* for a while, and then bend down and call him to you, sweetly. When he turns and heads in your direction, praise him and then get up and keep going, patting your leg and jollying him along. Introduce a command such as "Walk on" or "Let's go" for him to start associating with the idea of heading in your direction. A few minutes is enough. Try again later in the day, and maybe change direction once, saying "Let's go" and praising when the puppy follows.

TIP

The leash can be an important bonding tool for both puppies and grown dogs. After your puppy's comfortable with the feel of the leash, try tethering him to you for a few minutes at a time. With a six-foot leash, slip the leash handle through your belt and then snap the other end to the puppy. And then go about your business, hands off the leash. Doing so teaches the puppy to keep an eye on you, which in turn reinforces the idea of you as leader.

Puppy's first leash should be six-feet long, slender, and as light as possible, especially at the clasp. If you've got a heavy leash that you bought for your last dog, save it for later and get something appropriate for a puppy. Even a length of lightweight cord tied to a light snap is better than a leash that's too heavy. See Chapter 6 for more on leashes.

The leash is a symbol of your leadership, and when you let your puppy chew on the leash, you're letting him chew on your authority. Considering the sharp nature of puppy teeth, you'll also be spending money for new leashes pretty regularly. Neither of these is desirable. So *do not* let your puppy chew on the leash. Yank it upward an inch or so out of his mouth while delivering a stern "no." And praise — never, ever forget to praise — when your pup does what you ask!

Grooming

All dogs need to learn to be bathed and brushed, to have their nails trimmed and their ears cleaned out. Some breeds — Poodles, for example, as well as terriers and Cockers — need to be professionally groomed at regular intervals during their lives.

TECHNICAL STUFF

The hair of a Poodle is like ours — it never stops growing. If you don't keep them clipped, the coat will grow into twists called *cords* so long that they drag on the ground! As for other breeds, their coats are just difficult to live with if not kept clipped short.

REMEMBER

The time to start introducing your puppy to these experiences is the day you bring him home. Handle his feet and toes, lift and caress his ear flaps, all the time telling him what a wonderful puppy he is. Keep the sessions short and always end on an upbeat note.

For brushing and combing, put a towel on top of a high, solid surface like your dryer — it's easier on your back — and hold him while you brush. He'll wriggle and carry on, but don't let that stop you. Brush for a short period, and end the session with brushing in an area most dogs adore — their tummy. Then call it a day.

TIP

Expose your puppy to the concept of electric clippers by running a sweater depiller — or other small humming device — near him. Place the handle of it against him gently so that he can feel the vibration. Don't punish him for being scared: Let him get used to it for a second or two, and praise him afterward for being so brave.

If your puppy is of a breed that needs professional grooming, make his first appointment as soon as he's done with his puppy shots — at 14 to 16 weeks of age — to minimize the risk of exposure to disease. Make sure that the groomer knows you're bringing in a puppy so she can take a little extra time with him.

Sit for what you want

Teaching a puppy to "Sit" is almost effortless. You don't need to lay a hand on him. All you need is his food bowl and the force of gravity. Here's how it works:

TIP

Call your puppy's name and hold his food dish over his head, forcing him to raise his muzzle high to keep an eye on it. Soon he'll lose his balance and his back legs will start to fold. The microsecond this starts to occur, say "Sit." When his rump hits the ground, praise and give him his dinner. Within a short time — if you're consistent in asking — he'll be sitting automatically for his food.

Test that he understands the command by trying it at different times, pulling gently up on his collar and pushing his rump down to remind him and then praising and treating grandly for success (even if you helped engineer that success).

Once your puppy knows "Sit," expand the situations in which you ask for it. Have him sit before you put the leash on, sit before you go out the door for a walk, sit instead of jumping up (although you'll probably need to correct him for the bad behavior first). My dogs sit for *anything* they want — their dinner, their toys, to leave the house or car, or to be petted by guests. Not only does sitting make them easier to live with — especially the 75-pound retriever — but it also constantly and effortlessly reinforces my role as the boss. And like any gentle and generous leader, I *always* thank them for being good dogs with an ear or chest scratch, a sweet word, or a hug.

TIP

Molding good behavior by controlling food is why I don't recommend free-feeding for puppies. When you — and other family members — are the ones who offer the food and make your puppy sit before getting it, you're integrating puppy training into all of your lives seamlessly.

When food is always available, you lose the training tool. And you also lose this chance to reinforce your role as top dog, which can contribute to dominance problems later on. When you give your pup food, and make him earn it, you make it clear that you own the food and are giving it to him. He's eating with your *permission*. This understanding can help prevent food-guarding and growling.

"Sit" isn't the only command you can teach your puppy. "Down," "Come," "Stay" — puppies can and should learn them all. For step-by-step instructions on how to teach these obedience basics, see Chapters 14 and 15.

So use your imagination and teach your pup as much as you can. Remember, though, to be consistent in your naming — don't say "Off" one time and "Down" the next. (I prefer "Off" for asking for all paws on the floor and "Down" for lying down; it's less confusing for your puppy.)

Teaching your puppy to sit for what she wants helps to ensure she'll grow up to be a wellmannered pet.

Photograph courtesy of Richard D. Schmidt

Fixing the Things That Drive Puppy Owners Crazy

All dogs chew, jump up, bark, and nip. It's part of being a dog. Some dogs do more of these activities than others — some breeds are yappier, some are diggier — but these activities are all part of the genetic blueprint of every dog. If you aren't prepared to live with these activities — especially in the puppy stages — you're really better off with an iguana.

That's the bad news. The other bad news is puppies do not grow out of problem behaviors, so drop that idea right now.

The good news is that you can diminish, redirect, and control — and in the case of nipping, eliminate — these behaviors when raising your puppy. But be fair: You cannot expect a puppy — or dog — to spend boring, empty days without filling the time with activities you may not like. A dog requires a lifelong commitment of time for training and exercise.

Chewing

All puppies chew. So would you if your gums drove you as crazy as theirs do, especially when their adult teeth are coming in, around four months of age. The trick here is to redirect the behavior by keeping things you don't want your puppy to chew on out of reach and by giving her approved chews and praising her for using them.

TIP

One of the oldest pieces of pet advice in the world is to not give your puppy things that are like the objects you want her to leave alone. In other words, don't give her your old slippers to chew on and expect her to leave your new ones alone.

Some objects — like table legs and, in the case of one puppy I raised, walls — are not capable of being picked up and put away. Discourage chewing on these by applying Bitter Apple (available in pet-supply stores) to favorite spots — the taste is so horrible your puppy won't put a tongue on it again. Tabasco sauce is another pet-stopper

Puppies *must* chew. If you catch yours chewing on something you don't want her to, don't make a big deal out of it. Clap to distract her, give her an approved toy, and cue her by giving her a word to associate, like "Chewbaby." Then praise her for chewing on the approved item.

Never give a puppy free run of the house, allowing her to make her own decisions on what is and isn't chewable. If you cannot observe her, put her in a safe area — a crate, ideally, but also a small area like a laundry porch with a baby gate across the door. Make sure that you leave a chew toy or two.

Think cool when it comes to puppy's painful gums. I like to take a piece of beef leg bone (trimmed of fat) and put it in the freezer before giving it to a teething puppy. I look for clean shanks and have the butcher cut them into four-inch pieces, so the marrow can be chewed out. Alternately, look for sterilized bones at the pet-supply store, stuff the inside with a little peanut butter, and chill. The indestructible Kong dog toy — truly a pet toy Hall of Famer — can likewise be stuffed with peanut butter and chilled.

Improper greetings: Sniffing and jumping

What do dogs do when they meet? They touch noses and then check out each other's privates. Doing so is natural, normal, and unstoppable canine greeting behavior, and yet we *insist* our dogs do not use it on us. We don't want dogs who stick their noses in people's crotches, and we don't want dogs who jump up to touch our noses. The former we consider merely disgusting; the latter could be downright dangerous with children or people who are unsteady on their feet.

Of course it's not your dog's fault that he was born unprepared to deal with a species who prefers a handshake to a butt-sniff, and whose noses are so far off the ground you just *have* to jump to be friendly!

KEEPING PUPPIES FROM GROWING UP AGGRESSIVE

Aggression is a complicated problem for dog trainers and behaviorists and a serious public-health threat. Dogs bite because of fear, pain, dominance, and predation.

Despite statements by the owner to the contrary, bites almost never come out of the blue. They are almost always preceded by lots of warning signs that pet owners either overlook, misinterpret, or make excuses for. And sometimes encourage, taking pride in the "macho" behavior of their pet.

Puppies do not outgrow aggression. You must make sure, through training and socializing, that your pup understands every human is above him in the pack order and aggression to other dogs and predation upon smaller animals will *not* be tolerated.

Here are a few tips:

- **Never let your puppy chew on you or other family members, even in play.** Correct with a stern word and offer a chew toy instead, or go to the time out for more serious infractions.

- **Never let children and puppies play unsupervised, and never let them rough-house like littermates.** Instead of tug-of-war, teach your children to play fetch with your puppy.

- **Make sure that every member of the family acts as leader.** Teach your puppy manners such as sitting for his dish and then have everyone reinforce.

- **Teach your puppy that humans control the food.** Have every member of the family add food to the puppy's dish while he's eating so he learns to tolerate activity near his food. Correct verbally and sternly for growling.

- **Practice taking away and returning toys to your puppy.** Give the command "Give" then take the toy and praise him for obeying.

- **Have your puppy neutered.** Young, unneutered males are most likely to be involved in a serious bite incident than any other kind of dog.

- **Get a trainer's or behaviorist's help if you even suspect you have a problem, the sooner the better.** A professional can help you see ways in which you are encouraging aggression and help you to reorder pack structure to eliminate aggression.

Please note: These rules apply to puppies only. If you've got a grown dog with aggression problems, go right to the last step and bring in a trainer to help sort out the situation before a tragedy occurs.

These problems are fixed by redirection and consistency. When your puppy jumps up, throw a sharp "no" at her, followed by the command "Off," and then "Sit." If that doesn't do the trick, hold your puppy's paws and squeeze until it's uncomfortable, giving the "Off" command just as her paws head for the floor. How much pressure? You'll know the right amount when she drops to the floor — she'll give in before you can hurt her, I promise.

You may find it easier to put your puppy on her leash and invite a guest over. It's a simpler matter then to give the correction word "no," the command "Off," and pull the puppy sharply off your guest, quickly asking for a "Sit" and then praising.

WARNING

Consistency is the biggest problem here, I've found. People let puppies get away with jumping up and sniffing because they're *puppies,* so cute and so small. But remember they don't stay small for long, and making sure that your 20-pound Lab puppy never gets in the habit of jumping up is a lot easier than convincing your 70-pound, full-grown Lab to knock it off.

Barking

Some breeds and breed types are noisier than others. Terriers, Poodles, and Shelties can be truly obnoxious yappers, and it doesn't help that even reputable breeders think nothing of breeding the worst barkers if they can otherwise win in the show ring. For hounds, *giving voice* is a thing of beauty to connoisseurs, but not so widely appreciated by neighbors of a suburban Beagle whose melodious baying is a constant annoyance.

WARNING

A lot of barking is trained into dogs by owners who aren't thinking about what they're doing when raising their puppy. Puppy barks for attention, owners pick him up. Puppy barks for toy, owners give it to him. A friend of mine "discovered" that the only way to quiet her Golden was to give her a dog biscuit — and ended up with a nonstop barking problem and a very fat dog.

Realize that you can never turn a yappy breed into a hush puppy, but you *can* teach him to turn off the noise on command. When he barks, issue a sharp "no," the command "Quiet" or "Hush," and then praise him for quieting. *Never* yell at a puppy who's barking — he'll think you're joining in, too. A squirt in the kisser — discussed earlier in this chapter — can also be a good correction for barking.

By all means don't teach him to bark by rewarding him for the behavior. If he's barking for attention, to get out of his crate, for a toy, or whatever, tell him "no" then "Hush" before picking him up, letting him out, or giving him his toy. Better still: "Hush" and "Sit." A dog who sits for what he wants is a lot nicer to live with than one who barks for it.

More on barking problems and solutions is in Chapter 15.

Nipping and biting

Nipping and biting is serious, serious stuff, and you need to take it that way. Like jumping up and sniffing privates, dogs display this behavior naturally with each other, roughhousing with teeth fully — but gently — in play. That's fine for playing with dogs, but not for playing with people — our skin's a lot more tender, without a protective layer of fur. Puppies need to learn it's *never, ever* appropriate to use teeth on a human being. Not in play. Not ever.

All puppies nip, but some are worse than others. Those who were removed from their litters too young may never have learned how much those little teeth hurt and may be more inclined to use them than a puppy who was allowed to stay with his littermates for at least seven weeks. You can get this point across to the youngest puppies in the same way their littermates do — by crying out sharply and dramatically when those needle teeth touch your skin.

For some puppies, that may be enough. For others, you need to do more. Correct *sharply* with a "no" for nipping, stop play *immediately*, and put her in her crate to think about it for awhile.

If you can't seem to stop your puppy from nipping and biting — especially if the behavior is accompanied by growling — consult a trainer *right away*. Private consultation early on can prevent a tragedy later.

Working through the Rough Spots

Welcome to the canine equivalent of junior high, that oftentimes challenging period between the ages of three and six months, with growing proceeding one spurt after another, hormones raging, and your puppy's brain seemingly rewiring itself before your eyes. Some dogs, like some kids, go through a stage where they seem to be growing in the most awkward of ways — back legs longer than the front, bodies too long or too short. Your dog will emerge from the puppy uglies, of course, but at times you may doubt it.

REMEMBER

Other times you'll wish an ugly puppy is all you had to worry about. The canine phenomenon who learned to sit at 11 weeks — and was *soooo* proud of himself for doing so — may now give you a blank look as if he has never heard the word *sit* before, much less what you expect of him when you say it. Or maybe he recognizes the word just fine, thanks, but has something he'd rather do more than whatever it is you want.

Which is not to say your puppy becomes a complete heathen during this period. Sometimes he's just wonderful, sometimes not. This time is difficult for him, too, after all. His adult teeth are coming in, and they're driving him crazy — and you, too, with all the chewing he wants to do to feel better. You may even notice he seems tentative and shy for a week or so at a time — think of your first junior high dance to help you relate.

Your puppy's behavior is perfectly normal, but your behavior can mean the beginning of the end for your relationship. No matter how much he's driving you crazy, you must continue to socialize and train your puppy. Even if nothing seems to be getting through at times. If you give up at the first sign of trouble, you'll have more trouble later: This stage is when bad habits can really settle in.

REMEMBER

Remember above all that this, too, shall pass. At the end of this period, your pup will reach sexual maturity and become — gasp! — the canine equivalent of a *teenager!*

Age three to six months is an awkward but important time in a puppy's life.

Photograph courtesy of Randy Pench

3
Keeping Your Dog Healthy

In this part, you find the information you need on basic preventive care and coping with illness. The first line of defense against disease is good grooming: All that brushing, nail-trimming, and flea-control will help your dog stay healthy, and help you spot little problems before they become big ones. This part also gives you the run-down on such preventive-care measures as vaccinations, helps you find a veterinarian with whom you're comfortable working, and provides the information you need about common canine health problems. Senior dogs are the focus of the final chapter in this part, to help you keep your aging dog healthy and happy.

Chapter **10**

Good Grooming

When it comes to your dog's health, preventive care is easier on both your pet and your pocketbook. From head (teeth and ears) to tail (anal sacs), the emphasis today is on care that deals with little problems before they become big ones. Grooming is an essential element of any preventive-care regimen.

Are you surprised? Did you think grooming was just for show dogs, or for some fussy person's Poodle? Think again! While good grooming is a much larger task for someone who owns a Komondor than a Labrador — the Komondor's floor-length fur cords are a life's work to keep clean — regular coat care and more should be a part of every pet-lover's regimen. Grooming keeps your dog comfortable, helps you to spot developing problems, makes your pet easier to live with, and strengthens the bond between you. What a deal!

Grooming can't work miracles, though. All the brushing in the world won't keep your dog from shedding — although grooming can certainly lessen the amount of fur that gets on your clothes and furniture. (What you catch on a comb or brush won't end up where you don't want it.) Likewise, it won't turn a heavy-shedding dog, like a German Shepherd, into a neater one, like a Rhodesian Ridgeback. Some things only nature gets to decide.

Coat length and shedding are, of course, among the factors that must be considered when choosing a dog. For more information on how coat types factor into the selection process, see Chapter 1.

REMEMBER

While grooming can't change a shedder into a furless wonder, good stuff happens every time you pick up a comb or brush. You can spot a lump before it becomes deadly, stop a skin problem before it becomes itchy, and catch an ear infection before it becomes both painful to live with and expensive to treat. No fleas and no ticks on your dog now mean fewer health problems later. And, on top of everything else, your dog will look *gor*-geous.

Grooming is just one part of preventive care, but it is the part for which you're directly responsible. You'll need a veterinarian's help for the rest, including vaccinations, dental procedures, and more. Everything you need to know about preventive veterinary care is in Chapter 11.

Getting the Gear

Grooming tools can be an expensive investment, especially if you decide to show your dog. Serious dog-show folk travel with motor homes full of combs, brushes, scissors, thinning shears, nail clippers, nail files, forceps, and other tools of the trade. Scissors alone can be an investment in the hundreds of dollars for some of these competitors — for what looks, to most people, like just a fancy pair of scissors.

Although you don't need to spend *that* kind of money, investing in top-quality equipment is best: A few well-chosen pieces do the job well and last forever. Choose metal combs and brushes with sturdy bristles set into a comfortable wooden handle.

TIP

Two of the best mail-order sources for dog-grooming supplies are the J-B Wholesale Pet Supplies and Cherrybrook catalogs. These two companies are popular sources for those in the dog-show game and have an outstanding selection of top-quality grooming equipment.

Combs and brushes

For most dogs, the grooming kit starts with a comb and a brush. The ones you choose depend on your pet's coat type. If you bought your puppy or dog from a reputable breeder, you should be able to ask for equipment recommendations and grooming advice (you may even have gotten recommendations on a sheet when you picked up your puppy). For mixed-breeds, go with the tools best suited for the purebred your dog's coat most resembles. Remember, these are recommendations for keeping a coat in pet shape, but show grooming is considerably more involved and requires a lot more equipment. You could take years learning how to groom a dog for the show ring, and it would require another whole book to explain. (In fact, you can find books that cover nothing but show grooming for a *single breed* of dog, such as the Shetland Sheepdog.)

The following are the basic coat types, and the tools you'll need to keep them in good shape:

>> **Short, smooth coats (Labs, Pugs, Rottweilers).** You get off easy. You can either run a comb through to catch the shedding hairs or use a grooming glove, a tool you slip your hand into and run over your dog. It's like petting, and dogs love it!

>> **Curly coats (Poodles, Portuguese Water Dogs, the softer terriers).** Clipping is part of the regimen for these breeds. If you want to do the clipping yourself, you need an instruction book and a basic clipper set with a couple of blades. For daily grooming, a medium metal brush keeps tangles at bay, then follow by brushing with a slicker brush.

>> **Medium coats (Golden Retrievers, Australian Shepherds).** A medium steel comb and a natural-bristle brush keep these coats in fine shape.

>> **Long and silky coats (Afghan Hounds, Yorkshire Terriers, Maltese).** Use a medium steel comb and a natural-bristle brush — gently — to keep these glamorous coats from breaking. (Some people think that's too much work, and have their dogs kept clipped short by a professional groomer.)

>> **Wiry coats (Most terriers, Schnauzers, wire-haired hunting dogs).** A medium comb and a slicker brush get the dirt out. Terriers need to be clipped every two months to get rid of dead hairs and maintain their smart appearance, and if you're going to do this yourself, you'll need clippers. (For shows, terriers are *stripped*, a laborious task involving plucking out dead and dying hairs.) Wire-haired hunting dogs don't need to be kept trimmed, but do need brushing — that coat is a muck magnet.

>> **Long and double-coated (Shetland Sheepdogs, Collies, Keeshonden, Alaskan Malamutes, Pomeranians).** A wide-toothed, steel, "Collie comb," a natural bristle brush, and a dematting tool are needed. Bred to thrive in the coldest weather, these breeds shed plenty and require a lot of grooming. A thorough brushing against the grain and down to the skin keeps the downy undercoat from matting into a block of felt.

Keeping your dog wellgroomed is important, but one needn't get too carried away.

Sylvia/Photo courtesy of Christy Waehner

Nail trimmers

Because some — okay, most — dogs don't like to have their nails trimmed, this procedure is the most often neglected piece of a regular grooming regimen. A lot of people leave it to their veterinarian or groomer, sometimes waiting until the dog must be anesthetized for another reason.

TIP

Better you should trim a little bit yourself every week than let your dog struggle with long nails. If left unattended, overgrown nails can cause lameness. And no, a daily walk isn't enough to keep them worn down.

Three kinds of nail trimmers are widely available — guillotine style, scissors style, and an electric nail grinder. The latter is the most expensive — around $50 — but is a good way to keep nails short without nicking the quick, a common problem with nail cutters. A nail grinder may be more acceptable to dogs who don't like their nails trimmed — unless they're put off by the noise and the vibration.

Nail clippers are the most common, however, and which of the two kinds you use is a matter of personal preference — both do a good, fast job. Since I have a tendency to misplace nail clippers, I have at least one of both kinds and use whichever kind's handiest. I also use a nail grinder. You will need a small jar of blood-stopping powder on hand when you trim nails to stop bleeding, should you cut too far. There are a couple of brands on the market; Kwik Stop is probably the best known. Another good buy: a metal file, for cleaning up the rough edges.

Shampoos and conditioners

Remember that old saw about only washing a dog once or twice a year? Forget it! Who'd want to live with a dirty, stinky dog?

It's true that dogs don't need to wash as often as we do — because they don't sweat — but they get plenty dirty. Frequent bathing — as often as once a week — can make living with a dog manageable for many allergy sufferers, and a clean dog is just more pleasant for everyone to be around.

REMEMBER

Maybe you've heard that frequent bathing strips the coat of its natural oils. To some extent, that's true, although as a person who lives with retrievers, I can tell you that in some breeds there's plenty of oil to spare. If you need to, you can always put back in some of what you take out, by following shampoo with a conditioner. And good nutrition has a bigger impact on a glossy coat than bathing does — so go ahead, bathe that dog.

There are oodles of shampoos — some to keep dark coats dark, others to make white coats brighter. Shampoos with every imaginable scent, shampoos for fleas, shampoos for itchiness. If your pet has a skin problem, ask your veterinarian for a recommendation. Otherwise, experiment a little to find products you like working with.

Regular shampoos are almost as effective as flea shampoos at controlling fleas: They aren't very effective. When you wash your dog — with regular or flea shampoo — the result is the same: Fleas go down the drain. But the effect of a flea shampoo is short-lived. If you're planning to fight fleas by treating only your pet, you won't get anywhere.

Other niceties and necessities

Depending on what kind of dog you have, you may wish to add some other items to your collection of grooming supplies, including:

>> **Antiseptic liquid.** Nolvasan is probably the most common, a blue-tinted liquid veterinarians use for everything from cleaning ears to disinfecting exam tables. An absolute must-have for dogs with floppy ears who swim regularly or are otherwise prone to ear infections. Catalogs are a good source for this nonprescription item; your veterinarian is another.

>> **Bath mat** and **spray nozzle.** A wet bathtub is slippery, and nothing makes a dog more nervous than not being able to stand square on all four paws. A full bath mat is ideal, but in a pinch a towel in the bottom of the tub will do. Some people rinse dogs by pouring dirty bath water back over them, but that defeats the purpose of bathing a dog — to get him clean — so use a nozzle. An inexpensive option is the rubber kind that fits over the bathtub tap.

>> **Corn starch.** Useful for working out mats. Nonstick cooking spray can also be helpful in clearing a coat of burrs. (See the sidebar, "Getting the gunk out," later in this chapter).

>> **Cotton balls.** Great for cleaning the inside of the ear flap, and for wiping tear stains, skin folds, and eye gunk.

>> **Old towels.** Never throw a towel away! Even the most faded, worn, and torn towel is good for drying a freshly bathed dog or wiping off muddy paws. Also, old bathmats give your dog good footing in the bathtub.

>> **Spray bottle.** Makes brushing long-haired dogs easy, and keeps thing cool for short-haired dogs while you work.

>> **Tweezers.** Good for removing ear hair — especially important for Cockers and Poodles — and ticks.

Keeping Up Appearances

Good grooming has more benefits than keeping your pet looking beautiful and smelling clean — although that's certainly one of the pleasant payoffs. Regular grooming also relaxes the dog who's used to it, and becomes a special time shared between you and your dog. A coat free of mats, burrs, and tangles, and skin that is free of fleas and ticks, is as comfortable to your dog as clothes fresh from the wash are to you: It just makes you feel good. The effect is the same for your pet.

Properly trimmed nails make moving more comfortable, and keeping ears clean of wax and excess hair helps keep infections at bay — and eliminates another source of dreaded doggy odor.

Brushing and combing

With dogs, as with anything else, nothing succeeds like excess. Which is why the dogs who win in the show ring are the ones with lots of lovely coat. Breeds such as Cockers, Collies, and Afghans have lush, glorious coats that would be wholly impractical in their original lines of work, but all that lovely fur adds to their beauty at the end of a show leash.

Good grooming is essential, especially for longhaired dogs.

Friday and Edgar/Photo courtesy of Marilyn and Buckley Peterson

They're beautiful at the end of a regular leash, too, which is why many of these spectacular breeds are so popular. But there's a price to be paid for such beauty, and if you don't pay, your dog does. Consider a simple mat, so easy to overlook. Have you ever had your hair in a ponytail that was just a little too tight? A mat can feel the same way to your dog, a constant pull on the skin. Try to imagine those all over your body and you have a good idea how uncomfortable an ungroomed coat can be. Even worse, an ungroomed coat can be a health hazard, as skin becomes so badly damaged that flies will lay eggs in the wounds and maggots will result. Ick!

REMEMBER

Your dog need never know what a mat feels like if you keep him brushed and combed. You should go over him daily, clearing such things as mats and ticks from his coat — more on those later in this chapter — and brush him out completely every week. For short-haired breeds doing so is a cinch: Run your hands over him daily, a brush over him weekly, and that's it. One other benefit of short-haired (and some medium-haired) dogs: You can use a flea comb on them. Flea combs have narrowly-spaced teeth that catch the little blood-suckers where they eat: on your dog. To use one, comb from the skin out, a tiny bit at a time, flicking the pests into a bowl of warm, sudsy water as you go. When you're done, flush the fleas — most of them will have drowned by then anyway. Remember that combing fleas from your pet does *not* solve a flea problem. See the flea section later in this chapter for a total control program.

For other breeds, grooming is a little more involved. Double-coated, long-haired breeds such as Collies, Chows, Keeshonden, and Alaskan Malamutes have a downy undercoat that can mat down like a layer of felt against the skin if left untouched. To prevent this, divide the coat into small sections and brush against the grain from the skin outward, working from head to tail, section by section. In the spring and fall — the Big Shed times — you'll end up with enough of that fluffy undercoat to make a whole new dog. Keep brushing, and think of the benefits: The fur you pull out with a brush doesn't end up on the furniture, and removing the old stuff keeps your pet cooler in the summer and lets new insulation come in for the winter.

Lightly misting the part of the fur you're brushing with water from a spray bottle makes working the brush through the coat easier and helps keep the long outer coat from breaking.

Don't shave a long-haired dog down to the skin for summer. Why would you want to make your beautiful dog ugly for half the year? Double-coated dogs carry less coat in the summer than in the winter — they *blow* most of their undercoat in the spring — and keeping the remainder clean and well-brushed provides insulation against the heat as well as the cold. Some of the dogs *most* affected by summer heat, ironically, are short-haired: Dogs with short noses, such as Boxers and Pugs, and dogs with black coats, such as Rottweilers and some Dobermans. If you own one of these dogs, be especially careful to keep them cool in hot weather. If your long-haired dog is one big mat, however, you may have no choice but to clip — short, but not naked.

Silky-coated dogs such as Afghan Hounds, Cockers, and Maltese also need constant brushing to keep tangles from forming. As with the double-coated dogs, work with small sections at a time, brushing from the skin outward and then comb back into place with the grain for a glossy, finished look. Coats of this type require so much attention that having a groomer keep the dogs trimmed to a medium length is often practical.

Curly and wiry coats, such as those on Poodles and terriers, need to be brushed weekly, working against the grain and then with it. Curly coats need to be clipped every six weeks, wiry ones two or three times a year (but clipping every six weeks keeps your terrier looking sharper).

Learning to clip your dog yourself isn't that hard — if you don't mind a few bad hair weeks for your dog. Dog clippers are widely available in pet-supply and discount stores, and these kits contain basic instructions for keeping your pet shorn.

If your terrier doesn't come back from the groomer's looking like the show dogs you've seen, there's a reason: *hand-stripping*. The proper terrier coat is maintained for the show ring by painstakingly pulling dead hair by hand using a special grooming tool. Most pet groomers clip the coat instead, which presents an appearance just as neat but not as "correct" as hand-stripping. Clipping is a practical compromise for wiry-haired dogs whose job description is "household pet."

Every grooming session should end with a petting session, to make your dog's last impression of grooming time a pleasant one.

Giving a bath

Why is it that from the instant the first drops of water spill out of the tap, from the second you reach for the bottle of shampoo, your dog starts burrowing his way to the darkest, quietest, most hidden corner of the house? The dog who doesn't hear you when you scream, "Get off the couch!" is able to pick out the magic word when you whisper, "I think the dog needs a bath."

Like most dogs, your dog is content to live his life in dog-smell heaven, a place where water is to drink or swim in and never has soap added. Too bad. We make the rules, and dog-smell heaven is no paradise for us.

House dogs should be bathed monthly, more often still if they need it. Using a high-quality shampoo and conditioner babies the coat and replenishes some of the oils bathing removes. Another plus for frequent bathing: Fleas go down the drain!

Your dog should be brushed before bathing because mats and tangles, once wet, can never be removed — you need to cut them out. Let your dog chill for a minute while you set up, collecting your equipment. You don't want to be looking for shampoo while struggling with a dog determined to get out of the tub.

MASSAGE FOR A PET? YOU BET!

One especially nice way to end a grooming session is with a full-body massage. No, not for you — for your dog! Going over your pet with firm, gentle pressure can be very reassuring, and especially welcome by older pets.

In recent years, human massage techniques have been adapted for use on pets, and you should be able to find books or videos to help you learn the moves. Your dog will love you for it!

TIP

GETTING THE GUNK OUT

Many things your dog gets into — or that get onto him — have to be clipped out. But before hauling out the scissors, try some of these techniques:

- **Burrs:** Try spraying a little Pam cooking spray on the area, and then gently use your fingers to work the burr free from the now-slicker coat.

- **Mats and tangles:** Sprinkle the area with cornstarch and carefully slide sharp scissors through the base of the mat and slice it a couple times through the middle. If you're patient — and gentle — you should be able to work the fur free with your fingers. To finish the job, comb through the area with a wide-toothed steel comb and then a brush to remove the dirt and dead hair that caused the problem in the first place.

- **Fleas:** A flea comb will catch the pest, but you'll soon see more if you don't launch a flea-control program. More on fleas later in this chapter.

- **Ticks:** Never touch a tick with your hands. Use a tick remover or tweezers, grasp the body firmly, and pull with a steady motion. More about ticks later in this chapter.

- **Paint or tar:** *Never* use solvents to remove paint or tar: They irritate your dog's skin, are toxic if tasted, and they're flammable! Instead, clip the affected area out.

- **Gum or other sticky substances:** You can try a little peanut butter to lubricate the fur enough to slide the gum out, but it's rough going. Clipping is usually the answer.

A dog who's covered in burrs, mats, or dried paint or tar is best sent to a groomer to be clipped short. Not only is this solution easier on you both, it's considerably more attractive than having dozens of short-clipped areas. Don't worry: The hair grows back faster than you think.

Dogs have a keen sense of hearing and some are upset by the sound of bath water running when they know it's for them. After the tub is full, turn off the tap and let the water sit while you prepare the dog for the big plunge. Put a pinch of cotton just inside your dog's ears and a drop of mineral oil in each eye to help keep the soap out.

Oh, and you don't have to use the bathtub. Smaller dogs can be washed in a utility tub or sink. What about outdoor bathing? Dogs have been hose-washed for generations with no ill effect, but I think warm water is probably kinder, especially for older or arthritic dogs.

DO THE DIRTY DEED: EMPTY THE ANAL SACS

Many dog owners live in blissful ignorance of *anal glands,* two nasty little organs that produce fluid that carries the unique scent by which dogs identify each other (*anal glands* are one reason why dogs sniff each other's rumps when they meet). This ignorance is bad, though, because should one of the glands or the fluid reservoirs, the *anal sacs,* become impacted or infected, your dog will need veterinary attention.

The best way to prevent trouble is to empty the anal sacs every time you bathe your dog. The least repulsive way is to suds up the area, including your hand, and then place your thumb and forefinger on the outside of each gland, just below the skin on either side of the anus — you'll feel them as small lumps below the surface. Gently squeeze your fingers inward and together, and you should get a noxious mess for your efforts. Suds and rinse a couple of times and it'll be gone.

If your dog cries out when you touch the glands, or if the area is swollen, call your veterinarian. If you absolutely can't stand to empty your dog's anal glands, your vet or groomer will be happy to do it for you.

As you drag the dog toward the bathroom door, don't spare words of love and encouragement. In working with dogs, I've found that a good attitude can go a long way, but a bad one can go even farther. If your dog knows how much *you* hate bath time, how can he get a positive — or at least tolerable — opinion of the process? Keep your attitude high and don't let up on the praise.

Start shampooing by working a complete ring of lather around the neck, cutting off the fleas' escape route to the ears. Work forward and back from there, and don't forget to work some lather between your dog's toes — another favorite getaway for fleas. Empty the anal sacs (see the sidebar "Do the dirty deed: Empty the anal sacs") and suds the area thoroughly. Rinse thoroughly, and repeat the entire process if need be before conditioning. Then lift your dog out and put a towel over him loosely while he shakes. Your dog can get more water off by shaking than you can by toweling, so let him have at it, and then finish the job by rubbing him dry when he's done.

TIP

One of the reasons people don't like to wash their dogs is that it's messy! No matter how well-behaved your dog is and how fast you are with the towels, post-bath shaking can make a big mess of any bathroom. An alternative in many communities: Businesses that offer do-it-yourself dog bathing. They have the tubs and the water — usually elevated and warm, respectively — and will sell you soap and the use of towels if you don't bring your own. You walk out with a clean dog and leave the mess behind.

TIP

WHAT TO DO IF YOUR DOG GETS SKUNKED

Forget tomato juice. If your dog gets sprayed by a skunk, you'll want to be mixing up the miracle elixir that has people raving. No more stink, and your dog won't be pink.

Take 1 quart of 3 percent hydrogen peroxide (the ordinary stuff you can get at any grocery or drug store), ¼ cup of baking soda (sodium bicarbonate, for you science types) and 1 teaspoon of liquid soap, such as Ivory. Mix and immediately apply to the stinky pet as the solution is bubbling. Rinse thoroughly with tap water. Follow with a bath, if you like.

The solution is cheap and it really works. But it does come with a caution: You can't make up the brew in advance. The merging of the hydrogen peroxide and baking soda creates lots of oxygen in a big hurry. This chemical reaction is key to how the solution works, but it's also fierce enough to burst a closed container. So keep the ingredients on hand, but don't combine them until you need to.

If the weather is cold, keep your dog inside while he dries. With young or old dogs especially, set up a blanket or playpen by the heater or fire to make sure that they stay toasty while they dry. You can use a blow-dryer to speed up the process, but your dog would probably just as soon you didn't.

Let your dog dry while keeping him out of the yard, and he'll stay cleaner longer. And that's a bonus for you both.

Trimming toenails

Many dog owners avoid trimming toenails (but not for the same reason they ignore emptying anal sacs). Toenail trims can turn into a hard-fought war with bloody casualties on both sides. Because of that, many people leave the task of trimming nails to their groomer or veterinarian — but unless you're seeing these professionals a lot more than most people, your pet's nails aren't being trimmed often enough. Long nails can make walking uncomfortable and can even cause lameness, which is why trimming nails short — they should be just off the ground when your pet is standing — and then trimming them just a pinch every week is a better way to go.

The problem with nails is that each has a blood vessel inside. The trick is to trim to just beyond the end of this vein; if you nick it, the nail will bleed, and your dog will yelp. Everyone hits this vein on occasion, even veterinarians, which is why you should be sure to have blood-stopping powder on hand, such as Kwik Stop, before you start trimming. If your dog has light-colored toenails, the blood vessel is the pink area.

Black nails are harder to figure out, but you should be able to see the vein by shining a flashlight behind the nail. If you can't tell, just clip back a little at a time. If you draw blood, take a pinch of the powder and press it against the exposed bottom of the nail for a few seconds to stop the bleeding.

If your dog's nails are so long that they're forcing her foot out of position, you can take them back to where they should be in two ways. The first is to cut a little off them every few days: The *quick* recedes before you as you go. The second way is to have your veterinarian take them all the way back when your dog is under anesthesia, such as for a dental cleaning and scaling. After the nails are the proper length, in the front and back both, keeping them that way is easy with a weekly trim.

Whatever you do, don't ignore long nails. Long nails are one of the most often overlooked areas of basic dog care, and if you ignore them, you can cause your dog unnecessary discomfort.

If your dog's resistant to having her nails trimmed, work up to the task slowly by touching her feet, then her toes, then the nails, all while praising her for holding still. When she is used to having her feet handled, put the trimmer against the nail and praise more still. Then trim a little off, and so on. Praise and more praise! The process can take several weeks, working at it every night, but if you're patient, consistent, and persistent, you'll get there.

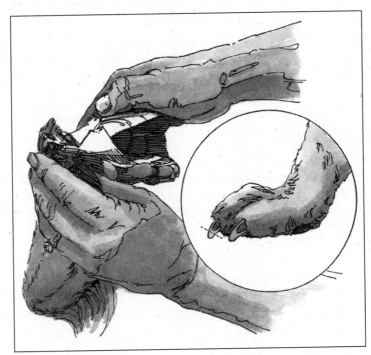

Trim the nail just beyond the quick to avoid any bleeding.

Not all dogs have *dewclaws* — a useless toe that can be found up on the inside of the leg — but for those who do, neglected nails can be a problem. They catch on things such as upholstery and can tear the toe partly off the leg, which is one reason why many breeders have them removed at birth. Keeping the nail on the dewclaw short is important, too. If dewclaws are a constant problem for your dog, discuss their removal with your veterinarian.

TIP

Another way around the Toe-Trim Wrestlerama is to try Karen Peterson's peanut butter trick. Peterson's Flat-Coated Retriever, Ciro, hates nail trims but loves peanut butter. So Peterson puts a big dollop of peanut butter on the door of her refrigerator, at Ciro's nose level. And while the dog's licking up the PB, she does his nails.

Controlling fleas

The experts say the bond with our pets was first formed over food. We had more of it than they did, and they figured if they were nice to us, we'd share. I have an alternative theory, however. Call it the *Rump Theory*, if you will.

See if this one works for you. The ancestors of our dogs figured our ancestors were their only hope to get those itchy places, which they couldn't reach on their own, scratched. Like the rump, see? It's probably no coincidence that fleas seem to prefer the spots dogs can't reach very well — above the tail, primarily. Even the most ardent attention from the sharpest human nails provides only fleeting relief during flea infestations.

Fortunately, flea control has gotten both safer and more effective in the last few years. Safer, because newer products break the flea's reproductive cycle without containing anything that can harm a dog (or person). More effective, because these products concentrate on keeping new fleas from advancing to the adult stage — where they bite.

WARNING

Fleas cause plenty of misery — not to mention annoyance to the owner who has to listen to that scratch, scratch, scratch. Some dogs are so allergic to flea bites they will tear themselves to pieces trying to satisfy the urge to itch, and even ones who aren't *that* sensitive can open up gooey patches called *hot spots* that need prompt veterinary attention.

The good news: Flea problems can be nearly eradicated by the use of spot-ons such as Advantage and Frontline. A few drops once a month is all it takes. Big difference from the years when we were told by veterinarians that every month we'd have to treat our pets, our yards, and our houses with various flea-killing concoctions. Forget sprays, powders, collars. See your veterinarian and get your pet on effective flea control.

What about a natural alternative? Electronic flea collars and various nutritional supplements such as garlic, brewer's yeast, and Vitamin B have all been touted for flea-control, but save your money. Any evidence as to their efficacy is purely anecdotal and has not stood up to scientific scrutiny. The best natural flea-control remedy on the market is already in your house: Your washing machine and vacuum cleaner. Weekly washings of pet bedding and daily vacuuming of pet sleeping areas do a great deal to help keep flea populations down.

Controlling ticks

While ticks have always been disgusting and annoying, they have been considerably more worrisome for dog owners since the discovery of Lyme disease, which affects dogs as well as humans.

While topical flea control solutions such as collars and spot-ons (liquids applied to the skin, usually between the shoulder blades) do have some effect on ticks, you'll likely still be picking them off your dog — favorite spots are behind the ears, and the places where the legs meet the body — whenever you head into tick country.

WARNING

For your own safety, *never touch a tick with your bare hand.* Instead, use a glove, tweezers, or tick remover. Grasp the body firmly, and pull with a steady motion. Wrap the ticks in tissues and flush, or drop them one by one into a small bowl of rubbing alcohol, and flush the lot when done. Don't worry if a piece of the head remains in your dog: It'll work it's way out in time — just put a little antiseptic on the spot to prevent infection. If Lyme disease is common in your area, discuss a vaccine against it with your veterinarian.

Special care for special ears

No matter what kind of dog you have, but especially if yours is of a floppy-eared variety, an important part of your weekly grooming routine should be to lift your dog's ear flaps and take a big sniff.

What are you checking for? It's hard to describe, but chances are you'll know it when you sniff it. Dogs with yeast or bacterial infections in their ears have a smell you can easily diagnose with a good sniff. All the crud in the ear will be a dead giveaway, too.

Ear infections can be very difficult to eradicate. You'll need your veterinarian's help, and you'll need plenty of patience. For more on ear problems, see Chapter 12.

If your dog's ears look and smell fine, you can help to keep them that way by regular grooming. All dogs can benefit from having the insides of their ear flaps cleaned with some rubbing alcohol or Nolvasan solution (available from your vet) on a cotton ball. Nolvasan, or a similar antiseptic product, can also be used to clear the ear canal. Fill your dog's ear with the solution, then massage the base of the ear to loosen dirt and debris. Let your dog have a good shake, and dab the ear and inner flap with a cotton ball to clean up the mess. Then do the same for the other ear.

Like nail-trims, ear cleaning may be a two-person job: one holding the dog, the other applying the cleaning solution. If you're gentle and patient, though, you should be able to get your dog to accept regular ear cleaning.

DOGGY BREATH

Controlling mouth odors is *both* a grooming and veterinary issue. Dental cleanings and scalings are an important part of preventive medicine — more on that in Chapter 11 — and keeping teeth clean between veterinary appointments is something that can, and should, be done by dog owners.

Plaque build-up on teeth causes gums to recede, opening pockets at the root line that are paradise to bacterial infections. Left unchecked, these infections can lead to tooth loss, make eating painful, and put the dog's immune system and internal organs under pressure, causing illness and premature aging. Rotting teeth and gums can become a powerful source of doggy breath — some pet owners treat this problem with products that may temporarily fix the smell, but do nothing about the real problem.

While some groomers and dog owners scale plaque themselves, this doesn't address the problem at the root line, so regular cleanings under anesthesia by a veterinarian are essential to ensure dental health. In between, attention two or three times a week with a toothbrush and a toothpaste designed for dogs slows the reformation of plaque and extends the time between dental scalings.

As with nail trimming, the key to getting a pet used to having his teeth cleaned is to take it in small steps, over time, being patient and encouraging.

Check your dog's ears weekly, and clean them out — well — monthly. If your dog's a swimmer, it wouldn't hurt to clean them out after every trip to the water — dogs get swimmer's ear, too!

WARNING

If your dog's ear is full of wax and debris, is tender to the touch, or is smelly, you need to take him in to your veterinarian for treatment. Some breeds seem to be born with ear infections — Cockers and Poodles seems especially prone, but any flop-eared dog is at high risk. Pulling excess hair from the ear canal seems to help, but it's a procedure many owners are reluctant to perform — it hurts! Ask your veterinarian or groomer to do it for you.

Don't take ear care lightly, and definitely don't ignore it altogether. Ear infections can be a source of considerable discomfort for your dog.

» **Finding the right veterinarian**

» **Understanding what's normal for your dog**

» **Recognizing an emergency**

Chapter **11**

Preventive Health Care for Puppies and Dogs

Where your dog's health is concerned, one person has the greatest impact on how long and how well your dog lives. Want to guess who that person is?

Your veterinarian, you say? Great guess, but that's not exactly right.

Make no mistake: Veterinary care is essential to your dog's well-being. You'll need a competent veterinarian, someone who cares about animals and keeps up-to-date on recent advances in veterinary medicine. You need someone who is comfortable with your dog, and with whom you are comfortable enough to ask all the questions you need to.

If the most important person when it comes to your dog's health is not a veterinarian, who is it? That's easy: It's you.

REMEMBER

You are the person who sees your dog every day, who feeds her, provides for her exercise and cleans up after her. *You* are the one who knows where she likes to sleep and how friendly she is to other animals and to people. *You* are the expert on the sound of her bark, which toys are her favorites, and the special games only the two of you know.

More than anything else, *you* are the person who knows whether anything about your dog isn't normal for her. Your powers of observation keep her healthy — and maybe save her life.

You need to be more than just a keen observer, however. Your role in keeping your dog healthy also includes at-home preventive care, as well as the important task of choosing the right veterinarian. The latter is essential, because even though you are the most important element in keeping your dog healthy, you have a partner — and that partner is your veterinarian. Choosing the right one for you and for your dog — and learning how to work with him and his staff efficiently — is essential for your pet's well-being.

Another part of preventive care is keeping your dog well-groomed and properly fed. Grooming is about more than good looks — it's another part of your dog's preventive-care regimen. For the right tools and techniques to keep your dog's coat and nails in good shape, see Chapter 10. For the lowdown on good nutrition, see Chapter 7.

Choosing a Veterinarian

If you're going to have a healthy pet, you need the help of a veterinarian. And although some people believe that these health-care professionals are pretty much interchangeable, distinguished only by convenience and price, perhaps, I've always believed that you're doing your pet a disservice if you don't put a little effort into choosing the *right* veterinarian.

To work effectively with your veterinarian, you need to develop a relationship over time so she can build a history and become familiar with you and your dog. Group practices are great — two, three, four, or more heads are often better than one when your dog is ill and the diagnosis is not immediately obvious. Within a group practice, though, working with one veterinarian as your pet's primary caregiver is best.

One of the biggest changes in veterinary medicine in the last decade is that many veterinarians who practice on their own aren't really alone anymore. With a subscription to the Internet's Veterinary Information Network (www.vin.com), a solo practitioner can be part of a group practice of more than 6,000 associates who help each other with difficult cases every day. My *Cats For Dummies* coauthor, veterinary cardiologist Dr. Paul D. Pion, is one of VIN's founders, and he's worked hard to make this service provide all the help your veterinarian needs so that she can provide the best and most up-to-date care for your dog. Ask your veterinarian if she's a VINer.

TIP

SHOULD YOUR DOG HAVE HEALTH INSURANCE?

Money is the 800-pound gorilla of veterinary medicine, looming over every suggestion a veterinarian makes and every decision a client considers. One way to tame the beast a little is to purchase health insurance for your dog.

While insurance doesn't cover preexisting conditions and has both a deductible and an annual limit on claims, the insurance can be the difference between life and death for the pet whose owner is looking at medical bills for something like cancer, which can effortlessly top the $1,000 mark and keep climbing.

With annual premiums between $100 and $200 — depending on the age of the pet — coverage could seem like a fantastic deal should a health catastrophe strike your dog. Talk to your veterinarian about insurance that could ease the bite of catastrophic health-care costs.

Your veterinarian should be technically proficient, current on the latest treatments, and willing to seek out more information on your pet's behalf or work with a veterinary specialist. She should be articulate, be able to explain what's going on with your dog in a way you can understand, and be willing to answer your questions so you can make a responsible decision on your pet's behalf. Above all, you must be able to trust your veterinarian. After all, knowing what goes on in a veterinarian's office after you leave your pet behind is impossible.

TIP

If you have any concerns, share them with your veterinarian. She will be happy to arrange a hospital tour and show you exactly how and where your dog goes when taken from you for care. Be understanding if the tour needs to be arranged. Like the ER you see on TV, things can get pretty hectic in the back areas of a veterinary hospital. The time when you ask for a tour may not be a good time.

TIP

Before you choose a veterinarian, ask friends, coworkers, and neighbors for recommendations. Over the years, animal lovers can tell which veterinarians are knowledgeable, compassionate, and hard-working. Those veterinarians are always talked up by satisfied clients. Other factors may help you narrow down your list of possibilities:

> **»** **Is the clinic or hospital conveniently located, with hours you can live with?** If you have a 9-to-5 job, a veterinarian with a 9-to-5 clinic doesn't do your pet much good. Many veterinarians are open late on at least one weeknight and for at least a half-day on Saturday, or they are willing to make other arrangements.

» **Does the veterinarian consult with veterinary college staff or independent or in-house specialists, or does she subscribe to an online veterinary service?** A willingness to discuss tough cases with colleagues is the sign of a veterinarian who's putting in effort on your pet's behalf. Online services are available the world over to assist veterinarians in getting to the bottom of a tough case.

» **What kind of emergency care is available, if any?** Although emergency veterinary clinics are prepared for any catastrophe, they are not familiar with your pet. If your veterinarian's practice does *not* offer 24-hour care, does it work with one that does?

» **Do you feel a rapport with this person? Are you comfortable asking questions? Discussing fees?** The final call on whether a particular veterinarian is right for you comes down to intangibles. If you don't feel comfortable, you're less likely to ask your veterinarian questions, and the lack of productive communication hurts your pet in the long run.

TIP

The Veterinary Information Network offers a free veterinary-referral service at www.vetquest.com. More than 25,000 veterinary practices are in the VetQuest database, and the service even shows you a street map to help you find the hospital or clinic you choose. You can search for the veterinarian nearest you, or for a specialist to suit your pet's particular health needs.

Working with Your Veterinarian

After years of listening to both pet owners and veterinarians, I've come to realize that what should be a team effort to protect and ensure the health of a pet is sometimes closer to a battle. The relationship between the client (that's you, not your dog) and the veterinarian can become adversarial if neither party respects the contributions of the other and both parties forget the reason that brought them together: helping the *patient* — in other words, your dog.

Sometimes, the task of figuring out what's wrong with a sick animal is like walking into a movie that began half an hour ago — for one brief moment you have no idea what the story's about and little chance of predicting the outcome. But given the opportunity to see a few more scenes, you start to under-stand what's going on. For the veterinarian, all too often that one glimpse is all he gets. The client wants an answer, a shot, or a pill to makes things better. He wants the problem fixed — now.

TRADITIONAL VERSUS ALTERNATIVE MEDICINE

Call it anything you like — including "Eastern" or "holistic" — alternative medicine is very hot in human medicine and, not surprisingly, in veterinary medicine as well. The growth of alternative medicine is in part a backlash against high-tech, impersonal (and expensive) care that sometimes seems more interested in the disease than in the patient, but it's also about getting back to the basics of sound preventive care. Alternative medicine includes a wide range of treatment options, from acupuncture to chiropractic to homeopathy to magnetic therapy.

In holistic medicine, the whole patient is the focus, rather than the specific disease. Traditional medicine tends to do better with acute illness, such as a bacterial infection, or with trauma, such as a broken leg. Alternative medicine's strength is in dealing with more chronic conditions that can be helped by a whole-body improvement in health.

Some traditionally trained veterinarians now embrace alternative care exclusively, and a great many others accept elements of alternative care as a complement to traditional medicine. My best advice is to seek a veterinarian who's open to using alternative approaches to problems that do not respond to traditional therapies. I'm not altogether keen on those veterinarians whose fervent embrace of alternatives sounds more like religious beliefs than medical recommendations. An open mind is a good thing in a veterinarian, no matter which side of this issue he's on!

The American Holistic Veterinary Medical Association is perhaps the best place to start finding out more about alternative veterinary medicine. You can access the AHVMA on the AltVetMed Web site (www.altvetmed.com) or contact the organization directly at 2218 Old Emmorton Road, Bel Air, MD 21015; phone 410-569-0795.

Although the client probably wants an immediate solution to his own health problems, too, he's resigned enough to say "yes" to diagnostic testing to find the right answer — as long as his medical insurance is footing the bill. Can you imagine the malpractice suits that would hit the medical doctor who didn't suggest appropriate tests in trying to diagnose a disease?

Isn't it strange that a physician who won't recommend diagnostic tests and the veterinarian who will are often criticized by their clients? What's the difference? In many cases, money.

Nearly every time, the client is footing the bill for veterinary procedures. And although veterinary costs are a small fraction of comparable procedures in human medicine, the fact that you're spending hundreds instead of thousands (or thousands instead of hundreds of thousands) of dollars isn't all that reassuring if your budget is stretched as far as it will reach. It's probably natural to wonder if everything you've agreed to on your pet's behalf is really necessary.

You and your veterinarian are on the same team — or you should be — working together to keep your dog in good health. Your dog deserves the best, and so do you. And so, too, does your veterinarian, who has spent years studying to be able to help your dog. So let him. For the good of your dog, take the time to develop a relationship with the veterinarian. You won't feel gouged and your veterinarian won't feel unappreciated if your dealings with each other aren't adversarial.

Choosing the right veterinarian is about more than price-shopping and convenience. The old saying, "You get what you pay for," very much applies to selecting a veterinarian; the lowest-priced veterinarian is not necessarily the best choice for your pet, or the most truly cost-effective.

REMEMBER

A proper diagnosis and an appropriate course of treatment are essential when your pet is ill. While learning all you can about a disease is a fantastic idea, you need to understand your limitations as a pet owner. Your veterinarian has trained for years to be able to treat your pet. No book, friend's advice, or Web site can make up for the expertise of a good veterinarian.

When Does My Dog Need a Specialist?

Although not as many specialists exist in veterinary medicine as in human medicine, they are a growing presence in the field of veterinary science. You can probably find at least a few specialists within a day's drive, and more specialists are likely to turn up in the future. Your veterinarian should be open to referring you to a specialist or consulting one on your behalf, if your pet's condition warrants it.

Although many urban areas can support independent specialists or specialty practices, in less-populated areas you're more likely to find a full complement of specialists at the closest university that has a school or college of veterinary medicine. Current companion animal specialties relevant to dogs include the following:

>> Anesthesiology

>> Behavior

>> Cardiology

>> Clinical pharmacology

>> Dentistry

- » Dermatology

- » Emergency medicine and critical care

- » Internal medicine

- » Neurology

- » Oncology

- » Ophthalmology

- » Radiology

- » Surgery

TECHNICAL STUFF

What's special about specialists? Becoming a veterinary specialist requires additional study in a two- to five-year residency program, as well as a specific examination for each specialty. The result is certification over and above that required to achieve a degree in veterinary medicine.

For veterinarians already in practice, the American Board of Veterinary Practitioners (ABVP) also offers specialty certification. This program does not require a formal residency program prior to examination but is still a very meaningful and rigorous demonstration of a veterinarian's commitment to excellence and lifelong education. Among the subspecialties of ABVP certification are companion animal practice (dog and cat), as well as avian or feline practice.

If your veterinarian doesn't suggest a referral to a specialist, and you wonder whether seeing one may help your dog, bring the idea up for discussion. If you have a good working relationship with your veterinarian, calling in a specialist is never a problem.

If your veterinarian is reluctant to refer, remember that the final decision in your dog's care is always yours. Keep the lines of communication open, though, and always be sure that your regular veterinarian is kept fully informed when you seek specialist care.

TECHNICAL STUFF

The relationship between your regular veterinarian and a specialist is a complementary one, each with respect for the skills of the other. Your veterinarian knows the specialist isn't out to steal clients, and the specialist realizes that, to get referrals, she needs to be clear on her limited role. To save time and money, your veterinarian shares your pet's medical history with the specialist and discusses your pet's case. The specialist probably requires additional tests to get the information she needs to make an accurate diagnosis and develop an appropriate course of care. A specialist doesn't practice shotgun medicine — if she's brought into the case, her purpose is to figure out exactly what's wrong, if she can, inform you and your veterinarian as to what to expect, and work with your veterinarian to do all that is possible to make your pet as comfortable as possible while working to restore your pet to health.

Two of the greatest challenges that those in veterinary medicine face are the small number of specialists and the lack of a central hospital system where practitioners have hospital rights in a facility with advanced diagnostic and treatment capabilities. This reality has created a system with many smaller, self-contained hospitals, while limiting the reach of specialists and interaction among colleagues.

Modern technology is changing the way veterinarians consult with colleagues. Members of the Veterinary Information Network (www.vin.com), for example, have access to a contingent of colleagues and online specialists, such as cardiologists and surgeons, who, although they may be thousands of miles away, can help diagnose and treat cases.

Other services accept and interpret transmitted ultrasound and radiographic images and other data. Laboratories maintain computerized databases of their animal-health records, and should your pet end up somewhere his records are not — such as at an emergency-care clinic on a holiday — the attending veterinarian can, in many cases, access recent test results for comparison and analysis. In some ways, it's a more efficient system than you'll find in human medicine!

Getting Puppies Off to a Good Start

Your puppy's first trip to the veterinarian is almost as much about educating you as checking out the puppy. Besides your many questions and concerns, you should bring two things with your puppy to the first exam. The first is whatever health information the seller or shelter provided to you, such as records of vaccinations and wormings. The second is fresh stool, which is examined for the presence of parasites.

While answering your questions, your veterinarian will likely do the following:

>> Weigh your puppy and check her temperature — 100 to 102.5 degrees Fahrenheit is normal — as well as her pulse and breathing rate.

>> Listen for heart and lung abnormalities and examine other internal organs by *palpating,* or feeling them.

>> Give your puppy's ears a going-over to ensure they not only look right but also *smell* right — no infections or parasites.

>> Check the puppy's genitals to ensure two testicles are present in males and there's no sign of discharge or infection in females.

>> Go over eyes, nose, skin, and the anal region carefully to check for discharge or other signs of disease or parasites.

>> Open the puppy's mouth to see that teeth and gums look as they should.

You'll find more on how to do basic health checks at home later in this chapter.

A puppy exam is one of the best parts of a veterinarian's job, and she works to keep it fun for the puppy as well. She wants to set up a relationship where your puppy accommodates being handled without fear or aggression. You are an important part of this learning process. Do not encourage shyness or aggression in your puppy by soothing her. Be positive and matter-of-fact in all of your pup's social interactions in order to raise a confident, secure dog.

TIP

Ask your veterinarian about *puppy plans* or other packages that save you money over purchasing services individually. Such a plan may include examinations, all shots and necessary wormings, heartworm tests, and even spaying and neutering.

WARNING

Because your puppy's immunity against disease is not yet like that of an adult dog, be sure to carry your puppy into the veterinary hospital, and don't let her interact with other dogs. Inside the exam room, the veterinary staff takes precautions to protect your pet, such as cleaning off the exam table with disinfectants and washing their hands between patients.

WARNING

MY, WHAT BIG TEETH YOU HAVE!

You will be delighted to see those sharp little puppy teeth replaced by adult teeth by the age of four months — going from 28 deciduous teeth to 42 permanent ones. But problems can occur.

Sometimes baby teeth are retained after the adult ones come in, a situation that can cause many problems, including the misalignment of permanent teeth, incorrect development of the jaw, and infections. Check your puppy's mouth weekly while adult teeth are erupting to ensure that the baby teeth aren't being retained — a double row of teeth, especially in the front, tells you that they are.

Have your veterinarian check out any suspicious developments. Retained baby teeth need to be surgically removed.

Growing up is exhausting work for a puppy, who also needs the help of a good preventivecare regimen to prepare for a healthy adulthood.

Puppy shots?

Vaccines are one of the most common reasons pets visit a veterinarian, but they're one of the least understood areas of pet health care. Most people don't even know what they're vaccinating their pets against, much less how often those vaccinations are needed. See the cheat sheet at the front of this book for some guidelines.

TECHNICAL STUFF

Puppy shots and boosters — covering five to seven diseases, depending on the part of the country and the individual veterinarian's recommendation — are weakened doses of the very diseases they protect against, and they're placed in an animal to teach the immune system to recognize and destroy a stronger attack of the disease. The system works because of *antibodies*, the body's warrior particles that surround and destroy viral and bacterial intruders.

A healthy immune system gives grown dogs a fighting chance against disease, but even seemingly strong puppies lack that ability.

TECHNICAL STUFF

Puppies are initially protected from disease by antibodies passed to them through their mother's milk. While this protection declines in the first few weeks of a puppy's life, it interferes with the preventive-care benefits provided by vaccinations. Since it's not feasible to pinpoint the moment when a vaccination will be effective, puppies are given a series of shots over the first few months of their lives. Most veterinarians now recommend a series of at least four vaccinations at three-week intervals starting at the age of 6 to 8 weeks.

Often the breeder himself gives the puppy her first shot, and your veterinarian administers the rest. Sometimes a veterinarian repeats the first shot, if she feels it has been given too early or is in doubt that the breeder correctly handled the vaccines. For your pup's sake, follow through on your veterinarian's recommendations — if you stop at just one shot, you're leaving your puppy at risk for disease.

TECHNICAL STUFF

Nearly all combination vaccines protect your dog against *distemper, hepatitis, parainfluenza,* and *parvovirus. Leptospirosis* is commonly included as well. However, this vaccine component seems to have an increased potential for side effects in some dogs. For this reason, many veterinarians leave it out of their combination vaccines, except when the patient is known to be at significant risk of exposure to this relatively uncommon disease. Depending on the risks in your area, your veterinarian may also use a product that protects against *coronavirus* and *Lyme disease.*

Parasite control

When people use the generic term *worms* in describing puppy parasites, they are usually talking about *roundworms,* or *ascarids.* That's because hardly a single puppy avoids being born infested with the pest. But puppies can also be plagued by other intestinal parasites such as *hookworms, whipworms, tapeworms,* and single-cell parasites such as *coccidia* and *giardia.*

WARNING

THE DEADLY DANGER OF RABIES

Rabies is caused by a viral infection of the nervous system. Most cases of rabies in the United States occur in wild animals. Because dogs share territory with wild animals, they're at risk of being bitten by a rabid wild animal. (Normally timid animals can become aggressive if rabid.) Most cases of rabies in dogs can be traced to skunks, foxes, raccoons, and bats, but any rabid mammal can transmit the disease.

The risk of contracting rabies from your dog is extremely small, but the disease is so deadly that, if your dog were to contract it, he would need to be humanely killed, and you would need to have a series of inoculations for your own protection.

A dog with rabies may hide, become agitated or nervous, get weak in the hindquarters, or become aggressive. Swallowing difficulties are also common. Whether he's vaccinated or not, and if you see symptoms or not, if you suspect your dog has tangled with a wild animal, contact your veterinarian and local public health officials immediately. Your life may depend on it! If your dog is current on his vaccination, he'll need to be quarantined, but if not, public health officials may require that he be killed. That's because the only way to tell for certain that an animal is rabid is to test brain tissues.

Can you possibly need any other good reasons to vaccinate your dog against this deadly, contagious disease? Don't take a chance!

Left untreated, intestinal parasites can stunt growth and weaken young animals. Worms — roundworms in particular — can present a danger to humans — especially to children, who often aren't as careful around pets as adults are. As with most diseases transmitted from animals to humans — rabies being the most deadly exception — sensible sanitary measures such as keeping pet areas picked up and hands clean minimize the risk of transmission.

The cure for intestinal parasites is easy, if a little repetitious. First, the puppy's stools are examined for signs of infestation at the veterinary hospital, and your veterinarian then prescribes the appropriate drug to kill the parasites. Puppies should be wormed every two weeks from birth on, until a fecal examination reveals no sign of parasites.

WARNING

Worming medication is available over-the-counter. The problem is, some intestinal worms and other parasites can be treated with medications available by prescription only. Treating your pet for worms he doesn't have is not a good idea; neither is mistreating him for worms he does — while thinking that the medication you've purchased is doing the job.

The only way to be sure which parasites your puppy is carrying is to have his stool examined by a veterinarian.

WARNING

The mosquito-transmitted *heartworm* is an internal parasite that's better prevented than treated, even though recent advances have made eliminating the pest safer for pets.

Puppies whose mothers were on preventive medication can continue on daily or monthly medication, starting from about the time of your puppy's first exam. The preventives often contain medications to control intestinal parasites as well. Once your pet has been started on preventive medicine from your veterinarian, a once-monthly dose for the rest of his life will keep heartworms from bedeviling your dog.

Information on controlling external parasites, such as fleas and ticks, is in Chapter 10.

Elective procedures

Depending on your pup's breed, you may also wish to discuss a few non-essential surgeries to alter your puppy's appearance.

REMEMBER

None of these procedures should be an automatic part of your puppy's first year. Consider the facts, and then make your own decision.

Tail docks and dewclaw removals

Many puppy buyers are not aware that breeds such as the Doberman or many of the terriers have their tails shortened (or *docked*) to a length dictated by their breed standard, or that the *dewclaw*, an unnecessary toe that's an evolutionary leftover, is often removed to give the leg a smoother look. If you purchase your puppy from a reputable breeder, either or both of these procedures may have already been done when the puppy was three to five days old. Some breeders are so skilled that they do the work themselves, with no apparent ill effect to the puppies, who recover quickly from the amputations.

While tail docking is sometimes performed for a medical reason, such as an injury to the tail, it is most commonly done to meet the appearance standards for the breed. Some advocates also tout the preventive value of docking, especially for hunting breeds, pointing out that a tail that isn't there is a tail that can't be injured. The logic is flawed, however: If injury prevention were the only issue, then *all* hunting breeds would be docked — and maybe all other dogs as well.

Tail dockings and dewclaw removals cause so little discomfort to three- to five-day-old puppies that they're usually performed without anesthesia. Both procedures are considerably more complicated on older dogs, however, requiring anesthesia, post-operative care, and more expense for the dog owner.

TIP

If your want your pup's tail docked and your breeder hasn't done it, be sure that your veterinarian is knowledgeable as to the correct length of tail for the breed. An incorrect dock may need to be done again, and a dock too short can take your pup out of the running if you hope to show him. If you do not intend to show your pup, I suggest that you leave his tail alone if it hasn't already been docked.

A stronger case can be made for the removal of dewclaws because injuries to them are common. It won't hurt to leave the dewclaws in place unless and until you do have a problem (these claws can occasionally get caught on objects). If you do have a problem, you can have the dewclaws removed, ideally when your pet is spayed or neutered.

Ear crops

According to reputable veterinary authorities, the only purpose of *ear cropping* is to change a folded-over ear to an erect one, for the sake of appearance. Like tail docking, ear cropping is required for the show ring in a handful of breeds. In some other breeds, cropped ears are not mandated, but the lack of them makes winning in the show ring almost impossible.

PUPPIES FIRST LEG-LIFT

Every year I get a few phone calls from puppy owners who are worried because their pet isn't lifting his leg. Male puppies start this scent-marking behavior — which some female dogs also do — as early as four months or so, but there are a lot of variables. A puppy who sees other male dogs lift their legs will likely start this behavior sooner, as may the dog who isn't neutered young.

Eventually, almost all male dogs lift their legs to leave their mark, although some are more enthusiastic about it than others. Some dogs stand on all fours to relieve themselves — leaning forward, but not really squatting as females do — and then lift their legs in a couple of places. Other dogs seem to believe that every drop of liquid they have is best deposited on a vertical object. All of this behavior is in the realm of normalcy and is nothing to worry about.

Ear cropping entails slicing an anesthetized puppy's ear flap to a shape and length preferred for the particular breed and then bandaging what's left on splints or racks to heal. This procedure is not painless by any definition, although untold thousands of dogs have come through it with no apparent long-term psychological damage.

Ear cropping is by far the most controversial of the elective procedures. Many veterinarians who have no problem with tail docks or dewclaw removals do not crop ears, and some are lobbying the American Veterinary Medical Association to condemn the procedure.

In England and Germany, ear cropping is banned as cruel. No such laws exist today in the United States and Canada. As long as the breed clubs that write the standards insist on this practice, many pet owners will follow suit.

I urge you to *not* crop your puppy's ears. Cropping is a matter of tradition and familiarity, and the more uncropped dogs are seen and loved, the more comfortable others will be with leaving their puppy's ears alone. Perhaps in time, even the breed clubs that defend ear cropping so vigorously will relax on the issue — and this senseless tradition will fade away.

WARNING

While experienced breeders can and do perform tail docks and dewclaw removals on very young puppies, under *no* condition should an ear crop be performed by anyone besides a veterinarian. Your breeder should be able to recommend a veterinarian who is knowledgeable about the look your particular breed requires, so be sure to ask her for a recommendation if you decide to have your puppy's ears cropped. Your veterinarian, too, may be able to refer you if he doesn't perform ear crops.

EARLY SPAYING AND NEUTERING

While spaying and neutering has traditionally been performed on puppies between the ages of four and six months, the procedure can be safely done at as early as eight weeks. If you adopt a puppy from an animal shelter, in fact, you may find that the operation has already been done — as a preventive measure to keep pets from reproducing. Some reputable breeders also have their pet-quality puppies spayed or neutered before they go to new homes.

What age should *your* puppy be spayed or neutered? The traditional six months is still fine. Earlier is fine, too; in fact, veterinary organizations have given their full approval to the early procedure. Some veterinarians are not comfortable operating on the youngest puppies, however, and if this is the case, follow your vet's recommendation.

The birds, the bees, and your puppy

Male dogs are early bloomers, showing signs of sexual behavior — mounting and thrusting both male and female littermates — almost as soon as they can walk. While female puppies also mount their littermates, this behavior is not as frequent or as common. While it's all perfectly normal, correct your puppy from mounting people. It's both a nuisance and a dominance challenge.

Females reach sexual maturity at different times, with small breeds attaining it more quickly than the largest ones. A dog's first *season*, or *heat* — and the accompanying vaginal bleeding — can occur anytime from about six months to 24 months, although most dogs come into season for the first time before reaching their first birthday.

The point when males become fertile is not so obvious, but they are capable of enthusiastic reproduction from about six months onward.

Don't panic if your female pup gets to her first birthday without showing signs of being in heat. Some dogs bleed very little, or they keep themselves especially clean. Chances are if you have a male dog in your house or nearby you *know* when your dog's in heat, but if that's not the case, you may miss it entirely.

Talk to your breeder about the age when most of her females come in season. If nothing has happened by the time you go in to get your pet's annual vaccinations, make a note to discuss the matter with your veterinarian.

REMEMBER

If you don't intend to show or breed your pup, you both are better off if you arrange for spaying or neutering. The surgeries are common, one-day procedures with few risks of complications in young, healthy animals. For more on these routine procedures, see Chapter 17.

Keeping Your Dog in Good Health

Once your pup grows up, you'll need to take him in annually for another of those thorough nose-to-tail veterinary check-ups and vaccinations as necessary. In between your veterinarian's evaluation, however, your dog relies on you to spot illness early.

Unlike cats and birds, who work to hide the signs of illness, your dog will likely demonstrate some clear-cut signs that he's sick. He might lose his appetite, for example, or be more clingy. Still, many pet-lovers don't recognize signs of illness that become obvious in retrospect, which is why it's important to learn what's right for your dog, and keep an eye out for anything that varies from the norm.

I learned these lessons years ago, with my very first dog. Then as now, my dogs had free access to a secure part of the yard, so they took care of their business on their own schedule. I started hearing the dog-door flap open and shut a couple times a night, but didn't take the hint that something wasn't right with my dog Lance. I finally noticed that his urine was tinged with blood. He had a tumor pressing against his bladder that eventually killed him. For a long time, I felt guilty for not having caught it earlier. Would it have made a difference? I'll never know, of course. But losing such a wonderful dog at such a young age taught me a valuable lesson I've never forgotten.

TIP

Make observing your pet a part of your everyday routine. A more thorough going-over should be on your weekly to-do list, but you don't have to make a big production out of it. Just incorporate the health check into a session that begins with petting and ends with more petting. After all, anything that you and your pet find enjoyable you continue to do on a regular basis, and routine health checks need to be regular to be useful.

The physical dog

To identify a potential health problem, you must be able to recognize what is normal for your pet. Hone your instincts and then learn to trust them! You know your dog better than anyone else, and you're the one who decides when to get help. Sometimes your dog's condition may be so serious it leaves no doubt that you need a veterinarian, but other times, changes are so subtle you could easily miss them — until your pet may be too ill to be helped.

TIP

One of the easiest ways to keep track of your dog's health is to keep a journal. A simple notebook and a few jottings are all it takes to spot some little problems before they become big ones.

If you examine your dog the same way each time, you'll be less likely to miss any problems. A list of things to check regularly should include:

>> **General appearance:** Before starting a hands-on exam, stand back and look at your pet for a few minutes. Consider his posture, activity level, gait, coat, and overall appearance for an impression of good health.

Abnormal: Exposed skin, thin or dry coat, ribs showing, sluggishness, outright limping or just lack of spring in the step, or other subtle signs you can pin down only as being "just not right."

>> **Weight:** Normal weight can be anything from three to four pounds for the smallest toy breeds to a couple hundred pounds for the largest dogs. Instead of worrying about what your dog weighs, pay attention to the fat on his body. Your dog should have enough fat to cover his ribs, but you should easily be able to feel those ribs if you press in gently with your hands. Look, too, to your dog's *waist* — that area just behind the rib cage. You should notice a definite "tuck in" at that point. It's normal for some dogs to have small seasonal changes in weight depending on their activity level — less exercise in winter, for example, may lead to an increase in size for an indoor dog. (You should try to compensate by feeding less.)

Abnormal: Too much fat or too little, and abrupt change in body type, either fatter or thinner. Swelling of the belly.

>> **Nose:** Moist and clean.

Abnormal: Dry, cracked, scabbed, or irritated; nasal discharge; or bleeding.

>> **Eyes:** Bright, moist, and clear, centered between the eyelids, with the pupils of equal size. The whites of the eye should not appear colored and should have only a few visible blood vessels. The pupils should shrink equally as bright light is shined into either eye (test this with a penlight) and enlarge if the dog is excited or scared, if the eyelids are held closed and released, or the room is darkened.

Abnormal: Eyes that are dull or sunken, that appear dry, or have thick discharge. One or both eyes not centered or pupils of unequal size. Yellow, muddy brown, or bloodshot eyes. Pupils that fail to respond or respond differently to changes in the intensity of light.

>> **Ears:** The skin should be clean, dry, smooth, and without wounds. The ear canal should be clean and almost odor free.

Abnormal: Swelling, wounds or scabs, or any sign of a rash. Crust, moisture, discharge, "crud" or strong odor in the ear canal. Pain at the touch or an unusual way of holding the head or ears.

>> **The mouth:** Your dog's teeth should be clean and white, with gums that are uniformly pink. Press on your pet's gum with your finger or thumb and release quickly. The color will become white where you pressed the gum but should return to the same color as the surrounding tissue within one or two seconds. This exercise checks the *capillary refill time,* or *CRT,* and is a crude assessment of how well the heart and circulatory system are working.

Abnormal: Loose or missing teeth, tartar (discolored, crusty buildup around the base of the teeth) or gums that are red or blue, pale, inflamed, or sore, as well as gums that recede from the tooth. A swollen tongue, lumps and bumps in the mouth, sores in the mouth, big tonsils visible at the back of the mouth. A rapid or slow CRT.

>> **Breathing:** You should find that hearing your pet breathe is difficult when he's at rest (panting is normal after exercise or in the heat), and his chest wall should move easily to and fro as he does. Most of the act of breathing should be performed by the chest wall. His abdominal (or stomach) wall should barely move.

Abnormal: Any unusual noise heard while the pet is at rest and breathing, such as crackles or wheezes, could indicate a problem, especially if you haven't noticed the sound before. Breathing that is labored and excessively involves the abdomen. Lumps, bumps, or masses on the chest and neck may also indicate a problem. (Panting is normal — it's how dogs cool themselves — but frantic panting is one of the signs your pet may be in need of emergency care for heat stress.)

>> **Abdomen:** Start just behind the ribs and gently press your hands into the abdomen. If your pet has just eaten, you may be able to feel an enlargement in the left part of the abdomen just under the ribs. Proceed toward the rear of your pet, passing your hands gently over the abdomen. You should find no lumps, bumps, or masses, and your pet should feel no discomfort as you press gently into him. Some bumps in the abdomen are normal — they're internal organs, such as the kidneys, and they belong there! Starting with a healthy dog is important, as is doing your health checks regularly, because you'll get a sense of what bumps belong there — and what do not.

Abnormal: Any lump, bump, or mass that you're not used to feeling but that is consistently present when you check. Your dog groans or has difficulty breathing as you palpate. A hard, tense, or swollen abdomen.

DOES YOUR DOG NEED SHOTS EVERY YEAR?

Up until a few years ago, annual shots were an automatic part of preventive health care for your dog. The veterinarian gave your dog a check-up, a combination vaccine, and a vaccine for rabies at the interval required by law — from one to three years, depending on the local regulation.

While the recommendations for rabies vaccines haven't changed — see the sidebar, "The deadly danger of rabies" elsewhere in this chapter — the rest of the annual shot ritual is under considerable debate. Many dog-owners, especially those who are interested in alternative or holistic veterinary medicine, prefer to check the status of their pet's immune system before revaccinating. This check is done by running a test of the animal's *titres,* or level of immunity. If the levels are adequate, vaccination can wait another year, or more. Running titres is currently more expensive than vaccinating, but the cost should come down as more people express an interest in skipping the practice of vaccinating every year. Be aware, though, that many veterinarians argue that titres do not accurately predict immunity. Keep talking to your veterinarian about how often to vaccinate and the value of titres.

If you elect to skip annual vaccinations, that doesn't get you off the hook for a yearly examination by your veterinarian. A thorough annual exam is one of the main elements of a preventive health care program.

>> **Fluid levels:** Check to ensure that your dog has enough fluids by pulling the skin just behind his shoulder blades into a tent and then releasing quickly. Your pet's skin should snap immediately back into position. Another good sign of proper hydration is that the gums just above the teeth are moist when touched.

Abnormal: The skin returns slowly or remains slightly tented. The gums are dry and tacky when touched, or the eyes have a sunken appearance.

Vital signs

Although a hands-on exam is an essential part of determining what's normal for your dog so you can spot problems early, three other diagnostic tools ought to be in every dog lover's bag of tricks: taking your dog's temperature, heart rate, and respiratory rate. This information is useful if you call your veterinarian and can help him determine whether you need to bring your pet in and what he may be facing after you get there.

REMEMBER

The time to learn how to take your pet's heart rate, respiratory rate, and temperature is *before* you're faced with a sick dog. Practice at home, whenever you and your pet are relaxed. If you're having difficulty, ask your veterinarian to demonstrate how to do these the next time you take your dog in for routine preventive care.

Here's how to perform these important skills:

» **Taking your dog's temperature:** Although you can find a special thermometer for pets in any pet-supply catalog or well-equipped pet-supply store, you can also use an ordinary glass mercury or digital-readout "people" device from your pharmacy.

If you use a people thermometer, be sure you put a piece of tape around it marked "dog" or something similar so you'll never accidentally use it on yourself. I don't care how clean it is — you won't want that thermometer in your mouth after it has been in your pet's fanny.

Lubricate the thermometer with petroleum jelly or a water-based lubricant, such as K-Y. Gently and slowly insert the thermometer about one or two inches into your dog's rectum. (If the instrument doesn't slide in easily or your dog objects, don't force it.)

Leave the thermometer in place for two minutes and then read and record the temperature. In a normal dog, the temperature should be between 100 degrees and 102.5 degrees (a little higher is fine in a normal dog on hot days), and the thermometer should be almost clean after it's removed. Call your veterinarian if your dog's temperature is below 99 degrees or above 103 degrees, or if you see evidence of mucous, blood, diarrhea, or a black, tarry stool on the thermometer.

» **Taking your dog's heart rate:** Feel your dog's heartbeat with one hand over his left side, behind the front leg. Count the number of beats in 15 seconds and multiply by four to get the heart rates in *beats per minute,* or *bpm*. A normal dog is between 80 and 140 bpm, with smaller dogs on the higher end of the scale. Call your veterinarian if your dog's heart rate is too rapid or too slow. Some irregularity in the heartbeat is normal for dogs.

» **Taking your dog's respiratory rate:** Stand back a bit and watch your dog breathe when he is relaxed and standing. Watch the abdomen and chest wall move. Often it is easier to count the respiratory rate when you watch the abdomen move. Count the number of movements in 60 seconds to get the respiratory rates in *breaths per minute*. A normal dog is between 15 and 30 breaths per minute, with small dogs on the higher end of the scale. Don't try to count the respiratory rate when your dog is hot, or excited and panting. Call your veterinarian if the dog's respiratory rate is too rapid.

You may find taking your dog's temperature and heart and respiratory rates easier if someone else holds the animal, especially if you're just learning.

If you go to the trouble of measuring temperature, heart rate, and respiratory rate, write it down in a log with the date. Compare future observations to what you measured before. Call your veterinarian if there are sudden changes or marked and gradual changes over time.

Your pet's attitude — energetic, playful, and outgoing — is one indicator of good health.

Katie/Photo courtesy of Mary Lou Kinnane

The emotional dog

You must be aware not only of your dog's body, but also of his personality. Many times, behavioral changes noticed by pet owners are later confirmed as illnesses through the use of such diagnostic tools as blood or urine tests. Again, your instincts are sometimes better than you know! Always be aware of the subtle changes in your pet's behavior, especially regarding the following areas:

>> **Changes in eating habits, especially loss of appetite:** Be aware of how much and how eagerly your dog eats and make a mental note of any changes.

A day or two without feeding is no reason for concern in an otherwise healthy dog — some dogs go off their food, especially in hot weather — but more than that is worth a call to the vet.

>> **Changes in activity level:** If a dog who's always ready to run and play suddenly would rather sleep, it's worth investigating.

>> **Changes in drinking habits:** Dogs drink more in the summer than in the winter, but even taking that into consideration, you should be aware of changes in your dog's drinking habits. Get an idea of what's a normal amount of water, and be aware of changes. You don't need to measure by the ounce: Just be aware of how often you're refilling that water bowl.

>> **Changes in voice:** Does your dog's bark sound different? Is his pattern of barking changing — is he more watchful, or less?

REMEMBER

Trust your instincts. I can't tell you how many times I've taken in an animal who was just barely getting sick — and saved money, time, and worry for myself, and suffering for my pet. I'd much rather pay for an occasional false alarm, based on being overly cautious, than miss the chance to catch a serious problem while it's still easily treated.

Emergency!

Anything is worth a call to the veterinarian if you're not sure, but some things require urgent attention. Here are some things that should have you heading for your veterinarian's — or for the emergency clinic:

>> Seizure, fainting, or collapse

>> Eye injury, no matter how mild

>> Vomiting or diarrhea, anything more than two or three times within a day or so

>> Allergic reactions, such as swelling around the face, or hives, most easily seen on the belly

>> Any suspected poisoning, including antifreeze, rodent or snail bait, or human medication

>> Snake bite

>> Thermal stress, either too cold or too hot, even if the dog seems to be recovered (the internal story could be quite different)

>> Any wound or laceration that's open and bleeding, or any animal bite

>> Trauma, such as being hit by a car, even if the dog seems fine

>> Any respiratory problem: chronic coughing, trouble breathing, or near drowning

While some problems don't classify as life-threatening, they may be causing your pet irritation and pain, and so should be taken care of without delay. Signs of pain include the following:

>> Panting

>> Labored breathing

>> Increased body temperature

>> Lethargy

>> Restlessness

>> Loss of appetite

Note: Some dogs may seek you out for reassurance; others will draw within themselves.

Giving Medication

I once asked readers to send me their best tip for sneaking pills down a pet, and the letters came in for weeks afterward. I can't imagine there's much edible that some dog lover hasn't popped a pill into, including an olive, as I recall. The most popular pill disguisers were hot dogs and peanut butter, but cheese (including canned cheese), liverwurst, and cottage cheese all got lots of votes, too.

Of course, you don't have to resort to such subterfuge if you don't want to. You can gently pry your dog's jaws apart by applying firm pressure from either side with your hand over the bridge of his nose and thumb and forefinger on either side, and then tuck the pill way, way back, at the base of the tongue, hold your dog's muzzle closed and skyward and then blow into his nose while stroking his throat.

Which is why most people use hot dogs.

If you're tentative or inexperienced, make medicating a two-person job: one to hold the dog, the other to apply medication. Some other tips include the following:

» **Liquid medication.** Ask your veterinarian for some large syringes, with the needles removed. These are marked on the sides to make measuring easy, and they're easier, too, for getting liquid medicine in the right place. Raise your dog's muzzle and lift her lip on one side. Ease the tip of the syringe to the back of the throat and then release the liquid in a slow, steady stream.

» **Ear medication.** Lay a large towel across your lap and coax your dog to put her head on top of it with gentle massage and encouragement. Apply ear drops, massaging the base of the ear gently.

» **Eye medication.** Have your pet sit between your legs and hold her muzzle up from behind. Gently apply a line of medication from the tube across the length of the eye, being careful not to touch the surface. Try to hit drops squarely in the center. Close the lid for a couple of seconds to let the medication distribute evenly.

Chapter **12**

Common Canine Health Problems

Your dog can live a longer and healthier life if you provide the benefits of preventive health care and protect him from accidents and infectious diseases. And if he does get sick, advances in veterinary medicine mean that the chances are better than ever that your veterinarian can help get your dog back to good health.

We consider our pets like family, and spend billions on them every year — and that has led to an explosion of interest in their health-care needs. Research into canine diseases is ongoing at the world's top schools and colleges of veterinary medicine, as well as at pharmaceutical companies, whose animal-health divisions have never been more active.

Then, too, the science of veterinary medicine has advanced as the diagnostic and treatment tools of human medicine have become widely available to pets. Such procedures as CAT scans, MRIs, hip replacements, and radiation therapy are now routine at veterinary colleges and specialty veterinary practices. The ranks of veterinary specialists have grown as well, bringing even more knowledge and options to dog lovers in the area of veterinary care for their pets.

What do all these advances mean for you and your pet? If you're careful to practice preventive health-care measures for your pet, and you're both lucky, you and your dog may barely be touched by the revolution in veterinary medicine. But if you need help, it's there — now more than ever, and it's getting better all the time.

Despite all the incredible advances in the diagnosis and treatment of canine illness, one of the most important elements in maintaining good health for your pet is still the laying on of hands — yours. For what you need to know to conduct an at-home examination — as well as a full discussion of other important preventive-health measures — see Chapter 11. And don't forget the importance of good nutrition! All you need to know to have your dog eat right is located in Chapter 7.

Things That Make Dogs Sick

Although I've heard that many dogs go through life without ever getting sick, no matter what they're fed or how they're cared for, I don't know anyone who has enjoyed the company of such a dog. I can guarantee I haven't had a pet like that: Over the years, the file on my pets at the veterinarian's office has grown wide enough to rival the phone books of many a good-sized town.

Everything that can go wrong with your dog may go wrong, it's true, but it's also true that some health problems are more common than others. In the rest of this chapter, I touch on some of the more common ones, and provide you with what you need to know in order to make an informed decision while working with your veterinarian.

REMEMBER

The most important role you play in keeping your dog healthy is preventive. Keep on top of the preventive-care measures your veterinarian recommends, and get into the habit of noticing changes in your dog's attitude, appearance, or behavior. For more on preventive medicine, see Chapter 11.

A few health problems are more common in older dogs, and so I've put them in the older-dog section in Chapter 13. These problems include difficulty moving and the decline of the senses, as well as dental problems brought on by neglecting your dog's teeth and gums.

Allergies

Achoo! Your dog lets fly with the sneeze of all sneezes. Does it mean that, like you, she has allergies? Typically, a dog sneezes because of an irritating smell, or in an attempt to jettison something that doesn't belong there — like the spiky seed pod of a pesky weed.

In dogs, allergies are more likely to assert themselves as skin problems. And that condition can pose a real problem for pet lovers, who see a skin eruption and often want to treat it with some cream or food additive they hope will return their pet's coat and skin to a healthy, normal state. Unfortunately, solving the problem is rarely that easy. The skin problems caused by allergies present something of a mystery to pet lovers and veterinarians alike, and it may take some time to sort out the clues and come up with the answer that will tame the allergy beast for good.

REMEMBER

A chronic skin problem cannot be fixed with guesswork and the occasional addition of a couple tablespoons of cooking oil. You'll need to work with your veterinarian on an accurate diagnosis and treatment plan to help your pet avoid the misery that can come with allergies.

Allergies in dogs are generally in response to one of three triggers:

» **Fleas.** Some dogs develop an allergy to the tiny amount of protein a flea leaves behind when it bites, triggering a bout of itching that quickly expands beyond the site of the bite. For these dogs, flea bites more than itch; they *torment*. The animals will tear at their own skin in their frantic efforts to quell the itching, making the situation even worse, often adding infection on top of the problems they already have. In the short run, a veterinarian will work to stop the itching and fight the infection, but the owner's diligence when it comes to flea control is the pet's only hope for the long-term. (Flea-control strategies are in Chapter 10.)

» **Food.** Often, a single ingredient found in dog food triggers an allergy — like beef or corn. The dog seems to itch all over, and may additionally have diarrhea or vomiting. Treating the allergy involves some educated guesswork on the part of the veterinarian and often a lot of trial and error in figuring out the source of the problem and then eliminating it from the diet for good.

» **Inhalants.** Dogs with inhalant allergies often become itchy on the front half of their bodies — rubbing their faces, chewing or licking their paws, or over-reacting to a scratch on the neck or chest. Pollen or dust can cause the problem, as can many other environmental triggers. Inhalant allergies can be some of the most difficult to pinpoint. They're also difficult to treat long-term, since eliminating the allergy triggers in the environment can be almost impossible.

Parvo and Other Nasty Viruses

The scourge known as *parvovirus* has claimed so many puppies and dogs and terrified so many dog lovers that it's sometimes hard to remember that we've been dealing with this disease for a relatively short time. The malady was first identified in 1978; it is widely considered to be a mutation of a virus that affects other animals.

Whatever its origin, parvo has been a nasty addition to the collection of things than can make dogs suddenly very, very ill — and can kill the young, the weak, or the old.

Fortunately, vaccinations provide protection against the virus, which is good news for adult dogs, but not always so hot for puppies. It takes a few weeks for a puppy's immune system to be able to protect him, leaving him especially vulnerable for attack by parvo. Once infected, some die before their owners even realize they are sick, while others come down with a high fever, violent vomiting, and bloody diarrhea. Aggressive veterinary intervention is essential, but it's no guarantee of survival.

Socialization is important for the emotional development of puppies (more about that in Chapter 9), but because of parvo, you need to be very careful when it comes to exposing your puppy to new things. Until the final series of vaccinations is in — at 16 weeks — don't take your puppy anywhere you know other dogs frequent, from parks to parking lots, and carry your pup when you must be in such a place, such as a veterinary office, to avoid physical contact with this hardy virus.

WARNING

The 16-week rule applies for most puppies, but Dobermans and Rottweilers seem especially prone to picking up parvo and should be kept from risky areas or puppy classes another month or so beyond the age of 16 weeks. Check with your veterinarian for what's best for your puppy.

Distemper is another virus that can be deadly to all dogs. We don't tend to worry about it much these days because widespread vaccination practices have limited the possibility of exposure. Pockets of distemper do pop up, though, and when it hits, it's ugly. A dog with distemper is as sick as you can possibly imagine: Difficulty breathing, seizures, diarrhea, and discharge from the eyes and nose are among the symptoms.

As with parvo, veterinary care is essential, but many dogs who contract distemper will not survive the encounter. And those who do may never be fully normal thereafter.

Distemper and parvo are among the diseases your pet is protected against by his routine vaccinations. For more on vaccines and other preventive-care strategies, see Chapter 11.

HOT SPOTS

Dogs with long hair or double coats (a fuzzy undercoat and harsh, long outercoat) are particularly prone to *hot spots*, a localized irritation that veterinarians call acute *moist dermatitis*. The problem usually starts on or near the fanny of the dog, with a minor irritation, perhaps a flea bite. The dog then attacks the spot enthusiastically, and soon the area is a gooey, infected mess.

If you catch it early enough, a hot spot can be treated at home; once it gets to the inflamed and gooey state, though, you'll need to be seeing your veterinarian.

Clip the fur away to allow air in and flood the area with an antibacterial cleanser. In some cases, giving your dog over-the-counter antihistamines such as Benadryl may help to quell the itching and encourage the dog to leave the area alone. Your veterinarian can give you an appropriate dose for these drugs, but be advised that antihistamines are not nearly as effective in dogs as they are in humans. If you have an old Elizabethan collar — a stiff plastic cone to keep dogs from chewing on themselves — from a previous vet visit, put that on your dog as well.

If you've caught the hot spot just as the dog himself started it, you may get lucky and see the area dry up quickly. If it gets worse, however, call your veterinarian without too much delay. The problem certainly isn't life-threatenting, but it's surely making your dog miserable.

Urologic Problems

The *kidneys* are the blood filters of the body. These organs help eliminate excess fluid if a dog drinks more than he needs; they retain fluid if the dog drinks less than he needs; and they eliminate waste materials from ingested food, drink, or medicine, and bodily by-products. The *bladder* stores urine until the dog is ready to eliminate it from the body. The system is not foolproof, however, and some dogs have problems, especially as they age.

Kidney problems

Kidney disease appears mostly in older dogs but is possible at any age. Initially, you may notice changes in urination or drinking (doing both more often), but as the disease progresses you may see weight loss and more severe evidence of a buildup of toxins in your dog's body, such as vomiting.

Be concerned if your dog is urinating and drinking excessively. These symptoms can mean any number of problems, including kidney disease. Observant owners may also note reduced appetite, more frequent vomiting, general weakness, and weight loss — but these symptoms are usually later-stage results of chronic kidney failure.

Some veterinary researchers have proposed that some chronic kidney problems may be caused by bacteria entering the blood of dogs whose gums are badly infected. Although the impact of an infected mouth is still under debate, research does suggest the importance of preventive dental care for your pet. For more information on preventive dental care, see Chapter 11.

Management of chronic kidney failure can include diet changes. Veterinarians have tended to advocate low-protein diets, with special attention to low salt if high blood pressure accompanies the problem. It now appears that traditional protein restriction may not be the best thing to do, so offering protein of high quality and digestibility is emphasized as perhaps a better feeding approach for dogs with kidney problems. Don't be surprised if these recommendations continue to change — such changes are part of the evolutionary nature of medicine. (See Chapter 7 for more information about nutrition.)

You need to work with your veterinarian to monitor the situation of a dog with kidney disease. Your pet will likely need regular blood tests to spot problems and changes. Your veterinarian may need to hospitalize your dog to give intravenous fluids and may even ask you to give your pet fluids under the skin at home. You can help monitor how your pet is coping with the illness by keeping a written, daily log of his attitude, appetite, and weight. This record helps you notice trends that may signal a need for additional attention from your veterinarian before the trends develop into a serious problem.

REMEMBER

Unfortunately, no true *cure* for kidney failure exists at this time. Treating kidney failure requires long-term effort on your part, and much progress has recently been made in managing this disease. Consult your veterinarian to learn the latest available options, from diet to drugs that stimulate production of red blood cells to blood pressure control to kidney transplants.

Bladder problems

The mineral deposits that, in people, become kidney stones, in dogs tend to find their way to the bladder instead. The mineral composition often varies by breed: The types of stones or crystals commonly found in Dalmatians may be different from those that plague another breed.

SMALL BEINGS, BIG PROBLEMS

Some of the deadliest things in our environment are so small you need a powerful microscope to see what they look like. Infectious agents or germs — veterinarians call them *pathogens* — are everywhere. These troublemakers can be put in three categories:

Bacteria. These one-celled life forms can be found inside and outside your pet, and most live in happy coexistence with their animal hosts. Some bacteria, called *normal bacterial flora*, are actually beneficial, serving as "squatters," keeping dangerous bacteria from settling.

Once properly diagnosed, the more dangerous bacterial infections can usually be fought with antibiotics. One thing to understand about bacteria is that they are capable of multiplying both inside a living thing and on surfaces of such things as food and water dishes, countertops, and toys. An example of a disease caused by bacterial contamination is food poisoning.

Viruses. Viruses are only "sort of" alive, and they rely on the cells of their hosts to reproduce. They vary greatly in their ability to survive outside the body of a host; some, like parvo, can survive for a long time, which is why it is important to check with your veterinarian about proper cleanup procedures before introducing a new dog or puppy into a household where another has died of an infectious disease. Antibiotics have no effect on viruses, and neither do most other medications. The scene is changing for the better, though, thanks to research into viral diseases that effect other species, such as HIV in humans and feline leukemia in cats. The fight against viruses is basically a preventive one: Some can be thwarted by vaccination, while others are best fought by preventive care — a pet in good health is more likely to withstand an assault by a virus.

Fungi. Primitive plant-like lifeforms, fungi flourish in moist, warm environments and shed spores that can be inhaled. Fungi are opportunists: They prey typically on those already weakened by disease, or with less-than-normal immune function. Long-term or inappropriate antibiotic treatment also gives them an edge, by killing healthy, normal bacteria that can keep fungal infections out. Antifungal medications, not antibiotics, are designed to fight fungal infections.

Dogs with stone or crystals will often dribble or struggle to release urine, or pass urine that has blood in it. They may also whine or cry when trying to urinate.

If left untreated, stones can block the urinary tract, a potentially life-threatening problem that requires immediate veterinary intervention. Feeding special diets, available from your veterinarian, can dissolve certain types of stones. Surgery, antibiotics, or a flushing of the urinary system may also be necessary.

Dalmatians are especially prone to certain types of bladder stones, and may need to be on a special diet for life.

Photo courtesy of Howell Book House/Winter-Churchill

Heart Disease

Heart disease is relatively common in dogs. Generally, your veterinarian detects heart disease in your dog in one of the following two ways:

>> **Hearing an abnormal sound** (a murmur or an irregular beat) with her stethoscope during a routine physical examination.

>> **Examining your dog** after you first notice your dog is slowing down, coughing, having a problem with exercise, fainting, breathing rapidly, or having trouble breathing.

What many dog owners see as a sudden change usually has been building to a noticeable state over time. This is why you'll find the information you need to take your dog's heart rate and respiratory rate in Chapter 11 — so you know what's normal and what's not before you're faced with an emergency situation.

Other signs of heart disease you may notice include:

>> **Changes in weight.** A noticeable weight gain or loss in a couple weeks' time is always a cause for concern.

>> **Not feeling well.** Sometimes, pinning down exactly what you believe is wrong with your pet is kind of hard, but often your instincts are better than you think.

If serious heart disease is found or suspected in your dog, the primary concern is to stabilize any life-threatening situations. Your veterinarian may suggest the removal of fluid from in or around the lungs by using medication or a needle and syringe.

If the situation is not as acute and you suspect heart disease — or if your dog was having trouble breathing and is now feeling better — your veterinarian is still going to want to know what's wrong with your dog. Diagnosis in such cases usually requires a good physical examination, chest radiograph (X-ray) and an echocardiogram (cardiac ultrasound). Electrocardiograms (ECG) may also be helpful, especially if an abnormal heart rhythm has been detected. In addition, your veterinarian may recommend some baseline blood and urine tests.

TIP

If you have limited funds, the most valuable money you can spend in this situation is often for the echocardiogram and an experienced veterinarian or specialist who knows how to read it.

After an accurate diagnosis is made, your veterinarian or the veterinary specialist works with you to determine the best combination of medications, diet, and monitoring that gives your dog the best chance at a long, healthy life. Nothing is guaranteed, however, and a dog with heart problems is always a candidate for serious complications or even sudden death. As difficult as this fact is to deal with, you need to be prepared.

TECHNICAL
STUFF

Heart disease in dogs is often inherited, and some breeds have more problems than others. Small-breed dogs have heart murmurs, most often caused by leaky valves, fairly commonly, while other breeds have different problems. When considering a purebred puppy, ask about congenital defects and commonly acquired problems in the breed you're considering, and don't buy a puppy of a high-risk breed unless the parents have been screened by a veterinary cardiologist for heart disease.

Tumors

Tumors are, unfortunately, a common problem for dogs. Some tumors can be ultimately fatal; others are of little concern at all.

The most important thing to remember about tumors is that you should carefully monitor your dog for lumps and bumps — he enjoys your loving rubbing, poking, and prodding, and the more you do this sort of thing, the more you get to know what's normal for your pet and what's a new growth. You should also be constantly aware of weight loss or other signs that your dog's not feeling well. At the first sign of a problem, consult your veterinarian. He will want to examine your pet and probably perform some diagnostic tests, including blood tests, radiographs (X-rays), and ultrasound. Your veteri-narian may also want to stick a tiny needle into the lump to draw out and examine its contents.

If cancer is suspected, the most important test to pursue is a biopsy.

Your veterinarian may recommend a consultation with a veterinary oncologist to assess the seriousness of the tumor and the options for care. Commonly available treatments include surgery, chemotherapy, and radiation — often a combination of treatments is used. Your veterinarian, perhaps with the help of a veterinary oncologist, can help you understand what to expect from the tumor type diagnosed.

Ear Problems

Because of their advanced auditory apparatus, our dogs have better hearing than we do. But they pay for the privilege. For the same reason humans cup their hands outside their ears when trying hard to hear a distant or soft sound, the outside of an animal's ear is designed efficiently to collect sound waves and channel them into the ear canal — along with foreign bodies and the infections that follow them. Some of the most common problems include:

>> **Ear infections.** Breeds with droopy ear flaps are more prone to infection in the ear canal than breeds where the ear canal is always open to the air. Your veterinarian will work with you to help keep your dog's ear canal clean of hair, debris, and ear wax. If you notice excessive head shaking, suspect infection or a foreign body (see below), and seek veterinary care.

>> **Foreign bodies.** Although almost any small item can — and probably has — caused problems for someone's pet, one of the most common foreign-body threats to the ear is the pointed seed pods of common weeds. Often called *foxtails*, these pods move in one direction — forward — and once in, must be removed by a veterinarian before too much damage is done. Foxtails can cause further damage by inviting infections, and the treatment will often include antibiotics for that secondary infection. A good indication of

a foxtail problem (and most other ear problems) is head-shaking, a move that only serves to drive the foxtail in deeper.

» **Aural hematoma.** The ear-shaking caused by problems inside the ear can cause a problem outside the ear, on the ear flap. A hematoma results when a blood vessel breaks in the ear flap. The flap swells noticeably, is hot to the touch, and is painful to the animal. Although the injury will eventually heal on its own, it will be a painful process and will leave the ear flap ridged and scarred permanently, a solution acceptable to few pet owners. The alternative is surgical intervention, in which the veterinarian will lance the area to relieve the pressure and let healing begin.

AN OUNCE OF PREVENTION

Veterinarians see plenty of illness that can't be prevented, but they also treat a lot of pets for problems that were completely avoidable. Few things are harder to cope with than losing a pet to an accident, for pet lovers and veterinarians alike. Here are some hazards to bear in mind:

Cars. Dogs end up in emergency clinics so frequently after tangling with a car that veterinarians even have an abbreviation for the problem: HBC, for *Hit By Car*. The best prevention: fences and leashes. Make sure your fences are solid, and don't let your dog off leash anywhere but in a safe place, such as a fenced dog park or run. *No dog is 100 percent trustworthy off-leash.* Near my house I see joggers with off-leash dogs working their way around the perimeter of a busy park, the jogging path just a few yards from the edge of a busy roadway. Believe me: It takes only one squirrel to lure even a well-trained dog into traffic. Don't risk it. Leash your dog.

Poisons. Household cleaners, pest-control products, antifreeze, prescription drugs, and even garden plants have claimed their share of pets. Read labels, store safely, and clean up spills promptly.

Heat. Dogs don't cool themselves as efficiently as we do, and they can get into a heat crisis easily. Don't exercise your dog when it's hot, and don't leave him in a confined space, such as a car.

Common sense? You bet. But I have a friend who's fond of saying that common sense is neither common nor sense, and that's certainly true when it comes to preventing accidents. Protect your dog, and if the unthinkable should happen, get him to a veterinarian right away. His life is in your hands.

Whatever the source, ear infections can be very hard to eradicate, usually because people are not good about following up. As a result, veterinarians tell me, ear infections are one of the most frustrating problems they deal with. People want to come in once with their dog, take home a prescription, give it (or give most of it) and then have the problem be gone, forever. With ear infections, however, it may take a longer course of antibiotics or a change to a different medication — and that requires more than one visit to the veterinarian. Yes, it's frustrating to be fighting a chronic problem, but it's even more difficult to be living with one the way your pet is. Be sure to follow your veterinarian's recommendation in the case of ear infections to the letter, including coming in for a recheck. I can't tell you how many dogs I've seen with painful ear infections that lasted for years, painfully, because the dogs' owners didn't recognize a problem or figured it was just normal. Things can get especially bad when an external ear canal problem is allowed to persist and progress to a middle or inner ear infection. If you've ever had an ear infection, you know how much they hurt!

Chapter **13**

Caring for an Aging Dog

People flip over puppies, but to me a well-loved older dog is one of the most beautiful beings on earth. An older dog has a nobleness about him, a look in the eyes that speaks of years of the special love only a pet can give — trusting, nonjudgmental, and unwaveringly true.

Your dog's health as he ages is not entirely in your control, but you can have a real impact on his attitude. When you see those first gray hairs appear on his muzzle, getting a little upset about them is natural. The normal lifespan of a dog isn't even remotely close to ours, after all, and those first signs of aging remind us that the years between a puppy's first gasp and the last sighing breath of a dying dog are not really that far apart.

But consider the following: Your dog doesn't know he's getting older. His gray hairs do not concern him, nor does he worry about the other visible effects of time, the thickening of his body, the thinning of his limbs. He doesn't count the number of times he can fetch a ball before tiring and compare that to his performance when he was a young dog and in his prime.

A dog lives in the now. Just as he doesn't reflect on his past, he can't imagine his future. He doesn't know his time is growing shorter, and that he'll get weaker, grow blind, perhaps, or deaf. He doesn't know that he'll die someday.

You know all of that, but this information is a secret best kept to yourself. Your dog takes his cues from you, and when you're upbeat, encouraging, and loving, he'll be at his best no matter his age. Keep your aging dog fit and healthy, and don't exclude him from your activities.

This time can be a special one for both of you, and it's up to you to make the most of it.

Dogs need love and special care to stay happy as they age.

Photograph courtesy of Gay Currier

Special Care for Seniors

Next to you, your dog's best friend as he ages should be his veterinarian. Preventive care is not only more cost-effective than crisis care, but it's also the only way to ensure that problems are caught *before* they lessen the quality of your dog's life.

I don't care if you've had such a healthy dog that you've rarely taken him to the veterinarian. Take him in for a thorough senior-dog physical when your dog hits eight or so (as early as six for giant breeds, as late as 10 for tiny ones), including whatever tests your veterinarian recommends — blood, urine, and so on. The information these tests provide can spot treatable problems early and provide baseline information against which your veterinarian can compare new data as problems develop.

I have nothing against group practices — in fact, the discussions within them can be beneficial to your pet's overall care — but for my dogs, I prefer to work with one veterinarian. Ours is in a top-notch specialty group, but he is the one we always see, because he is most familiar with my dogs, their needs, and their idiosyncrasies. This information and rapport is never more important than when you're guiding your pet through his senior years.

Nutrition

Your pet's nutritional needs change as he gets older and so, in most cases, should his food. If you have been satisfied with a particular food, you may be able to switch to the brand's formulation for older dogs. If not, your veterinarian may be able to suggest something suitable.

The biggest food-related problem for older dogs is obesity, which puts pressure on joints and internal organs that aren't able to withstand the pressure. If your pet is portly, talk to your veterinarian about safe ways to thin him down slowly. Remember that unlike us, dogs have no control over how much they eat: Your dog's weight is dependent on *your* self-control, not his. Dogs with chronic health problems may end up on a special diet available only through your veterinarian. These diets — which come in both canned and dry varieties — are formulated to address your pet's particular health needs. Some pets may not like them, especially compared to the fat- and treat-based diet they were on before, but don't sabotage your pet's care by adding goodies to the mix. A simple strained broth made from boiling chicken bones with a crushed garlic clove or two — no added salt — may make the diet more palatable. Check with your veterinarian, though, before adding anything else to a prescription diet.

For the rundown on dog food — what's in it, what your dog needs, and how to choose — see Chapter 7.

Exercise

"If you don't use it, you lose it" is true for both humans and dogs. Exercise keeps your dog's body in good condition and brightens his outlook.

The secret here is increasing the frequency and diminishing the intensity. Instead of taking your dog to the park once a week to chase tennis balls until he's exhausted, take him for a daily walk. If you are going to throw a tennis ball, keep it low to avoid leaps, twists, and hard landings, and consider walking to the park and back instead of driving. Warm-ups and cool-downs are important for older dogs, whose bodies aren't as able to withstand the pounding a younger dog endures without pause. Inactivity punctuated by bouts of overexertion isn't good for any dog, but for the older dog it can be painful or even dangerous.

PUTTING JUNIOR IN HIS PLACE

If you have an older dog and a younger one, the competition between them can be frustrating to the older dog. Here's an exercise that lets the older dog win and improves the obedience of the younger:

After your younger dog has chased a few balls to get rid of his excess energy, put him on a "Down-Stay" (see Chapter 14). If you've never tried this exercise before under such tempting conditions, leave his leash on and then stand on it. Repeat the "Stay" command and then throw the ball — a short throw — for your senior dog. Let him get the ball a few times, and then release the younger dog and praise him. Then tell them both they're wonderful.

TIP

Despite your best intentions, sometimes an older pet is going to make like a puppy and play hard. The next morning, she'll surely feel it. Give her a buffered aspirin, 5 milligrams per pound of body weight every 12 hours. If the stiffness lasts for more than a day, consult your veterinarian. If she's on other medications, check with your veterinarian first.

Walking is a good exercise for older pets; supervised swimming is another, if you have a dog who enjoys it. (Choose a lake or pool rather than a river, and keep her close to the bank.) Whatever you choose, just keep her moving, every day. Push her a little on the distance and the time, or at least try to maintain what you've got going, but don't overextend her — let her set the pace.

TIP

Think about games she can do just as well — or better! — than when she was younger. In my house, senior dog Andy no longer chases tennis balls at a gallop. Instead, I put him on "Stay," show him a toy and hide it for him to sniff out. He's so good at this game that I'm thinking of loaning him to the government to sniff out contraband. And he's so *proud* of his cleverness that watching him strut about makes me smile.

Very few dogs, even young ones, get enough exercise to keep their nails short without trimming; senior dogs never do. Arthritis and muscle stiffness makes moving around hard enough for older dogs; overgrown nails make things worse, and they're something that you have the power to fix — so do! (See Chapter 10 for tips on how to keep nails short.)

Swimming is wonderful exercise for dogs of all ages.

Lucy/Photo courtesy of Desiree Weber

Dentistry

One of the most important recent advances in the care of older dogs regards their mouths: Canine dentistry is an area of preventive care you ignore at your pet's peril.

Preventive care involves brushing your dog's teeth — two or three times a week is fine — using gauze wrapped around your finger or a toothbrush, whichever your pet tolerates best. Toothpastes made just for dogs are available, with flavors that appeal to the canine palate and ingredients that can be swallowed. (Because dogs can't spit and rinse, people toothpaste or baking soda, which is high in sodium, aren't recommended.)

Before you start your at-home regimen, your pet will likely need some help from your veterinarian. A complete dentistry under anesthesia takes 45 minutes to an hour, and involves not only cleaning and polishing the teeth, but also treating broken or rotting teeth, cavities, abscesses, and periodontal disease. This procedure is especially important if you've neglected your pet's mouth: Brushing prevents plaque from forming, but it won't help much with the muck that has already built up — and it won't fix bad teeth or infections.

Dental care is very important in older dogs. Especially small ones, who tend to have mouths crowded with teeth. Neglected mouths can make eating painful. Infections are a problem, too, and the adverse effect of bacteria from chronic mouth infections take their toll on your pet's internal organs and can overwhelm her immune system. Bacteria can even travel through the blood stream from your dog's mouth to her heart and infect her heart valves.

ANESTHESIA AND THE OLDER DOG

As common as anesthesia is in veterinary medicine, many misconceptions exist about its use where older animals are concerned. The idea that the risk of anesthesia outweighs the importance of preventive veterinary care, such as dentistry, is no longer supported by veterinary findings.

The risks can be greatly minimized by a few basic tests, including a laboratory evaluation of blood and urine, a chest X-ray, and possibly an electrocardiogram. While these tests admittedly add to the cost of a procedure, they allow your veterinarian to provide the life-enhancing and life-extending benefits of preventive care to the pets who need them most.

Your veterinarian may also recommend IV or subcutaneous fluids while your pet is under anesthesia, and, for dental procedures, pre- and post-surgical antibiotics.

No discussion of anesthetic danger can be complete without a few words on your responsibilities where anesthesia is concerned:

- Follow your veterinarian's instructions on preparing your pet for surgery. If no food is specified, then make sure that you deliver a pet with an empty stomach. Following this one piece of advice is one of the easiest and most basic ways to reduce risk. Under anesthesia, the contents of a full stomach can be inhaled into the lungs.

- Be prepared to provide special home care for your pet after surgery. Releasing animals before the preanesthetic sedation wears off is common practice. Such animals must be kept safe from hot or cold environments, because their reflexes are reduced. If you do not feel comfortable caring for a sedated pet, arrange for your veterinarian to extend the care.

- Don't hesitate to ask questions. Make sure that you understand what the procedures are and what to expect. For example, pets commonly have a cough after anesthesia, because the tube used to deliver the gas may cause some irritation. If the cough does not clear in a couple of days, call your veterinarian.

No matter what the age of the pet, chances are very high that the anesthetic will present no problem if both you and your veterinarian work to minimize the risks.

The benefits of such care extend to more than the elimination of bad breath in an older dog: Once your pet is no longer fighting infections and pain, his spirits lift along with his health — all of which can spark his appetite.

Some Common Problems

While every dog is an individual, a few age-related maladies seem to strike many of them. You should, of course, discuss how they affect your dog and the best approach to treating them with your veterinarian, but knowing a little bit about what you're dealing with before you go in is helpful.

Here are a few old-dog problems, along with some things you can do to help:

>> **Decline of the senses.** Deaf and blind dogs do just fine, as long as you do your part to keep them out of any danger their disabilities may cause. Blindness, in particular, is a problem dogs adjust to with an ease that stuns their owners. But consider the following: Dogs don't have to read the newspaper, they don't care about TV, and they count on you to read the ingredients label on a bag of kibble. Sight isn't their primary sense anyway; they put much greater stock in their sense of smell. After they learn the layout of the land, they rarely bump into things (as long as you don't keep moving the furniture). Handicapped pets should never be allowed off-leash on walks, because they can't see danger and cannot hear your warnings.

One time I had a foster dog who I suspected was totally blind, and I took her in to the veterinarian to be sure. "Wait here," he said after examining her. "I have to get a special piece of equipment." He came back with . . . a Nerf ball! He bounced it off her nose and those eyes didn't even blink. We had our answer.

Even if your older dog *is* blind (or deaf — check by clapping your hands behind his head), there *may* be something that you can do. Ask your veterinarian for a referral to a specialist like a veterinary ophthalmologist. Problems such as cataracts may be treatable with medications and surgery.

>> **Incontinence.** I get letters all the time from frustrated owners wondering why their older dogs are no longer house-trained — and how they can get them back on track. The first rule of any sudden-onset behavior problem is to make sure that it's not a health problem, and I can think of no case where this rule is more true than with an older dog who's suddenly urinating in the house. Your pet could have an infection or, if she's an older, spayed female, she may be suffering from the loss of muscle tone related to a decrease in her hormone levels. Both are treatable; see your veterinarian. At a certain age, a little dribbling of urine is practically inevitable, especially while your older dog is

sleeping. With my old dogs, I've placed old rubber-backed bathmats in their favorite sleeping areas. They catch the dribble and are easily washable, keeping odor, dampness — and flea eggs! — under control. Living with pets, like living with children, can be one big mess — literally. For tips on removing pet-specific stains from carpets and furniture, see Chapter 6.

» **Lumps and bumps.** Benign fatty tumors are common in older dogs, and the vast majority are nothing to worry about. Benign tumors are round and soft, with well-defined edges. You can usually get your fingers nearly around them, and they don't seem well-anchored. Showing them to your veterinarian for a more complete evaluation is important, and you should inform her of any changes in size or shape, especially if they happen rapidly. Your veterinarian may be concerned enough about the size, appearance, or location of a mass to suggest its removal and a biopsy; most bumps, however, are left alone. The best time to check for lumps and bumps? During regular grooming, weekly, at least. Run your hand over every inch of your dog, and don't forget to talk sweetly — she'll think it's petting.

Know your breed. Some breeds — Boxers, for one — are much more prone to cancer, and you should be more aggressive in investigating lumps and bumps. Work with your veterinarian closely to catch any problems early.

» **Stiffness.** Your veterinarian can help you determine if the stiffness is because of temporary muscle soreness — say, from overdoing it — or the onset of arthritis. Many dogs are worse in cold weather and first thing in the morning. Arthritis is common in older dogs, and while no cure exists, treatments are available that can make your pet comfortable. Your veterinarian may prescribe buffered aspirin, food supplements, or anti-inflammatory medications, all of which your pet may need to take for the rest of her life. For your part, you need to be sure that your pet is not overweight and is kept consistently, but not strenuously, active.

WARNING

Nonsteroidal anti-inflammatories — the best-known is Rimadyl — have made life bearable for tens of thousands of older dogs, but they are not without risk. Rimadyl has been implicated in the deaths of many dogs — Labradors, especially, seem to be vulnerable. Don't let these tragedies dissuade you from considering a medication that can work wonders, but do press your veterinarian to explain all the risks and benefits so you can make the best decision for your pet.

TIP

Some dogs lose strength in their hindquarters as they age or become paralyzed because of a spinal injury. This condition need not mean euthanasia. A company called K-9 Carts manufactures wheeled devices that support a pet's weight and allow him to be mobile again. For information, write to the company at P.O. Box 160639, Big Sky, MT 59716, or call 406-995-3111.

Reasonable Accommodations

Your dog has no real sense of shame or embarrassment, so she has no loss of face if you come up with some ideas to make her life a little easier. I once bought a wagon so that an older dog with bad legs could go to the park — the best part was the harness that let the younger dog pull the load! Truly, the number of ways you can give your oldster a break is limited only by your imagination. Here are a few tips to get you thinking:

>> **Beds.** Think soft. Think cushioned. Think low. Think heated. Your dog will thank you for all of these thoughts, especially in cold weather.

>> **Clothes.** Canine clothing isn't just for Poodles anymore. Older dogs, like older people, have a harder time maintaining their body temperature. This problem is even more pronounced in slender, short-coated breeds like the Greyhound or Whippet. So check out the sweater selection at your local pet-supply store, or consider altering one of your own for the task.

My favorite of these custom-designed dog-warmers was the brainchild of my friend Judy Harper, who put a worn-out sweater with the sleeves hacked off on her old Irish Setter, Shannon. "It's a fashionable Capri length," she observed. Shannon thought it was swell.

TIP

OLDER DOG VERSUS NEW PUPPY

All the trials of old age can make a dog downright cranky and make some people long to have a puppy in the house. Of course, you want to be sure that your older dog enjoys the change, or at least tolerates it. So should you add a puppy to an older dog's life?

That depends. For some older dogs, a puppy is a big boost to the senior's enthusiasm. For others, a puppy's energy and attention are enough to make an older dog want to leave home. You must determine which of these attitudes your older dog has.

In general, older dogs who are still fit and full of life probably get the most out of an addition to the household; elderly or severely debilitated dogs enjoy it least. No matter your dog's age, try to keep tabs on the interaction until you're sure how things are progressing. Don't let your older dog overextend himself, and put the puppy in his crate or behind a baby gate to give your oldster a break from time to time. Finally, save some energy and time for dog No. 1: Spend time together, just the two of you, so he realizes he is still very much loved.

>> **Dishes.** Raised food and water dishes are a kindness to tall dogs of any age, but they are especially easy on the back of an oldster. You can find them at pet-supply stores or you can make your own.

>> **Ramps and steps.** If your dogs are allowed on the couch and the bed — and mine are — you should be able to find or build something to help out the dog who can no longer make it in one jump. You wouldn't want to watch TV without your dog at your side, would you? I thought not.

Knowing When It's Time

Euthanasia, the technical term for putting a dog to sleep, is one of the hardest decisions you will ever make, and it doesn't get any easier, no matter how many times over the years you face it. Your veterinarian can offer you advice and your friends can offer you support, but no one can make the decision for you. When you live with an elderly or terminally ill pet, you look in her eyes every morning and ask yourself: Is this the day?

To know for sure is impossible.

Some owners do not wait until their pet's discomfort becomes pain and choose euthanasia much sooner than many people would. Some owners use an animal's appetite as the guide — when an old or ill animal is no longer interested in eating, they reason, he's not interested in anything at all. And some owners wait until there's no doubt the time is at hand.

Each guideline is the right one, for some dogs and some owners at some times. You do the best you can, and then you try to put the decision behind you and deal with the grief. Ironically, the incredible advances in veterinary medicine in the past couple of decades have made the decisions even more difficult for many people. Not too long ago, the best you could do for a seriously ill pet was to make her comfortable until that wasn't possible anymore. Nowadays, nearly every advantage of human medicine — from chemotherapy to pacemakers — is available to our pets.

If you can afford such care and have a realistic expectation that it will improve your pet's life — rather than simply prolong it — then it is an option that should be pursued. But let nothing push you into making a decision based on guilt or wishful thinking.

Euthanasia is a kindness extended to a treasured pet, a decision we make at a great cost to ourselves. It is a final act of love, nothing less.

Euthanasia options

Should you be with your pet at the end? What should you have done with the remains? The questions are all difficult, but no answers are wrong. As performed by a veterinarian, euthanasia is a quick and peaceful process. The animal is unconscious within seconds and dead within less than a minute; the euphemism *put to sleep* is a perfect description. Those who attend the procedure usually come away reassured that their pet felt no fear or pain.

Some people stay with a pet at the end and some don't, but no decision you make regarding the last few minutes of an animal's life will change the love you shared for the years before those final moments. If you wish to be there, then by all means stay. But leaving euthanasia to your veterinarian is no less a humane and loving gesture.

WHAT ABOUT THE REMAINS?

You can handle your pet's remains in many ways, and doing so is easier if you make your decisions beforehand. The choices include having your municipal animal-control department pick up the body, burying the pet in your backyard or at another site (where it's legal and with the land owner's permission, of course), arranging for cremation, or contracting with a pet cemetery for full services and burial. Some people even choose to have their pets preserved like hunting trophies, or have a part of them cryogenitically saved for cloning later. Again, no choice is wrong. Whatever feels right to you and comforts you best is what you should do.

The next topic is difficult, but it must be considered. If your pet dies unexpectedly or while under the care of your veterinarian, and there is any question as to the cause of death or your veterinarian believes there are lessons to be learned by performing a postmortem examination, I encourage you to agree. This may not help your dog but it may very well help hundreds or thousands of others. What better way to demonstrate your love of your dog than to assist in the advancement of care for other pets with similar health problems?

Call ahead to set the appointment, and make it clear to the receptionist what you're coming for. (Your crying might tip her off, anyway.) That way, the practice can ensure that you don't have to sit in the waiting room but can instead be immediately ushered into an exam room, if you choose to remain with your dog. Your veterinarian will do his best to be sure that all your questions are answered and that you are comfortable with everything before proceeding. He may clip the fur on your dog's foreleg to have easier and quicker access to the vein for the injection of the euthanizing agent; he may also choose to presedate your pet. Remember: Crying is normal, and your veterinarian will understand. So, too, I believe, will your pet. I always hold my hand near my dog's nose, so the last breath will have my scent in it; I don't know if it eases my pet's mind, but I do know it eases mine.

You may wish to spend a few minutes with your pet afterward, and your veterinarian understands that, as well, and will give you all the time you need alone to begin the process of coming to grips with your loss.

You may be more comfortable with having your pet euthanized at home. If this is your wish, discuss the matter with your veterinarian directly. Many vets extend this special service to long-time clients. If yours doesn't, you may alternately consider making arrangements with a mobile veterinarian.

TIP

Several manufacturers offer markers for your yard to memorialize your pet; they are often advertised in the back of magazines like *Dog Fancy*. Other choices include large rocks or slabs of stone, or a tree or rose bush. Even if you choose not to have your pet's body or ashes returned, placing a memorial in a special spot may soothe you.

Another way to celebrate the memory of your dog is to make a donation to your local humane society, regional school of veterinary medicine, or other favorite animal charity. A donation in a beloved pet's name is a wonderful thing to do for a friend who has lost a pet as well.

YOU'RE NOT ALONE

You may find talking to others about your pet's death helpful. Ask your veterinarian about pet-loss support groups. Almost unheard of a couple decades ago, such groups are available in many communities today. You may also want to see a counselor; this, too, can be helpful.

Veterinary schools and colleges have been among the leaders in creating programs to help pet lovers deal with loss. A handful now operate pet-loss hot lines staffed by veterinary students trained to answer questions, offer materials that may help you (including guidelines for helping children with loss), and just plain listen. These are wonderful programs, and they're free for the cost of the call. (If you call during off hours, they call you back, collect.)

Locations, operating hours, and phone numbers of pet-loss hot lines are as follows:

Cornell University
College of Veterinary Medicine
Ithaca, New York
Hours of operation: 6 to 9 p.m. eastern time, Tuesdays through Thursdays
607-253-3932

Iowa State University
College of Veterinary Medicine
Ames, Iowa
Hours of operation: 6 to 9 p.m. central time, Monday through Friday
888-478-7574

Michigan State University
College of Veterinary Medicine
East Lansing, Michigan
Hours of operation: 6:30 to 9:30 p.m. eastern time, Tuesday, Wednesday, and Thursday
517-432-2696

Ohio State University
College of Veterinary Medicine
Columbus, Ohio
Hours of operation: 6:30 to 9:30 p.m. eastern time, Monday, Wednesday, and Friday
614-292-1823

Tufts University
School of Veterinary Medicine
North Grafton, Massachusetts
Hours of operation: 6 to 9 p.m. eastern time, Monday though Friday
508-839-7966

Virginia-Maryland Regional College of Veterinary Medicine
Blacksburg, Virginia
Hours of operation: 6 to 9 p.m. eastern time, Tuesday and Thursday; calls referred to Ohio State when school is out
540-231-8038

(continued)

(continued)

Washington State University
College of Veterinary Medicine
Pullman, Washington
Hours of operation: 6:30 to 9 p.m. Pacific time, Mondays through Thursdays; 1 to 3 p.m. Saturdays
509-335-5704

University of California
School of Veterinary Medicine
Davis, California
Hours of operation: 6:30 to 9:30 p.m. Pacific time, Mondays through Fridays; Tuesdays through Thursdays during summer
530-752-4200

University of Florida
College of Veterinary Medicine
Gainesville, Florida
Hours of operation: 7 to 9 p.m. eastern time, Mondays through Fridays
352-392-4700, ext. 4080

University of Illinois at Urbana Champaign
College of Veterinary Medicine
Urbana, Illinois
Hours of operation: 7 to 9 p.m. central time, Tuesday, Thursday, and Sunday
217-244-2273

Dealing with loss

Many people are surprised at the powerful emotions that erupt after a pet's death, and they are embarrassed by their grief. Remembering that pets have meaning in our lives beyond the love we feel for the animal alone may help. Often, we don't realize that we are grieving not only for the pet we loved, but also for the special time the animal represented. When a friend of mine lost her very special German Shepherd, her grief was a double-whammy: The dog had been given to her as a puppy by her father, not long before he died of cancer. Suddenly, she was grieving for them both.

Taking care of yourself is important at this difficult time. Some people — the "it's just an animal" crowd — will not understand your feelings and will shrug off your grief as foolish. The company of other animal lovers is very important. Seek them out to share your feelings. In some areas, pet-loss support groups may be available. The Internet offers another alternative: Search for "pet loss" to come up with sites that can help. And don't forget pet-loss hotlines: I've included a list in this chapter.

A difficult time, no doubt, but remember: In time, the memories become a source of pleasure, not pain. There is no set timetable, but it happens. I promise.

TIP

A handful of books and one really fine video may help you help your child with the loss of a pet. From Fred Rogers (yes, Mr. Rogers of the Neighborhood) comes the book *When a Pet Dies* (Putnam) and the video *Death of a Goldfish*. Rachel Biale's *My Pet Died* (Tricycle Press) not only helps children cope better, by giving them pages to fill in, but also offers parents advice in special pages that can be torn out. Finally, Judith Viorst's *The Tenth Good Thing About Barney* (Aladdin) is a book that experts in pet loss have been recommending for years.

What if You Go First?

First things first: You can't leave your estate to your dog, because in the eyes of the law, an animal is an it, with little more legal status than a chair. Nor can you set up a trust for your pet for the same reason. The beneficiary of a trust must be a bona fide human being, and the fact that you think of your dog as a person does-n't really matter, because the courts don't.

Although you, of course, should discuss this matter with your attorney, talking it over with your friends and family is even more important, because finding one of them whom you trust to care for your pet after you're gone is what you must do. You must leave your canine "property" to that person, along with enough money to provide for the animal's care for life. You have no real control over the outcome, which is why you need to choose someone you trust and then hope for your dog's sake that things turn out okay.

No one likes to think about dying. But you have a responsibility to those you leave behind, and that includes your pets. Talk to your friends, family, and even your veterinarian. Call an attorney. Don't rely on the kindness of strangers to care for your pet if something happens to you. Your dog deserves better than that.

The Association of the Bar of New York City offers a low-cost pamphlet on provid-ing for your pet when you no longer can take care of her. To order "Providing for Your Pets in the Event of Your Death or Hospitalization," send a $2 money order or check made out to the Association of the Bar and a self-addressed, stamped, legal-size envelope to the association's Office of Communications, 42 W. 44th St., New York, NY 10036.

4

Living Happily with Your Dog

IN THIS PART . . .

Everyone wants a well-mannered dog, and in this part you find the tools you need to train your dog right, with not only the basic parts of dog obedience — "Sit," "Down," "Stay" — but also some other behaviors that will just plain make your life with your dog easier. And what about behavior problems: digging, barking, and so on? Here, you find a strategy for turning the situation around, making both you and your dog happier as a result. You also find what you need to know about breeding your dog. And finally, you get lots of ideas on how to have fun with your pet in the chapters on dog sports and traveling.

Chapter 14

Teaching Your Dog Manners

An old dog-training adage still applies today: *Every handler gets the dog he deserves.*

In other words, the most important factor in training is not your dog, but *you*. You're the leader — or you should be — and you need to know enough about canine language so you can teach your dog *your* language. You need to show your dog what you want her to do and give her a reason for doing it — and an understanding that not doing the very reasonable things you ask of her is unacceptable.

Your dog gets trained, whether you do anything or not. If you don't guide her toward good behaviors, and praise her when she accomplishes them, she will fill her life with behaviors you don't like. If you don't lead, she will. And that's bad news for a dog. Shelters, rescue groups, and newspaper classifieds have plenty of dogs like that: dogs with problems. Their chances of finding happiness — or even staying alive — aren't very good at all.

That's not the way things have to be.

REMEMBER

Resolve that you *must* train your dog, and that training is not a one-shot deal, but an intrinsic and ongoing part of the promise you make to your dog when you bring her into your life.

Then, think of the rewards of dog training. The obvious reward is good manners, but the bigger payoff is that as you train your own dog, the bond between you and your dog grows stronger, the love deeper.

The special relationship between an owner and a well-mannered dog is the Total Dog Experience, and I don't want either one of you to miss it.

I show you the importance of socialization and early training for puppies in Chapter 9. House-training solutions are in Chapter 8, and help with fixing other annoying behaviors is in Chapter 15.

A Few Words about Aggression

If you have ever, even for a moment, been afraid of your dog or what he may do, read the rest of this segment carefully and then put the book down, for now. The rest of this chapter and the next is not for you. Not yet, anyway. You need serious one-on-one help, whether you realize it or not.

Aggression in dogs has both genetic factors and learned ones. Some dogs are born with the potential to be aggressive, and that potential can be fully realized in a home that either encourages aggressive behavior or is ill-equipped to cope with it. Other perfectly nice dogs can become unreliable because of abusive treatment.

Is your dog potentially dangerous? Answer these questions, and be brutally honest:

>> **Has your dog ever stared you down?** I'm not talking about a loving gaze — my dogs hold those for minutes at a time. I'm talking about a hard, fixed, glassy-eyed stare that may be accompanied by erect body posture — stiff legs, ears forward, hackles raised.

>> **Do you avoid doing certain things with your dog because they elicit growling or a show of teeth?** Are you unable, for example, to approach your dog while he's eating or ask him to get off the couch?

>> **Do you make excuses for his aggressive behavior, or figure he'll grow out of it?** Or do you think a growling puppy is cute?

>> **Do you consider your dog safe — *except* around a particular group of people, such as children?** When he growls at the veterinarian, do you tell yourself the behavior is reasonable, and a veterinarian should be able to cope with it, after all?

>> **Has your dog ever bitten anyone, even only once, because it was an accident, he was scared, even though he's usually so good, or some other equally inexcusable rationalization?** People often make excuses for the behavior of little dogs, but growling and snapping is no more acceptable from a Pomeranian than from a Pit Bull.

WARNING

If, after answering these questions, you suspect that you have a problem, get help. *Now.* You should no more attempt to cure aggression yourself than you should try to treat cancer. The reason is the same: You haven't the training and the expertise to do so. If you suddenly try to eliminate your dog's self-appointed role of leader of your pack, there'll be trouble. If you even attempt to make eye contact with such a dog, you may get bitten. So don't.

Ask your veterinarian for a referral to a trainer or behaviorist with experience handling aggressive dogs. And realize from the start that, just like cancer, aggression is a disease that is sometimes not curable. Have your dog neutered — most dogs involved in attacks are young, unneutered males — and follow the expert's advice. But if, in the end, you have a dog who still cannot be trusted, have him euthanized. I'm sorry if that upsets you, but this is the only responsible thing to do. If your dog is aggressive, he'll probably end up euthanized eventually. The difference is that if you wait, someone will get hurt first.

REMEMBER

Finding an aggressive dog a new home — one with no children, perhaps — is not the answer. Children are everywhere, and you may be responsible for one of them being hurt if you pass a problem dog on to someone else. Especially if you do so without admitting the real reason you're finding him a new home, knowing that no one wants to adopt a biter. You do the dog no kindness, and you put the new family at risk.

Maybe you prefer to live in a state of denial, hoping nothing awful involving your dog will ever happen. More than 4.5 million American dog owners are jolted into reality every year — 4.5 million being the number of bites estimated by the U.S. Centers for Disease Control and Prevention. Of those attacks, 800,000 required medical treatment in 1994 — and 15 were fatal. Children were the most frequent victims.

Need more reasons to act? You could lose your homeowners insurance — or more. U.S. insurance companies shell out more than $1 billion a year to settle dog-bite liability claims. The companies say claims are rising both in number and value. Even one "minor" bite claim could cost you your homeowner's insurance — and a vicious attack could cost you a lot more than that.

Aggressive behavior never improves on its own. It only gets worse. So get help. Now.

Developing the Right Attitude toward Training

If you don't have an aggressive dog, consider yourself lucky. Chances are, though, you probably have a dog who's a little out of control. One who drives you just a little bit crazy. A canine adolescent, more often than not. You've given up waiting for her to outgrow her bad behavior — they never do! — and figure it's finally time to . . . (big sigh) . . . train her. You're thinking you can't avoid training; it just has to be done, like cleaning leaves out of the rain gutters.

Stop!

Now, consider the following: If you have a bad attitude toward training, so, too, will your dog. If you think training is a joyless chore, she'll hate it, every minute. If you walk around jerking on her collar and swearing, she'll wonder what she's done to deserve your anger, and she'll be too busy worrying about that to learn anything.

If you tell her she's stupid, she will be.

REMEMBER

Expect success from her and be willing to work for it. Praise her not only for succeeding, but for trying. Learning is hard for her, and stressful. Think of your dog as a person who has just moved to your house from a country where the language and customs are different — a trans-species exchange student. She was born, after all, a dog, and you're asking her to live as a member of a human family. You're asking her to learn the language and follow the rules.

The fact that this feat is ever accomplished at all is nothing less than a miracle. So celebrate it. With her.

Consider dog training not as a mechanical thing — if you do X, your dog does Y — but rather as something organic — alive, interconnected, and ever-changing. A well-mannered dog becomes that way from the inside out. "Sit" and "Stay" are the least of it, really, and are only the visible manifestations of what that dog is on the inside: a confident, comfortable, and secure member of a loving, human pack. A dog who is, quite simply, a joy to live with.

WARNING

We all get cranky sometimes. If you've had a horrid day at work, a fight with your spouse, or the mechanic just told you the cost to fix your car is $2,700, you're probably better off skipping any efforts at teaching your dog something new. Instead, use your dog to help you ease out of your funk: Play fetch, or just hang out with her. Pet her while you watch TV — it's good for your blood pressure.

Likewise, if you start out a training session fine and feel yourself getting frustrated and angry, don't push things. End on a positive note. Ask your dog for something you know she knows well and, when she does it, praise her. Then call it a day. If you can't manage even that, just stop before you both get even more frustrated.

In either case, remember: Tomorrow is another day.

DOG FIGHT!

Anyone who has ever walked a dog has experienced that terrifying moment when a vicious, unleashed dog is intent on doing harm to your dog. It's a dangerous situation, even for owners of big dogs; for small dogs, it could be a fatal encounter.

With male dogs, one thing that can help keep your dog out of fights is to get your dog neutered. Even if your dog is a cupcake, there will always be one dominant unneutered male who takes your dog's very presence as an insult to his masculinity. If *your dog* is neutered, this particular fight trigger is usually not an issue.

You should always try to avoid dogs who appear aggressive — those with erect body stances instead of the relaxed, ears back attitude of a dog coming over to play — but sometimes there's no escape from a dominant dog.

If the other dog's owner is nearby, demand he put his canine terrorist on leash. Should he be clueless enough to say "mine's friendly," yell back "mine's not" and make your demand again.

If a fight starts, stay out of it. You could be badly hurt. If you're willing to risk a bite and there's another person to help, pull the dogs apart by their tails — not their collars! If you're alone and there's a hose nearby, hitting them in the chops with a high-volume water spray usually stops the action.

If your own dogs are constantly fighting, call a trainer or behaviorist to help you develop strategies to make it clear you require your dogs to get along. Realize, however, that peace might never be possible, and you may have to find a new home for one of the dogs.

Keys to Success

Ask a person who has never owned or trained a dog to teach one to sit and I bet he can come up with a successful plan without any prompting. Hold the front end up, push the back end down while saying the command word of choice — "Sit," "Plant it," or even "Keyboard," as long as you're consistent. The mechanics of training aren't that hard to understand. But to get your dog to mind you consistently and happily, you're going to need to know a little more.

Dog training is not about eight Thursday-night group classes and the training is over, forever. The training is *never* over. You teach, and then you practice, in ever more challenging circumstances. You correct or ignore the behavior you don't want. And you integrate your dog's lessons into everyday life so that the lessons are never, ever lost. Remember the French you learned in high school? How good are you at it now? If you don't use it, you lose it, and the same can be said of skills you teach your dog.

After he knows the language, keep asking him to use it. Following are some tips that will help both of you.

Be on the same team

Don't think of training your dog as a you versus your dog endeavor. Think, instead, about the two of you being on the same team, albeit in different positions. Consider yourself the quarterback, if you like: You call the plays. Maybe you've noticed that the quarterback doesn't get very far without folks to follow those plays. Winning is a team effort.

Of course, your dog has to learn the plays first, and you're the one to teach him. But this relationship is still not an adversarial one. You show your dog the things he needs to learn, and you do so with love and respect, which your dog will return in kind.

To bring your dog onto your team and show him the plays you'll be calling, you need to spend time with him. Bring him into your life. Let him sleep in your bedroom and practice his "Sits" in the kitchen. The more opportunities for interaction and practice you have, the faster and more reliably your dog performs.

Be positive

This tip goes back to having the right attitude, of course, but it's more than that. Rewards — treats and praise — that are well timed and appropriate are essential to your dog's learning process. If all you ever do is tell your dog "no," your relationship isn't going to be a very good one. How would you like to work with a boss like that?

In particular, praise is cheap — free, in fact! — so use it, lots. Use praise when your dog tries to get it right. Use it more when your dog succeeds. Use it when your dog just pays attention to you, because as you find out in a moment, that's the first step in the training. You don't have to be some gushing goof, but you *do* need to let your dog know when you're proud of her.

Be fair with corrections

Make sure your dog understands what you want before you correct him for not doing it. And let the punishment fit the crime.

A correction should *not* be a release of anger, a clearing out of pent-up feelings by unloading them on the apparent cause of the problem, your dog. Instead, a correction is another way to communicate with your dog, to foster in him a clear understanding of his place in your human pack. As such, a proper correction is another way to strengthen the bond between you and your pet.

A correction can be the absence of praise, the denial of attention, or a sharp rebuke. I want you to remember to always ask yourself if you're being fair before you give in to a desire to respond negatively toward your dog. A correction is a tool, one of many in the trainer's kit. It's not about anger or revenge. Negative reinforcement needs to be used selectively, and always fairly. You should never punish a dog for something he didn't know was wrong.

Be consistent

How would you do in your job if your boss kept changing the names of your tasks or asked you to do two things at once? Or had different rules for different places and times? It would drive you nuts, wouldn't it? And yet, that's exactly what people do to their dogs, all of the time. Here are some things to think about:

>> **Training consistency.** Two things to remember: After your dog knows a command, and demonstrates that knowledge consistently, use it the same way each time and never change its meaning. The most common of these is probably saying "sit *down*" to a dog when you really mean "Sit." Now, you know when someone says "sit down" to you, it's the same thing as "Sit." But if you teach your dog "Sit" and "Down" as two separate commands, you can understand why it's confusing. Which do you want?

Same for saying "Down" when you really mean "Off." I was visiting someone once when her Cocker Spaniel jumped on the couch beside me. "Down!" commanded her owner, and the dog laid down beside me. "She's so *willful*," said the woman, who didn't realize the dog had in fact obeyed her perfectly.

» **Situational consistency.** Some dogs start to recognize situations where ordinary rules don't apply. They learn, for example, that when you're in a hurry you'll shrug off disobedience: You're in a rush to feed your dog, for example, and when you say "Sit," he doesn't. And you throw the food down anyway.

If "Sit" doesn't always mean "Sit," eventually it will never mean "Sit." Teach your dog that "Sit" means "Sit," no matter where or when you request the behavior.

Another kind of inconsistency is when you never expect your dog to mind until you've repeated the command a few times. After a dog knows a command, follow through in having her perform the behavior. Then praise!

PHONE CALL FOLLIES

I got a call once from a person who worked as an order-taker for a catalog company, and he wanted the answer to something that had been driving him crazy: Why do dogs bark when their owners are on the phone?

Because you teach them to, that's why.

The problem starts when a dog barks at you once when you're on the phone. If he did that while you were home, by yourself, watching TV, you'd likely not reward the behavior — you'd ignore it or correct it. But you don't want to do that when you're on the phone — you're busy, after all, and you don't want the person on the other end to think a) you have a bad dog or b) you're a mean person. So instead, you pet your dog to shut him up.

Before too long, you have a dog who starts yapping every time you pick up the phone — you've inadvertently taught him to do so! I have one friend who took this a step further. She discovered that if she gave her dogs treats while on the phone she could get them to be quiet for the time it took them to crunch the treats up. What she didn't realize was that she was rewarding them big time for a behavior she didn't like. Soon, she couldn't have a phone conversation without a box of dog cookies beside her. Talking to her on the phone involved listening to high-pitched, demanding barks punctuated by sounds of crunching. And her dogs became butterballs very quickly!

On behalf of catalog order-takers everywhere, don't let this happen to you and your pet. Arrange to have some friends call you expressly for the purpose of convincing your dog he's expected to behave no matter what you're doing. Show him the meaning of consistency while you chat.

Build on your successes

Dog training succeeds by degrees and creativity. You continue to expand the length of time and the number of situations in which your dog will execute a command, and you look for new ways to use what he knows so you can continue to develop and strengthen the bond between you.

The half-hour "Down-Stay," for example, is great for reinforcing your position as leader. With just a couple of words and no more effort than it takes to watch TV — which you can certainly do during that half-hour — your dog will spend a pretty solid chunk of time reflecting on your status as a god. A reasonable and loving god, but still a deity, and don't you forget it, furball. What else does he have to do, after all? He's stuck there until you say otherwise.

"My dog would *never* sit for thirty minutes." Not today, he won't. First he has to learn "Down." Then he has to learn "Stay." Then he has to learn to do both for one minute, then five, then fifteen, and so on. And he has to learn that if the phone rings he can't move. If you leave and return, he can't move. If you sing, he can't move. This behavior is taught step-by-step, over time.

So build. A little bit at a time, celebrating every step along the way. Living is learning, and learning is good.

TECHNICAL STUFF

What good is the half-hour "Down-Stay"? Think of it not as some draconian measure but instead as canine meditation. Your dog will *not* be uncomfortable, and you are *not* being unreasonable. During that time you've asked him to "Stay," the one topic he's meditating about is your status as leader of his pack, and that's exactly what you want him to be thinking — that you're the boss. A nice boss, a reasonable boss, but a boss nonetheless. The half-hour "Down-Stay" helps to build an obedient dog from the inside out, and complements all your other efforts to teach your dog good manners.

Tools for Teaching

Dog training isn't expensive, or it needn't be. You need a leash, some treats, and a properly fitted collar, but the other things you need are free for the asking. The trick is knowing what they are, how they work, and when to use them.

A six-foot lead you can handle easily — leather or nylon, neither too wide nor too thin — is a must, as is a collar that is properly fitted and put on.

Some trainers recommend a slip-chain collar for training; others prefer a flat collar, a head halter, or even a prong collar. All of these pieces of equipment are right for some dogs and some people in some training situations. Start with what's easiest on you and the dog — a head halter or a flat collar, and focus on teaching, not forcing. Slip collars are less in favor these days because they're often put on incorrectly — choking the dog, instead of correcting him — and because the collars are difficult for most novice dog-trainers to use properly. If you use a slip collar, you must keep the chain loose, except for the split second when it tightens and releases to correct your dog.

In practical terms, a head halter or flat collar — or even a prong collar — is easier for a novice trainer to use properly than is a slip collar, and as a result, all of them are more reliable training tools than the slip collar. I don't recommend a slip collar unless you're working with a trainer who can help you to use it properly.

Getting your dog's attention

You're not going to be able to teach your dog anything if you can't get his attention. One of the best ways to do so is to teach him to give you eye contact at your request.

Eye contact is one of the most important areas of communication for dogs, and mastering eye contact, dog-style, immediately strengthens your relationship. Catch your dog's eye by swooping your hand under his chin, bringing your fingers back up near your eyes while you make a clucking noise, and saying his name, followed by "Look" or "Watch." The motion upward and the sound orients your dog's eyes up so that he's looking right into your own. When they lock in, hold for a split second, smile, and praise. This command may take time to learn, because dogs avoid eye contact to show respect. Build up your time until your dog gives and holds eye contact until you release him. Practice this several times a day and always be loving and encouraging.

As your dog learns to respect and trust you more, you find that he looks at you more. He wants to see what you're doing, because you're where the action is.

TECHNICAL STUFF

Some dogs get a little bit carried away with this devotion thing, to the point where it becomes a way of controlling *you*. The phone follies dogs are like that (see the sidebar "Phone call follies"). If your dog is becoming an attention addict, give him something to do to earn your praise — ideally, a half-hour "Down-Stay" on the other side of the room. Think of this activity as tough love, if you will, but it's better than spending the rest of your life unable to read your newspaper because your love-junkie dog is sticking his nose through it.

Your dog should know his name not as a command to go to you or as a swear word but as a request for his attention. Praise him for looking at you when you use his name, and then build on that to help get his attention before giving a command. If you're doing your eye-contact exercises, he'll start looking at you at the sound of his name, before he even hears "Look." Praise him! Eventually you won't even have to give the "Look" command. The sequence will be: "Bosco (not yelled, but clear and encouraging) . . ." and then a slight pause, and then the command. Finish with praise, always.

TIP

ON THE CUTTING EDGE: CLICKER TRAINING

One of the most exciting developments in dog training in recent years has been the widespread use of a little piece of plastic and metal known as a *clicker* (or sometimes a *cricket*). The clicker brings classic operant conditioning to dog training, and first became known for training dolphins and whales for those popular shows at marine parks.

Consider the dolphin, if you will. You can't put a leash on him, and he's really too big — and too slippery — to force him into doing what you want to do. (Trying to wrestle in the water with an orca would be even harder, and dangerous too!) So trainers had to come up with a way to communicate, to shape behavior in a nonphysical way. Enter the clicker.

Trainers — dog and dolphin alike — begin by associating the sound of the clicker with the reward: Fish in the case of dolphins, a dog treat for a canine pupil. Soon the animal understands that the clicker — which is easier to time properly than verbal praise — means they did right, and that they've earned a reward. This technique is especially good for shaping complex behaviors — in the obedience ring, for example, where high-scoring dogs must not only sit, but sit square on their haunches and in proper position relative to their handlers to get a high score.

This level of precision is attained by shaping the behavior. The dog gets a click and treat for sitting, and when that's mastered, the trainer waits to click/treat until the dog offers a behavior that's just a tiny bit closer to the goal, and then a tiny bit more, and so on. Soon the dog is being clicked/treated for the perfect position only.

Clicker training is fun for both owner and dog — and it works on any animal! My colleague Steve Dale, who writes a column for Tribune Media, trained his cat to play a toy piano by shaping the animal's behavior with a clicker and treats!

If you have a click trainer in your area, take a class — you'll enjoy it! If not, the best selection of books on clicker training can be found at the Dogwise Web site, www.dogwise.com.

One thing for sure: You'll be hearing more about clicker training for dogs in the future, and more trainers will be switching over to this novel way to train.

Giving praise

All praise is good, but praise specially tailored to connect with the dog's way of reacting is ten times as effective. Here are some tips:

Teaching your dog to make eye contact is one of the first steps in training him.

>> **Use the right tone of voice.** Dogs communicate with one another through sounds easily duplicated by humans. If you're angry with your dog, for example, dropping your voice to a low rumble closely approximates the growling of a dog. For praise, use a sweet, high-pitched crooning voice: "Gooooooooood, dooooogggg. Aaaren't youuuu a gooood doooog?"

>> **Tailor your petting style to your dog.** Some dogs go crazy when petted; others hardly notice. Use a little chest pat or scratch for those who tend to be overly enthusiastic, and be a little more boisterous for the ones who really warm to being jollied. Don't let the dog use petting as an excuse to go crazy — lighten up on the pats, but don't correct him — and let your voice do most of the praising.

>> **Smile!** Dogs understand many of our facial expressions because they use similar ones to communicate with each other. A smiling face is understood in both species, but if you really want to get through, make the smile as wide open as you can. You're trying to approximate that big, panting grin a happy dog has. Panting is optional (but kind of fun).

What about using treats to train your dog? They're a wonderful way to get through to your dog quickly, and probably the easiest way for beginning dog owners to train. Since I wrote the first edition of this book, dog trainers have come a long way in developing training techniques using food. Unfortunately, many people take away the wrong lesson: They come to believe in the treat not as a way to shape behavior, step by step — for which treats can work *very* well — but rather as the wages for obedience. Dog sits, dog gets a treat. Dog sits, dog gets a treat. And guess what happens? You end up with a dog who won't pay attention to you if you aren't in a position to pay the edible going rate.

And what about the relationship that's supposed to be developing from the inside out, that special bond? It doesn't. To your dog, you're a vending machine, not a leader. Food helps to form the bond with your dog — dogs quickly become attached to the person who feeds them, after all — but there's more to developing a solid relationship.

USING A SLIP COLLAR AND LEASH CORRECTLY

TECHNICAL STUFF

Dog trainers these days are split into two camps: those who think the slip collar is an instrument of torture, and those who believe it to be an important training tool. The debate will rage on for years to come, but there's one thing that both sides agree on: Used *incorrectly*, a slip collar is ineffective and cruel.

If you're going to use a slip collar you have to know how to put it on and use it properly. With your dog at your left, put the loop of the leash over your right thumb and let the leash drape across your palm and in front of your body. Measure out enough leash so that it's loose, but not drooping. Fold the extra into your palm and close your fist. Now put your left hand on the leash, too. *The collar should always be loose.* A dog can't learn if a dog can't breathe, and if the collar's always cinched down, you're being cruel, inadvertently or not. When the collar corrects the dog, it takes but a split second. The collar tightens. The collar loosens.

If the collar doesn't loosen easily, you probably have it on wrong. The moving end should go over the dog's neck, not under.

The best way to learn to use a slip collar is to enroll in a group class or get private lessons so that you can get a little one-on-one coaching with a trainer. That way, you'll be sure you're using ir properly. After all, a tool that's being used wrong flat-out won't work.

Treats are great for training — they're especially useful for trick training, or for teaching any behavior that requires your dog to be in precise positions, such as those demanded of top-level competitors in obedience trials. But they're for training, not for life. You should not be carrying around a pocketful of treats to bribe your dog into doing what you want. Your dog needs to learn his proper place in your pack by using the commands *without* food after he learns them, or you're not really teaching him much of anything. And that means varying his rewards — always praise, but don't always treat, once the lesson is learned.

When you teach a dog to figure out that a particular behavior gets him what he wants (food and praise), then put a word on it (the command word), you are truly teaching, and he is truly learning.

Maintaining control and giving correction

During training, control and correction is handled by a collar and leash, and by your body, all of which are used both to help guide your pet into correct position and to keep him from getting into wrong ones — such as a full-out gallop, heading away from you.

You also correct your dog with your voice, and you need to be sure that you're using both your voice and your vocabulary properly. I don't use the word "no" much because it's so overused. Instead, I use my "bad dog" sound, kind of a honking "Augh," often preceded by a very loud and dramatic intake of air, like the gasp you make involuntarily when you find your dog has chewed your favorite shoes. The word or sound you use should be sharp, guttural, and dramatic. You should throw the sound at your dog, like a rock. Put the emphasis on the correction word, not on your dog's name, to which there should never be any negative connotations.

Using a release word

The last thing you need is a word to let your dog know he is through with the command you gave him. Probably the most common in use is "Okay" — regrettably, it's the one I use — but a real obvious reason exists to choose another: Some of us say "okay" practically every other word, like, okay, you know what I mean, okay?

If this is you, pick another word. "Release" is a fine one. I also like the one the sheepdog people use at trials: "That'll do." It sounds very gracious!

Whatever you use, though, just be sure that you're consistent in the use of it.

Your release word can mean more than the end of an exercise, allowing your dog to move about, for example, at the end of a "Stay" command. The release word is also a sort of an all-purpose at ease word. If your dog is heeling along at your side, staying out of trouble on a crowded sidewalk, for example, you can use your release word to let him know doing a little sniffing is fine, and maybe a little leg-lifting, too.

A slip collar must be fitted properly and put on correctly to be effective.

Basic Things Every Dog Should Know

In the preceding sections I explain *how* to train and *why* to train; in this section I tell a little bit about *what* to train. The basics are the ones taught in every obedience class and done to high-gloss perfection in obedience competitions.

Deliver commands in a sensible, no-nonsense tone, loudly and clearly enough for your dog to hear — but never yell. Don't whine a command — "Tiiiigerrrrr, ssiiiiiiiitttttttt, baaaaabbbyyy" — and don't say it angrily or rough. Give the command as if you expect it to be obeyed and are confident that it will be.

How often should you train your dog? When you're trying to introduce something new, short lessons twice a day are ideal. You don't have to teach everything at once just because you're in a five- or six-week obedience class. Just do the "Sit," twice a day for a week, if that's all you have time for. Then train the "Down," and so on. Just be — oh, here's that word again — consistent. If you take up the same lesson for a day or two and then drop it for two weeks, you'll never get anywhere. After your dog knows the command, look for every opportunity to practice — and praise.

Sit

Two variations exist on this theme. In both, you take the slack out of the leash with your right hand, but don't tighten it. Offer a treat slightly over and behind your dog's head, with your right hand, and give the command "Sit." He might sit just from being off balance, and if he does, praise and treat. If not, you can spread the index finger and thumb of your left hand and place them on either side of your dog, just in front of his hip bone, the underside of your finger and thumb resting on his back. Say "Sit" and exert *gentle* pressure inward and down. He should fold up to avoid the pressure, and when he does, even if only for a minute, praise and treat.

Some trainers prefer to tuck, and that's fine, too, if this method works for your dog. Slide your hand over his rump and apply pressure to the back of his legs right at the bend, tucking his legs and tail comfortably beneath him. Praise and treat.

TIP

You can teach a puppy to sit without putting a hand or leash on him. All you need is gravity and a bowl of food. If you hold his dish above and slightly behind your pup's head, he'll look up, lose his balance and . . . sit! Just remember to fit the word in there, and you have it made.

For more tips on puppies, see Chapters 6 and 8.

Down

The "Down" builds on "Sit," so make sure your dog completely understands that behavior first. Start with the dog sitting at your left side with the slack taken out of the leash.

Give the command "Down," and use a treat to guide your pet into position, drawing the treat between his legs and forward. When he's in position, give him the treat and praise.

WARNING

Some training methods suggest forcing a dog into a "Down." While this has worked, and still does, it's an especially bad idea when working with a dominant dog. Dominant dogs don't like being forced into a "Down" position because in the dog world, crouching is a sign of submission. If your dog passes the aggression test elsewhere in this chapter and rumbles when you put a hand on him in a down position, stop. If you're truly amazed because your dog is a major wimp, have your veterinarian take a look. Your dog may have a problem that's causing him pain when you attempt to place him into either a "Down" or "Sit" position. If you're *not* that surprised, call a trainer for advice and admit you probably fibbed on the aggression test. Either way, stop. Doing so could save you a nasty bite.

Stay

"Stay" is a command used in conjunction with another command, a request of your dog to hold whatever position you put him in, whether it's "Sit," "Down," or "Rest on the couch." After your dog learns "Stay" in relation to one position, applying the command to the other positions is pretty easy.

Start with the "Sit," and with the dog at your side, hold the leash in a straight line up from his head with all the slack out. Flash an open palm in front of your dog's nose — you can use hand signals in conjunction with any and all commands, but they work especially well here — and then say "Stay." Step out in front of your dog so that you can block his forward motion. If he moves, flash your hand and repeat the "Stay" command. If he stays, return to your position alongside him, and after a second or two, praise and treat, then give him your release word and praise him again.

From there, you want to build up time and distances in slow increments. When you're working at the end of the six-foot leash and your dog is staying reliably, tug on the leash a little without making a sound. If he moves, go back and correct him verbally, repeat the command sequence, and try it again. When he resists the tug, return to position alongside him, praise, and then release him.

Heel

Two kinds of "Heels" are floating around, and most people only want one of them. In competitive obedience circles, heeling has been raised to an art form as demanding as ballroom dancing, where one false step on the part of handler or dog ruins the performance. The dogs prance at their trainers' sides, practically wrapped around their legs, head turned in, muzzle raised, eyes up. Handler and dog aren't much more than a hair's breath apart, and they glide together so gracefully.

Lovely, you say, but I just want my dog not to drag me down the street. Don't worry, there's that, too. To teach it, your dog should be sitting on your left. Call his name, say "Heel" and step off on your left leg so he can see that you're leaving. Praise him for leaving and for staying alongside. If he darts forward, however, turn and head in the other direction, repeating "Heel," and praising and treating him for responding. Keep your dog focused on you and keep praising and treating for trying. When you stop, ask your dog to "Sit" at your side. Eventually, that "Sit" becomes automatic.

To watch a professional trainer teach "Heel" is impressive: She works quickly, dazzling the dog to the point where he has no choice but to pay attention and stay close. And that's what you should try for: Keep the dog moving on *your* terms, focused on you. Keep it fast, keep it upbeat, *keep it going.*

Keep the leash loose, and let the leash and collar do the correcting. Praise and treat your dog! More praise! And above all, keep that collar loose. Remember, if your dog can't breath, he can't learn, and if the collar's tight, you're hurting him and losing your leverage to boot.

Of all the basic commands, this one probably demands the most coordination on your part. It you can't walk and chew gum at the same time, you're probably going to have trouble saying, "Stanley, Heel!" stepping out on your left foot, praising, and keeping the proper amount of slack in the leash so that the collar stays loose. If your head spins just thinking about it, you'll probably do better with the help of a trainer, in either a group class or a private session.

Heel position is on your left, with the leash loose and your dog's shoulder even with the seam of your pants leg.

TECHNICAL STUFF

Why is heel position on your left? Because you'll be carrying your shotgun on your right, of course! The heel exercise is derived from gun-dog training: The dogs would walk *at heel* on the left so they would not be shot when their owners raised their weapons to their right shoulders to shoot birds. The dogs would then be sent to retrieve the downed game, give it to their owners, and return to heel. Now, heeling on the left is just tradition. Can you teach your dog "Heel" on your right side? You bet. But if you ever walk with friends and their dogs, go to an obedience class, or try to compete in obedience, you're going to get tangled.

Come

Teaching the "Come" is easy. Put your dog on a "Sit-Stay" on leash, call his name, say "Come," reel him in with praise, and give more praise and treats when he gets to you. Easy, sure, but have you ever noticed that the majority of dog owners have to cross their fingers when they call their dogs?

Although "Come" is in theory easy to teach, it's not performed very well in everyday life. Are you a finger-crosser? Here are a few reasons your dog may not respond to the "Come" command:

>> **Your dog is afraid to come to you.** Recognize this scenario? Your dog slips past your 10-year-old daughter as she comes in the front door and takes off. You run after him, screaming "Come" in all it's variations — "SANDYCOME!" "HERE! Sandy, I said HERE! NOW!" "YOU'RE DEAD! COME!" and so on. Sandy's running, but you finally corner him. He knows you're hot, so to try to appease you maybe he rolls over or takes a step forward. You grab him by the collar and scream at him — or worse — for not coming to you. You tell me: What is he going to do the next time? Keep running? You got it.

The trick here is to be welcoming. Kneel down. Spread your arms. And when he moves in your direction, praise; when he gets there, praise more. Even if you want to ring his neck. *Never correct a dog for coming to you.*

>> **Your dog doesn't really know the command.** Few people practice this one. You probably use "Sit" a half-dozen times a day, just around the house, but you probably never say "Come" when you want your dog to come to you in the house. You probably just use his name. Or maybe not even that, since the opening of the refrigerator door gets you a canine appearance at the speed of light. But the dog doesn't know "Come"; he knows if he's sitting *in just the right* place you may drop something. Big difference.

>> **Your dog doesn't see why he should.** "Come" is where all that work in developing the relationship from within really pays off. A dog who knows what's expected of him and respects you is going to mind. A dog who knows you're not a deity but a flat-footed slow-poke who couldn't catch a bus is going to treat you like the fool he thinks you are.

How to fix this? Train your dog to "Come" in increments, on-leash and on longer leashes and lighter lines still. In different places, too: in the house, in the yard, in the park, with your cat walking by, with your kids playing. Never let him get into a position where he learns you really can't do much about it when he bolts. Practice, not just in formal training but in everyday life. Build on your successes. Don't forget the treats, and don't forget the praise.

TIP

If your untrained dog slips out and takes off, try to use a command he knows well — like "Sit" — instead of "Come." This is an emergency after all — a wrong move and he could be road pizza. Most dogs know "Sit" so well they'll plant their rumps and, once they're planted, you can praise and take their collars. Another possibility is to run *away* from your dog, enticing him to follow you — the chase instinct is very strong in dogs.

Remember, a loose-dog situation is not about dog training, but about dog *saving*. A near-disaster such as this one should convince you it's time to train your dog. If you don't, the next time he slips out you may not be so lucky.

Great Things They Don't Teach in Obedience Class

The things you can teach your dog have no end, and you needn't stop with the five basic commands described in the preceding section. My friend Gay Currier, who started learning about dog training when she worked at the service-dog organization Canine Companions for Independence, got me thinking years ago about expanding my dogs' vocabulary. Gay's wonderful Doberman, Laramie, has passed on, but in her time she knew dozens of useful commands. In this section I've put in a few I like so much that I've taught them to my dogs and recommended them to my readers for years.

REMEMBER

Don't let your mind stop because a trainer's — or author's — suggestions do. After reading this chapter you know how to train a dog, so build on your *own* success. If you have something you want to teach your dog, give the behavior a name and do so!

Wait

This is different from "Stay" because the dog is not required to hold a position, just to not cross an imaginary line of your choosing. To teach this command, position your dog in a doorway, call his name, say "Wait," and draw your hand from frame to frame in front of his eyes. Walk back into the room and allow him to move around, and then step back out. If he follows across the imaginary line, give a voice correction, and repeat the command and hand signal. Praise and treat for staying on the other side of the line, then release him to more praise and treats.

This command has many uses. I tell my dogs "Wait" when I open the car door, so they don't jump out into traffic. They "Wait" before entering people's homes or leaving our own.

The "Wait" command can help keep your landscaping from taking a beating. See Chapter 22 for tips on combining a dog and a garden.

Go to your bed

This one builds on "Down," but is not so formal. It means "go there and plant it, pal" and is a great command for getting your dog out from underfoot. Call your dog's name, tell him to "Go to your bed," lead him there, and tell him "Down." With practice — and consistency — the "Down" becomes automatic.

My friend Laura taught this one in reverse: Instead of teaching her Border Collie, Pancha, where she *should* be, she taught her where she *couldn't* be. The command: "Out of the kitchen," which meant: "Anywhere else but in this room."

Off

"Off" is what people often mean when they say "Down": "I want all four of your paws on the floor, *now*." This is not a punishment: It's a command. If your dog's on the couch or the bed without an invitation, take her by the collar, say "Off," and then lead her down and praise. Likewise with the jumping dog, though then the command is best taught with a leash and slip collar. "Off," then use the leash in a downward motion until those feet hit the ground, ask for a "Sit," and praise.

Don't touch or Leave it

Gay uses "Don't touch" and I use "Leave it." You can use "Apple juice," as long as you're — what's that word? — consistent! Teach this command with a physical correction from the get-go. With your dog in a "Sit-Stay" and your hand in a fist, flat surface up, offer your dog a biscuit with the other. As she reaches for the biscuit, say "Don't touch," and bop her under the chin, enough to close her jaw but not lift her off her feet. Offer the biscuit again, repeating the "Don't touch" command and, if she hesitates or turns away, praise her. Few dogs need this demonstrated more than twice.

This command is another with many useful applications. A dog leads with his nose, after all, and a dog who knows "Don't touch" isn't going to head in a direction you don't want him to go in. Use this command when you're walking and he dives for some dreadful leftovers in a fast-food bag. Use it to keep him from lifting his leg where you don't want him to on walks — since the sniff is the prelude to the leg-lift, this command works well. If you drop your sandwich in front of him, "Don't touch" assures you get to finish it — assuming you still want to, of course.

Retrieving

I have to admit that with the dogs I have, retrieving is the easiest command to teach. They're retrievers: They were born with the desire to retrieve. You throw something, they bring it back. That's the way they're wired.

On the other hand, I have good friends who have Rhodesian Ridgebacks, dogs who were developed to hunt lions — prey that's too big to be carried to the hunter in a dog's mouth. Retrieving isn't one of their natural interests. With the Ridgebacks, you throw something, and they look at you as if to say: "Well, you obviously didn't want it since you threw it away. Surely you don't expect me to do something about it. Fetch? You must be kidding!"

Some dogs are born retrievers. Some take to it like a retriever to water, once you start teaching them. Others warm to the idea of retrieving slowly, at best. But it's worth trying to teach your dog to retrieve if only because it's the world's best way to get your dog the exercise he needs without you exerting all that much time or energy. You don't have to jog, you can just throw!

If your dog isn't a natural-born retriever, realize that you must be very patient, and be content with small advances. The dog who first makes even the tiniest move forward to take an object on command has made a huge achievement! Recognize it, and build on your successes. Don't lose patience!

Before you start, go to pet-supply store and get a *dumbbell*, a wooden or plastic retrieving tool that's a dowel with wide pieces on both ends to help keep it from slipping out of your dog's mouth. Dumbbells come in various sizes and weights; pick one that wide enough for your dog to get his mouth on the dowel part comfortably, without being squeezed by the side pieces.

Several different methods exist for teaching the retrieve, including ones that involve force. For most people, a positive, patient approach will work fine. Remember: Think short, upbeat sessions, small increments, and lots of praise and treats. Work at your dog's own pace, and don't rush to the next level.

Start by teaching the dog to open his mouth. Say "Take it" and offer your pet a treat. Once your dog is opening his mouth in expectation when he hears the "Take it" command, slip the dumbbell inside for a second. Praise and treat! Try this a few more times, then end the lesson.

After your dog is accepting the dumbbell, put it in his mouth and ask him to "Hold it" while you gently hold his mouth around the dumbbell for three or four seconds. Then tell him "Give" and let him spit the dumbbell out. Treat and praise.

The next step is to hold the dumbbell just in front of the dog's mouth and say "Take it." If you need to pull his head toward the dumbbell with the collar, that's fine. If he moves forward on his own, even better. Treat and praise.

From that point, it's a matter of building the distance slowly, lesson by lesson. A foot, two feet, then picking it up from the floor, then picking it up from the floor three feet away, and so on. You should be working separately on practicing the "Hold it" and "Give" commands, as well as the "Come" command described earlier in this chapter.

REMEMBER

Retrieving isn't just one skill: It's a combination of skills. Taking the object is one part of it. Holding the object is another, and so, too, is bringing it to you. Releasing the object on your "Give it" command is the final part. Each piece must be taught, and then merged into a seamless behavior. Some dogs put it all together quickly and naturally; other dogs don't. But if you work slowly and patiently, your dog will learn.

Chapter **15**

Problem-Solving

One of the things that has surprised me the most in the years I've been writing about dogs and listening to dog lovers is not how many times problems, even some minor ones, put dogs in shelters — to that, I've quite sadly become accustomed — but how many times they *don't*. I've heard some amazing stories over the years of what people have put up with — dogs who've eaten thousands of dollars worth of furniture, dogs who lift their legs on their owners, dogs who bark a thousand times a day in staccato bursts that would outpace a machine gun.

Do people like living with beastly dogs like this? Who would? But some dog lovers hang in there, sometimes for years, hoping the problems will end before the dog does and just getting by as best they can in the meantime.

Others aren't anywhere near so tolerant. Some try a little, some try a lot but, in the end, many people throw up their hands and figure someone else — someone with more time, more space, no children, or whatever they imagine will be the key to solving the problem — will fall in love with their dog behind the chain-link of a shelter run and everything will work out fine.

Neither approach to dog problems is a good one.

I'm not going to tell you that all your dog problems can be fixed. Some can't. Sometimes the best you can do is make adjustments so that your life with your dog is easier. Sometimes you have the wrong breed type for your lifestyle (see Chapter 2 for more on breed choices) or a dog with problems caused by bad breeding, a lack of early socialization, or a history of abuse before you got her. All of which is why I put such emphasis elsewhere in this book on choosing the right dog from the right source and then putting some real effort into getting the relationship off to a good start. The time to decide that a hyperactive, unsocialized Rottweiler, produced by a clueless or careless breeder, isn't the best match with your work as a home day-care provider is before you buy the dog, not after.

Still, you *can* do a great deal, no matter your past mistakes or your dog's unfortunate history. And that's what this chapter is all about.

As with basic training, though, you first have to be willing to work with your dog, and you *must* realize that you're in for a long haul. Changing your relationship with your dog is often the only way to alter a problem behavior. Such problems as too much digging and too much barking are often only symptoms of a larger problem. Treating the symptoms won't solve the problem.

WARNING

If your dog's showing aggressive behavior, you haven't got a problem, you've got a potential disaster. Stop here and turn to "Teaching Your Dog Manners," Chapter 14. Read the section "A Few Words about Aggression." If you see your dog in those words, make a phone call now to a trainer or behaviorist. You need more help than a book can give you.

If your dog has become a delinquent, working with him can help you to solve the problems.

Photograph courtesy of Kerry Drager

Curing Problems from the Inside Out

As with teaching basic obedience to your dog, you have to look at the big picture when approaching problem behaviors. That's because problems are often a symptom of something larger — most commonly, a dog who's not having his needs met, physically, socially, or mentally.

You must keep in mind that dogs are social animals whose ancestors, long ago, lived as part of a pack, working together to hunt and raise young. More recent history has seen the development of dogs who work to serve humans, as hunting dogs, sled dogs, or sheep dogs. Is it any surprise that an intelligent breed such as the Border Collie, developed to work closely and diligently with a human companion, isn't going to be happy left alone for hours without a job to do? Should it shock you that an Alaskan Malamute, whose relatives pulled sleds across the tundra, has so much energy that the only way he can release it — alone in a barren backyard — is to reduce a picnic table to splinters or dig holes deep enough for a new basement? And what about that Lab-Shepherd cross, whose parents both come from long lines of intelligent, active, and hard-working dogs? Do you expect her to just hang out every day waiting for a few minutes of your time?

Be fair! While human-dog comparisons don't always work, this one does: How would *you* feel if you never went anywhere and no one ever expected much out of you? What would *you* do to relieve your boredom and anxiety? After a few weeks, you'd be ready to chew a picnic table, too.

So, you've got a problem, or two. You want to scream at your dog. You want to hit your dog. Neither will help you with your problem, and both may damage your loving relationship with your pet. Anger isn't in the trainer's tool kit. Remember always to:

>> Keep your cool.

>> Remind yourself that bad behavior is often a symptom, not a disease.

>> Work to avoid behavior problems by meeting your dog's needs.

Avoid problems by picking a breed that's right for your lifestyle. Chapter 2 includes a description of each of the AKC's twenty most popular breeds — if you're thinking about getting a popular breed, make sure that you read this section!

Trying Recipes for Fixing Behavior Problems

Although I *do* give you pointers on dealing with specific behavior problems in the upcoming sections, the basics for addressing bad behavior — from the inside out — are more valuable than any specific strategy. I once listed some of the behavior problems people have asked me about over the years and I came up with more than a hundred — many of which were variations on a few very common themes.

If you learn what goes into behavior problems, you're better equipped to deal with anything that comes up. It's like that old saying: *Give a man a fish and he eats for a day; teach him to fish, and he eats for the rest of his life.* I want you to develop the problem-solving skills you need to live happily with your dog forever, no matter what odd problems may pop up.

Besides, if all I did was show you how to stop one problem behavior without showing you how to fix the underlying cause, your dog may simply start a new habit in place of the one you eliminate. He might trade barking for digging, or digging for chewing.

Some dogs have problems because they don't feel that their place in the household is secure. For some tips on giving your dog the help he needs, start using leash-bonding and the "people first" rule in the "Establish a routine" section in Chapter 5. Going back to these basics is a good refresher course in "me person, you dog," an important base for good dog behavior.

Ensure good health, inside and out

The first step to solving a behavior problem is to make sure that it's not a health problem, *especially* if nothing has changed in your life, except suddenly you have a dog problem. For example, a dog who starts throwing fits when you try to brush out the mats that form in the feathery hair behind his ears may have a painful ear infection. Two more examples: Some kinds of chewing can be attributed to nutritional deficiencies, and some house-soiling problems can be the result of a urinary-tract infection.

My friend, Kathy Diamond Davis, is a dog trainer and the author of books on pet-facilitated therapy and how to train your dog to be a responsible canine citizen. She's also the online dog behavior expert for the Pet Care Forum Web site (www.vin.com/petcare). She told me a story about a sweet Border Collie who would turn over on his back to get a tummy rub but then growl when being petted. The owners were concerned about the dog's "viciousness." Turned out the dog had hip problems and was *in pain*. Once his medical problems were addressed, they never heard another growl from him.

WARNING

Don't try to solve a behavior problem until you've made sure your dog is healthy. Any behaviorist will tell you that the first rule of sorting out any behavior problem is to make sure it's not a medical problem. Don't guess at the problem and throw a home remedy at it. See *your veterinarian*. Pop for the diagnostic tests your veterinarian suggests: They're necessary tools in finding the clues that solve the mystery of errant behavior.

REMEMBER

Even if your dog's behavior problem isn't directly related to some physical malady, if your dog isn't healthy he'll have a hard time focusing on learning to behave more appropriately. To have any chance of fixing your dog's behavior problems, you must work with your veterinarian to fix any health problems. Doing so will probably save you money in the long run, and you'll certainly spare your pet some misery.

After your dog checks out okay on the medical front, you need to start addressing the other necessary parts of a healthy doggie life:

>> **Mental exercise.** Training is for life. Your dog needs to keep learning, and keep using all he he's been taught. That doesn't mean, however, that you have to make formal obedience sessions a permanent part of your life. Think, instead, of creative ways to expand your dog's working vocabulary and integrate the skills he has learned into your life together.

When you play fetch, for example, vary the routine: Make him do a "Sit" or "Down" before you take the ball from him. Put him on "Stay," throw the ball, and then send him. Have two family members play recall games with him in the house: One calls and praises, and then the other does the same. These games keep him engaged, and they also help enforce his place in your family, which makes him feel confident and secure.

>> **Physical exercise.** Probably the biggest contributor to behavior problems is that dogs don't get nearly enough exercise. (Lack of exercise is also a big contributor to health problems: Too much food and not enough exercise makes dogs fat, which leads to other health problems.) By exercise, I don't mean a walk around the block, stopping and sniffing at every shrub, street light, and fire hydrant. These outings are important, too, for your dog's mental health, but they don't satisfy his physical needs.

Your dog needs 30 to 40 minutes of aerobic exercise that gets his heart pumping, and he needs it three or more times a week to stay fit, burn excess energy, and alleviate the stresses of modern life, which for many dogs includes being a latchkey pup. This kind of exercise is especially important for dogs with a working heritage, such as sporting or herding breeds.

Keeping dogs on the move

The good news is that you don't need to live in the country to keep your dog well exercised. Folks in Manhattan manage it as well as anyone around, arranging doggy play groups and visiting dog runs. You just need some time and some creativity.

First, consider your dog. An animal bred for a day's hard work — herding, for example, or pulling a sled — is going to require more exercise than one whose job it was to sit in someone's lap, or wake up now and then to discourage an intruder. What follows is an idea of exercise needs, depending on the kind of dog you have, divided by AKC group. (If your dog is a mix, determine his needs based on his dominant breed background — a German Shepherd mix, for example.

WHAT DOGS DON'T KNOW — AND WHAT PEOPLE SHOULD

Dogs don't know guilt, they don't know a behavior is "bad" until you teach them so, and they don't know how to be spiteful. They're just being dogs. They live in the now, and revenge is not in their gene pool. Barking, chewing, and digging are another story: They're natural, normal behaviors, part of every dog's DNA.

A lot of the motives people attribute to dogs for their behavior just can't be. They don't chew because they're mad at you for leaving them; they chew because they're stressed about being alone; chewing fills the time and makes them feel better.

"Aha!" you say, "if that's true, how come when I come home and find a mess my dog looks guilty and tries to find a place to hide?"

Look at this scenario through his eyes. Your owner comes home, and you're trotting happily down the hall to meet him when you hear . . . swearing. You pause, uncertain. Then . . . yelling, and *you hear your name* in the middle of that diatribe. And you realize: He's mad at *me!* Why, you have no idea — you've long forgotten chewing all his underwear — but you're scared and fairly certain the most prudent plan of action would be to take off.

When he finds you, he's so angry it scares you, and so you do your best to appease him, dog style. You roll over and show your belly, or maybe you release a little urine. A dog would see both as efforts to say, "I'm sorry, I'm sorry, I don't know what's making you angry but I apologize, anyway," but instead . . . more yelling, and maybe a smack.

Get the point? A display like this one doesn't teach your dog anything except that you're an unpredictable lunatic. And that doesn't get you any closer to solving the problem.

If you find your dog among the ones I've noted as not needing as much exercise, don't breathe a sigh of relief. You're not off the hook! All dogs need exercise; some just need a lot more of it than others. And remember that even those breeds that mature into easygoing couch potatoes often have high exercise requirements when they're growing up — to the age of two, generally.

>> **Sporting group.** The setters, retrievers, spaniels, and pointers of the sporting group were developed to do a long day's work in rough conditions. You simply cannot give these dogs enough exercise. Thirty to sixty minutes every day would be ideal; three thirty-minute aerobic sessions a week is the bare minimum.

>> **Hound group.** Two kinds of hounds, with two different kinds of exercise needs. The hounds developed to follow animals with their noses — Beagles, Foxhounds, Coonhounds — have exercise requirements similar to the sporting breeds — every day would be ideal. The dogs known as sighthounds, such as Greyhounds, Afghan Hounds, and the deerhounds, aren't quite as demanding. Bred to expend their energy in short, intense bursts, sighthounds would rather sleep than run. An easy daily walk and a twice-weekly hard workout suits them fine.

>> **Working group.** A mixed bag here. The breeds that were developed to guard, such as Rottweilers, Mastiffs, and Great Danes, don't need as much exercise as a breed like the Portuguese Water Dog, which was developed to work retrieving fishing nets in cold water. Everyday aerobics suit a Portie fine (especially if the exercise involves swimming), but some of the other big dogs in the group are quite happy with a good walk and an occasional aerobic workout.

>> **Terrier group.** The dogs most people identify as terriers — small, wire-coated dogs such as Scotties — are such incurable in-your-face busy-bodies that they get a lot of exercise on their own. And their small stature and short legs makes a brisk walk an aerobic workout for them. As such, a good walk three times or more a week suits them fine. The other kind of terrier — typified by the American or English Staffordshire — are powerful dogs who really benefit from a three-times-a-week aerobic workout.

>> **Non-sporting group.** Alas, it's impossible to generalize about this bunch, which is the AKC's version of a grab-bag — any breed that didn't fit elsewhere ends up here. So you have to look at the background of the breed and go from there. A breed like the Schipperke is a lot like the wire-haired terriers — energetic, diminutive busy-bodies — and should be exercised as such. For all their fluffiness, Poodles are sporting dogs at heart, and need all the exercise you can give them. As for the bulldogs, they'd rather sleep, thanks, but a couple easy walks a week will keep them in good form.

>> **Toy group.** Like the terriers, toy dogs don't need a lot of help from you to get their exercise — they're always moving, and their short legs make your brisk walk a good workout. Teach these bright little guys to fetch, and you can have serious aerobic time in your home's hallway. Like all dogs, toys need exercise, but they don't need all that much room to roam.

>> **Herding group.** Like the sporting dogs, herding dogs have very high exercise needs — thirty minutes to an hour daily would be ideal, twice that for the super-athlete known as the Border Collie. Neglect the bodies and minds of these dogs at your own risk.

So what should you be doing to get your dog's heart pumping? The possibilities are endless!

Fetch is a fantastic way to give your dog aerobic exercise. Get an old tennis racket to get some real distance on those tennis balls.

Jogging is another great exercise. If you don't jog but your dog is well-behaved on-leash, you may have a friend or neighbor who'd welcome the company and the added security. Swimming is a natural for retriever types, and if you're lucky enough to be near an off-leash dog park, playing with other dogs is a first-rate way for your dog to exercise.

Bicycling is another great exercise, and three products are on the market designed to help you bicycle safely while with a dog. They attach to the bicycle and allow you to keep both of your hands on the handlebars — a much safer plan than holding onto a leash with one hand and the bike with the other.

Roadwork, such as jogging or tagging alongside a bicycle, can be good for dogs, but remember to pace your dog properly: A brisk trot is ideal.

WARNING

A few warnings about exercise, especially roadwork. Have your veterinarian sign off on any exercise program, making sure that your dog doesn't have any joint problems that rule out any particular kind of exercise. Make sure that you build up slowly, especially if your dog is overweight. Let your dog set the pace, and often check the bottoms of his feet (the smooth parts are called *pads*) for tears or cuts.

Exercise when the weather is cool — dogs aren't as efficient at lowering their body temperature as we are — carry water, always, and know the signs of heat stress: glassy eyes, frantic panting. If your dog gets in trouble, get him wet and call your veterinarian *immediately*.

A gentle stroll is interesting to your dog, but he also needs exercise that gets the heart pumping.

A handful of manufacturers make it easy to exercise your dog while riding a bike.

WARNING

Do *not* force puppies to sustain a pounding pace, especially on pavement, lest you injure their developing bones. That means no jogging or bicycling until they're through adolescence — two years old is a good ballpark figure, but check with your veterinarian.

Minimize mischief opportunities

As with any relationship, you're going to have to make some adjustments for living with your dog. One of those is that you're probably not going to be able to put meat scraps in an open-topped kitchen trash can that just happens to be at perfect nose height for your dog. Yes, you can correct your dog when you catch her in the trash and, yes, you can booby-trap the garbage to make it less appealing (see the upcoming section "Let the situation teach the dog"), but sometimes the best answer is to get a trash can with a lid, or one that fits under the sink or behind a door you can close. Sometimes doing things a little differently just makes sense with a dog in the house. Not that I want to add even more to the toilet seat wars that rage in some households, but if you want to know how to keep your dog from drinking out of the toilet, how about looking for the obvious answer: Close the lid. (Come to think about it, that solves the gender war over this issue, too.)

Some adjustments are forever, some not. When you have a dog who goes nuts when you leave her alone, the answer — while you're building up her confidence and taking care of her exercise needs, of course — is not to give her more choices, but fewer. That may mean putting her in a crate or a small area with a chew toy while you're gone, and then slowly building up the space available to her, room by room.

Again, the crate comes to the rescue as one of the best ways to deal with dog problems. For more on choosing a crate for your dog, read the section on them in Chapter 6.

Substitute other behaviors

Instead of jumping on your dog for what he *can't* chew, show him what he's allowed to chew and praise him for doing so. Make his toys more appealing than your shoes or the remote control: One tactic is to take a destruction-proof Kong toy — more on this marvel, and other top toys, in Chapter 6 — and put peanut butter inside it. Your dog stays busy for hours.

For a special discussion on puppies' chewing — a normal part of the teething process — see Chapter 9.

Another kind of substitution is to put an activity you approve of in the place of one you do not. For example: Teach the dog who jumps up on people that sitting, not jumping, gets her the attention she's looking for. And be consistent: If you don't want your dog to jump up in greeting, don't ever let her. No fair saying that jumping is okay when you're in jeans, but not when you're dressed for an evening out.

Dog parks, where offleash play is legal and encouraged, help make good citizens out of dogs and their owners.

Photograph courtesy of Joan Mahone

Let the situation teach the dog

You can help steer your dog away from inappropriate behavior by making the objects you want to protect do their part to discourage your dog. You can do so in three ways:

>> **Make the object taste bad.** Coat the object with something dogs find hateful, such as Bitter Apple, available in any pet-supply store. Tabasco sauce is another disagreeable taste to most dogs. No matter what you choose, remember to test it on a small area first, in case the product you use causes a staining problem.

TIP

THREE CHEERS FOR DOG PARKS!

When it comes to running my dogs, I'm a lawbreaker. And I'm not alone. In veterinary waiting rooms, in pet stores, at dog shows, and on the Internet, a massive underground of determined dog lovers trade information on places to run our dogs.

We hate being criminals; we'd rather be legit: Give us some dog parks.

I'd choose a dedicated dog park to run my dogs in anytime. But I can't always drive out of town, so I also drive to local places where I let my dogs go off-leash illegally. I go at odd hours, when I know a park will be empty, and never on weekends. My dogs are friendly and well-socialized, they are under voice control, and yes, I clean up after them.

Why should dog lovers have to play this game? In terms of sheer numbers, we are a larger population than either tennis, soccer, or softball players, all groups whose needs are recognized and addressed by those who plan public facilities. Our dogs are our chosen form of recreation, and we deserve facilities as much as any other group.

What worries me even more is not the people who run their dogs illegally, but those who never run their dogs at all. Destructive and antisocial behaviors find their roots in boredom and unspent nervous energy. How many dogs would be spared a trip to the shelter if only they had a place to be socialized and exercised on a regular basis? Considering that behavior problems are a top reason for abandonment, the numbers could be considerable.

Dog parks work, and they're just as good for dog haters as dog lovers. If the recreational needs of dog lovers are covered, it's perfectly fair to crack down on them elsewhere. Steep fines for off-leash dogs are justified in areas of high human use, just as long as there are alternatives elsewhere for off-leash play. And dog parks encourage responsible ownership, with the result being healthier, happier, better-socialized dogs. Such dogs are good citizens.

I don't like being a criminal, and I wouldn't be if my legitimate needs as a dog lover were recognized. If you feel the same way, let your elected officials know about it. Every community is capable of putting aside some space for dogs to run.

>> **Make the object startle him.** Balloons and mousetraps make sharp noises that startle your dog and help him decide that maybe he'd better leave the booby-trapped area alone. Some products give off a piercing noise when motion is detected near them, and these can work, too. (The mousetrap won't hurt your pet: It's the noise of it snapping shut and the motion that scares him.)

>> **Make the object shocking.** Vinyl mats and strips that give off a tiny static shock can be very effective in teaching dogs to stay off furniture and countertops.

Mousetraps don't hurt dogs, but the noise they make when triggered can startle a dog into leaving things alone.

Controlling Problems That Put Dogs in the Shelter

Ready to problem-solve? Let's see how your new skills apply to some of the problems that really endanger dogs' lives by putting them at risk to go to the shelter.

Two problems that also often put dogs on the road to the shelter are covered elsewhere. House-soiling is in Chapter 8, and biting, or any sign of aggression, is in Chapter 14.

Barking

This one puts your dog at risk from the people in your neighborhood: The poisoning of a nuisance barker is all too common. Even if your neighbors aren't the kind to take things into their own hands, a barking dog can run you afoul of the law, and not dealing with the situation marks you as an irresponsible and inconsiderate dog owner.

Vicious dogs may be what you read about in the papers, but the barking dog is truly the bane of urban and suburban life.

LITTER-MUNCHING DOGS

I hear constantly from readers who are astonished that their dogs consider the contents of a litter box as some kind of special treat. These folks are always desperate for an end to this disgusting habit.

As incredible as the thought seems to humans, many dogs do indeed consider cat feces to be every bit as wonderful as dog biscuits — they're drawn to the undigested protein.

When faced with a constant supply of litter munchies and ready access to them, no dog can resist for long, which is why efforts to train a dog to leave the litter box alone are rarely successful. The better plan is to restrict access, which you can accomplish in many ways. Here are a few suggestions:

- Purchase covered litter boxes. Some cats don't like them, and cats with asthma can't use them. If your cat falls into either category, this solution isn't going to work for you.

- Change the litter box's location. You must be careful not to upset your cat. But experimenting with such ploys as gradually moving the litter box to a location above the dog's reach usually doesn't hurt.

- Provide barriers. One way is to rig the door to the room containing the litter box so that it stays open wide enough for the cat but not for the dog. Another possibility is to put a cat-sized door through the door to the litter box room if your dog is medium-sized or larger. For small dogs, try a baby gate — the cat can jump it, but the dog can't.

- Keep it clean. Don't forget to keep the box scooped: A dog can't eat what a dog can't find.

TECHNICAL STUFF

Dogs bark to express a variety of emotions: anxiety, boredom, territoriality, aggression, playfulness, and hunger, to name a few. In addition, barking sessions can be triggered by certain conditions in the dog's environment. For example, a dog who barks a warning when strangers are near will bark constantly and frantically if one side of a fence separates his area in his yard from a well-traveled public sidewalk. Likewise, an intelligent, high-energy dog, neglected and bored in a lonely back yard, often rids himself of that excess energy by indulging in barking sessions that can last for hours, day or night.

Breed characteristics factor in, as well. Expecting an arctic breed or mix not to engage in an occasional howl — or a hound not to give voice when on the trail of a squirrel or rabbit — is unrealistic. Some herding dogs drive livestock by nipping and barking at their heels, and even their suburban relations, many generations removed from the farm, may still yap joyfully at the heels of the family's children at play.

Figure out the kind of barking your dog indulges in. Is he a fence-runner, trading insults with the dog on the other side of the back fence? Consider reworking the yard to deny him access to that activity. Is he a bored outside dog? Make him a part of your life, bring him in the house, and make sure that his needs for physical and mental stimulation are being met. Another advantage of having him in the house: Many of the sounds that trigger barking are masked inside. (You can help this masking even further by leaving a radio on when you leave.)

Train him not to bark by teaching him the "Quiet" or "Enough" command. Allow him a bark or two — let him get his point across — and then say "Enough" and put your hand over his muzzle. Praise him for stopping. If he's loose, you can also get the point across with a shot from a spray bottle: Allow him a bark or two, say "Enough," squirt, and then praise him for stopping.

PROBLEMS PEOPLE PRODUCE

Sometimes dog owners inadvertently teach their pets bad habits.

Do you think your dog would ever have learned to beg if the first time he tried it he got nothing for his efforts? After this habit starts, some dogs can be very persuasive, either by being cute or annoying. How to stop this behavior? Stop giving in, and substitute a "Down-Stay"— see Chapter 14 for tips on training — for begging at the table. As your dog gradually becomes convinced that he will never again see another piece of food delivered from under or over the table, he'll stop asking.

Another people-produced problem results from inconsistency. Say you're replacing an old couch with a new one, and while there wasn't much your dog could do to hurt the old one, you'd rather he stay off the new one. If you work with him, he'll eventually get the idea, but it isn't really very fair of you. If you don't want your dog on the furniture, ever, don't let him up on the furniture, ever.

And what about nervousness? Many people train their dogs to be afraid by soothing them when they show shyness. When a dog is acting shy, don't pet him and say, "There, there, it's okay," because doing so just reinforces the behavior. Instead, be matter-of-fact with him: Jolly him along and keep moving. Show him he has nothing to be worried about.

Remember, preventing problems is *always* easier than fixing them later.

TIP

It's not a quick fix — you still have to address the underlying problems of boredom, stress, and inactivity — but one kind of training collar offers real promise in fighting the battle of the bark. The ABS Anti-Barking System is a collar that releases a mist of harmless yet annoying citronella spray when the dog barks. This device is a good alternative to an electric collar, which is really not a product that should be used without the guidance of a trainer or behaviorist.

Digging

Filling up the holes and putting the dog's own stools inside is one oft-toted solution that can help — assuming your dog's not into eating stools; many are — but digging is a classic case where looking at the bigger picture is essential. If your dog is left outdoors while you're gone — or all the time — and never gets worked or exercised, he'll destroy your yard. Add to that the fact that some dogs — such as terrier types — simply live to dig and the fact that your yard is as holey as swiss cheese is no surprise.

Three things that can help: Work and exercise your dog. Limit his unchaperoned access to the parts of the yard you'd like preserved. And give him an area where digging is okay — and tell him so!

More hints on having both a nice yard and a dog are in Chapter 22.

Destructiveness when left alone

This is *the* classic problem with the dog you adopt as an adult. He's had his heart broken once and his hopes rekindled, by you. And then you leave him and he copes with his anxiety — will you ever return? — by going nuts, chewing, most typically.

You help build his confidence by getting him into a routine — more on this in Chapter 5 — and by training him. You relieve some of that excess energy by exercising him. And finally, while the cure is working from the inside out, you minimize the damage potential by confining him to a crate or small space.

A couple of other tips for dealing with separation anxiety:

>> **Feed your dog his biggest meal before he's about to spend his biggest chunk of time alone.** What dogs do after they eat is sleep and, if you're lucky, he'll sleep most of the time you're gone.

» **Give him something special to chew on just as you leave.** Have a really good chewy that's just for his alone time, and hand it to him as you leave. He may even become a little glad to see you go!

» **Leave a radio on to mask outside noises.** Something soothing, please. Classical music. Your dog's anxious enough without having to listen to talk radio.

» **Practice no-fuss comings and goings.** Some people unwittingly make matters worse by staging hellos and good-byes that look like scenes from *Gone With the Wind*, and I'm thinking of the ones where Ashley leaves Melanie in Atlanta and then reappears after the war. Emotional stuff, and your dog doesn't need it. New rule: no pats. When you leave, tell your dog "guard the house" and give him his special chewy — it makes him feel important. When you return, tell him to "Sit," and then praise slightly — I mean *very* slightly — and ignore him for the next ten minutes. Read your mail, check your answering machine, visit the bathroom. And then sit down, call him to you, and tell him how your day went. The message here is that all this in-and-out is no *big deal*, so chill already.

» **Consider medication to help with retraining.** Separation anxiety is one behavior problem that's addressed by some of the new medications that have come into veterinary medicine in the last few years. (See the sidebar, "Does your pup need Prozac?") It wouldn't hurt to talk to your veterinarian about some calming medication.

Disobedience

You say your dog's a holy terror, doesn't mind you when you say "Sit" and drags you down the street? He needs exercise and training and lots and lots of practice. See Chapter 14 for the basics.

If your dog's an adolescent, he'll calm down some as he matures, but not enough to make living with him tolerable if you *don't* train him. So do.

New baby worries

Some people in this world — and maybe you're related to them — consider a dog as kind of a parenting trial run, and suggest that when you're ready to try parenting "for real" you should find your dog another home. Because of this mentality, some dogs end up in shelters in kind of a preemptive strike against any potential problem interactions of dog and baby.

Sometimes those worries are justified. If you have a dog who has an aggression problem — and I hate to keep harping on aggression, but I must in hopes of saving even one child from a bite, or worse — get help from a trainer or behaviorist with experience in dealing with these problems. And realize that a chance exists that you may *not* be able to trust your dog around children, which means you have some very difficult decisions to make.

More likely, though, you've just got a dog whose exuberance worries you. The best exercise for this is a solid "Down-Stay." Practice 30 minute "Down-Stays" in the couple of months before the baby arrives, especially in the nursery. When the baby comes home, practice them while you're nursing.

TIP

Want your dog to love your baby? Give him positive attention — praise and treats — only in the baby's presence for several weeks. He'll soon make the connection that the baby's a cool thing. If you pay attention to your dog only when you're away from the baby and ignore him when the baby's around, he never makes the connection between *cool thing* and *baby*.

Aside from that, the usual rules apply: exercise and training. Managing both an infant and a dog in the first few months is hard, so maybe a neighbor kid can help you out with walks or you can find another creative solution.

WARNING

Some parasites and contagious diseases can be passed from a dog to a child, but the risk of these is minimal if your veterinarian checks out your dog and you make sure that proper sanitary conditions are met in your home and yard.

TECHNICAL STUFF

THE SURGICAL OPTION FOR BARKERS

Call it the "final solution before the final solution," if you will, but one method of controlling barking that works well in almost all cases is available: debarking. The procedure is, however, as controversial as it is successful.

Debarking is the surgical altering under anesthesia of the vocal cords, changing them so that the dog can still bark, but at a greatly reduced volume. The debarked dog ends up with a bark that sounds like a harsh whisper, although the unpredictable final outcome, in terms of tone and volume, will vary from dog to dog.

While other options should be explored first, debarking is certainly better than euthanasia. It can be a good call in some cases, especially with dogs who simply like to yap. The dog still gets to bark, but the owner — and the neighbors — can live with it.

Talk to your veterinarian about this bark-control option.

Help your dog love your baby by training him, and by praising him in the child's presence.

Photograph courtesy of Gay Currier

HELP FOR THE STORM-CRAZED DOG

Some people who live in those parts of the world where thunderstorms roll in on a constant basis have reason to look at clouds with concern: Their dogs are terrified of the noise.

Thunderstorm fear can be very difficult to resolve, especially if your dog has a severe case of it. In some cases, you can train the dog to be more calm during storms by getting a tape or CD of storms (some nature stores offer them) and gradually increasing the noise level over time while engaging your dog in something she enjoys. The problem with this approach is that some dogs aren't fooled: They don't believe it's the real thing.

Positive (reward-based) obedience training can also help by building a dog's confidence. So, too, can medications prescribed to calm dogs. Some people report success with a holistic aid sold for people called Rescue Remedy that can be purchased from most health-food or vitamin stores.

Because of the difficulties in treating thunderphobia, a good place to start is with a trip to your veterinarian. Medication can help, and so can your vet's referral to a trainer or behaviorist.

DOES YOUR PUP NEED PROZAC?

Three times more dogs die because of behavior problems than because of cancer in the United States, and that sobering figure has caused a boom in the study of behavior in veterinary schools. One thing to come out of all that work — the one that has caught the public's fancy — is the use of human psychiatric drugs such as Prozac and Valium in treating some canine behavior problems. More recently, drugs such as Clomicalm have been introduced specifically for the veterinary market.

These findings are promising, no doubt, but there's still no quick fix. Whether an expert learned about dogs from years in academia or the School of Hard Knocks, you find very similar recommendations for proper health: exercise and training.

For a thoughtful read on canine behavior problems and the use of medications to treat them, pick up Dr. Nicholas Dodman's *The Dog Who Loved Too Much: Tales, Treatments and the Psychology of Dogs* (Bantam Books).

You're more likely to be able to find a veterinary behaviorist if you live in an urban area or near a veterinary college; ask your veterinarian for a referral. Whether you choose a veterinary behaviorist or a trainer, though, get help if you feel you're getting nowhere with your dog's problems. Sometimes a dog's owner isn't able to see what the real heart of the problem is and needs assistance in setting up a program that works.

> » Competing in dog shows and obedience trials
>
> » Enjoying games for working dogs
>
> » Introducing some hot new sports
>
> » Getting involved

Chapter 16

Canine Competitions: Fun Things to Do with Your Dog

Nearly all sports have their origins in some real-life activity, and dog sports are no exception. Likely not a minute had passed between the time our ancestors figured they could get a hound to hunt for them and the instant one ancestor turned to the other and said, "Yeah, well I bet *my* hound is faster!" The races haven't stopped since.

The games today are for more than the swift, however. In some competitions, looks take the day and in others agility — literally — is the point of it all. Some sports are meant to show off a breed's original function, such as hunting, sledding, and herding, and others stress precise teamwork the likes of which a ballroom dancing pair would be proud. Some sports are for a particular breed or a handful of related breeds only, others are only for purebreds, and a few are open to every dog. Some are as old as the relationship between humans and dogs, and others are taking shape even as you read this chapter.

Although some canine sports require top physical performances from both dog and handler, others are within the abilities of people slowed by age or disabilities. I have seen people in wheelchairs compete, and at a national obedience competition I once covered, the oldest competitor was nearing 90. And speaking of age: In no other collection of sports would a 12-year-old win over adult professionals at a top-level event — a feat that happened a few years ago at the Westminster Kennel Club dog show.

There is, truly, a competition for everyone — and every dog. To the uninitiated, dog sports can be a little hard to follow, which is why learning a little bit before you go is a good idea. Whether you're planning to attend with an eye toward competing someday or you're just looking for a pleasant family outing, this chapter contains plenty of information to get you started.

Be careful: Dog sports can be addictive. For some, a casual introduction to canine competitions ends up as a whole lot more than they reckoned for. Before they know what's happening, they're buying air-conditioned motor homes for the comfort of their dogs on the road and homes in the country so the ever-growing canine family can practice on agility or obedience equipment that's permanently set up. They have dog classes and club meetings nearly every night of the week, and they plan their vacations around such events as the national specialty show.

All this activity costs money, and the entry fees — which start at around $10 for a practice match and climb to $50 or so for the more prestigious events — are the least of it. Equipment and travel are expensive, and if you hire a professional to show your dog around the country for you, you're looking at potentially thousands of dollars in handling fees alone.

Go to the dogs if you must; the folks who love dog sports have no complaints. Just don't say I didn't warn you.

The Benefits of Organized Activities

Ribbons and trophies are all well and good, and I wouldn't suggest you ever turn one down should you and your dog get to such a level of proficiency that you start earning them. But I find the true benefits of canine competition are in the way they encourage a tighter bond between humans and dogs, and a camaraderie among the human participants, united as they are by the common thread of enjoying the company of dogs.

Preparing a dog for competition takes time, and time is the greatest gift you can give your dog. Training, practicing, grooming, traveling to events, and hanging out while waiting for your turn to compete all take time. While some humans (say, your spouse) may find all this hanging out decidedly less than entertaining, your dog couldn't be happier. After all, she's with *you*.

At times, you'll be particularly happy to have her around, too. Like any competitive endeavor, all is not supportive good sportsmanship in the world of canine competitions — you'll be happy for the unconditional support of your canine partner. In canine sports, the beginners compete against the experienced, the young against the old, the amateurs against the professionals — and every dog has his day. While the whole thing works a lot better than seems possible, these differences are a source of grousing, at the very least, and shouting, on more than a few occasions.

TIP

Dog events are happening nearly every weekend, but they can be a little hard to find. Calendars of events are listed in the general-interest dog magazines like *Dog Fancy*; the American Kennel Club and Canadian Kennel Club offer complete lists of their sanctioned events in their respective magazines, *The AKC Gazette* and *Dogs in Canada*. You may even keep an eye out in the events calendar of your local newspaper. A good listing of U.S. and Canadian events can be found on the Web at www.infodog.com.

If you get involved with a particular sport, you'll land on mailing lists event organizers use to keep entry forms constantly in prospective competitors' mailboxes.

Making Sense of It All

Although the point of some dog sports is rather obvious — you chase it, you pull it, you find it, or you bring it back — others aren't so easy to follow. The most popular dog sport of all — a conformation show (see the section "Dog Shows" later in this chapter) — is one of the hardest to follow. Sometimes determining who won in a given class is hard enough, much less understanding where that dog goes from there.

A dog show is surely the only sporting event in the world where the overwhelming majority of spectators — and even competitors — neither know nor care who won the final round (with the exception of the Westminster Kennel Club dog show and Crufts in England, both of which function, in essence, as national championships for the sport). Most competitors go to show their own dogs and then leave, and most spectators go just to look at the dogs and maybe buy a few canine accessories.

Still, if you get the basics down, you soon start understanding the nuances. And even if you don't stay for the finale, you will better enjoy the time you spend at the event.

TIP

No matter what kind of canine competition you attend, you need to take your comfort into your own hands. Dog shows are held both indoors and out, in all weather. Wear casual clothes and shoes you can walk in, and bring a lawn chair and shade if you plan to spend the day. (For indoor shows, just the lawn chair will do.) Although big shows have concessions, smaller events don't, so pack a lunch and make sure you've plenty to drink.

WARNING

Unentered dogs are not allowed on the grounds of events where dogs are competing for titles or points, so leave them at home until they're ready to enter. They are allowed at practice events, called *matches*, and these events are where exhibitors first expose their young dogs to the sights and sounds of competition.

TIP

An excellent resource on canine competitions is Cynthia D. Miller's *Canine Adventures: Fun Things To Do With Your Dog* (Animalia Publishing). The book covers every dog sport, and helps readers to evaluate which may be the best for any particular dog. Conditioning tips, too, make this book a must-have for anyone considering canine competitions.

WHAT'S THE BIG DEAL WITH WESTMINSTER?

If you had to pick the world's worst spot to put 2,500 freshly bathed and perfectly groomed show dogs, you'd be hard-pressed to top midtown Manhattan in the middle of February.

No dog in his right mind would choose the noise and the grime over the comforts of home. And yet every year, the second Monday and Tuesday of February find the few blocks around Madison Square Garden crowded with purebred dogs of all description, all there for the Westminster Kennel Club dog show.

Westminster, it's been said, is just a dog show the way that the Kentucky Derby is just a horse race. The comparison is especially apt considering that the Derby is the only major American sporting event with more history than Westminster: The great horse race is a scant 20 months older. Westminster is one of only two canine events with instant name recognition — the Iditarod is the other — and the prestigious dog show draws society's elite to its finals, along with millions of at-home spectators.

A win at the Westminster is the dream of a lifetime for those who breed, own, or handle show dogs; and only the best of them can even think of going. The Westminster Kennel Club allows in none but champions. Even with that restriction, the demand for the show's 2,500 slots is so keen that all are claimed within an hour of the time that show officials start accepting entries.

A victory by a particular breed at Westminster can trigger a jump in public demand for pups, a trend that goes back at least as far as the popularity of Cocker Spaniels in the '40s and '50s, helped immensely by a flashy two-time Westminster winner by the name of Ch. My Own Brucie.

A Best in Show win at Westminster is the ultimate honor in the sport, but the show is run pretty much the same as any of thousands of American Kennel Club–approved shows held every year. For Best in Show, the dogs are judged not against each other (for who, really, can compare a Chihuahua to a Great Dane?) but by how well each of the dogs conforms to the written standard of the breed. As with any dog show, the competition is first for Best of Breed, then a winner is chosen in each of the various groups — hound, herding, sporting, and so on.

Nearly all of the 2,500 dogs who come to Westminster will be on their way home or sleeping on a nearby hotel bed when the seven group winners enter the ring for Best in Show judging at the end of the show. In the hotel bars across Seventh Avenue, where the big TVs will surely be turned to the finale, exhaustion and disappointment will breed a litter of complaints: the venue is too small, the judging too political, the weather too brutal.

A few may swear they'll never enter a dog again, but most don't really mean it. The next time they have a dog with a chance of winning, they'll be back, no matter the difficulties.

Because . . . well, it's Westminster.

Dog Shows

Although the registries such as the American Kennel Club, United Kennel Club, and Canadian Kennel Club sanction field, agility, and obedience trials, most of the action is in *conformation competitions*, what most people think of when they think "dog show."

A dog show is, at its heart, a single-elimination tournament, with quarter- and semifinal rounds leading up to the selection of one winner — the Best in Show. The competition starts in the breed ring, where dogs of the same breed and similar characteristics square off against one another.

Each dog is judged against a *breed standard* — a set of rules and guidelines that define an ideal specimen of that breed. Parts of the standard may be quite specific — eliminating dogs over or under a certain size, for example — or quite vague, as in standards that ask that the dog have "dignity." Breed clubs set the standards and the AKC's breed standards are all listed in *The Complete Dog Book* (Howell Book House). *The Complete Dog Book* is updated and reissued every few years; in the interim, up-to-date breed standards are available from the kennel club. (You can also check out the kennel clubs' Web sites for breed standards.)

On the breed level, dogs are divided by sex and then again into smaller classes such as *puppy, bred-by-exhibitor,* and *open.* Some of these classes may be further divided by such factors as coat color — in Shelties, for example, separate classes will be held for *sable* dogs (little Lassie look-alikes) as well as for *tri-colors* (black, tan, and white) and *AOACs* (which stands for *Any Other Allowed Color*).

Just to make things even more confusing, colors and markings are treated like separate breeds for the purpose of judging for some breeds, but not others — for no real reason other than that's the way it has always been done. That's why you'll see only one Sheltie in the final rounds of competition, the top dog out of all the Sheltie colors allowed — but a handful of Cocker Spaniels, one of each allowed color combination. It may not be fair, but it's tradition, and tradition is big in the dog-show world.

The judge chooses a winner from each of these classes and then the best male and female from those winners. This pair then competes against established champions for Best in Breed honors. The best dog from each breed (or variety, in those breeds that get extra chances based on color or another factor, such as size) goes on to the semifinal round, against other dogs in the *group.* The best dog in each group — seven dogs in all — are all that remain at the end of the show, and one of those seven will be the top dog — Best in Show. Whew!

Obedience Trials

The sport of *obedience* started out as little more than a traveling exhibition more than 50 years ago, as its early proponents struggled to establish a friendly competition that challenged the intelligence and promoted the companionship ability of purebred dogs. They succeeded in creating a sport, but only just. For years, obedience competition languished in the shadows at dog shows, its classes small, its top dog-handler teams overlooked.

There were three levels of competition, three titles to attain, and when a team reached the top level, there was little incentive to stay involved. But then the AKC tossed the top trainers a meaty bone: a championship of their own. The addition of this obedience-trial championship, along with an ambitious series of national competitions and awards, shook up the sport.

At the highest levels of obedience competition today, the scores of the top dog-handler teams are often separated from each other and from perfection by the smallest of margins, sometimes by as little as one-half a point, the penalty for a slightly crooked sit.

But unlike the breed ring, where the difference between a first- and second-place finisher is difficult for the casual observer to spot, the difference between top-performing dogs and the others in the class are easy to see. Top-performing dogs work happily, willingly, and speedily, tearing through exercises that include jumping, retrieving, and heeling with the polish and panache of a true performer. These dogs are always "on," eyes glued to their handlers, muscles tensed in anticipation of a word or hand signal. The work is fast and exacting, but it's also apparent that the dogs are having fun.

The top dogs come from a relatively small handful of breeds — Golden Retrievers, Shetland Sheepdogs, Border Collies, Poodles, and Dobermans, for the most part — but almost all breeds are represented in the sport as a whole. They're all trying for the same thing — a perfect score of 200 on the road to an obedience title.

TECHNICAL STUFF

Why do some breeds do better overall in competitive obedience than others? It doesn't really have as much to do with intelligence as you might think — although the breeds that do well are certainly among the smartest. The breeds that do well in the obedience ring share the common traits of biddability — they learn easily and love the intricate tasks required by the sport — along with agility, high energy, and a certain level of flashiness.

TECHNICAL STUFF

To attain an AKC obedience title, a dog-handler team must receive a qualifying score, at least 170 points out of a possible 200, under three different judges on different days.

At all three levels — called *novice, open,* and *utility* — the dogs start with a perfect score, from which points are deducted for such violations as slowness, inattention, or whining. Some offenses are more serious than others: If a handler is forced to repeat a command, the team is disqualified.

After a dog has attained a degree at each of the three levels (a goal that can take two or three years to attain, and which most never reach) comes the hardest test of all — the pursuit of an obedience trial championship. The dogs are awarded points for first- and second-place finishes in the two highest classes, with the value of the win determined by the number of dogs in each class.

Obedience competitions used to be for purebreds only, but that's no longer true. While AKC-sanctioned events are still for purebreds only, some events — including the prestigious national championship series — are open to all dogs. The American Mixed Breed Obedience Registry (AMBOR) is the governing body for non-purebreds in the sport. The United Kennel Club also accepts mixed breeds for obedience competition.

Working Events

While dog shows and obedience trials attract the majority of competitors every year, several more sports are available to you and your dog. Most of these fall into the category of working events — competitions designed to prove a purebred dog still possesses the ability to do the job for which his breed was developed.

Some of these sports are governed by a major registry such as the AKC, UKC, or CKC, while others have their own governing body. Each sport is involved enough to warrant its own book — and most have them. In this book, I give you a brief overview to get you thinking.

The ability to compete successfully at a working event has been virtually lost in some breeds. As a result, some breeds, such as the Cocker Spaniel, have nearly abandoned their hunting heritage, while other breeds have split into *field* and *show* lines, with the dogs in each quite different in appearance. This split is perhaps most obvious in the Labrador Retriever, where show dogs are heavier in appearance than their leaner cousins in the working events.

Field trials

These competitions are designed to duplicate situations that would face hunting dogs at work. They break down by breed type:

>> **Trials for scent hounds.** Beagles are the most popular entrants in these events, which are designed to show how well a dog is capable of trailing game. Basset Hounds, Dachshunds, and Coonhounds have their own events, too.

>> **Trials for sight hounds.** Coursing events — usually using an artificial lure, not a live animal — test the enthusiasm of these most ancient of breeds to hunt using their awesome speed. Sight hound breeds as small as the Whippet and as large as the Irish Wolfhound find these events a blissful way to accomplish what many don't get the chance to do in more developed areas: Run like the wind.

>> **Trials for pointing breeds.** Here the point is to search for and find a bird, indicate its location with a classic point, and hold that position while the handler fires to prove that the dog isn't gun-shy.

>> **Trials for retrieving breeds and spaniels.** These events test the ability and endurance of these hunting breeds to retrieve game under a variety of conditions. Spaniels, usually English Springers, must additionally find and flush the game.

>> **Trials for terriers.** The courage and tenacity of these "earth dogs" — the name *terrier* comes from *terra*, for *earth* in Latin — is tested in a covered trench where they must race through the darkness to attack a caged and protected quarry, usually a rat.

Sled dog events

The International Sled Dog Racing Association serves as the primary governing body of this sport, which offers a variety of events for teams of all sizes and breeding. (Collies, hounds, and even Poodles have competed in these events.) Races of different lengths are usually run over a groomed snow course — although some are run in snowless areas, using a *gig* — a sled on wheels. Freight- and weight-pulling events are also run, as are long-distance races such as the Iditarod and those of lesser fame.

One of the hottest sports on snow is now *skijoring*, a cross between cross-country skiing and sled-dog racing. Handlers on skis are harnessed to one or more dogs, who run full-tilt to the finish line. Even those who don't compete still enjoy skijoring — it's a great way to exercise a dog. As in sled-dog racing, most of the dogs who compete are some combination of Huskies, but skijoring also attracts participants from the ranks of retrievers and other breeds.

Breeds that were developed to pull loads not on sleds but on wheels — such as Bernese Mountain Dogs — compete in *carting* events, where the aim is to show that the dog is as well-mannered and biddable in harness as a horse would be.

Protection dog events

Schutzhund — German for *protection dog* — is an international sport that tests the intelligence, endurance, and courage of dogs trained for police work. Competitors work their dogs through progressively harder levels of competition including tests of tracking, obedience, and protection. German Shepherds, Belgian Malinois, Rottweilers, and Dobermans are among the breeds most popular in this sport.

Herding dog events

These range from trials of real working sheep dogs to events that test the ability of a herding breed dog to move instinctively toward sheep or ducks as if herding. In the United Kingdom, sheepdog trials are so popular they're televised. The movie *Babe* gave millions of people a taste of the intensity and grace demonstrated by working sheepdogs.

Water dog events

Breeds that were developed for water search and rescue, such as Newfoundlands, can enter competitions designed to show off their skills in the water.

New Sports for the New Millennium — and Beyond

Some of the fastest-growing dog sports around are less than 20 years old, and some are of even more recent origin. What they have in common is that they're *fun*, for dogs, for handlers, and even for spectators.

Even better, they're open to all breeds, purebreds and mixes alike.

Agility

In agility competitions, the dogs race the clock over a course that includes a variety of obstacles to go through or jump over. The teams are penalized for missing or knocking down obstacles or not completing the course within the designated time. Both dogs and handlers have to be in decent shape for this one, because the handlers run the course while directing their dogs over the obstacles.

Agility is one hot sport, probably because the dogs get as much of a kick out of it as the people do, and because it's one of the few canine activities that show great promise as a spectator event — many agility competitions are now televised, to a loyal and enthusiastic audience.

Flyball

At the heart of the flyball competition is a launching device that releases a tennis ball into the air when the dog steps on a triggering board at the front of the device.

Picture two such devices, side by side, at the end of a series of low jumps, and a relay team of dogs and handlers, and you can imagine just how fast and exciting flyball can get.

Agility competitions are growing in popularity because the sport is fun for both dog and handler.

Fang/Photograph courtesy of Jack and Samantha Russell

The dogs leap over the series of jumps, trigger the launcher, grab the ball, and jump, jump, jump back to the beginning of the course — all in a few seconds. After these actions are complete, the dogs must cross the finish line, which allows the team's next dog to be released. The team that gets all its dogs up and back the fastest wins.

Freestyle obedience

The latest competition to be developed, freestyle obedience, consists of dog-handler pairs performing original and intricately choreographed routines set to music. Think dancing or figure skating with your dog. The latter comparison makes sense if you think of traditional obedience as the compulsory figures and freestyle as the creative program, complete with costumes!

Flying disk competitions

This competition is probably the only dog sport that started because of a single dog — Ashley Whippet, who in the '70s became a media superstar performing gravity-defying leaps at nationally televised sporting events. Today, hundreds of dogs compete in regional events, leading up to a world invitational tournament — where style, height, and daring in the art of the retrieve separate the winners from the other competitors.

The fastmoving sport of flyball is nearly as exciting for spectators as it is for competitors.

Photograph courtesy of Gay Currier

Getting Started

So maybe now you want to quit watching and get out there and *compete* with your dog. Good move, but where do you begin?

Some dog sports — or events, anyway — are clearly not for beginners (the Iditarod comes to mind). Others aren't open to all breeds, and some rely much more on your dog's natural attributes than anything you can contribute to make him more competitive. So the first step in getting involved in canine competitions is to take a look at what you've got, and by that I mean your dog.

Choose a sport

No dog can compete in all sports, so the first step in deciding what canine competition suits you both is to take a good look at your dog. First, is he purebred or mixed? Many dog sports are for registered purebreds only. If your dog is truly an original in appearance — the result of some illicit dalliance between a Golden Retriever and a Basset Hound, say — you're going to have to stick to those events open to all.

If your dog *is* a registered purebred, is he a good representative of his breed? If so, you may decide to go the dog-show route. Be warned, however, that what a lot of puppy sellers call *show quality* isn't really *show winning:* What they're guaranteeing is a dog who has no disqualifying faults, such as being too tall or the wrong color.

You need only a few minutes with the breed standard — available from a governing registry such as the American Kennel Club or Canadian Kennel Club — to get an idea of how your pet stacks up. A person with experience breeding and showing dogs like yours should also be able to explain the good and bad points of your pup and assess his chances in the show ring.

TECHNICAL STUFF

No matter how lovely your dog, he or she can't be a show dog if you've already spayed or neutered your dog. Because a dog show is supposed to be about evaluating breeding stock, altered animals aren't eligible.

The dog-show game is a hard one to break into, a super-competitive blend of big money, professional handlers, and some very hot dogs. But beginners can do well now and then. A few years ago, a couple's very first show dog, a lovely Doberman, had a spectacular show career capped by a win in Madison Square Garden, where she was named Best in Show of the prestigious Westminster Kennel Club dog show.

For more on breed standards and researching a breed, see Chapter 2.

So maybe your dog's markings aren't right, or one of his ears sticks up when it should fold over, or maybe you've already done the responsible thing and neutered him. Although he isn't going to be a show champion, he has plenty of titles left to work for. If he's one of a working breed, a group is probably around that's prepared to honor him for showing he can still do the job for which he was bred.

Some of the best competitions for beginners — open to all dogs, purebred, mixed, or neutered — are sports of a more modern development, such as obedience, agility, or flyball. The latter two would get many a dog's vote as "best," too, for they are full of high-flying canine competitors who can barely stand to wait their turn to compete.

TECHNICAL STUFF

Although you cannot enter your pet in a dog show if he hasn't full registration with a governing body such as the AKC, you may be able to make him eligible for other canine competitions run by the same group. The AKC has a designation called *Indefinite Listing Privilege (ILP).* This designation is a way into competition for dogs who aren't eligible for full registration. For more information on ILP registration, contact the American Kennel Club.

Take a class, join a club

After you decide on a sport for you and your dog to try, you need to find other people who are interested in it and willing to share their expertise with you. You find those people in dog clubs and in training classes.

TECHNICAL STUFF

Dog clubs come in several varieties, and plenty of them are available. The AKC, which is itself a club made up of smaller breed and activity clubs, reports that more than 4,000 clubs are holding shows and other competitions around the United States.

You can find all-breed kennel clubs, such as the Louisville Kennel Club or the Kennel Club of Northern New Jersey. Every breed has a national club, such as the Afghan Hound of America Club or the American Bouvier des Flanders Club, and hundreds of local or regional single-breed clubs, such as the Greater Atlanta Fox Terrier Club or the Papillon Association of Puget Sound, exist as well. Some clubs exist because of a particular sport, such as the Fresno Dog Training Club, the Snake River Retriever Trial Club, or the Haute Dawgs Agility Group. Such groupings of fanciers exist all over the world.

Clubs exist to put on competitions, provide training facilities and advice, and share information between club members. These are the folks with whom you need to be associating if you're going to get started in competition.

TIP

Classes are another good opportunity to get started. Group or individual classes exist to teach dog-show handling, competitive obedience, agility, or nearly every other canine endeavor. Some of these classes are sponsored by clubs, others by top individuals who make their living competing in canine sports. For example, some people who are professional show-dog handlers give classes in handling. And if you discover you're just too uncoordinated to show your own dog, then they're often happy to take you on as a client and show your dog for you.

Making the connections

So where do you find these clubs and classes? Following are a few ideas:

>> **Breeder.** If you bought your dog from a reputable breeder, chances are she's already involved in her local and national breed club and has attended plenty of classes and seminars. She should be happy to mentor you or point you in the direction of people who can.

>> **Registry.** You can also work your way from the top down, by asking the AKC, CKC, or UKC (or other dog registry or governing body) to provide you with a contact name and address in your area, or at the very least, a contact for the national breed club.

>> **Publications.** Hundreds of national, regional, and local canine publications are available, from the simple newsletter for a small, local, breed club to slick magazines dedicated to a single breed or sport. Such publications can quickly increase your knowledge and competitive edge, and I highly recommend them.

Keeping Things in Perspective

Whatever you do, try to keep in mind the original purpose of getting involved was for you and your dog to have something fun to do *together*. Sometimes people lose sight of that, constantly replacing one dog in favor of another who they hope will be better. And while it's true that to be truly competitive you're going to need a very special dog — and a large amount of time and money — it's also true you can pick up many titles with the dog you have now, if you work with her.

Your dog will be happier if you keep the love of dogs primary in your mind, not the love of competition. You'll both have a better time if you remember it's just a game — win or lose, your dog goes home with you afterwards.

PAWS FOR A CAUSE

TIP

Not everyone who likes to get out and about with a dog is chasing ribbons; a great many people gauge their success in smiles, and you and your dog can be among them.

Animal-assisted therapy is a growing field of volunteerism that uses friendly, well-mannered dogs to make a difference in the lives of people in institutional settings. Children in hospital wards, residents of nursing homes, people in hospices — all of these and more have benefited from the visits of these marvelous dogs and their caring owners.

Therapy work is not for every dog — or every person. Although breed and breeding don't matter, therapy dogs do share the ability to behave calmly and predictably in all surroundings. For their handlers, perhaps the most important trait is commitment, because people come to depend on the visiting dogs.

If you think animal-assisted therapy is something you'd like to do, find out more. The rewards of making a difference in the lives of others are truly breathtaking.

The Delta Society is an excellent resource for information on animal-assisted therapy, service dogs, or any other expression of the human-animal bond. Contact the organization at 289 Perimeter Road East, Renton, WA 98055-1329; 800-869-6898; www.deltasociety.org

Chapter **17**

To Breed or Not to Breed

Somebody has to breed dogs, or there wouldn't be any. And I certainly want dogs to be in my life — and yours — for a long, long time. Good breeders have always existed, and I hope they always will. They care about their breed and the dogs they produce. They put years of study and effort into breeding dogs who are healthy and temperamentally sound — dogs who closely match the standards for their breed.

These breeders, unfortunately, are the minority. All is not right in the dog world, and it hasn't been for a long, long time. The reason: too many. Too many what?

» **Too many dogs** dying for the want of a home. Not just mixed breeds, either. Shelters and rescue groups deal with plenty of purebreds.

» **Too many dogs** with health problems that could be eliminated through conscientious breeding.

» **Too many dogs** with inherited personality problems, such as aggression or shyness or even yappiness.

» **Too many dogs** with personality problems caused by improper handling in the first weeks of their lives.

People who shouldn't be breeding dogs cause these problems. If you care about dogs — your dog and all dogs — you need to consider breeding very carefully. You need to educate yourself about your breed and the congenital health and temperament problems within your breed. You need to have a plan for breeding, and a plan — as well as a fund — for dealing with emergencies. You need time to help the puppies be born, to care for them, and to socialize them. You need to know how to find good homes for those babies. You can be a good breeder, but you have to work at it. There are no shortcuts.

WARNING

Be prepared to deal with the puppies you can't sell. Also, some puppies may be returned to you. They are your responsibility, too. If you can't say that you will do all of the things that a reputable breeder does, you need to spay or neuter your dog. Neutering, or at the very least making a decision not to breed your pet, is in the best interest of your dog and all dogs. It also makes your life easier.

The Case against Breeding

According to a 1995 survey by the American Animal Hospital Association, nearly 80 percent of all U.S. pets are spayed or neutered. The American Kennel Club's findings back this up — most AKC-registered puppies are never bred.

What do these people know that you don't? Spayed and neutered dogs make happier, healthier, safer, and less expensive pets.

Health and behavior

Spaying and neutering have benefits that extend greatly beyond birth control. A neutered male:

>> Is less likely to roam, less likely to fight, less likely to leg-lift in the house, and less likely to bite. The latter is especially significant: A dog involved in an attack on a human is typically a young, unneutered male.

>> Is less likely be involved in a dog-fight. Aggressive dogs find the presence of another unneutered male a challenge they take very seriously. If yours is a large dog he may escape such an attack with only a bite or two; a small dog could be killed.

>> Is spared from testicular or prostate cancer.

SPAYING AND NEUTERING: WHAT'S INVOLVED?

Spaying and neutering are the everyday terms for the surgical sterilization of a pet — spaying for the female, neutering for the male. Neutering — or *altering* — is also used to describe both procedures. The clinical terms for the two operations are *ovariohysterectomy*, for the female, and *castration*, for the male. (Which is obviously why most people call the procedures something else!)

Both spaying and neutering must be done only by a veterinarian, and both require general anesthesia. The procedures have traditionally been performed starting at the age of six months but, in recent years, *early spay-neuter* on puppies as young as 8 weeks has been widely approved by veterinary groups and is gaining favor.

Spaying involves the removal of the female's entire reproductive system: The uterus, fallopian tubes, and ovaries are taken out through an incision in the abdomen. Your veterinarian may require you to return to have your dog's stitches removed in about 10 days, or he may use stitches that are absorbed into the body. Recovery is fast, taking just a few days, during which you should limit your dog's activities — no jumping or boisterous play. Most owners notice very little difference in their female's personality.

In neutering, the male dog's testicles are removed through an incision just in front of the *scrotum,* the pouch holding the testicles. Self-absorbing stitches are the norm in this relatively minor procedure; your veterinarian will inform you if your dog needs any postoperative care.

Many dog owners are surprised to see that their dog doesn't "look" neutered at first, since the scrotum remains in place and may be somewhat swollen. The loose skin will gradually shrink away over a few weeks.

Behavioral changes can be dramatic in some neutered males. Such hormone-linked behaviors as mounting and dominance-related aggression will diminish in a good percentage of young adult males. In older ones, there may be little behavior change at all, and in dogs neutered before sexual maturity — before six months or so — sex-linked behaviors will likely never develop.

Spaying and neutering are among the most common medical procedures in the United States and Canada, and carry very little risk for your dog. Your veterinarian will discuss your role to ensure that any complications that *do* develop are dealt with promptly.

For females, the behavior benefits aren't as remarkable, but the health benefits are more so. A spayed female:

>> Is safe from breast cancer if you spay her before her first season.

>> Is protected from other cancers of the reproductive system.

>> Will not develop *pyometra,* a life-threatening infection of the uterus.

>> Will not spot your carpets with the twice-yearly mess caused by the vaginal bleeding of a dog in season.

>> Will not attract male callers.

Time and money

Breeding a dog takes time and money, especially for the owner of the female. Your dog and the dog you breed her to need to be certified clear of inherited problems such as hip dysplasia, deafness, and inherited eye diseases. Both dogs need to be tested for venereal diseases, and they need to be current on their vaccinations, free of parasites, and on heartworm-preventive medication. This all costs money, easily into the hundreds of dollars.

After the male dog has all his health clearances, his job is easy. He gets to the party early and leaves the scene before too long. But the female's job has just gotten started after the coupling. Most of the costs are borne by her owner, starting with the stud fee. But even before you can pay that, you'll have to find a stud dog. You're not likely to find a suitable mate around the corner, or even in your town, which means you have to spend more money to drive or ship your female.

Your dog will need high-quality food in greatly larger amounts than usual and possibly supplements, if your veterinarian recommends them, for the last few weeks of her pregnancy and the entire time she's nursing. If the litter is too much for her, you'll be hand-raising at least some of the puppies, and maybe all of them if she becomes unable to nurse. Above all, you have to be prepared to deal with a long list of medical emergencies that can threaten the life of both mother and puppies and can result in very large veterinary bills.

If your breed requires tail docking and dewclaw removals, you'll need to pay for that, along with vaccinations and other health needs. Have I mentioned puppy food for the last three or four weeks you have the puppies (after they've been weaned)? And that's assuming you can sell the puppies promptly — sometimes you can't.

You have to take time off work when your dog's *whelping*, or giving birth, and you should take still more time off to socialize your pups to ensure that they become good pets for the people you sell them to. You need to expose your puppies to children, men, women, cats, and the normal noises of a human household. A litter of puppies is a constant mess-making machine: Your washing machine will be going around the clock and you'll be begging your neighbors for their old newspapers and towels within a week. You need more than free newspapers, though: You need a whelping box and hot-water bottles or a special heating element or lamp to keep puppies warm when they're young, because they can't regulate their own temperature well. When they're up on those pudgy little legs, you need an exercise pen to keep them safe and away from the many, many things those puppy teeth can decimate.

What if you can't get the price you want for your puppies? The popularity of fad breeds means that, before long, too many puppies are around and prices fall accordingly. You may be playing *Let's Make a Deal* with the last couple, or even giving them away. And it's not unheard of for desperate first-time breeders to drop the remains of a litter off at a shelter.

TIP

Ask a reputable breeder to help you determine what producing a high-quality litter costs. Chances are you'll find even more items in the expense column than I've listed here, things such as ultrasounds to verify pregnancies or the cesarean deliveries that are common in some breeds. Litter announcements and advertising costs money, too, and hardly a breeder alive hasn't dealt with a disaster that has wiped out an entire litter of dreams and left nothing but huge veterinary expenses behind.

What if you meant to spay your dog and come home to find her mating with the dog from three doors down? She doesn't have to carry the litter to term. Spaying can be done on a pregnant dog, and the sooner the better.

A Dog-Breeding Primer

The business of dog breeding hasn't changed much over the years: You breed the best to the best, and hope for the best. The ways of determining quality have changed a great deal, though, and will change even more as health screenings move to the chromosome level in the future.

The whole thing would likely make the owner of a working sheep or hunting dog shake his head. In the old days, if a dog didn't earn its keep, it didn't live long enough to breed. In some circles today that's still the bottom line, although more — but not all — of the less-gifted career dogs today find homes as pets, be they Greyhounds, Beagles, or Border Collies.

Donald McCaig, who is one of the best writers around when it comes to dogs, tells a story in one of his books about how folks with working Border Collies will sometimes resort to sneaky methods to breed their dogs to the best around: They wait until the dog's owner has tied up his dog outside the refreshment tent at a trial and tossed back a couple, and then put the two dogs together when no one's paying attention.

Because few breeders work their dogs as a shepherd does his, they rely on other factors to determine which animals they should breed. They show them to have judges evaluate their *conformation* — a measure of how closely they conform to the blueprint for the breed, called the *standard* (more on standards is in Chapter 2). They may test their working instincts or put hunting or other working titles on them in competitions that recreate the conditions of the real thing. They certainly have them tested for hereditary defects and consider temperament before breeding. High-quality dogs are produced through this selective process. For more on canine competitions, see Chapter 16.

REMEMBER

If you're thinking of breeding your dog, you want to go to the best stud dog you can, and that means the best stud dog for *your particular dog*, one who is a good match for her pedigree, her conformation, and her temperament. The person who can best help you find such a dog is an experienced, reputable breeder with knowledge of your dog's breed in general and her pedigree lines in particular. A better deal still is if you can convince this person to mentor you through the mating, pregnancy, delivery, raising, and placing of the puppies — everyone has to start somewhere, and good breeders know this.

If your dog's neither titled nor of reasonable conformation, such a person may not want to work with you or allow her stud dog to breed with your female. It doesn't hurt to ask, though, because this is a much better way to go than breeding your dog to one that your neighbor, cousin, or coworker owns. The latter may be your only option, however, if your dog is not of a quality that should be bred. Which means, of course, that you shouldn't breed her.

Mating, gestation, and whelping

Your dog should be at least two years old before you consider breeding her, because she needs to be more than a puppy herself to be a good mother to her babies. She should be in good health, to withstand the rigors of pregnancy, whelping, and nursing. Her vaccinations should be current, and she should be clear of parasites and on heartworm-preventive medicine. Test for genetic defects in her breed should have come back clear, as should a test for *brucellosis*, a disease passed through mating that causes sterility in dogs. All of this means, of course, that you need to be see your veterinarian.

The stud dog, too, must meet these criteria and should be chosen before your dog is ready for breeding. Females are usually sent to the stud for breeding, and some are shipped thousands of miles for just the right match.

TECHNICAL STUFF

Some breedings take place without the dogs ever so much as sniffing each other, thanks to frozen semen and artificial insemination. Some stud dogs have even sired litters after their demise! If the stud dog that suits your dog is too far away, discuss this option with the owner of the dog and with your veterinarian. This procedure is increasingly common, and the puppies are eligible for full registration with the AKC and other organizations.

A female *comes into season* (or *heat*) for approximately 21 to 30 days every five to seven months. Her heat begins at the first sign of bleeding and ends when she loses interest in breeding. The female does not become interested in breeding until a week or so after her season begins. While your veterinarian can pinpoint when she is most likely to be successfully bred, the dog has a pretty good idea herself, flirting with the males and standing with her tail up in her best canine come-hither behavior.

The males don't need that much encouragement. Her smell from the first day of her season has been driving them wild, and the only thing that has kept them from mating with her sooner has been her refusal to allow it.

TIP

As soon as the first signs of season appear, you should finalize arrangements with the stud dog's owner and send your dog to the stud so she can be there when she's ready to breed.

An experienced breeder can best handle your dog at this point. She allows the dogs to become comfortable with one another and, after the female is interested, the breeder does what it takes to get the job done, including holding the female for the male and even inserting the male's penis into the female if the stud is inexperienced. Far from being embarrassed about such things, the experienced breeder considers it just another job that must be done to produce puppies.

TECHNICAL STUFF

The male starts to ejaculate soon after he starts thrusting, but the most sperm-rich semen is released after the action appears to have stopped and the so-called *tie* begins. The base of the canine penis swells while inside the female, locking the dogs together to give the sperm a chance to impregnate — and keeping competitors at bay. After the tie begins, the male turns away from the female so that the two are positioned rump to rump. This stage can last for more than a half-hour before the swelling goes down and the dogs break apart. If it lasts for more than two hours, call your veterinarian.

Pregnancy ranges from 58 to 70 days, during which you should follow your veterinarian's instructions on prenatal care. A couple of weeks before her due date, you should prepare a *whelping box*, a place for her to have her puppies, in an out-of-the-way corner of your home. For large breeds, a plastic kiddy pool lined with layers and layers of newsprint works well; smaller breeds may use the bottom half of a shipping crate. The most important characteristic in a whelping box is that it can be easily cleaned.

TIP

Printed newspapers are messy, so try to get unprinted newsprint. Your local newspaper may sell — or give away — the ends of the giant newsprint rolls that go onto the presses.

Final preparations for long-coated breeds include clipping the hair on her hind end very short, to keep puppies from getting caught, and on her belly to make the nipple area neater. Don't worry about how awful she looks; she'll lose even more fur on her own before it's all over and look even more dreadful!

Talk to your veterinarian one last time about what to expect. Ideally, if you've been working with an experienced breeder, she'll be there to help you as your dog starts labor. He may suggest an ultrasound or X-ray to aid in predicting the size of the litter and any potential problems with the delivery.

A day before the big date, your dog will probably lose her appetite and become more restless. She may dig in laundry piles; show her to her whelping box, instead — you may need to be persistent, but she should have her litter where *you* can care for them best. Take her temperature: A dip to 99 degrees shows that labor is near. *Make sure that you know where your veterinarian is — or the closest emergency clinic — and cancel all your plans, because the time is near.*

Take the puppies and their mother to the veterinarian's within the first day after the birth to make sure that everything's okay with them all. If dewclaws are to be removed and tails docked, discuss these procedures with your veterinarian right away — these minor surgeries (both elective, neither necessary) need to be done before the age of three days. While experienced breeders often complete these procedures themselves, a novice breeder should not even attempt it — have your veterinarian take care of it. (For more on cosmetic surgeries, see Chapter 11.)

TIP

Another job in those first few days: Paperwork! Send in litter registration so that you get individual registration forms back in plenty of time to provide to puppy buyers. Contact the registry for more information on what's required.

WARNING

BIRTHING EMERGENCIES

Most dogs are natural whelpers and may not need your help at all. Many a pet owner has fallen asleep waiting for the big event only to wake up to a box full of puppies born, cleaned up, and nursing. If your dog isn't quite so efficient, you have to release the puppies from their amniotic sacs within 30 seconds or so and help them to breathe on their own. Clean the fluid from their mouths and noses by supporting their heads and swinging them between your legs, stopping sharply. You can also remove fluid with a bulb syringe. Rub the puppy with a clean towel and put her on a nipple. Above all, keep the puppies warm.

If the mother doesn't sever the umbilical cord, you may need to do that, too: Tie it off about an inch from the puppy with a thread soaked in alcohol and then snip with clean scissors. Dab the ends with Betadine to combat infection.

While many experienced breeders are sometimes as capable as any veterinarian when it comes to saving puppies, the novice breeder should not hesitate to get veterinary help quickly. You *must* take your dog to the veterinarian when:

- She fails to enter labor 24 to 36 hours after her temperature dips to 99 degrees.

- She's in labor and more than four hours lapse with no puppy being born, especially if a dark green fluid passes.

- She seems very uncomfortable and is panting heavily.

- A puppy gets stuck while being delivered.

- She has a puppy, and 30 minutes pass without another puppy being born, yet she's having strong contractions.

- If she doesn't expel an afterbirth, or *placenta*, for each puppy. Retained afterbirths can trigger infections.

If in doubt about anything, call! She may need more help than you can give her, including a cesarean section. If everything goes well, clean the mother up with Betadine while she cleans up the nest — eating the afterbirths is a normal part of the process.

An important after-birth problem to look out for: If your nursing mom becomes restless, agitated, and trembling, call the veterinarian's and tell them you're on the way. She may need calcium treatments for a condition called eclampsia.

Mother and puppies should visit the veterinarian within the first 24 hours after birth.

Raising Good Puppies — and Finding Good Homes

If you want to increase the chances of raising your puppies right — and be reassured that your puppies are "normal" — knowing a little about how puppies mature is helpful. As with children, these stages each have their wonders and their challenges. These stages pass too quickly, so to get the most out of the *puppy experience* clear your calendar of nondog activities and keep your eyes open.

All puppies look much the same when they're born. You find size and marking differences, but they each come into this world looking something like a sausage, with tiny ears, tiny legs, and tightly closed eyes. Things start to change before long.

TECHNICAL STUFF

Although people have raised puppies for thousands of years, most of what we now know about how people can influence a puppy's development — and about developmental stages in puppies — goes back only about four decades, starting with the work of John Paul Scott and John L. Fuller in the '50s. From their "school for dogs" in Bar Harbor, Maine, came the basis of what trainers and breeders have been using to get the most out of dogs ever since.

Animal Behavior, (Paul Scott, University of Chicago Press) is a fascinating place to start a study of dog behavior. Fuller and Scott teamed on *Genetics and the Social Behavior of Dogs*, also from the University of Chicago Press. Although out of print, these books are in many libraries, and a good second-hand bookseller should be able to find copies without too much trouble.

A more recent — and less academic — treatment of the subject can be found in many subsequent books. Three I like to recommend are Carol Lea Benjamin's *Mother Knows Best: The Natural Way To Train Your Dog* (Howell Book House); *How To Raise a Puppy You Can Live With*, by Clarice Rutherford and veterinarian David H. Neil (Alpine Press); and *The Art of Raising a Puppy* by the monks of the New Skete Monastery (Little, Brown).

Birth to 3 weeks

Puppies are pretty helpless at birth. They can't see or hear and need their mother for everything. She is their source for food, warmth, and protection; they cannot even eliminate waste without her gentle licking to stimulate the process.

Newborn pups can crawl and right themselves when turned over, and they can seek out food by smell. They can also seek out the warmth of their littermates — they are unable at this stage to regulate their own body temperature.

TIP
On the outside, this time seems quiet — puppies at this age sleep almost constantly — but a lot of development is going on inside their brain and central nervous system. Leave them alone, except for one thing: Handle them briefly and gently on a daily basis, and subject them to the tiniest amount of stress in the process. Puppy-raising experts believe this stress — such as placing them on a scale — is as important as handling in the development of a confident dog.

Even this early in a puppy's life, some temperament patterns are set. If you watch, you can already see which puppies will later become dominant with their siblings. These are the ones who push others out of the way at nursing time — an impression confirmed during frequent weighings: The pushier pups will grow faster. Other pups are more wiggly, nervous, or cry during handling. You should note all these things.

Towards the end of the second week, the puppies start to open their eyes, although they see little more than light at this point. In the third week, the first teeth appear and puppies start to hear. By the end of the third week, the sausages look like puppies, and they're ready to start exploring the world.

TIP
What if you have a litter of black Labrador puppies? How can you possibly tell one from another enough to follow and record changes in the early weeks when personalities are not so obvious? Use this trick: Make little collars of *rickrack*, a decorative zigzag trim material available in fabric stores, a different color for each puppy. You won't have to resort to this tactic, of course, if you can note the puppies' markings to keep things straight.

3 to 5 weeks

During this stage puppies start relying less on their mother and start to learn from each other. They learn to play and to eat solid food.

Even as all of this activity is happening — a wealth of new experiences, overwhelming their new senses of vision and hearing — the puppies are learning the rudiments of canine communication and social structure. Puppies start to learn to use their sharp little teeth and, more importantly, when they cannot use them. Their mother teaches them some of this behavior, using her teeth to correct, but not hurt, them. In play with each other, an observer hears plenty of cries and squeals as bites are delivered just a little too hard, and puppies learn to *inhibit* their biting, delivering them with a force that matches the situation. (When puppies don't learn to inhibit biting from their mother and littermates, problems are bound to occur when they're in their new homes. More on this in Chapters 9 and 15.)

REMEMBER

While the puppies are most interested in each other at this stage, you should be busy reminding them that there are people in the world, too. Make sure their environment is always changing, and continue to handle the puppies, making sure that each gets individual attention. Expose the puppies to both genders and to children as well as adults. If a cat lives in the house, even better — although do your cat a favor and let him choose his interactions. His mere presence is enough to expose the puppies to the existence of felines.

Start weaning the puppies after three weeks. Discuss with your veterinarian or mentor the type of soft food you'll offer the puppies and help the pups get the idea by putting the food on your finger and helping it into their mouths. Puppy pans — doughnut-shaped dishes with a low outer rim — are ideal for giving every pup a place at the "table."

After puppies are eating semisolid food, the mother will quit cleaning up the nest by eating their waste — so the task of keeping puppies clean falls entirely to you now. About this time the mother will start helping the weaning process by spending more time away from her babies — she's getting a little sick of them!

Watching a litter is a wonderful way to spend some time. Although I've seen many, many litters, one in particular seems special to me: my dog Andy's. I saw Andy at least twice before he came home with me — the first time he was just hours old. He wriggled a little in my hands and settled down as I stroked the tan patches on the sides of his face. It was as if he recognized me and, years later, he still sighs in happiness when I run my hands along the sides of his face.

5 to 7 weeks

The biggest mistake you can make in this period is to remove a puppy from the litter and send him to a new home. This practice is probably based on the idea that weaning is the logical time for puppies to be sold — puppies can start on hard kibble around six weeks — but the research emphatically insists that this "logic" is wrong.

REMEMBER

Puppies have a lot more learning to do during these two weeks, and they need to be with their littermates to do it. Think of this period as the *time of more*. Puppies can see more, hear more, and play more at this stage. They are starting to become more interested in the world beyond their enclosure. They are especially attracted to those funny, two-legged dogs who have spent the last few weeks picking them up, talking to them, and petting them. Suddenly, they think humans are pretty cool.

This stage is when humans think puppies are pretty cool, too. Puppies are absolutely adorable now, with the softest fur and the cutest faces. They run with a rolling, bouncing, puppy gait, tripping over their big paws at times. They roughhouse with each other and stalk their toys. They drive their mother crazy — she is interested in spending as little time with them as possible now.

They are still learning, but what a fun time they're having.

TIP

You should spend a lot of time with them at this stage, for socializing is in full swing. Keep exposing them to the sights and sounds of life all the way up to the time they go to their new homes — ideally, after their seventh week.

Finding proper homes

If you've done your job right, you have something truly remarkable to offer puppy buyers: Fat, friendly, well-socialized puppies who promise a lifetime of good health and companionship. You want to be sure that the people who take them are worthy of such wonderful pups.

This means you need to be extra-careful in screening homes, not just accepting money from the first half-dozen people who walk through your door. If you've been working with a reputable breeder, ask for her help in placing the puppies. Some questions you should ask:

>> **What is your living arrangement?** You don't need a house with a yard — some dogs, even large ones, do just fine in apartments — but you do need a person who's aware of what a dog needs and is prepared to deliver it. Just say no to anyone who plans to stick one of your pups on a chain in the yard.

>> **Have you had dogs before? What kinds, and what happened to them?** Wrong answers include "lots" and "they ran away," "we moved," or "he got hit." Accidents happen to even the most conscientious of dog lovers, but a pattern of mishaps says a great deal about the way the prospective buyer treats dogs — and it's not well.

>> **Do you have any experience with this breed? What do you expect of it?** You want to educate — and possibly eliminate from contention — anyone who isn't prepared to deal with the reality of living with a dog like yours. A person who isn't prepared for the shedding of a long-haired dog or the activity level of a terrier, for example. Be honest with buyers about the drawbacks of the breed, and you're much more likely to put your puppies in homes that will keep them, because they know what to expect.

>> **Do you have children? What ages?** Some dogs, such as delicate toys, just don't work out well with children. Still, be flexible. A thoughtful, gentle child could work out fine. Discuss your concerns and see what answers you get.

>> **Do you intend to breed your dog? Show your dog? Train your dog?** Your pet-quality puppies — ones with obvious show faults, such as wrong markings — should be sold on contracts that require them to be spayed or neutered. (Some breeders have the surgery taken care of before their puppies go to their new homes.) People who are interested in training and competing with their dogs plan to be involved in their pup's life, and that's the kind of thing you like to see. Look, too, for people who travel with their pets or obviously treat them like the family they are — or should be.

Be cordial and informative, but be persistent. Check references, including calling their veterinarian. A person who has had numerous pets and *doesn't* have a veterinary reference is another to cross off your list. Don't be afraid to turn people down. While it may not be pleasant, you must do what's best for your puppies. You've put a lot of effort into them, and you want them to live with someone who will continue to love and care for them as you have.

Remember, always, that you want your puppies to go to good homes, and the only one who has a chance at making that happen is you. So do your best.

If you are considering breeding your dog again, you need to skip at least a season to give her time to recover. In any case, one or two litters are about all you should ask of her if she's to enjoy just being a member of your family. As soon as her motherhood days are behind her, arrange for her to be spayed to give her the best chance at a healthy life.

OLDER DOGS NEED HOMES TOO

Puppies aren't the only dogs who need responsible, loving homes. Oftentimes, older dogs do too. If a stray follows your son home from school and you can't find an owner, or you inherit an older dog from a sick relative, or you end up with an extra dog for any other reason, you want to find the best home for the dog you can. Here are some tips:

- Do everything you can to make the animal more adoptable. The pet has a better chance if she has current shots, is house-trained, and neutered. It also helps if she's socialized and friendly with children, with other dogs, and with cats. Try to fix behavior problems before placement, or you may see a quick return. (For more on basic manners and problem-solving, see Chapters 14 and 15.)

- Ask a price. People show more respect for something they've paid for, and a price tag dampens the interest of profiteers, such as those who collect "free to a good home" pets for sale to research labs or to dogfighters. A good rule: Charge an amount to cover the cost of the spaying/neutering and vaccinations. That makes sense to prospective adopters, because it's money they would have had to spend anyway.

- Don't lie about the pet's problems, or why he's being placed. Although finding a new home for a pet with behavior problems takes longer, it can be done. But the person who gets such a pet without warning is likely to bring him back or place him somewhere without your knowledge, maybe into a horrible situation.

- Ask lots of questions and verify that the answers are true. Ask for a telephone number and call back to check it. Ask to see a driver's license. Check out the home in person, and bring along a friend. Don't forget to ask prospective adopters if they've had pets before and what happened to them. Make sure that you're dealing with people who realize owning a pet is a long-term commitment.

WARNING

Another reason to spay her quickly: If you keep a puppy, you may be positively shocked to find your girl pregnant again — thanks to her own son. I once got a call from a woman who wanted me to convince her husband their dog could not possibly be pregnant, because the only male she'd been around was a pup from her last litter. "But that's incest!" yelled the woman when I gave her the bad news. "Don't they know better?"

Unfortunately, they don't.

IN THIS CHAPTER

» **Deciding whether to travel with your dog**

» **Finding care for the stay-at-home pet**

» **Preparing to travel**

» **Traveling by car and air**

» **Choosing a dog-friendly vacation**

» **Ensuring that dogs remain welcome**

Chapter **18**

Traveling with Your Dog

For some folks, a beachside vacation isn't complete without a big stick and a wet, smelly dog to chase it.

These are the people who travel with water dishes, leashes, and plenty of towels. People who trade information on good dog beaches and pet-friendly inns the way gourmands talk about new restaurants. People who would no more think of leaving the dog at home during vacation than leaving the children with neighbors.

Their numbers, travel-industry watchers say, are growing. And you and your dog can be among their happy ranks.

Still, traveling with a dog is sometimes no picnic. Finding lodging is hard, inside-dining is largely sacrificed in favor of eating takeout in the car or in a park, and hours spent tripping through quaint shops becomes a thing of the past. Traveling with *dogs does* offer some challenges, but nearly all are surmountable with common sense and creativity.

Traveling with dogs is not new, of course. The unique combination of companionship and protection that dogs offer has made them welcome on trips from the very beginning of our centuries-old partnership with them. They've gone along with every mode of transportation we've invented — accompanying us on foot or alongside our horses, trotting under carriages, riding in our planes, trains, ships, and automobiles. They've even been in space.

Although most dog-related travel is strictly for pleasure now, such was not always the case. Breed historians tell us that dogs such as the Rottweiler once helped their human partners take goods to market and carried the profits home in a pouch attached to their collars to deter thieves. While the idea still has appeal, not many dogs are so intimately involved in business travel today.

REMEMBER

Recreational travel for dogs, however, has never been more popular. Dogs can be seen at the roughest campsites and the swankiest hotels. Several books and Web sites cover traveling with dogs, and some travel agents have carved out a niche booking canine-centered vacations. People in the travel industry have learned that many travelers with dogs are exceptionally grateful for pleasant accommodations and return to the places that treat them well year after year. As a result, some entrepreneurs have gone to great lengths to attract dog lovers: You can even find canine camps where people do nothing but share a piece of dog heaven with their pet for a week or more at a time.

Should Your Dog Travel?

A pet who is very old, not in good health, or nervous or untrustworthy in new situations is probably best left behind with a friend, a sitter, in a kennel, or at your veterinarian's. (See the section later in this chapter, "If Your Dog Can't Go with You," for more information.)

REMEMBER

The best canine travelers are reasonably well-mannered — more than can be said for many human tourists. They must also be in good health. That said, don't count your aging or sick pet out without a little consideration and a trip to your veterinarian. Your pet may be in better shape than you think, after all, and any behavior problems she has may be fixable.

Health concerns

Before you hit the road, make sure that your pet is fit for travel. If your dog's last check-up was a few years ago, this is a good time to schedule another one. You'll have to if you're shipping your pet by air or going to another country, because you'll need a health certificate signed by a veterinarian. But even if you're only driving to a state park four hours away, you want to know your pet is in good health, and you need to know he's current on his vaccinations, especially rabies.

TIP

Because you'll be picking up after your pet on vacation — more on that coming up in this chapter — make sure that he has been wormed so clean up's not a total gross-out (just a partial one).

Car travel is pretty easy on a dog; air travel, however, is another matter. Because of the stresses of traveling in an airline cargo hold, some experts suggest dogs who are not designed for easy breathing — pug-nosed breeds such as the Boxer, Bulldog, and, of course, the Pug — should never travel by air. Old dogs and those in marginal health are likewise not good candidates. Your veterinarian can help you make an honest appraisal of your pet's condition.

If your pet doesn't have a regular veterinarian, tips on how to find a good one are in Chapter 11.

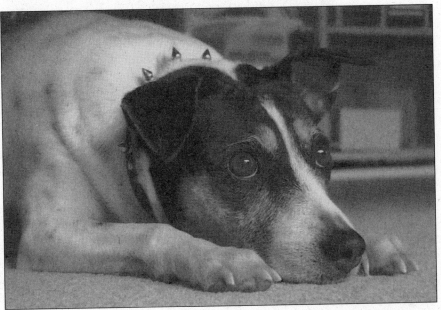

Don't leave me behind! While those sad eyes may be hard to deal with, some dogs are better off not traveling with you.

Tucker Junior/Photograph courtesy of Joanne Losenno

Travel manners

The *minimum* requirement for canine travelers is that they be able to behave themselves on-leash in some very exciting circumstances — around strange people, strange dogs, and strange scenery, sounds, and smells. If you plan to let your dog off-leash, you'd better be sure that she'll come when called and leave something — like a dead fish on the beach — alone when you ask her to. She should also be trained to stop barking on command.

"Sit?" "Down?" "Stay?" Are these foreign concepts to your dog? All you need to know to make your dog a well-mannered companion is in Chapters 8 and 14.

Wellmannered dogs make all the difference when traveling.

Cooter and Annie/Photo courtesy of Natalie Hollifield

TIP

THE AKC CANINE GOOD CITIZEN PROGRAM

One of the best things to happen in the dog world in recent years is the growth of the AKC Canine Good Citizen (CGC) program, which gives formal recognition to dogs of all ages, sizes, and backgrounds who prove themselves — and their owners — to be ambassadors of goodwill to those among us who wish dogs would stay home or simply go away.

The certification program was designed to duplicate the everyday challenges a well-mannered dog should be able to handle in good grace. In order to be granted the Canine Good Citizen title, the dog must accept the attention and handling of a friendly stranger, sit politely for petting, walk on a loose leash, walk through a crowd, demonstrate an understanding of the commands "Sit," "Down," "Stay" and "Come," and behave politely around other dogs, distractions, and when separated briefly from his owner.

Some owners have used this program to prepare their dogs for therapy work in hospitals and nursing homes, and the program is one more tool in helping to keep lodgings, parks, and other areas open to canine travelers.

For a free information kit on the Canine Good Citizen program, write to The American Kennel Club, Attention: CGC, 5580 Centerview Drive, Suite 200, Raleigh, NC 27606, call (919) 233-9780, or send e-mail to: info@akc.org.

If Your Dog Can't Go with You

You need to know what to do if you can't take your dog — even if you end up taking him most of the time. Business travel is necessary, after all, as is that emergency trip cross-country to handle the estate of the relative you haven't heard from in 15 years (but who you hope left you money).

TECHNICAL STUFF

You may even decide to go someplace where canine tourists aren't welcome, such as Hawaii or England, both of which have strict animal import requirements to keep rabies away from their shores.

Another place you may go where your dog can't — and I hope you don't, because I've been there and didn't like it much — is the hospital.

In any case, you're better off checking out your options ahead of time.

Ask your friends, neighbors, and coworkers what they do with their pets when they're gone. Ask your veterinarian, too, for referrals to pet sitters or kennels. Remember, the people you ask may have different criteria for selecting a service than you do. I find that for some people, the closest or cheapest kennel (or veterinarian) is the one that always gets the nod, while I would drive to the next city — and have — for the *right* trainer, kennel, or veterinary specialist for my pet.

TIP

When you have a service in mind, whether a kennel or sitter, call and ask for references, and then check them out — a step few people take. Ask about professional affiliations, such as the American Boarding Kennel Association or National Association of Pet Sitters, both of which offer materials and training to U.S. and Canadian members to encourage a higher degree of performance.

TIP

No matter what kind of care you choose for your pet while you're gone, make your arrangements early. Pet sitters and boarding kennels are booked weeks and sometimes months in advance for peak travel times such as summer or the winter holidays.

Prepare for emergencies

One of the easiest things to overlook when leaving your pet behind — whether with a friend, a pet sitter, or kennel — is how you want him cared for should he become ill. Discuss care options with your veterinarian in advance, and then clue in the person who'll be caring for your dog.

Setting up emergency-care arrangements works best if you have a good relationship with your veterinarian — but then, so does everything else concerning your pet's health. My veterinarian knows the kind of health care I expect for my pets, and I trust his judgment if he cannot get in touch with me. In my dogs' records is a note from him saying that no matter who shows up with my dogs, his hospital is to provide care, and my credit card number is on file to handle the charges. Every so often I touch base with my veterinarian on this topic so no misunderstandings come up.

For the ultimate in preparing for a trip where you can't take your pet, see the information in Chapter 13 on providing for your pet in your will.

Considering pet sitters

A wide range of services are lumped under the general title of pet sitter covering everything from a reciprocal agreement between friends to care for each other's dogs, to paying a neighbor kid to look in on your dog, to hiring a professional pet-sitting service to care for your pet either in your own home or, less commonly, in theirs.

The benefits of having your pet stay in your own home are that she's familiar with the surroundings and gets to sleep in her own bed — or, because you're not looking, on yours. Additionally, if your pet is not well-socialized, she won't be stressed by the presence of other dogs in a boarding kennel. And pet sitters can do more than just look in on your pet: They can take in your mail and newspaper, water your houseplants, and turn lights on and off.

REMEMBER

Make sure that you discuss services and prices beforehand and, if you're dealing with a service, make sure that they are bonded and insured.

The biggest drawback is that your pet is left alone a great deal of the time, because most professional pet sitters have a list of clients to drop in on every day and are probably not able to spend all that much time giving your pet individual attention. (An arrangement with a young person — or a house sitter to stay in your home while you're gone — may get your pet more time being walked or played with.) If your pet becomes ill or manages to escape, it may be a while before a pet sitter comes back to notice. And finally, some people just aren't comfortable with having people in their home when they're gone.

WARNING

Informal arrangements for house-sitting (having the person move in) or pet sitting (having them drop in) can be even trickier than hiring a professional service. Just ask the friend of mine who left her house and pets in the care of a friend's college-aged daughter, only to find the young woman had been anything but a quiet resident. She'd had guests and even parties. The house was a bit worse for wear, but the pets were fine.

If you're going to go with a young person — and many people do, with no regrets — be sure that parental oversight is part of the picture.

TIP

One of the best solutions is to *trade* dog care. If your dog is socialized, well-mannered, and gets along well with other animals, he may be able to stay with friends while you're gone — as long as you reciprocate when your friends need help. If your pet won't be comfortable in another's house, then trade in-home care, with your friend looking after your house and pets in your house while you're gone, and you doing the same for them when they are gone.

Although I have, on occasion, used both professional pet sitters and boarding kennels with no complaints, trading care is the solution I prefer for my own dogs. My dogs are familiar with the people and pets with whom they stay, and they love having another playful dog around in their own house from time to time. Having dog-loving friends who knew my dogs and upon whom I could rely was crucial to me at one point, when I unexpectedly ended up in a hospital for a week. The friends with whom I share dog care had the homefront secured within hours, and I never worried about my pets during my recovery.

REMEMBER

Trading care is a solution that's both reassuring — I know my friends care for my dogs as I do — and inexpensive.

Boarding kennels

Boarding kennels are another option, ideal for friendly, well-adjusted pets. Despite all the recommendations in the world, don't, even on short notice, leave your pet at a kennel you haven't inspected yourself. You should see clean, comfortable, and well-maintained facilities; if you don't, go elsewhere.

WARNING

Ask where your pet will stay. Some kennels leave pets in crates for most of their stay, so as to maximize the number of animals they can take in, especially during peak vacation periods. While I have nothing against keeping a pet in a crate for a short while, I would not want my pet spending a couple of weeks so confined. Make sure that your pet has a comfortable run of his own — your own pets can share a run, but bunking with strangers is not recommended. You pet should also get individual attention such as walks or time in a securely fenced play area. Areas for cats and other animals should be separate — for the good of all!

The kennel operators should seem sincerely interested in tailoring their facility to make your dog's stay more comfortable. They should be prepared to feed your dog as you do, especially if he's on a special diet, and they should be willing to allow you to leave toys or articles with your smell — like a dirty sock — behind to reassure your pet.

TIP

Boarding your pet at a kennel has a few advantages. Boarding kennels are usually very secure — more than most people's backyards — and the best ones always have someone onsite to check in on your dog. Some kennels make up for the fact they're out in the sticks by picking up and delivering your pet.

AVOIDING KENNEL COUGH

TECHNICAL STUFF

Boarding kennels take some heat over kennel cough, an upper-respiratory infection that's as contagious as sniffles in a daycare center. In fact, some kennel operators even find the name a little pejorative, insisting that the ailment be called by its proper name, canine infectious tracheobronchitis, or even bordetella, after its most common causative agent.

And maybe that's fair, because dogs can pick up kennel cough any place they come into contact with a dog who has it — and that means anywhere. Parks, dog shows, the waiting room of your veterinarian's office, or the fund-raising dog walk thrown by your local humane society — these are all possibilities for infection.

Fortunately, the ailment is not usually serious, even though the dry, bellowing cough can sound simply awful. For most dogs, the disease runs its course in a couple of weeks; others, especially yappy dogs who keep the airways irritated, may develop an infection requiring antibiotics. See your veterinarian for advice; he may recommend nothing more than over-the-counter cough suppresant and rest.

Although not completely effective against the disease, a vaccine is available against the ailment. A boarding kennel should demand proof of it. The rub: It requires two doses a couple of weeks apart, which means you need to call your veterinarian at least three weeks before a kennel stay — or a trip to a dog-dense area.

TIP

If you don't have a home yet in a city you're moving to, a reputable kennel may meet your pet at the airport in advance of your arrival and care for her until you get there. Alternately, you can often leave your pet while you're house-hunting and arrange for the kennel to ship her after you find proper lodgings.

Many veterinarians have boarding facilities, and if yours is among them, this option may well be the best kennel choice for your pet. The biggest advantage is that the staff is already familiar with your pet and her medical background — a real plus if your dog is elderly or has a chronic health condition.

WARNING

Do not patronize a kennel that does not ask you for proof of up-to-date vaccinations. If they do not insist that *your* pet is healthy and well-protected from disease, they are not asking these questions of other boarders, either, and that puts your pet at risk.

No matter what, I would not recommend boarding a puppy who hasn't had all his vaccinations — which means no boarding before 16 weeks. The increased possibility for disease isn't worth the risk.

BOOT CAMP FOR BOWSER

If your dog has some behavior problems you'd like to see fixed, you may want to consider boarding your pet with a dog trainer while you're gone. While a board-and-train arrangement will likely be more expensive than boarding alone, coming home to a dog who's better behaved than when you left can be a wonderful thing indeed.

You'd be surprised what a good trainer can accomplish in a couple of weeks, even if you haven't managed to train your dog in the years that you've had him. While it's probably not the answer for dogs with such serious problems as biting, a couple weeks with a trainer is great for brushing up on or introducing basic obedience — "Sit," "Down," "Stay," "Come," and so on.

Ask your veterinarian for a referral, and be sure to check out the kennel and the references of any trainer you choose. Ask about follow-up lessons, both for your dog, and to help you learn how to handle your pet. Above all, remember that a well-mannered pet doesn't happen in two weeks: A trainer can lay the foundation for good behavior, but it's up to you to follow-through in the home.

Many boarding kennels also have a grooming shop, and even those that do not are usually equipped to groom their boarders. Arrange to have your dog freshly groomed when you pick him up. The extra cost is well worth the price, because even in the most fastidious of facilities a dog can get a little rank during his stay.

Travel Preparations

Enough of this stay-at-home talk! You're ready to think about hitting the road. Although dogs aren't as complicated to travel with as, say, babies, you do have to pick up and work out a few things in advance of any trip.

The well-equipped travel dog

You can really go crazy packing things to ensure your dog's safety and comfort. My friend Maria Goodavage, who has written a couple of books on traveling with dogs, even packs her dogs' *beds* in the camper shell of her battered pickup truck. I don't bring along all that much less. Whenever I've thought "I really don't need that," I've been wrong on the very next trip.

What should you bring? First, some basics.

>> Your dog should be wearing a sturdy collar with a license and an up-to-date ID tag with at least one number, area code included, that's not yours — someone who'll be there to answer the phone should you lose your dog miles from home.

If your dog is more comfortable in a harness, put the tag on that, but remember, a harness isn't a good option for a dog who doesn't behave well on-leash, because you have less control with a harness.

Ideally, your pet should also be carrying an imbedded microchip for unshakable, permanent ID. See Chapter 6 for more information on microchipping, and on tracking services like 1-800-HELP4PETS.

TIP

My friend Judy Jordan got me started carrying paper key tags for disposable IDs while traveling. You can buy a bag of a hundred of them at any hardware store for not a lot of money and throw a couple dozen in a baggie in your glove box. Every time you change location on a vacation, write the day's information on the tag, for example: "Russian Gulch Campsite No. 15," or "Sea Dog Inn, Room 32, 707-555-DOGS." If you're going where your dog might get splashed, use the heavier plastic key tags, with the paper that inserts into the splash-proof housing. It won't help for swimming, but it'll take a splash or two, which a paper tag won't.

>> Bring along a six-foot leash. A longer leash is handy, too, especially a reel type leash such as the Flexi, which is great for giving your dog a little room to stretch his legs in areas such as rest stops.

I always bring an extra leash, as well as a nylon, one-piece slip lead like those veterinary hospitals and kennel operators use. (The one-piece lead, which is like a very long choke collar with a handle on the end, is in permanent residence in my glove box, for coping with the occasional stray or dog in trouble.)

>> Two bowls, one for food, one for water.

Water bowls that either collapse for easy storage or don't spill are perfect for travel. I take the spill-proof one on all my trips and keep a collapsible bowl in the trunk, along with a bottle of water, always, because you just never know when you're going to run across a thirsty animal.

>> If your dog's on a widely available brand of food, just pack enough to get you started and pick up the rest on the road, if you're going to an area with a market or pet-supplies store. Prescription food or anything out of the ordinary you'll have to bring along, enough for the trip. If your pet eats canned food, you need a spoon or fork, and a can opener unless your pup's brand comes in pop-tops.

>> Don't forget some treats!

>> A comb, brush, and tweezers or ready-made device for pulling ticks come in handy, especially on back-country trips.

- Some basic first-aid supplies — scissors, gauze, tape, and Pepto-Bismol, for diarrhea — are handy to have around. Your veterinarian can prescribe some motion-sickness medication, if need be, and you certainly want to pack that.

- Don't forget to pack any regular medication your pet takes.

- Bring along cloth towels, for drying off wet, dirty dogs, and paper towels, for cleaning up more things than you can imagine.

   I also pack an old sheet and blanket, for covering bedspreads, furniture, and carpets in motel rooms, and a multipurpose cleaner in a spray bottle. I'm very conscious of what a privilege it is to be able to stay in hotels, motels and inns, and I will not ruin things for other dog lovers by making a mess.

- Plastic bags are a must-bring, too, for poop pick-ups.

- I've purchased dog shampoo on a couple of trips; now I just bring it along. Trying to find shampoo at 10 p.m. in a resort town after your dog has rolled in something vile will convince you, too, to travel with shampoo.

- For the owners of little dogs only: A shoulder bag for carrying your pet. With this — or any oversized bag — you can slip your dog into areas the big dogs can only dream of, and most of the people around you will never notice.

- Last, but certainly not least, from your dog's point of view: a couple of his favorite toys!

The standard travel advice has been to bring water from home, but that's just unfeasible for a trip of any decent length. Your dog will be fine drinking the same water you do in unfamiliar places. That said, I always travel with a couple gallons of bottled water, either from the tap or the store, because I often stop to water and walk my dogs in areas where a source of safe drinking water isn't readily available.

More on first-aid kits is in Chapter 21; other tips including, tick removal, are in Chapter 10.

The well-prepared dog lover

As with anything else, the key for traveling with a dog is *prepare for the worst, hope for the best.* Carry some ready-made LOST DOG! flyers with your dog's picture on them and a place to write a phone number with a big marker, which you should also pack. (More on preparing these flyers is in Chapter 21.) Don't forget your pet's health records, including microchip number, and especially proof of rabies vaccination. The latter is absolutely imperative should the unthinkable happen: Your dog bites someone or tangles with a rabid creature in the wild.

LOOKING FOR MR. GOOD CAR

From the time I first learned how to drive, I've been looking for the perfect dogmobile. I know it's an obsession not all pet lovers share; in fact, I've been stunned to learn that some people don't consider their pet at all when shopping for a vehicle.

My brother, for example, once pulled into my driveway, beaming with pride over the acquisition of the perfect midlife-crisis car: a cherry-red, two-seat convertible. "Whaddaya think?" he said. "Pretty sweet, huh?"

"I think it's gorgeous," I replied. "But . . . are you sure Taz will be comfortable in it?"

The perplexed look on his face made it clear he had temporarily forgotten his beloved Boxer. Blinded by the showroom shine and imagining young women drawn to the car like flies, he hadn't even noticed the lack of space behind the seat for the dog. "I guess he'll just ride shotgun," he shrugged, sliding his hand over the soft upholstery.

There are no "I guesses" when I go to buy a car. Either it works for the dogs or I don't buy it. I remember one fellow who pushed really hard to sell me a small wagon where the rear seats only folded partially. He tried to convince me the dogs would enjoy the elevated view, or that when the weight of the dogs was added, the seats would indeed lie flat. I made him crawl in to demonstrate, and proved him the liar. He then tried to steer the conversation to air conditioning — how economical it was on this model, and how powerful. I nodded. "Do you think it'll keep the dogs cool in the back?" I asked him, and he lost it. "Lady," he sputtered. "They're just a couple of damn dogs. You gonna buy this car, or not?"

Sorry, no sale.

Finally, I started fantasizing about minivans. I guess it had something to do with my own midlife situation — call it acceptance more than crisis — but I finally gave up any pretense of looking cool and started shopping for something that would fit us all: dogs, dog gear, and my own middle-aged fanny. I found more than a few salesmen happy to talk about dog-friendly features. The one who won out, though, was the fellow with big dogs of his own. He happily talked about their comfort in the minivan he drives. "If you set the front air-conditioning vents to arch over the seats and open the rear ones, your dogs will always be comfortable," he volunteered. "And if you pull out the back seat, you can fit some nice dog beds back there."

Clever man. I was writing out a check before you could say "extended warranty."

I still haven't counted the number of cup holders back there — the dogs don't care, nor do I — but I'm happier than a retriever in water with my minivan.

And so are the dogs, which was all I really cared about in the first place.

I also travel with a directory of pet-friendly lodgings. Some travel guides, such as AAA, mention whether pets are accepted, but calling ahead is always a good idea: Policies and ownership can change, after all.

My favorite dog travel book is Maria Goodavage's *The California Dog Lover's Companion* (Avalon Travel Publishing). If you live in or are planning to visit California, this book is a must buy. Others in the series are just as wonderful.

As with so many other things, the Internet has changed travel, and that's just as true of travel with dogs. I've found some wonderful places to stay with my pets by searching the Web, and I've shared my favorite pet travel Web sites in Chapter 23.

Travel by Car

Given the worries most pet lovers have about air travel, it's no wonder that most doggie vacations are conducted in the family car. After they understand car rides end up in exciting places like the beach, most dogs greet the prospect of a car ride with unabashed enthusiasm — a little too much, for some drivers.

Making car rides safer

As with all other training, ending up with a good car rider starts with molding correct behavior when your dog is a puppy. No matter how cute or how small, do not allow your pup to ride in your lap, and don't make a fuss over him while you're driving. On short neighborhood trips, ask your pup to sit quietly, and praise him for proper behavior.

Traveling with your dog in a crate is often easier and definitely safer. Depend- ing on the size of your dog and the size and shape of your car, a crate may not be feasible. Crates should always be considered, though, especially for those dogs who are so active they distract the driver. Collapsible crates are available for easy storage in the trunk when not in use.

Another safety tool is a doggy seat belt, which fits into a standard seat-belt buckle and then attaches to a harness on the dog. Also good for keeping a pet in her place, if you have a station wagon or similar vehicle, are widely available metal barriers that fit between the passenger and cargo areas.

Uneasy riders

If your dog's only exposure to riding in a car is an occasional trip to the veterinarian's, don't be surprised if he's not the happiest of riders. Try to build up his enthusiasm by increasing his time in the car and praising him for his good behavior. The first short trips should be to pleasant locations, such as parks.

TIP

Dramamine prevents car-sickness in dogs as well as people, but other remedies are available — talk to your veterinarian. A dog-handler's trick: Your dog should travel on little or no food, and the dog should get a jelly bean — or any other piece of sugar candy, except chocolate — before hitting the road.

Because most of the problems come from fear, not motion sickness, building up your pet's tolerance for riding in a car is a better long-term cure than anything you can give him. Although fresh air is a wonderful thing, don't let your pet hang his head out of the window. Small debris kicked up by other cars can strike him in the eye or nose and injure him. Roll the window down enough for a sniff, if you like — but no more.

On the road, remember to stop at regular intervals — about as often as you need to for yourself — for your dog to relieve himself and get a drink of fresh water. Remember to always keep your dog on-leash for his safety.

For information on heat stroke and other canine emergencies, see Chapter 11. The Humane Society of the United States offers free *Hot Car* flyers to slip under windshield wipers to inform others of the risks of leaving a dog in a car. Send a self-addressed, business-sized envelope to Hot Car, HSUS, 2100 L Street, N.W., Washington, D.C. 20037. If you see a dog in danger, contact local police or animal-control officers immediately.

TIP

If, when you're on the road, you want to spend a few hours kicking around an area where dogs are not welcome, a local veterinary clinic is a safe place to leave your dog. I've always managed to find one amenable to a short-term boarder within a couple of calls, and I know my dogs are in safe and secure surroundings while I'm not with them. The price for this service is negotiable — a half-day's boarding is a good starting point — and on a couple of occasions I wasn't charged at all.

Another possibility is your motel room. Although leaving a dog loose in a strange room is not a good idea — most places forbid doing so, in fact — you can leave a *crated* dog alone, provided he's not a barker. Just another reason why a crate is one of the most versatile pieces of canine equipment your dog can have.

Travel by Air

If you don't take your dog by car in the United States, air is your only other option. The major bus lines and Amtrak don't allow any animals except those serving the disabled. Other countries are far more liberal on this point — dogs are welcome in restaurants, too, in some places — but it's still hit and miss.

Although horror stories make the news, the truth is that airline travel is relatively safe for most dogs, and it will be for yours if you play by the rules, plan carefully, and are prepared to be a little pushy on your pet's behalf.

TECHNICAL STUFF

Animals move through the airline system in two ways: as cargo or as accompanied baggage. Either way, almost all of these animals will travel in a pressurized cargo hold beneath the passenger compartment. Although the accommodations aren't any nicer, it's better for your pet if he is traveling as your "baggage," so you can ask about him in person.

TIP

Some airlines allow small dogs in the cabin, if their carriers can fit in the space beneath the seat. This is by far the best way that your dog can fly, because he never leaves your care during the course of the trip. Not all airlines allow dogs to travel in the cabin, however, and others put a limit on the number of dogs in the cabin, so making your arrangements far in advance pays.

The only larger dogs allowed in the cabin are service dogs traveling with a disabled person.

The Air Transport Association estimates more than a half a million dogs and cats are transported on commercial airlines in the United States each year, and the industry group insists 99 percent reach their destination without incident.

To make sure that your dog is one of them, pay careful attention to the following:

>> **Talk to the airline.** Some carriers — especially the no-frills companies — don't take animals at all. Even those that do have limits to the number of animals on a flight because a set amount of air is available in the sealed cargo holds. You also need to know where and when your dog has to be presented, and what papers — health certificate, and so on — you need to bring.

>> **Be sure that your dog is in good health, and isn't one of the pug-nosed breeds.** These dogs find breathing a little difficult under the best of circumstances, and the stress of airline travel may be more than they can handle.

>> **Be sure that your dog is traveling in a proper carrier that has contact phone numbers at both ends of the journey.** (Your home number won't help if you're not home.) The crate should be just big enough for your dog to stand up and turn around in.

Be sure that all the bolts securing the halves of the carriers are in place and tightened.

REMEMBER

HOT DOG!

WARNING

Just about everyone understands that dogs shouldn't be left inside a car on a hot day, but fewer realize the danger is just as great on a warm one.

It's a horrible way to die.

A car functions similarly to a greenhouse, and heat can build up to lethal levels in minutes, even on a pleasant day in the 70s or low 80s. Even with the windows rolled down, a dog can show signs of heat stress — heavy panting, glazed eyes, rapid pulse, dizziness or vomiting, or a deep red or purple tongue — in the time it takes you to get a six-pack through the Ten Items or Less line. Brain damage and death can follow within minutes.

An overheated dog needs prompt veterinary attention to have a chance at survival. Don't delay! Better yet: Don't risk your dog's life by leaving him in the car.

Another danger to the unattended dog is theft, which, when combined with heat dangers, means a few minutes looking through that cute little shop really isn't worth the risk that is posed to your pet.

While he cannot wear a collar in his crate — it's not safe, because it can get caught on other objects — put an ID tag on a piece of elastic around his neck; in addition, you may want to consider having him micro-chipped before travel. (See Chapter 6 for more on microchipping.)

>> **Don't ship your pet when the weather is bad, or when air traffic is heaviest.** Avoid peak travel days such as around the Christmas holidays, and be sure to choose flights that are on the ground when the temperature is neither too hot nor too cold, not only at the departure airport but also at the connecting and arriving airports. In summer, a night flight is likely better, while the reverse is true in the winter.

>> **Fly with your dog whenever possible.** Keeping on top of things is easier when you're on the same flight.

>> **Choose a direct flight; if that's not possible, try for a route with a short layover.** Most canine fatalities occur on the ground, when dogs are left in their crates on the hot tarmac or in stifling cargo holds. Direct flights eliminate layovers, and short layovers reduce the time on the ground.

>> **Remember, your dog's life relies on the attentiveness of airline personnel.** Most of these employees are excellent and caring, but mistakes do happen. You should be prepared to pester airline personnel to confirm your dog has been loaded and has made the same connections you have. If your pet is flying unaccompanied, talk to freight-handling personnel at every airport your dog will visit. Be polite but persistent; don't take "I'm sure he's fine, have some delicious honey-roasted peanuts" as an answer from a flight attendant. Make the staff *check* and report back.

WARNING

Contrary to popular belief, it's generally better that your dog *not* be tranquilized before flying. The combination of high altitude and limited oxygen is a challenge your pet's body is better prepared to meet if she's not sedated. Still, your pet may be an exception. In the end, you and your veterinarian should decide on this issue.

TIP

The Air Transport Association has a free booklet, *Air Travel for Your Dog or Cat*. The booklet is available by sending a self-addressed, stamped, business-sized envelope to: ATA, 1301 Pennsylvania Blvd. N.W., Suite 1100, Washington, DC 20004.

Dog-Friendly Vacations

Just as vacations with children are different from adults-only trips, traveling with your dog works out better if you plan the journey with an eye to finding places where dogs are not only welcome but are also able to enjoy the surroundings.

In general, that means an emphasis on the outdoors. But as you'll soon find in traveling with your dog, all parks and beaches are not the same. In some cities and towns, dogs aren't even *allowed* in municipal facilities; in other open areas, too many humans may make things tough for dogs.

Even camping can be a disappointment. The U.S.'s national parks aren't much fun for dogs, but national forests are. The difference: The crowded national parks — such as Yosemite — have strict leash laws and require dogs to stay off most trails. National forests, on the other hand, have wide open spaces with few people and fewer leashing requirements — although that doesn't relieve you of the responsibility for your dog's poor behavior. The requirements in other parks vary, so check them out in advance.

TIP

A PIECE OF DOGGIE HEAVEN

It used to be that dog lovers were happy just to find lodgings that accepted dogs. How things have changed — some vacation options today are designed with dogs first in mind. These doggie vacations take two forms: Dog resorts with planned activities, and dog resorts without.

Those places with planned activities are known as *dog camps*. The organizers rent a campground, school campus, or a similar location for part of the year, and bring in trainers, lecturers, and other experts to teach campers and their human companions about various dog sports. It's not as serious as I made it sound, though: Dog camps leave plenty of time for hiking, fetch, silly games, and just plain hanging out with other dogs.

Camp Gone To The Dogs is the prototype, and still a place many dogs and dog lovers dream of visiting someday. (I'm included in that list!) Honey Loring puts the camp together every year, offering everything possible to keep human and canine guests deliriously happy. For information, write to Loring at P.O. Box 600, Putney, VT 05346, or check out the Web site at www.camp-gone-tothe-dogs.com.

The other kind of dog resort is typifed by one of my favorite places to visit, the strangely named Sheep Dung Estates in Northern California. Sheep Dung's cabin's are dog-friendly to the maximum extent possible, with tile floors and easy-to-clean furnishings. And each cabin is set in a private setting away from the others, so staying at Sheep Dung is like having your own ranch — your dog can be off-leash the entire stay. For more information, write to Sheep Dung Estates at P.O. Box 49, Yorkville, CA 95494, or visit their Web site at www.sheepdung.com.

While Camp Gone to The Dogs and Sheep Dung Estates are definitely pioneers, their trail-blazing efforts have not gone unnoticed by others in the travel industry. The great example set by these dog-friendly businesses has been followed by others — and the trend is sure to grow.

I prefer to head for a generally pet-friendly area and stay in lodgings where dogs aren't just tolerated — they're welcomed. The owners of dog-friendly inns and motels are often dog lovers, and they're happy to give you clues on the best things to do in the area. A less-popular resort area is almost always more laid back and tolerant where dogs are concerned.

TIP

Whatever you do, *call ahead!* Even the most dog-friendly places may have only a couple of rooms available for dog lovers, and if these are in popular resorts areas, they can be booked months in advance for prime vacation weekends. Better still, plan for an off-season vacation (and still call ahead).

A day at the beach can be great fun — even if you can't leave your winter coat at home.

Friday on the beach/Photo courtesy Joyce Munz

Getting Past "No Dogs" — It's Possible!

If you travel with your dog a lot, a time will come when you're going to be stranded somewhere you weren't counting on — because of a car problem, perhaps — and you're going to be trying to find a place to stay. This has happened to me more than once, and although I've gotten plenty of definitive no's at registration desks, I've also managed to convince some motels to let the rules slide. Here are some tips:

» **Offer a deposit.** If you're confident your dog isn't going to cause any damage — and if you aren't, you shouldn't be traveling with her — put your money where your mouth is and offer to guarantee your pet's good behavior.

>> **Show off your dog's good manners and well-groomed appearance.**
Obviously not a plan for someone with a muddy, out-of-control, 125-pound
shedding machine. But if your dog is clean and well-behaved, show him off!

>> **Show the manager a crate.** A dog who's going to sleep in a crate and not be
left to his own devices is a much better risk for the manager to take.

I would never, never, encourage anyone to sneak a dog into a motel room, but
I've heard doing so works best if your room is far from the office and you're
prepared to sleep in your car, just in case. If you're planning to have your *dog*
sleep in your car, you'd better be with him: Leaving your pet unattended is *never*
a good idea.

Even a casual reader of this chapter will get the idea that crates are a very useful
item, and indeed, they are. They're good for training, good for travel, and indispensable in disasters. For more on choosing a crate, see Chapter 6.

TO LEASH OR NOT TO LEASH

My favorite travel story regarding dogs and leash laws happened in a state campground
on the drop-dead gorgeous northern coast of California, where my dogs and I go as
often as we can. As we pulled next to the ranger station to check in, one of the two rang-
ers leaned out and started explaining the rules in a loud voice.

"No dogs on trails. No dogs on these two beaches, marked on this map. Dogs must be
in the car or in the tent at night. And remember: We *absolutely, positively* will not tolerate
any off-leash dogs. It is *expressly* forbidden in California state parks."

And then she leaned out a little more, and dropped her tone so the other ranger could-
n't hear her. "Two miles up the road is the beach where I take my dogs," she said. "We
never, ever patrol there." And then she smiled and waved us through.

She was one of us!

At this point, a confession is in order: I am a chronic breaker of canine leash laws, like
probably three-quarters of the nation's dog lovers. I am very careful about where and
when they're allowed off-leash: Early in the morning or late at night, far from people,
traffic, and wildlife. They are under voice control, and leashed at the first sign of
trouble.

Should you let your dog off-leash? I'm not going to tell you to break the law. Just be careful out there. And be considerate.

RUFFING IT!

Some people spend their vacation not in some fancy resort, but in the great outdoors — and they want to take their dogs with them. Fortunately, sturdy, well-designed packs are on the market designed to let your dog carry his share of the load, and even some of yours. An adult dog in top condition can carry up to a quarter of his weight, evenly distributed in a properly fitting pack. Get your dog used to the feel of the pack on short walks and trips and gradually build up the weight and distance.

Dogs aren't welcome everywhere, and the biggest danger to the future of canine backpacking is other hikers more than wild beasts. Don't give the dog haters any ammunition: Keep your dog under control, and that means on-leash in areas with other people or animals. Take something to bury waste, or supplies to pack it back out.

You won't take much into the back country — food and water are the basics — but you will need a few extra things. Grooming tools — a brush or comb, and tweezers or a tick remover — keep your pet healthy and comfortable. Basic first aid supplies for human and canine packers should be included, as should a light rope for tethering your dog when necessary.

Charlene G. LaBelle's *A Guide to Backpacking With Your Dog* (Alpine) is an outstanding little book offering invaluable tips on how to train and equip your dog, and where to take him. I also recommend Cheryl S. Smith's *On the Trail with Your Canine Companion* (IDG Books Worldwide).

Keeping the World Safe for Canine Travelers

Even though more people than ever are traveling with their dogs, plenty of people are still out there who don't like sharing their space with the four-legged tourist. Some of them, unfortunately, own motels, and others are politicians like those in my home town, who seem to tolerate drug dealers and muggers at the margins of an outdoor street fair but absolutely forbid the presence of dogs there.

Still, you can see how the decisions to ban dogs get made. There are the liability concerns over dog bites and the sanitation worries over dog mess. But our job as caring, responsible dog lovers is to make sure that people realize more good dogs are around than bad ones. Here are a few things to do on the road:

>> **Keep 'em clean.** Your dog should always be well-groomed and clean-smelling. Always dry off wet dogs and wipe off muddy feet — using *your* towels, not the

motel's — before allowing your dog inside. Cover furniture, carpets, and bedspreads with your old sheets and towels, and if you need to bathe your dog, be sure, again, to use *your* towels and to clean up all the fur.

» **Keep 'em under control.** Your dog should be obedient, friendly but not annoying, and *never* aggressive, not to people, not to pets, and not to wildlife. Do *not* allow your dog to bark uncontrolled in a car, camper, or motel room. Use your best judgment on when to let a dog off-leash — even in areas where doing so is allowed — and be sure that your dog isn't annoying other people or dogs.

» **Pick up after 'em.** I am always astonished that well-mannered people who would never consider tossing a soft-drink cup on the ground will look the other way when their dog deposits something 5,000 times more vile. Don't give me that "it's biodegradable" excuse, either. **Pick up after your dog.** Did you get that? No? Then let me repeat it: Pick up after your dog. Dog mess is the single biggest complaint dog haters have against our being in public areas, so don't give them any ammunition. When you check into a motel, stress that you intend to pick up after your dog, and inquire if they have a place where they prefer you take him to relieve himself. Don't let a male dog lift his leg on the shrubs while you're walking there, either: Teach the "Leave it" command — see Chapter 14 — to get his nose up. No sniff, no lift.

TIP

EASY WAYS TO SCOOP THE POOP

In the couple of decades since urban areas started fining people for failing to pick up after their dogs, a zillion products have come and gone in an effort to make the task easier and less disgusting. The latter is just not possible. The only thing that helps is time, over which you get so used to the feel of warm dog poop that your stomach doesn't even shimmy anymore.

Forget the long-handle gizmos. The easiest way to get the job done is with a plastic bag. Fold-over sandwich bags are fine for small dogs, but for larger ones I prefer to use plastic grocery bags, which tie off nicely at the top. In either case, here's how it works:

Pull the bag over your hand like a loose mitten, then pick up the poop. Pull the outer edges of the bag over your hand while still holding the poop, until your hand ends up on the outside of the bag and the mess is inside. Then close, either by flipping the flap or tying the tie, and drop in the closest garbage can.

Clean-up bags become one of those signs of a real dog lover, as in "You know you're a real dog lover when there are plastic bags in the pockets of every coat and jacket you own."

They are in mine. They should be in yours, too.

5

The Part of Tens

So many fun and important things don't fit anywhere else, but are just too important to leave out. Like some ideas on how to have a nice yard and a dog — yes, it's possible! And what about all those things people "know" about dogs. Which ones are true and which are not? The answers are in here, along with what questions to ask when you're buying a puppy and how to be ready for a disaster. And what about looking for dogs on the Internet? You'll find some of the best Web sites for dog-lovers, along with tips on making your canine-themed Web browsing both fun and educational.

» Examining why dogs eat grass

» Answering whether or not dog kisses are good for you

» Explaining the truth about spaying and neutering

Chapter **19**

Ten Dog Myths — Debunked!

S ome of those old wives were pretty smart cookies, because more than a few old wives' tales aren't that far off the mark. Of the ones still floating around about dogs, however, the accuracy rate isn't all that high.

I'm not sure why, but when it comes to myths, cats have it over dogs by far. Cat myths are more . . . *mythical,* if you will. No one ever claimed a dog has more than one life, and black dogs are thought to be just as lucky or unlucky as any other kind. (I'm glad, since I share my home with a couple of them!) Dog myths tend to be of the practical variety; cat myths are more magical: Cats are just flat-out more mysterious, I think, and cat myth reflects that perception.

Dog myths may be more often about proper care than about good (or bad) luck, but bad information still needs to be set straight. Here are some of the most common misconceptions about dogs — and the facts.

One Dog Year Is Equal to Seven Human Years

You can see how this one started. Something in the neighborhood of 70 is a decent life span for a human being, while 10 is probably average for a lot of dogs — although some, especially small ones, live far longer. Divide 70 by 10 and what do you get? You got it: 7.

But if you look at a year-old dog you can see that he's an adult, or nearly so — physically, mentally, and sexually. These characteristics don't compare with the attributes of a seven-year-old human child. So the rule of thumb has been changed, but it's nowhere as easy to remember.

Age is as much a state of mind in dogs as humans. Exercise can keep us all feeling young.

Photo courtesy of Jack Russell and Bill Newcomb Photography

REMEMBER According to the American Animal Hospital Association, the first eight months of a dog's life equals 13 years in human terms — birth to puberty, in other words. At a year, a dog's a teenager, equivalent to a 16-year-old human, with a little filling out still to do. After the age of two, when a dog's about 21, every dog year equals approximately five human ones.

These are ballpark estimates, because the fact is dogs age at very different rates. Small dogs may hit puberty at five months, while some large ones may be more than a year and a half old before a female comes into heat for the first time.

So when is a dog "old"? Giant breeds such as Great Danes are senior citizens at six; a Lab may be considered old at eight. A little dog like the Pomeranian, however, could behave like a healthy adult well into her teens.

Two things go a long way to keep your pet acting young longer, and they should come as no surprise, because they have the same effect on human longevity. Proper nutrition and regular exercise keep dogs active and happy for as many years as possible. The biggest risk to an older dog? Obesity. Not only does obesity shorten lives, but it makes the years that remain miserable, especially for older dogs with arthritis.

To give your pet the best shot at a healthy, long, and happy life, keep him trim and keep him moving. It's good for you both!

For more on caring for an older dog, see Chapter 13. You'll find the skinny on good nutrition in Chapter 7, and on preventive care in Chapter 11.

A Hot, Dry Nose Means a Fever

A dog has a fever when a thermometer properly inserted into his fanny exceeds 102.5 degrees. His nose has nothing to do with it.

Thermometers for dogs and cats are available at any good pet-supply store, or through mail order. A thermometer is an essential element of a home-care kit for your pet, along with a tube of lubricating jelly to make the task of temperature-taking easier for you both. (For more on temperature-taking, see Chapter 11.)

While a nose check isn't a reliable sign of a dog in trouble, other physical symptoms are well worth watching for. A dog who's overheated may die if not promptly identified — frantic panting and glassy eyes are classic symptoms. A dog in this condition needs to be helped with the application of cool — not cold — water on his belly and a very prompt trip to the veterinarian's. For more on heat and dogs, see Chapter 18.

A Dog Should Go through One Season before Being Spayed

Wrong, wrong, wrong. You don't need to wait. In fact, the opposite is true: Spaying *before* your puppy comes into season reaps health benefits. Vet-erinary experts are now saying you can have your puppy spayed at the age of eight weeks, and an increasing number of shelters do just that!

Spaying before the first season reduces to almost nothing the chances of your pet getting mammary tumors — breast cancer — later in her life. And of course, without the uterus and ovaries, your pet is also safe from cancer in those parts of the body, as well as life-threatening infections. (See Chapter 17 for more on spaying, neutering, and why most every pet should be altered.)

REMEMBER

Dogs are better, healthier pets after altering, and they don't add to the numbers of unwanted pets — which many people don't realize includes oodles of "valuable" purebreds. All things considered, the sooner you get your pet altered, the better.

Spaying and Neutering Makes Dogs Fat

The basic truth for pets is the same as for people: Too much food and too little exercise make dogs fat.

You may need to adjust the levels of both after your dog has recovered from surgery to make sure that he or she stays in shape. The activity level of male dogs, in particular, may decrease after neutering because they are not so anxious to get out and roam after the alluring scents of females in season.

Grown dogs are less active than puppies, and if you do not adjust your feeding routine when your puppy nears maturity — about the same time as neutering — he will put on weight.

Obesity is a completely human-driven problem for dogs who, after all, are incapable of opening the refrigerator, getting a second serving of kibble, or taking the dog cookies out of the cupboard.

REMEMBER

Spaying and neutering offer important health benefits to your pet. Don't offset those by allowing your pet to get fat. Feed your dog an appropriate diet in the proper amounts, use treats sparingly — even better, substitute rice cakes and carrots — and don't share your meals with your dog. (For more on proper nutrition, see Chapter 7.)

TIP

Look no further than the dogs at canine competitions such as agility and obedience (discussed in Chapter 16) and dogs who work for a living (such as service dogs) to see examples of properly fed, well-exercised, neutered dogs without a touch of fat on them!

A Dog's Mouth Is Cleaner than a Human's

Some folks have taken this idea so far as to say that letting your dog lick your cuts as they lick their own is a good idea to aid your healing.

Whoever thought this one up apparently never observed the things a dog takes into his mouth, some of which are quite disgusting, as any dog lover knows. One of my dogs thinks that the contents of a litter box are the best treat imaginable — and I know from my mail that he's certainly not alone!

For tips on how to thwart the litter-cruising dog, see Chapter 15.

So you shouldn't go out of your way to get a dog kiss, but should you avoid your dog's preferred form of greeting? Unless he's just eaten something disgusting, let him lick. A slurpy dog kiss isn't going to hurt you, but the good it does you isn't anything more than psychological.

TIP

Apple slices are a great canine breath-freshener, and some dogs really love them. One of my dogs also goes nuts for citrus fruit, to the extent of stealing oranges off the low-hanging limbs in my back yard. Remember, though, that bad breath can be a sign of serious dental problems that need to be addressed by your veterinarian. See Chapter 11 for more on the importance of good dental care.

Dogs Eat Grass when Their Stomachs Are Upset

The common wisdom on this one is that grass makes dogs throw up, so they seek it out when they've got a tummy ache. But many dogs eat grass constantly, with no after effects.

One theory as to why dogs seek out grass is it fulfills some nutritional deficiency caused by a diet too heavy on meat. In the wild, the thinking goes, wild dogs and wolves consume vegetable matter when they devour the stomach contents of prey animals.

The reasoning may be this simple: Some dogs eat grass because they like to, nothing more.

Unlike cats, dogs are not pure carnivores. They can live on a vegetarian diet — although given their druthers, they'd probably rather not — and commercial dog foods have high percentages of vegetable matter. Advocates of freshly prepared diets, such as veterinarian Richard Pitcairn, author, along with Susan Hubble Pitcairn, of the immensely popular *Dr. Pitcairn's Complete Guide to Natural Health for Dogs & Cats* (Rodale Press), recommend putting fresh raw vegetables such as carrots, parsley, and zucchini in the mix. If you'd like to try cooking for your pet with fresh meats, grains, and vegetables, Pitcairn's book, now in its second edition, is a wonderful resource.

A growing number of people are taking the idea of preparing food for their dogs to a new level, offering a diet of raw meats and vegetables and no commercial kibble whatsoever. For more information on the *BARF* diet — short for *Biologically Appropriate Raw Foods* — see Chapter 7.

Adding Oil to a Dog's Diet Solves Skin Problems

Some people have what I call "add-in-itis" — they aren't happy unless they're adding oils, vegetables, herbs, cottage cheese, or eggs to their dog's meals. A lot of what people add falls into the "can't hurt, might help" category — no proven benefits, but it makes the human feel better.

It's true that some skin and coat problems can be helped by oils — including some oil supplements veterinary dermatologists prescribe. But that doesn't mean you should just start chucking things into the mix whenever your dog's coat or skin doesn't look right to you.

WARNING

Making sure that skin problems are correctly diagnosed is important before treating with a blanket cure-all like oil, which, after all, adds fat to the diet of a pet who may not need more. Skin problems caused by fleas or allergies are not magically cured by the addition of oil, nor are those problems produced by intestinal parasites or hormonal imbalances.

REMEMBER

Before adding anything to your dog's diet, check with your veterinarian to make sure that the supplement is doing what it's supposed to and is not causing any other problems for your pet. Your veterinarian may give the go-ahead, or he may suggest a treatment that's more precisely targeted to what's bothering your pet.

Brewer's Yeast and Garlic Control Fleas

If only controlling fleas could be so easy! Adding garlic cloves and brewer's yeast isn't going to do much of anything — no solid evidence exists that either ingredient deters fleas when taken internally. Some believe brewer's yeast makes an effective flea powder, although the evidence on that, too, is largely anecdotal.

Many dogs love the taste of garlic and brewer's yeast, though, so adding some to your pet's food if you want to won't hurt anything — if you don't mind a little garlic breath! (In fact, adding a little garlic is a great way to get an old or sick dog to eat.)

In the last few years, safe, effective strategies for flea control have become available through veterinarians. In my home, we don't remember what fleas look like! To check out these new products, see Chapter 10.

A Barking Dog Won't Bite

A really, really, dangerous myth, and probably most in need of correcting. Either barking or growling can telegraph the intention to attack, which is why watching a dog's *body language* for signs of aggression is important.

Some of the warning signs of a dangerous dog include standing tall on his toes, and leaning forward a little. His ears are forward, too, and his eyes have taken on a steely, glazed expression. The fur over his shoulder — his *hackles* — stands on end. He may be barking or growling — or neither — but if he is barking, the sound is low, no-nonsense, and guttural.

Leave this dog alone — as well as any others you don't know, just to be safe.

Chapter **20**

Ten Questions to Ask When Buying a Purebred Puppy

Y ou can find many poor-quality purebreds around. Vicious Golden Retrievers, crippled German Shepherds, and deaf Dalmatians — virtually every breed has some kind of genetic problem that reputable, knowledgeable breeders work to eliminate. Defective dogs most often come from two kinds of breeders: the clueless and the careless. The first group is blissfully ignorant of the potential for congenital problems; the second group knows full well and could not care less.

Weeding out poor breeders doesn't take much, if you know what to ask. Following are ten questions, along with the answers you want to hear.

You should ask lots of other questions, of course, that are more breed-specific, involving shedding, drooling, aggressive tendencies, size, or life span. Make a list and ask them all. A reputable breeder is reassured by your interest. Also, if you want to know some questions to ask when considering an adult dog, see Chapter 5.

REMEMBER

One sure sign of a reputable breeder is that she asks you more questions than you ask her. Don't be put off by this questioning: Someone who cares about her dogs is just the kind of person from whom you want to buy a puppy.

See Chapter 4 for more on how puppies develop and for temperament tests you can do when looking at litters.

WARNING

Every day — yes, *every single day* of my life — I hear from some person or another who has a dog problem that relates specifically to the source of the puppy. The pup can't be house-trained because she grew up in filth. The dog doesn't like other dogs because it was taken from her littermates too early. The pup needs surgery on both hips because her breeder put together two dogs who had crippling congenital hip problems. Don't be one of these people. *Don't buy from a less than reputable breeder!*

How Long Have You Been in This Breed, and What Others Have You Bred?

You're looking for someone who has worked with one or two breeds, at the most, and studied them for years or, possibly, someone who has bred a litter with help from a mentor in the breed. (Everyone has to start somewhere!)

WARNING

Someone who has jumped from popular breed to popular breed is, more than likely, in the business to turn a fast buck and won't have the expertise you're looking for in a breeder. And an outfit that can get you any breed of puppy? Run!

Remember, though, that people can be involved in just one breed of dog and still do a bad job of matching the parents, or of training and socializing the puppies. Still, a person who's committed to just one or two breeds is definitely your best option — if the rest of the criteria check out!

What Are the Congenital Defects in This Breed?

Every breed has some problems, be it *hip dysplasia* (a painful malformation of the hip socket), *progressive retinal atrophy* (an eye disease), increased cancer susceptibility, epilepsy, or a dozen others.

The breeder who answers "none" or "I don't know" is to be avoided. She's not screening for what she doesn't know about, and you don't want to pay the price for her ignorance.

A good breeder tells you every possible problem in the breed, from droopy eyelids to ear infections.

What Steps Have You Taken to Decrease Congenital Defects in Your Dogs?

You want to hear words like "screened" and "tested" and "certified." You want to see documentation. You want to go elsewhere when you hear, "The mother's plenty healthy. We've never had to take her to the vet!"

TECHNICAL STUFF

In breeds with the potential for hip dysplasia — almost every large breed — look for PennHIP or Orthopedic Foundation for Animals certification. These are expert, unbiased evaluators who know exactly what to look for. Don't take: "My vet X-rayed her, and he says she's fine." Insist on expert documentation on both parents. And their parents, too.

Do You Have the Parents on Site? May I See Them?

This is a bit of a trick question. You should *always* be able to see the mother — unless she died giving birth — but reputable breeders usually don't have the father on hand. That's because the best match for any particular dog may be owned by another breeder, and the female is sent away for breeding.

WARNING

People who have just a pair of dogs and keep breeding them over and over for the money or the "fun" of having puppies are not the breeders that you should be looking for.

As for the mother, she may be a little anxious with strangers around her puppies, but on her own you want to see a well-socialized, calm, and well-mannered dog. So, too, should be the rest of the breeder's dogs. If you don't like the temperaments of a breeder's grown dogs, what makes you think you'll get a good temperament in one of her puppies?

What Are the Good and Bad Points of the Parents, and What Titles Do They Have? Will You Explain Their Pedigrees?

You may be looking for a pet-quality purebred, but you want to buy him from someone who knows what top-quality examples of the breed are — and uses such dogs in her breeding program. The only way for a breeder to maintain top-quality dogs is to constantly be testing breeding stock — in the show ring, in the field, and in public. Look for titles, titles, titles. Titles from shows, like *Ch.* for champion. Titles for working dogs, such as field trial titles for hunting dogs. Obedience titles, agility titles, whatever. CGC, for Canine Good Citizen, is nice to see, too; this certification shows a breeder who cares about the impression her dogs make in public. (For more on titles and the competitions in which a dog can earn them, see Chapter 16.)

It doesn't matter if you never compete with your dog, or if you go home and throw that fine pedigree in a drawer. Recent titles on both sides of a pedigree show a breeder who's making a good-faith effort to produce healthy dogs who conform to the breed standard.

WARNING

A couple of champions two or three generations back proves nothing. Especially if they're only on one side of the pedigree — either the mother's or father's side. It's a typical ploy for a backyard breeder to claim "champion bred" for a pup with one titled dog generations back. Don't fall for it!

There's more to a dog than his papers, however, and the breeder should be able to go over the mother and the other dogs in the house, explaining where their good and bad points lie — too thick a backskull, for example, too short a tail, or an imperfect gait when trotting. A breeder who cannot explain the good and bad points of her dogs is someone you should avoid.

Where Were These Puppies Raised?

"Underfoot" is the best answer. "In the basement," "in the garage," "in the kennel," or "in the barn" is not a great indicator. You want a puppy who knows what the dishwasher sounds like, whom you don't have to peel off the ceiling when a pan drops, who has set a paw on linoleum, carpet, and tile.

REMEMBER

Dogs live in our world, and the sooner they're introduced to it, the better.

Raising a litter of puppies in the house is a massive undertaking — the constant clean-ups alone prove a degree of commitment on the part of the breeder. Raising pups underfoot demonstrates more than puppy love — it also shows a knowledge of the importance of socialization.

How Have You Socialized These Puppies?

Environmental socialization is important, but so, too, is the intentional kind. The best breeders make sure that their puppies have been handled by adults of both genders and by children, even if they have to borrow children to accomplish the task. They expose the puppies to all kinds of noises and all kinds of objects.

You want to deal with a breeder who clearly demonstrates in her discussions that she knows the importance of socialization and has taken steps to provide the puppies with many experiences during the first, extremely important, weeks of their lives.

How Have You Evaluated These Puppies?

You're looking for someone who not only knows the difference between *show* and *pet* pups — and can explain the difference — but also has a feel for the temperament of each pup as an individual. Within each litter are shy pups, bold pups, and some in-betweens. Depending on the breed and your family, the wrong pup chosen from the right litter can be just as big a mistake as choosing the wrong breed.

TIP

A reputable breeder will help you choose the right pup. Too many puppy buyers buy a pup "because he chose us," when in fact that puppy would have chosen anyone — he's the most outgoing in the bunch. For most people, one of the "middle" pups — not too pushy, and certainly not too shy — is the best choice. You can find more on evaluating pups in Chapter 4.

What Guarantees Do You Provide?

Bad breeders forget your name after your check clears. You want to buy a puppy from someone who provides you with a health record on the puppies to date — vaccinations and wormings — as well as a contract laying out her responsibilities to you should the puppy develop a congenital ailment. In most cases, such contracts state either replacement with a new puppy or refunding of your purchase price.

The contract also states *your* responsibilities, mind you, such as neutering your pet. You may also be required to return the dog to the breeder if you can no longer keep him. A reputable breeder will always take a dog back.

REMEMBER

Read and discuss the paperwork with the breeder. The best breeders offer contracts that protect not only the buyer and seller, but also the most vulnerable part of the transaction: the puppy.

When Can I Take My Puppy Home?

Some breeders start selling puppies when they're weaned, at five or six weeks of age. But puppies still have lessons to learn from their mother and littermates and should not go to new homes until seven weeks at the earliest.

Reputable breeders don't let puppies go until they're a week or so older than seven weeks, and maybe longer for a tiny breed. Beware of the breeder who keeps a puppy until he's a few months old, just to make sure she's not letting a prime dog with show potential slip away. You may end up with a puppy who's more dog-oriented than people-oriented, unless the breeder's been careful to continue socialization. (And the good ones do!)

Chapter **21**

Ten Things You Need to Know to Prepare Your Dog for a Disaster

urricanes, earthquakes, floods, tornadoes, fires, and even volcanoes have brought home to us all in recent years that a disaster can happen at any time, to any community. In the aftermath of such natural calamities has come a new awareness of the need for disaster planning for our pets, both on a community level and in our own homes.

Although animals aren't allowed in most disaster-relief shelters, an increasing number of animal shelters and veterinarians are better prepared now than ever before to take in animals during an emergency.

Some regional veterinary associations work to appoint a volunteer veterinarian in each community to help coordinate animal-relief efforts. And veterinarians certainly aren't alone in the effort to help animals when a disaster strikes. Prob-ably the most influential group in the field of animal disaster relief is the Emer-gency Animal Rescue Service (EARS), a group based in Sacramento, California, that is prepared to do for animals what the Red Cross does for people. EARS-trained volunteers have worked on behalf of animals all over the world.

TIP

Terri Crisp, founder of the Emergency Animal Rescue Service, has done more than any other person to change how animals are dealt with in times of disaster. Her story is a compelling read for any animal lover, and she shares it in her book *Out of Harm's Way: The Extraordinary True Story of One Woman's Lifelong Devotion to Animal Rescue* (Pocket Books).

Behind the big changes of recent years is a growing realization that animals need help, too, and that some people choose to put their lives in danger rather than abandon their pets.

WARNING

Natural disasters aren't the only concern. Have you considered what would happen to your pets if you were in an accident or became ill suddenly and landed in a hospital with no time to prepare? Sometimes people who end up critically ill can't even tell anyone they have pets at home who need caring for!

Just as you can't leave preparations for your human family members to chance, you need a plan to ensure the safety of your dogs (and other animals!). Living in California as I do, I'm very disaster-savvy — we seem to get more than our share of fires, floods, earthquakes, and so on. I've dealt with personal emergencies, too, ending up near-death in an emergency room a few years back.

REMEMBER

Even if you feel safe from natural disasters, an all-too-human kind of an emergency is a possibility in anyone's life. Which means everyone should plan.

Here are some tips from disaster-planning experts.

Have a Plan

Prepare for all possibilities, including the possibility that you may be away from home when disaster strikes. Make sure that everyone in your family — children, too! — is prepared in the event of an emergency. Make a plan and go over it until everyone knows what to do.

TIP

Find other pet-lovers, and prepare to help each other. People need to rely on each other during emergencies, and this is just as true when it comes to your pets. Get to know your neighbors, and put a plan in place to help each other out. Find out from local shelters and veterinary organizations what their emergency response plans are and how you fit into them in case of a disaster.

Know What Your Veterinarian's Plans Are

Ask your veterinarian if he has a disaster plan and how he plans to work with other veterinarians in case of an emergency. If he's never thought of it, pushing him a little on the subject won't hurt.

TIP

Your regular veterinarian may not be the owner of the hospital or clinic, and as an employee, may not feel comfortable doing anything more than her day-to-day job. Find out who owns or runs the place, and write a note expressing your interest in discovering if the hospital can be counted on in a crisis. It's just good business sense for everyone to have a plan!

Maintain Your Pet's Permanent and Temporary ID

Most animals will survive a disaster. But too many will never see their families again unless there is a way to determine which pet belongs to which family. That's why pets should always wear a collar and identification tags. Better still is to add to the tags by using a permanent identification that can't slip off, such as a tattoo or imbedded microchip.

Keep temporary ID tags at hand, too, to put on your pet if you're forced to evacuate. (Your pet's permanent ID isn't much use if you aren't home to answer the phone, if you even have a phone or a home after the disaster.) One of the easiest forms of ID: Keep cheap key tags around the house. You can jot a current number on the tag, slip it into a plastic housing, and then attach it to your pet's collar.

TIP

A tracking system like 1-800-HELP4PETS is an excellent idea as well. The number always works, and the company will arrange for the care of your pet until you can be reunited.

Pet tags are essential and can make the difference between life and death — especially in the middle of a disaster situation.

Tae Beau/Photo courtesy of Becky Ogden

Keep Vaccinations and Records Current

Infectious diseases can be spread from dog to dog through floodwaters, which is why keeping pets' vaccinations up-to-date is essential. Kennel cough, although not serious, is common in sheltering situations and is also preventable through vaccinations.

You can find the information you need on vaccinations — who needs them, what kind, and why — in Chapter 11.

Prepare a file with up-to-date medical and vaccination records, your pets' microchip or tattoo numbers, your veterinarian's phone number and address, feeding and medication instructions, and recent pictures of your animals. Trade copies of emergency files with another pet-loving friend — it's a good idea for someone else to know about your pet should *anything* happen to you.

Have Restraints Ready

Even normally obedient dogs can behave rather strangely when stressed by an emergency. Consequently, you should be prepared to restrain your pet — for his safety and the safety of others.

TIP

Keep leashes and carriers ready for emergencies. *Ready* means *at hand* — the means to transport your pet shouldn't be something you have to find and pull from the rafters. Harnesses work better than collars at keeping panicky pets safe.

TIP

Shipping crates are probably the least-thought-of pieces of emergency equipment for pet owners — but are among the most important. Sturdy crates keep pets safe and give rescuers more options in housing pets. They give *you* more options, too, in the homes of friends or relatives or in shelters outside of the area. Depending on weather conditions, crated pets may also be safely left overnight in vehicles.

Another item to keep on hand is a muzzle, because frightened and injured dogs are more likely to bite.

For more information on crates and muzzles, see Chapter 6.

Rotate a Supply of Food, Water, and Medications

Keep several days' worth of food and safe drinking water as well as any necessary medicines packed and ready to go in the event of a disaster. Rotate your supplies so they do not get stale. If your pet eats canned food, be sure to keep an extra can opener and spoon tucked in among the emergency supplies.

TIP

Don't forget to pack plastic bags! Include the kind you usually use for picking up poop, as well as bags that seal to put the poop into.

You do clean up after your dog now, don't you? You should! For the lowdown on the easiest, neatest way to scoop the poop, see Chapter 18.

Keep First Aid Supplies on Hand — with Directions

Pet-supply stores sell ready-made first aid kits, or you can put your own together fairly easily. You can find the ingredients of a good basic kit in Chapter 11.

Keep a canine first-aid book with your supplies, but give the book a quick read before you store it.

TIP

Veterinarian Michelle Bamberger's *Help! The Quick Guide to First Aid for Your Dog* (IDG Books Worldwide) is well organized and easy to follow. Dr. Roger Gfeller is one of relatively few veterinarians board-certified in critical care. His book, *First Aid: Emergency Care for Dogs and Cats,* is another I like to keep at hand. It's kind of hard to find, although Amazon.com stocks it.

TIP

Pet-Pak, Inc., manufactures animal first-aid kits in five sizes, all neatly packed in a plastic container (the four largest have handles). The kit contains the basics for emergency care, along with a pamphlet on using the supplies. For information, contact the company at P.O. Box 982, Edison, NJ 08818-0982; 800-217-7387; www.petpak.com.

Know the Locations of Other Veterinary Hospitals and Animal Shelters

Your veterinary hospital may become damaged in the disaster, which is why having some backup plans for boarding and care is a good idea. Know where to find other veterinary hospitals in your area, as well as animal shelters and animal-control facilities. Boarding facilities should also be noted, as well as groomers — all these places may be able to help out in a pinch. Photocopy the appropriate pages from your local Yellow Pages — or compile and print a list on your home computer — and tuck the pages in with your emergency supplies.

TIP

If you lose your pet, these facilities are going to be among the first places you look, in hope that she turns up.

Keep a "Lost Dog" Kit Ready

In case of a disaster, you probably won't be able to get flyers printed up, so make up some generic ones and keep them with your emergency supplies. In the biggest type size you can, center the words *LOST DOG*, along with a clear picture of your dog. Below, provide a description of your dog, including any identifying marks, and a space to add the phone number where you can be reached, along with any backup contacts, friends, relatives, neighbors, or your veterinarian. Print a hundred copies and keep them in a safe place.

TIP

A staple gun allows you to post your notices; keep one loaded and with your supplies, along with thumbtacks and electrical tape.

If your dog becomes lost, post flyers in your neighborhood and beyond and distribute them at veterinary hospitals and shelters. While relying on the kindness of strangers is nice, offering a reward makes many strangers just a little bit kinder.

Be Prepared to Help Others

You may be lucky and survive a disaster nearly untouched, but others in your community won't be so fortunate. Contact your local humane society and veterinary organization now to train as a volunteer so you can help out in a pinch. Disaster-relief workers do everything from distributing food to stranded animals to helping reunite pets with their families — and helping find new homes for those who need them.

REMEMBER

Volunteering in a pinch is not only a good thing to do — it's the right thing for anyone who cares about animals and people.

Chapter **22**

Ten Ways to Have Both a Dog and a Nice Yard

I s having both a dog and a nice backyard possible? Nancy Dyson says it is, and she offers living proof.

Dyson is a University of California–trained master gardener *and* a dog trainer of considerable accomplishments. Her retrievers are models of canine decorum, top winners in the obedience ring. But they're still dogs, quite oblivious to their owner's desire to have plants left unmolested.

The key, says Dyson, is being realistic about the needs of the garden — and of the dogs. Following are a few tips, gleaned from Dyson and others.

Give Your Dog Lots of Exercise

A dog with too much energy isn't one you want to leave alone all day in a nice yard — and yet, that's exactly what many people do. If you don't take care of your dog's exercise requirements, he's going to take care of them on his own — by digging a hole to China or removing the shrubs in your yard.

Exercise is the missing element in most owners' attempts to fix behavior problems such as digging. Dogs, like people, need a half-hour of aerobic exercise three or four times a week — jogging, playing fetch, or swimming, for example.

Giving your dog plenty of exercise is a good way to ensure that she doesn't take up annoying or destructive habits.

Chase/Photo courtesy of Joan Mahone

TIP

Dogs who don't get the exercise they need are likely to expend that energy and cure boredom doing things people don't like — digging, chewing, and barking. Dogs who are well exercised are more likely to sleep while you are gone.

Give Your Dog Mental Stimulation

A tired dog is a happy dog, and that means more than physical exhaustion. Dogs need to exercise their minds as well as their bodies, which means working on basic training regularly — teaching new commands and practicing those your dog already knows. It's good for your dog's overall manners, and it wears your dog out mentally so he's more likely to snooze when you leave him.

When you leave, you should also offer your dog alternatives to choosing his own amusements: Provide him with chew toys. You can make them more appealing by praising him for using them and, also, by stuffing hollow toys — such as a Kong — with something delicious, like peanut butter.

For more on Kong and other great toys, see Chapter 6.

Don't Leave Dogs Unsupervised in the Yard

Dogs don't know a wisteria plant from a weed, and they never will. That's why it's up to you not to leave them unattended around plants you want left alone. When you leave for work, limit your dog's space for his, and your plants', safety. Most of a dog's time alone is spent sleeping, anyway, so he doesn't need to have the entire run of the house and yard. Outings — for jogging, walking, fetch, or swimming — should be done with your supervision.

If you don't want to leave your dog in the house while you're gone, a well-protected kennel run is a fine way to keep him out of trouble. Remember, though, that these small, chain-linked areas are not the place to spend a life. The run should have shelter, toys, and plenty of fresh water.

WARNING

Whatever you do, don't leave your dog chained. Dogs who are always on tie-outs often develop aggression problems. For more on chaining and kennel runs, see Chapter 6.

A WHOLE LOT OF DIGGIN' GOIN' ON

My friends Ellen and Darryl have a Golden Retriever they named Cap, short for Capability Brown, the noted English landscape architect. He got the name after rearranging a few shrubs in the yard. Not as blatant a reference as with another friend's Jack Russell terrier, Digger, who'd paw his way to the center of the Earth if he could, just for fun.

One of my readers named his Labrador Retriever Cat, an unusual name for a dog, to be sure. The name, though, was really short for Caterpillar, as in the giant manufacturer of earth-moving equipment.

If your dog is allowed in your yard under your supervision only, the chance of him digging or chewing is just about nil — you can stop him before the damage is done and redirect his behavior.

Discourage Digging

Some breeds were developed to dig, and expecting them not to is unfair. You can find most of these digging dogs in the Terrier Group — the word *terrier* derives from *terra*, Latin for *earth*. These breeds were developed to dig after and kill pests such as rats.

You can keep many dogs from digging if you keep them exercised, limit their access to dirt, and make the digging experience unpleasant. Sometimes putting the dog's own stools in the hole and covering the stool with dirt deters the dog. Many dogs won't dig if their own mess is under the surface.

TIP

If you don't mind the mess, you may think about giving your dog a *dig zone*. While hardly clean fun, it is good fun, especially for dogs who are happiest with their noses in the dirt and their paws flying.

If your dog is digging not for pleasure, but for escape — along the fence line, for example — the habit may be hard to break. The first step is to reduce the desire for roaming by neutering and by making sure that he's kept well-exercised. For persistent problems, you may need to bury wire fencing beneath the ground and pour a concrete curb or run a hot wire — available at farming-supply stores — around the base of the fence. None of these solutions is inexpensive or easy, but they could save your escape-artist pet's life.

Heather is the only dog in my family who likes to dig, and she takes to it very enthusiastically. She has but one hole — and I let her have it, in the spirit of compromise. Her excavation is impressive: The hole is really a den, with a small opening at the mouth of a cavern so vast she can disappear into it completely, and even turn around! I let her enjoy her den, but I do have some limits: When she gets around to ordering furniture for her summer home, I plan to put my foot down.

Teach the Wait Command

Living with your dog is all about communication; after all, how else is she going to know you don't want her jumping up into the raised beds if you don't tell her? Instead of yelling at her to get out of the garden, teach her the "Wait" command to keep her from going in.

TECHNICAL
STUFF

"Wait" is different from "Stay." "Stay" means "don't move until I tell you to," while "Wait" means "you can move anywhere you want except across this line." The line can be the edge of a flower garden, or it can be the open gate of a vegetable garden while you're inside picking tomatoes. It's anywhere you deem to be off-limits for your dog.

For information on teaching the "Wait" command, see Chapter 14.

Boundary training such as "Wait" is not to be relied on when your dog is alone. "Wait" is a command to be used in your presence so you can correct transgressions if you need to.

TIP

Although I don't recommend electronic fencing to keep a dog contained — more on that in Chapter 6 — it can be a useful tool to keep dogs out of gardens.

Give Your Dog Space of His Own

If you have space, take the "potty zone" concept a bit further and give your dog a yard of his own. Dyson advocates a place where dogs can run and play and not hurt anything.

This play area can be worked into the landscaping of your yard in clever ways. The dog area can wrap around an ornamental garden or be along one side of it. A low fence to separate the play area from the rest of the yard can be made of attractive wood or chain link and covered with vines.

SEEING SPOTS — YELLOW ONES!

Dick Tracy, the now-retired garden writer from the *Sacramento Bee* newspaper, has long kidded me about how we can become rich on the money we'll earn when we come up with the "cure" for urine burns on the lawn. (Or for dog mess in the flower beds, but that goes in another book!)

We aren't going to be retiring anytime soon. Trust me.

The best way to keep urine from ruining your lawn is to make sure that your pet puts it somewhere else — like in a potty area. But you can reduce the potential damage to your lawn by flushing the piddled-on area immediately with water. But I do not recommend — as I've seen some do — giving your pet extra salt to encourage her to drink more water and so produce a more diluted urine.

A friend of mine used to use another trick. She kept a roll of sod growing in a side yard, and every weekend she'd cut out the yellow patches and replace them with fresh sod.

REMEMBER

Ideally, a dog space is not one that isolates your pet, but is instead a place to share. A place for fetch or other games. The area should be designed for your pet's enjoyment, with things to jump on and to play with, and perhaps a kiddie pool for water-loving dogs. Trees for shade, and sunny spots for resting in the warmth, are also important. Provide access to your house through a dog door, and you're talking pet paradise.

TIP

Small trees and big dogs often are not a good combination, but large trees are important to make the dog space more pleasant. This is why you need to protect the trees as they grow. They should be staked to get a head start on growing straight and tall, and Dyson suggests putting wire cages around them to protect them from being knocked over or dug up.

What kind of grass works best in a dog area? I've had the best luck with weeds, kept watered and mowed. They look fine from a distance and are well-nigh indestructible. If you want the perfect lawn, you're going to have to be perfectly resolute about keeping your dog — and your kids — off of it.

Work with the Patterns in Your Yard

If you must share yard space with your dog, put paths in high traffic areas and plants in low ones. If you have a dog who runs along the fence line, for example, don't put plants in the area in front of the fence — dogs will run right through them, even the thorny ones. Dyson suggests leaving a *running track* along the fence line, with plants along the edge of it.

Fence-running is one of the things that can trigger unacceptable barking. If your dog is *just* running — and you don't mind the wear on the area near the fence — then it's fine, fun, and good exercise. But if every step is matched with a bark, you may need to close that area off to keep the peace. For more strategies to keep barking to a minimum, see Chapter 15.

Keep Things in Perspective

Remember, the secrets to having both a nice yard and dogs are planning and training. Still, keep in mind that tolerance is a must, too. Accidents *do* happen. Few love a nice yard as much as Nancy Dyson, but her final words of advice: Plants are just plants, and you can always replace them. You can't say the same about your dog.

TOXIC PLANTS

WARNING

Dogs can be deadly to plants, but more than a few plants are quite capable of getting revenge. Here are some bad seeds. Most "just" make your pet sick, but a few of them can kill. If your pet has tangled with any of these, call your veterinarian.

- American yew
- Angel's trumpet
- Apricot, almond
- Arrowgrass
- Azalea
- Bird of paradise
- Bittersweet
- Black locust
- Buttercup
- Castor bean
- Cherry tree
- China berry
- Coriara
- Daffodil
- Delphinium
- Elderberry
- English holly
- English yew
- Foxglove
- Hemlock
- Jasmine

- Jimsonweed
- Larkspur
- Lily of the valley
- Locoweed
- Lupine
- Mescal bean
- Mistletoe
- Mock orange
- Moonweed
- Mushrooms and toadstools
- Oleander
- Peach tree
- Pokeweed
- Privit
- Rhododendron
- Rhubarb
- Skunk cabbage
- Soapberry
- Spinach
- Tomato vine
- Wisteria

Chapter **23**

Ten Must-See Dog Sites on the World Wide Web

The worldwide network of computers we know as the Internet is an incredible resource for any dog lover. You can shop for your dog, research breeds and health topics, enjoy some canine humor (some of it far too gross to mention here, a lot of it having to do with flatulence), or just plain look at dog pictures, of which the Internet seems to have millions — and the number climbs every minute.

One of the easiest ways for beginners to poke around is to use the graphical part of the Net, called the World Wide Web. You also might enjoy joining an e-mail list, which is an online discussion group dealing with a specific topic — a breed of dog, for example, a sport such as dog agility, or holistic dog care. Arguably the largest collection of e-mail lists can be found at the Egroups site (www.egroups.com). Just enter the name of a breed, an interest (such as holistic pet care), or an activity (such as agility) in the site's search engine and join the groups that interest you. You can also *chat* (the lingo for real-time type-talking) about dogs on commercial providers such as America Online or on Web sites such as the Pet Care Forum (www.vin.com/petcare).

A list of ten sites can't begin to hit all the best dog sites on the Web. A hundred wouldn't do the job, nor would a thousand. If you feed the word *dog* into any search engine (a site that searches the Web), you'll find that the subject triggers millions of suggested Web sites. And that's just when *I* did it. By the time you read this book, you're likely to find millions more such references — such is the Internet's speed of growth.

Try out my humble offerings and don't be shy about exploring on your own. Many pages offer connections, called *links*, that take you to related sites if you click them with your mouse; in fact, some pages are nothing *but* links. Following some of these links can turn up some real gems.

REMEMBER

Please forgive me if some of the Web sites I've offered turn up missing. The Internet is a very fast-changing place, remember, and things move and even disappear. You should be able to locate sites that have moved by using any search engine, such as www.google.com.

Finally, avoid any Web site selling — or worse, auctioning — puppies or dogs. No reputable breeder would ever place an animal that way, so you'd likely be dealing with backyard or high-volume commercial breeders. (See Chapter 3 for a rundown on good breeders and those to avoid.)

WARNING

BOWSER BROWSER BEWARE!

Framed in my pet-centric home office is a print of a New Yorker cartoon: a dog sitting at a computer, one paw on the keyboard. "On the Internet," reads the caption, "no one knows you're a dog."

Meant to poke fun at one of the basic truths of the online world — no one knows what anybody looks like — the cartoon always reminds me of the pet-friendliness of the Internet. I've touched on just a handful of my favorite sites in this chapter, but millions exist, and a lot of them offer great information.

You need to be aware, however, that a lot of junk makes its way online and gets passed around like gospel. Don't rely on online veterinary advice for anything more than general information. Such advice is no substitute for a veterinarian who can examine your dog in person. Be cautious, too, of home remedies you may find. Many are a waste of your time and money, but a few can be downright dangerous. When in doubt, check with your veterinarian.

The Mother of All Canine Web Sites

Cindy Tittle Moore is an Internet pioneer who deserves some kind of medal for the work she has done to help dog lovers. Her library of canine *FAQs* (Frequently Asked Questions) has some of the best information available anywhere on all aspects of choosing and living with a dog. You'll find no sugarcoating here: The breed *FAQs* are full of detailed descriptions of what living with each breed is like, written by experienced fanciers who are just as keen on sharing the problems as they are on talking up the good points. (Unlike quick-buck breeders who'd sell any dog to anyone, good breeders want their dogs with families who fit the animal's characteristics.)

Breed descriptions aren't all you'll find, either. Also included are FAQs on raising a puppy and on health care, on canine organizations and publications, on dog breeding and canine competitions. An exhaustive resource, first started in the Stone Age of the Internet, *waaaaaaaayyyyyyy* back in the early '90s.

The jumping-off site for all this information is the rec.pet.dogs FAQ homepage, at `www.k9web.com/dog-faqs/`. This site is an absolute must-see. I'd tell you that every dog lover who has ever signed on to the Internet should send Moore an e-mail of gratitude, but I know she gets more e-mail than she can possibly handle, so I won't suggest it. So instead I'll thank her for all of us.

TIP

It's no surprise to anyone that the Internet is a highly commercial enterprise these days. Nothing wrong with that, of course, but it's still wonderful to see what folks like Moore and the rest of the dog FAQs contributors have done for no other reason than to help out dogs and the people who love them.

A Doggy Dictionary

I tried to print Kyler B. Laird's glossary of dog terms for my files and had to hit Cancel as fast as I could — the text is 40 pages long! But what a great site — everything from A (Abdomen) to Y (Yorkshire Terrier), with lots of information and dozens of links to other places in between. Want to know what a *stop* is? First dog in the AKC stud book? It's all here, and much, much more.

Laird's site should be good for hours of entertaining and informative Web cruising. Save your visit to this site for a winter's day, though, so as not to cut into prime dog-walking weather. (My dogs make me type these things.)

SIT . . . ASSIS . . . ZIT . . . OH, JUST DO IT!

Now here's something that will impress all your friends: Teach your dog commands in another language. With the help of Mark Plonsky, a psychology professor at the University of Wisconsin, Stevens Point, you can start today.

The good Dr. Plonsky is a dog lover who has put together a terrific site at www.uwsp.edu/psych/dog/dog.htm with articles on a variety of dog-related topics as well as some excellent links. Dr. P's overall site is a solid and thought-provoking resource, but his dog commands page is what really caught my eye, at www.uwsp.edu/acad/psych/dog/languag.htm. He has even added audio files so you can hear the commands spoken. In all, he has translations for German, French, Czech, Dutch, Hungarian, Polish, Hebrew, and Finnish.

I had a lot of fun with this page, especially the translations for "good dog!" I tried them on my dogs and got tail wags for every one. Before I give them credit for being multilingual and oh-so-smart, though, I should confess my crooning voice probably tipped them off. Try them on your dog, and be sweet: "So brav" (German); "bon garcon" (French); "hodny" (Czech); "okos" (Hungarian); "dobry pies" (Polish); or "kelev-tov" (Hebrew).

The page is at www.ecn.purdue.edu/~laird/dogs/glossary. Don't expect any fancy graphics here, though. It's just one big list. A very, very big list. Since my last visit, Laird has improved the site with the addition of lots of links, including some to information on the rarest breeds in the world. He's still missing a few of the AKC breeds, though.

And a *stop*, by the way, is that area where most dogs' skulls step down, right where the eyes hit the nose. The first dog registered with the AKC? That would be a pointer named Adonis, who's also pictured on the logo of the prestigious Westminster Kennel Club. (You can see that logo at www.westminsterkennelclub.org.)

Another interesting site is the Dog Fanciers' Acronym List, which offers an explanation of every title that can be given to a dog in every imaginable canine sport. You can find it at www.k9web.com/dog-faqs/lists/acronym-list.html.

Hitting the Road

I love to travel with my dogs, and the fact is that I just don't have as much fun when I leave them behind. And the funny thing is, when I must go somewhere without them, I'm usually heading to a place where I can get a major dog fix — like to New York City to cover the Westminster Kennel Club dog show.

Lots of folks take their dogs along when they leave home, so I know I'm in good company. Fortunately, traveling with pets is a lot easier than it used to be thanks to the Internet. Two sites in particular are must-sees, with lots of information on making the trip easier. The third isn't specifically a pet site, but it's one you'll want to make note of before you go.

My favorite site is TravelDog (www.traveldog.com), which combines great-looking graphics with loads of helpful advice. The site offers state-by-state listings of hotels, motels, and inns that take dogs. The list isn't exhaustive, but it does include lots of nifty lodgings that aren't part of chains, as well as those that cater nearly exclusively to dog-loving clientele, such as the remarkable Sheep Dung Estates (www.sheepdung.com), which has to be any dog's idea of off-leash heaven. TravelDog also offers links to pet policies for most major airlines and quarantine information for those hoping to take their dogs abroad.

Like TravelDog, Petswelcome.com (www.petswelcome.com) offers a mix of listings and advice — and these folks have thought of everything, including what to do in case of an emergency. Exhaustive listings, too, including chain hotels, lodging in various countries, and more. The site also has feedback from visitors, although too many people post on topics other than travel, which makes plowing through all the comments a drag.

Finally, you can do your quick-and-dirty searching at Travel Web (www.travelweb.com), which is a fast search engine that lets you search for lodgings that meet your needs — including, of course, those that accept pets.

TIP

You can make online reservations from all three sites, or just take the phone numbers down and call. When I was traveling across country with my show dog, Heather, I used my laptop every day to access these sites and book lodgings for the next night.

Just for Kids

Since I wrote the first edition of this book, the quality of Web content has improved in some remarkable ways, none more astonishing than in these two Web site gems designed with dog-loving children in mind.

How to Love Your Dog (www.geocities.com/~kidsanddogs) advertises itself as "A Kid's Guide to Dog Care," and you'll be able to turn your kid loose here and feel good about the experience. The site offers oodles of fascinating information on dogs, along with kid-friendly tips on training and care, riddles, quizzes, and games. I love the areas where the kids themselves contribute to the content. The sections on what dogs cost, and what they need, help children to understand those circumstances when getting a dog just isn't possible. For those children who can't have dogs, a list of suggestions is included, from alternative pets to walking a neighbor's dog.

TIP

The creator, Janet Wall, also maintains a mailing list for parents and teachers who'd like to be kept informed when new content goes on the site. The Kids and Dogs Web site (www.geocities.com/Heartland/Meadows/2344) was fun to play with — you "pet" dogs with a mouse click to enter various content areas. The site has other graphic-oriented games, including one where a child is invited to click on pictures of kids who aren't caring for their dogs responsibly.

For the Literary-Minded

The Bark (www.thebark.com) started out as a community newsletter advocating off-leash dog parks in the Oakland-Berkeley area of northern California. *The Bark* still does push for off-leash dog parks, but nowadays it does so as a literary journal for dog lovers. The magazine has been compared to *The New Yorker*, and with good reason: Some of the world's best writers have appeared in the pages of *The Bark*, writing about — what else? — dogs. *The Bark's* Web site doesn't offer everything the magazine does, but it's a fun place to kick around anyway.

And speaking of off-leash dog parks, you can find out if there's one in your area by checking the lists on dogpark.com. If you're interested in getting your own work about dogs published, a great place to start is by visiting the Dog Writers Association of America online (www.dwaa.org). The organization has been around for decades and offers an annual writing competition. A yearly seminar for writers and photographers is also offered in conjunction with the Cat Writers Association (www.catwriters.org).

For Dog Sports Fans

The Dogpatch (www.dogpatch.org) is another of those Web sites that has been around since the days when few people were online. It was one of my favorite sites then, and it remains so today. Creator Mary Jo Sminkey has never been one to rest on her laurels, and the Dogpatch has grown and grown.

Although the whole site offers lots for dog lovers, the best part of the Dogpatch is its collection of information on and links to various canine sporting events (www.dogpatch.org/dogs/shows.cfm). You can pick any dog sport and find information here on how it works and how to get started. The strongest collection of information has to do with the very popular sport of agility. The main agility page (www.dogpatch.org/agility) offers just about everything you need to know, but you can also find tons of great links to other agility sites.

Because Sminkey has a soft spot for Shelties, you can also find great information on this breed on the Dogpatch site.

For Purebreds Only . . . Mostly

Not much on the American Kennel Club's Web site will interest the owner of a mixed-breed dog, and the AKC isn't shy about saying so. Consider the mission statement of this breed registry, founded in 1884:

>> "Maintain a registry for purebred dogs and preserve its integrity."

>> "Sanction dog events that promote interest in, and sustain the process of, breeding for type and function of purebred dogs."

>> "Take whatever actions are necessary to protect and assure the continuation of the sport of purebred dogs."

See any themes here? Women once weren't all that welcome either, if it's any consolation.

Still, the AKC isn't half as snooty as it seems, and its Web site is proof of that. The organization is a tireless fighter against antidog legislation and promotes responsible care of *all* dogs (including mixed breeds) through its Canine Good Citizenship program. Their Companion Animal Recovery service, a registry of microchips and tattoos, is open not only to all dogs, but also to other animals — cats, sure, but also exotic pets such as pot-bellied pigs. See? They're not so bad. If you're looking for a purebred dog or puppy, this site is one of the best places to start finding that reputable breeder or breed-rescue group. Information on every AKC-registered breed is available, as well as links to many breed Web sites.

This site is worth a good look, at www.akc.org. And while you're wandering the Web, don't forget to check out a few other dog registries, including the Canadian Kennel Club/Club Canin Canadien (www.ckc.ca/), United Kennel Club (www.ukcdogs.com), American Rare Breed Association (www.arba.org), the United Kingdom's Kennel Club (www.the-kennel-club.org.uk/) and the Fédération Cynologique Internationale (www.fci.be).

TIP

If all you want to do is go to a dog show, check out InfoDog (www.infodog.com). A resource for American and Canadian dog-show competitors, InfoDog offers schedules of nearly every canine event.

Veterinary Resources

Dr. Paul D. Pion, my *Cats For Dummies* coauthor and a board-certified veterinary cardiologist, runs the Veterinary Information Network, Inc., an online service that offers its subscribing veterinary professionals access to continuing education, top-quality specialty consultants, bulletin boards for discussing cases with colleagues, and searchable databases of dozens of professional journals. Through the Pet Care Forum (www.vin.com/petcare), these professionals share their veterinary expertise with pet lovers, especially in the Veterinary Hospital, where veterinarians respond to questions on the many bulletin boards. You can also find my weekly syndicated pet-care column on the site.

Probably the best-known veterinary site on the Web is NetVet (netvet.wustl.edu/vet.htm), put together by Dr. Ken Boschert, a veterinarian in Washington University's division of comparative medicine in St. Louis, Missouri. His dog section offers a lot of solid information and many good links.

Another site worth a look is the U.S. Food and Drug Administration's Center for Veterinary Medicine (www.fda.gov/cvm), which keeps its visitors up-to-date on the latest approved drugs for veterinary uses. The site also offers links to other animal-related government resources, as well as colleges of veterinary medicine, which themselves offer more links.

Shop! Shop! Shop!

Enough of this serious stuff! Time to go shopping. You can find almost as many pet-supply vendors on the Web as you can dog pictures, and you can find links to them from practically every dog-related site on the Web. You can also put the words *pet supplies* into a search engine and let it rip.

Since I wrote the first edition of this book, the online retail world has gone mad with huge and well-funded Web sites such as Pets.com, Doctors Foster and Smith (www.drsfostersmith.com), and Petsmart.com. These sites are hotly competitive, to say the least, and offer up some good content along with the toys, food, bowls, beds, and more. Pets.com, in fact, is the home of an exclusive weekly essay on pets by yours truly, and they've also sent me out to cover numerous other pet-related stories, such as the Westminster Kennel Club dog show.

With their multi-gazillion-dollar advertising budgets, these big sites don't need my help in promoting them. So I also want to draw your attention to a niche player I've enjoyed buying from over the years.

Dogwise (www.dogwise.com) surely isn't selling as many dog books as Amazon.com, but it's the place to go to stay on top of trends in training and dog sports. The site caters to serious dog lovers, those who spend their leisure time training their dogs and their weekends attending seminars and competitions. The Dogwise folks have a good eye for what's hot and what's not, and although most of what they sell is books, they're also a great place for cool new toys and equipment.

A Memorial Space

One of the saddest places to find dog pictures on the Web is on sites dedicated to the memory of beloved pets who've passed on. I find such places sad, true, but I also find them beautiful and inspiring. One such site is the Rainbow Bridge Tribute Pages (www.rainbow-bridge.org/bridge.htm).

The Rainbow Bridge refers to a lovely story that has given many pet lovers comfort over the years. After our animal companions die, the story goes, they're restored to health and vigor and are well cared for in a special place. They're happy, except for the fact that they miss us. After we die, we see them again and cross the Rainbow Bridge together. A wonderful story, and I hope it's true, for I'd like to see many, many animals again.

The site offers stories, poems, and pictures, each and every one guaranteed to tug at your heartstrings. The last page notes that this site was "made with love," and I have no doubt about that. Creators Meggie O'Brien and Kathie Maffit are providing a much-needed service to us all.

If you've just lost a pet, you may also find a call to a pet-loss hotline comforting. Most veterinary schools and colleges offer these services, staffed by compassionate veterinary students. I've put a list of them in Chapter 13.

Index

American Board of Veterinary Practitioners (ABVP), 197

American Boarding Kennel Association, 325

American Eskimo Dog, 46

American Foxhound, 37

American Holistic Veterinary Medical Association (AVHMA), 195

American Mixed Breed Obedience Registry (AMBOR), obedience trials, 296

American Society for the Prevention of Cruelty to Animals (ASPCA), 72

American Staffordshire Terrier, 40

American Water Spaniel, 35

amino acids, 126

ammonia-based cleaners, avoiding, 144

anal sacs, cleaning, 183

anesthesia, senior dog risks, 250

Animal Behavior, 314

Animal People, 73

animal-assisted therapy, 303

animal-based chews, 138–140

animal-control shelters, 70

antibodies, 200

antiseptic liquid, grooming uses, 177

appearance, physical examination element, 207

The Art of Raising a Puppy, 315

ascarids, control methods, 201–202

aspirin, senior dog stiffness/ache treatment, 230

Association of American Feed Control Officials (AAFCO), 130–131

Australian Shepherd, 45–48

Australian Terrier, 40

automobiles
  barriers, 333
  behavior issues, 333–334
  car-sickness prevention techniques, 334
  crate advantages, 313
  doggy seat belt, 333
  dramamine, 334
  heat stroke concerns, 334–335

B

baby gates, 108

backpacking, dog-friendly vacation, 341

backpacks, 341

bacteria, 221

bad breath, dental problems, 349

balls, 122

BARF diet, 132, 350

barkers
  ABS Anti-Barking System, 284
  debarking, 286
  phone calls, 252
  problem behavior control techniques, 281–284
  puppy training, 168
  reasons for, 281–284

barriers, automobile travel, 333

Baseball Aquatic Retrieval Korps (BARK), Portuguese Water Dogs, 38

Basenji, 37

Basset Hound, 36

baths, grooming techniques, 181–184

Beagle, 36, 51

Bearded Collie, 47

beats per minute (bpm), heart rate testing, 210

Bedlington Terrier, 40

bedroom, puppy's sleeping arrangements, 89–90

beds
  oval cuddlers, 111
  senior dogs, 235
  uses and types, 109–112
  washability issues, 112

begging, avoiding table scraps, 102

behavior
  adult dog evaluation questions, 96
  aggression avoidance techniques, 167
  automobile travel issues, 333–334
  barkers, 281–284
  barking, 168
  begging, 102
  biting, 169
  board-and-train arrangements, 329
  chewers, 165–166, 278–279
  consistency of training, 157–159
  diggers, 284, 370–371
  disobedience, 285
  eliminating health problems, 272–273
  jumpers, 278
  jumping, 166–168
  litter-munchers, 282
  mental exercise strategy, 273
  minimizing mischief opportunities, 278
  new baby jealousy concerns, 285–288
  nipping, 169
  physical exercise strategy, 274–278
  problem behavior substitution strategies, 278–279

D

Dachshund, 35–36, 51

Dalmatian
Non-sporting group, 44–45
deafness issues, 33, 45

dam, viewing at purchase, 355

Dandie Dinmont Terrier, 40

danger, indicated by body language, 351

Davis, Kathy Diamond, 272

deafness, Dalmatian issues, 33, 45

Death of a Goldfish, 241

Delta Society, animal-assisted therapy information, 303

dewclaw removal, reasons for, 203

dig zone, 370

digestibility, protein issues, 126

diggers, problem behavior control techniques, 284

digging, discouraging, 370

disaster preparation
current vaccination/ records, 362
develop a plan, 360–361
first aid supplies/ directions, 364
food/water/medication supplies rotation, 363
help others, 365
know alternate veterinary clinics/shelters, 364
know your veterinarians plan, 361
Lost Dog kit always ready, 365
maintain pet ID, 361
muzzles, 363
pet tracking system, 361
restraints available, 363

diseases
brucellosis, 310
children's cautions, 286
coronavirus, 201

distemper, 201, 218

hepatitis, 201

kennel cough, 70, 328

kidney, 219–220

leptospirosis, 201

Lyme disease, 201

parainfluenza, 201

parvovirus, 70, 201, 217–218

rabies, 201

veterinary hospital cautions/ concerns, 199

dishes, senior dogs, 236

disobedience, problem behavior control methods, 285

distemper, 201, 218

Doberman Pinscher, 39

Doctors Foster and Smith, 112

dog camps, dog-friendly vacations, 338

dog doors, 108

Dog Fancy, 62, 291

dog fights, dangers of, 249

dog ownership
activity level issues, 17–18
avoiding love at first sight, 14
cost considerations, 25–26
domestic dog development history, 11–14
family work patterns, 56
indoor dog advantages, 106
intelligence issues, 21–22
large breed issues, 16–17
locating a puppy, 55–58
locating reputable breeders, 59–65
male/female selection guidelines, 24–25
mixed breed resources, 68–73
paperwork types, 66–67
puppy versus adult dog, 22–24
reasons for attending dog shows, 28
shedding issues, 19–21

size guidelines, 15–17
small breed issues, 17

dog parks, exercise opportunity, 278–279

dog resorts, dog-friendly vacations, 339

dog shows
Best in Show honors, 293
Best of Breed honors, 293
bred-by-exhibitor class, 294
breed standard judging, 294
breeder resource, 62
class divisions, 294
coat color divisions, 294
Crufts, 291
group judging, 294
male/female class divisions, 294
open class, 294
popularity of, 291
puppy class, 294
show quality versus show winning puppy, 301
Westminster Kennel Club, 291–292, 301

dog space, garden/yards, 371

Dog Who Loved Too Much: Tales, Treatments and the Psychology of Dogs, 288

Dog World, 62

dog years versus human years, 340–347

doggy seat belt, automobile travel, 333

doghouses, 109

Dogs in Canada, 62, 291

Dogs USA, 62

dominance
puppy personality testing, 83
tug-of-war concerns, 122

Don't touch command, 265–266

Down command, 260–261

Down-Stay command, new baby jealousy problems, 286

K

K-9 Carts, 234

Keeshound, 45–46

kennel clubs, conformation/ obedience classes, 302

kennel cough

boarding kennel concerns, 328

shelter cautions/concerns, 68

kennel runs

safe place, 108

save yards, 369

kennels, travel alternative, 325, 327–328

Kerry Blue Terrier, 40

key tags, travel uses, 330

kiddy pool, whelping box uses, 312

kidneys, urologic problems, 219–221

Komondor, 39

Kong toy, 121, 137, 278

Kuvasz, 39

L

Labrador Retriever, 33–35, 50

Lakeland Terrier, 40

lamb ears, 139

large dogs, who should own, 16–17

leads. See leashes

leash-bonding, adult dogs, 102

leashes

Flexi, 119

off-leash law breaking, 340

size ranges, 119

traffic, 119

training, 162–163, 253, 258

travel uses, 330

Leave it command, 342

leptospirosis, vaccinating against, 201

Lhasa Apso, 46

links, defined, 378

lint rollers, dealing with shedding, 21

liquid medications, giving, 214

litter boxes

controlling litter-munchers, 282

house-training uses, 151

littermates, cautions/concerns, 85–86

litter-munchers, control techniques, 282

Lixit, outdoor waterer, 113

long-haired dogs, shedding issues, 19–21

loss of appetite, illness indicator, 211

loss support groups, 238

Lost Dog Kit, disaster preparation, 365

lost dogs

prevention/recovery techniques, 100, 120

recovery service 1-800-HELP4PETS, 100, 120, 330

Lowchen, 43

lumps, senior dogs, 233

Lyme disease

ticks, 187

vaccinating against, 200

M

Maddie's Pet Adoption Center, San Francisco, CA SPCA, 68

Maffit, Kathie, 383

magazines, breeder resource, 62

mailing lists

breeder resource, 62

treat recipe source, 138

males

brucellosis testing, 310

first leg-lift time frame, 204

intact, 24

intact/attack issues, 13, 24

leg-lifting issues, 149

mating process, 310–313

neutering advantages, 306–307

new owner advantages/ disadvantages, 24–25

sexual maturity issues, 205–206

Maltese, 43, 54

massage therapy, health benefits, 188

Mastiff, 39

matches, dog show practice events, 291

mats, removing, 183

McCaig, Donald, 310

meats, 127

medications

Clomicalm, 288

delivery methods, 213

disaster preparation, 364

Prozac, 288

separation anxiety uses, 284

travel uses, 330

Valium, 288

memorials, Web sites, 383

mental exercise, behavior problem strategy, 273

mental stimulation, daily workout, 368

microchip implants, lost dog recovery, 100, 120, 330

Milk Bones, 137

minerals, 128

Miniature Bull Terrier, 41

Miniature Pinscher, 43, 54

Miniature Poodle, 46

About the Author

Gina Spadafori writes an award-winning column on pets and their care, which appears in newspapers across the country through the Universal Press Syndicate. Her writing also appears frequently on Pets.com, where she is the special correspondent and essayist, and on the Veterinary Information Network's Pet Care Forum Web site.

Gina has served on the boards of directors of both the Cat Writers' Association and the Dog Writers Association of America. She is a three-time recipient of the DWAA's Maxwell Medallion for the best newspaper column, and her column has also been honored with a certificate of excellence by the CWA.

The first edition of her *Dogs For Dummies* was given the President's Award for the best writing on dogs and the Maxwell Medallion for the best general reference work, both by the Dog Writers Association of America

Along with coauthor Dr. Paul D. Pion, she was given the CWA's awards for the best work on feline nutrition, best work on feline behavior, and best work on responsible cat care for *Cats For Dummies*. With top avian specialist Dr. Brian L. Speer, she has also written *Birds For Dummies*.

Gina is affiliated with the Veterinary Information Network, Inc., of Davis, California, the world's largest online service for veterinary professionals. She and her pets divide their time between Northern California and South Georgia/North Florida.

About Howell Book House

Committed to the Human/Companion Animal Bond

Thank you for choosing a book brought to you by the pet experts at Howell Book House, a division of IDG Books Worldwide. And welcome to the family of pet owners who've put their trust in Howell books for nearly 40 years!

Pet ownership is about relationships — the bonds people form with their dogs, cats, horses, birds, fish, small mammals, reptiles, and other animals. Howell Book House/IDGB understands that these are some of the most important relationships in life, and that it's vital to nurture them through enjoyment and education. The happiest pet owners are those who know they're taking the best care of their pets — and with Howell books owners have this satisfaction. They're happy, educated owners, and as a result, they have happy pets, and that enriches the bond they share.

Howell Book House was established in 1961 by Mr. Elsworth S. Howell, an active and proactive dog fancier who showed English Setters and judged at the prestigious Westminster Kennel Club show in New York. Mr. Howell based his publishing program on strength of content, and his passion for books written by experienced and knowledgeable owners defined Howell Book House and has remained true over the years. Howell's reputation as the premier pet book publisher is supported by the distinction of having won more awards from the Dog Writers Association of America than any other publisher. Howell Book House/IDGB has over 400 titles in publication, including such classics as The American Kennel Club's *Complete Dog Book*, the *Dog Owner's Home Veterinary Handbook, Blessed Are the Brood Mares, and Mother Knows Best: The Natural Way to Train Your Dog.*

When you need answers to questions you have about any aspect of raising or training your companion animals, trust that Howell Book House/IDGB has the answers. We welcome your comments and suggestions, and we look forward to helping you maximize your relationships with your pets throughout the years.

Dominique C. De Vito
Publisher
Howell Book House/IDG Books Worldwide

Dedication

First edition: For Bruce Rubin, who makes things happen, and for Jan Haag and Carol Lea Benjamin, who always knew I could.

Second edition: For Joan Frazzini, who keeps me sane. And for Drs. Carla Weinberg and Paul D. Pion, world-class veterinarians and very dear friends.

Author's Acknowledgments

So many people are involved in the making of a book it doesn't seem fair only one name goes on the cover. My first wish would be to thank the readers who have let me know they've enjoyed my books, essays, and columns over the years.

The staff at IDG Books is amazing. I'll be forever grateful to Kathy Welton, who had the idea for this book and asked me to write it, and to project editor Jennifer Ehrlich, who shepherded the first edition through with the grace and dedication of a border collie. Keith Peterson, project editor for the second edition, has both a keen eye and an unflappable disposition. I'm grateful for both. Other IDG people who've had a hand in this edition include Dominique De Vito, Pam Mourouzis, Cynthia Kitchel, Scott Prentzas, Tracy Boggier, and Ben Nussbaum. Also worthy of acclaim is the IDG production staff, without whom this book would never have become a reality. Special thanks to Valery Bourke, Angie Hunckler, and Clint Lahnen.

The contributions of illustrator Jay Gavron are positively first-rate, and Rich Tennant's "The 5th Wave" cartoons prove he has a good handle on the sweet quirkiness of the canine soul. Photographers Gay Currier (who's also a fine dog trainer) and Dick Schmidt brought their unique vision to this book. My thanks, too, to the readers who sent me photographs for this edition, and to the Humane Society of the United States for the use of their pictures. Dr. William G. Porte, MBA, DVM, of Sacramento Veterinary Surgical Services again has my thanks for reviewing the text for medical accuracy.

Special thanks to my friends Drs. Carla Weinberg and Paul D. Pion, outstanding veterinarians who are always there to answer a quick question or review a chapter. Thanks, also, to my family and friends, especially those who carefully refrained from asking "Isn't that book done yet?" at the most stressful moments. I'm most grateful to Carol Lea Benjamin, Peg McGraw, Jan Haag, K.T. Jorgensen (whose dog Sirene is my dog Heather's best friend), Kathy Diamond Davis, Kelly Graham, Peggy Conway, Kevin Salt, Christie Keith, Linda Batson, Jack Russell, Tonya Machen, Ben Silverman, and to my brother, Joe Spadafori. The members of the Dog Writers Association of America and Cat Writers' Association have also been supportive, and I blow kisses to them all, especially Amy Shojai, Darlene Arden, and Ranny Green.

More thanks are due to very patient other editors: Heather Mackey and John Hollon at Pets.com, and Greg Melvin and Alan McDermott at Andrews McMeel Universal. Good editors make good writers, and these talented people prove that every day.

I cannot close without acknowledging the dogs who have shared my life, especially Lance, the Original Demo Dog, whose spirit will always be with me. Andy, Benjamin, and Heather, who share my life now, could not be more perfect. That's my story and I'm sticking to it.

Publisher's Acknowledgments

Editorial Manager: Pamela Mourouzis

Project Editor: Keith Peterson (Previous Edition: Jennifer Ehrlich)

Acquisitions Editor: Scott Prentzas

Technical Editor: Dr. Bill Porte

Editorial Assistant: Carol Strickland

Project Coordinator: Regina Snyder

Cover Image: © Tereza Jancikova/Getty Images

Leverage the power

Dummies is the global leader in the reference category and one of the most trusted and highly regarded brands in the world. No longer just focused on books, customers now have access to the dummies content they need in the format they want. Together we'll craft a solution that engages your customers, stands out from the competition, and helps you meet your goals.

Advertising & Sponsorships

Connect with an engaged audience on a powerful multimedia site, and position your message alongside expert how-to content. Dummies.com is a one-stop shop for free, online information and know-how curated by a team of experts.

- Targeted ads
- Video
- Email Marketing

- Microsites
- Sweepstakes sponsorship

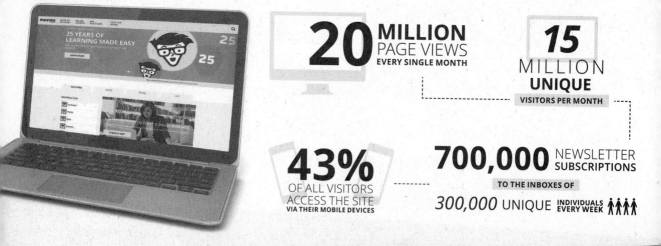

20 MILLION PAGE VIEWS EVERY SINGLE MONTH

15 MILLION UNIQUE VISITORS PER MONTH

43% OF ALL VISITORS ACCESS THE SITE VIA THEIR MOBILE DEVICES

700,000 NEWSLETTER SUBSCRIPTIONS TO THE INBOXES OF *300,000* UNIQUE INDIVIDUALS EVERY WEEK

# of dummies

Custom Publishing

Reach a global audience in any language by creating a solution that will differentiate you from competitors, amplify your message, and encourage customers to make a buying decision.

- Apps
- Books
- eBooks
- Video
- Audio
- Webinars

Brand Licensing & Content

Leverage the strength of the world's most popular reference brand to reach new audiences and channels of distribution.

For more information, visit dummies.com/biz

PERSONAL ENRICHMENT

Staying Sharp
9781119187790
USA $26.00
CAN $31.99
UK £19.99

Facebook
9781119179030
USA $21.99
CAN $25.99
UK £16.99

Guitar
9781119293354
USA $24.99
CAN $29.99
UK £17.99

Investing
9781119293347
USA $22.99
CAN $27.99
UK £16.99

Beekeeping
9781119310068
USA $22.99
CAN $27.99
UK £16.99

Digital Photography
9781119235606
USA $24.99
CAN $29.99
UK £17.99

Meditation
9781119251163
USA $24.99
CAN $29.99
UK £17.99

Pregnancy
9781119235491
USA $26.99
CAN $31.99
UK £19.99

Samsung Galaxy S7
9781119279952
USA $24.99
CAN $29.99
UK £17.99

iPhone
9781119283133
USA $24.99
CAN $29.99
UK £17.99

Crocheting
9781119287117
USA $24.99
CAN $29.99
UK £16.99

Nutrition
9781119130246
USA $22.99
CAN $27.99
UK £16.99

PROFESSIONAL DEVELOPMENT

Windows 10
9781119311041
USA $24.99
CAN $29.99
UK £17.99

AutoCAD
9781119255796
USA $39.99
CAN $47.99
UK £27.99

Excel 2016
9781119293439
USA $26.99
CAN $31.99
UK £19.99

QuickBooks 2017
9781119281467
USA $26.99
CAN $31.99
UK £19.99

macOS Sierra
9781119280651
USA $29.99
CAN $35.99
UK £21.99

LinkedIn
9781119251132
USA $24.99
CAN $29.99
UK £17.99

Windows 10 All-in-One
9781119310563
USA $34.00
CAN $41.99
UK £24.99

SharePoint 2016
9781119181705
USA $29.99
CAN $35.99
UK £21.99

Fundamental Analysis
9781119263593
USA $26.99
CAN $31.99
UK £19.99

Networking
9781119257769
USA $29.99
CAN $35.99
UK £21.99

Office 2016
9781119293477
USA $26.99
CAN $31.99
UK £19.99

Office 365
9781119265313
USA $24.99
CAN $29.99
UK £17.99

Salesforce.com
9781119239314
USA $29.99
CAN $35.99
UK £21.99

Coding
9781119293323
USA $29.99
CAN $35.99
UK £21.99

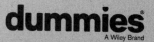
dummies®
A Wiley Brand

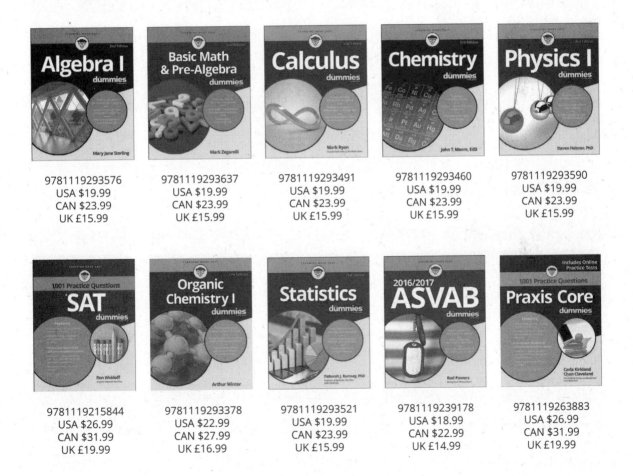
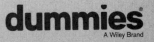